GAMES AND
DECISION MAKING

GAMES AND DECISION MAKING

Charalambos D. Aliprantis
Purdue University

Subir K. Chakrabarti
Indiana University Purdue University at Indianapolis

New York • Oxford
OXFORD UNIVERSITY PRESS
2000

Oxford University Press

Oxford   New York
Athens   Auckland   Bangkok   Bogotá   Buenos Aires   Calcutta
Cape Town   Chennai   Dar es Salaam   Delhi   Florence   Hong Kong   Istanbul
Karachi   Kuala Lumpur   Madrid   Melbourne   Mexico City   Mumbai
Nairobi   Paris   São Paulo   Singapore   Taipei   Tokyo   Toronto   Warsaw

and associated companies in
Berlin   Ibadan

Published by Oxford University Press, Inc.
198 Madison Avenue, New York, New York 10016
http://www.oup-usa.org

Library of Congress Cataloging-in-Publication Data

Aliprantis, Charalambos D.
    Games and Decision making / Charalambos D. Aliprantis, Subir K.
Chakrabarti.
      p.   cm.
    Includes bibliographical references and index.
    ISBN 0-19-512609-2 (paper)
    1. Game theory.   2. Decision-making.   I. Chakrabarti, Subir K.
II. Title.
QA269.A44   1999
519.3—dc21   98-45396
                                                            CIP

9 8 7 6 5 4 3 2 1

Printed in the United States of America
on acid-free paper

To my family: Bernadette, Claire, and Dionissi

—CDA

To my parents: Sunil and Maya

—SKC

CONTENTS

Foreword **ix**

Chapter 1   Choices   1
    1.1   FUNCTIONS   **1**
    1.2   THE OPTIMIZATION PROBLEM   **3**
    1.3   FIRST-ORDER CONDITIONS   **7**
    1.4   OPTIMIZING USING THE LAGRANGE
        METHOD   **13**
    1.5   UNCERTAINTY AND CHANCE   **17**
    1.6   DECISION MAKING UNDER UNCERTAINTY   **26**

Chapter 2   Decisions and Games   40
    2.1   TWO-PERSON MATRIX GAMES   **42**
    2.2   STRATEGIC FORM GAMES   **49**
    2.3   APPLICATIONS   **54**
    2.4   SOLVING MATRIX GAMES WITH MIXED
        STRATEGIES   **68**

Chapter 3   Sequential Decisions   74
    3.1   GRAPHS AND TREES   **74**
    3.2   SINGLE-PERSON DECISIONS   **79**
    3.3   UNCERTAINTY AND SINGLE-PERSON
        DECISIONS   **88**

Chapter 4   Sequential Games   95
    4.1   THE STRUCTURE OF SEQUENTIAL GAMES   **96**
    4.2   SEQUENTIAL GAMES WITH PERFECT
        INFORMATION   **104**
    4.3   SEQUENTIAL GAMES WITH IMPERFECT
        INFORMATION   **116**

Chapter 5   Sequential Rationality   128
    5.1   THE MARKET FOR LEMONS   **129**
    5.2   BELIEFS AND STRATEGIES   **133**
    5.3   CONSISTENCY OF BELIEFS   **138**

5.4   EXPECTED PAYOFF   **141**
5.5   SEQUENTIAL EQUILIBRIUM   **143**
5.6   APPLICATIONS: SIGNALING GAMES   **151**

Chapter 6   Auctions   163

6.1   AUCTIONS WITH COMPLETE INFORMATION   **164**
6.2   INDIVIDUAL PRIVATE VALUE AUCTIONS   **169**
6.3   ENGLISH AUCTIONS   **178**
6.4   COMMON-VALUE AUCTIONS   **182**

Chapter 7   Bargaining   190

7.1   THE NASH SOLUTION   **191**
7.2   MONOTONICITY IN BARGAINING   **205**
7.3   THE CORE OF A BARGAINING GAME   **214**
7.4   ALLOCATION RULES: THE SHAPLEY VALUE   **226**
7.5   TWO-PERSON SEQUENTIAL BARGAINING   **238**

Bibliography   **251**

Index   **253**

FOREWORD

In the fall of 1995 the National Science Foundation awarded a grant to Indiana University System for the project *Mathematics Throughout the Curriculum,* whose objective was to develop inderdisciplinary undergraduate courses with substantial mathematical content. The primary focus was to expose students in a wide variety of subjects to the usefulness of mathematical techniques. We were asked to design a course that would include topics from economic theory. Our response was a course that put together material from decision theory and game theory in a novel way. This book is the culmination of that effort.

The book evolved from the need to offer a course in *decision theory* that would include the classical material on optimization theory as well as from the newer and more recent literature in game theory. Since no existing text covered the topics in the manner required for the project, we put together our own material that included classical optimization theory, game theory, auctions, and bargaining. We wrote the book with the objective of introducing the rather sophisticated concepts of modern decision theory to a readership that is familiar with only elementary calculus and elementary probability theory. It is a self-contained treatment of almost everything that can be called decision theory—from classical optimization theory to modern game theory. We have included applications from economics, political science, finance, and management. Examples are used to show both the need for a theory and to demonstrate the framework within which the theory can be applied. Thus the examples and applications are used as a major pedagogic device.

This text can be used for a course at the undergraduate level as well as at the introductory graduate level. It is aimed at the undergraduate student who wants to take a serious look at decision theory, for instance, the economics major or the business major or even the mathematics major. The book is also appropriate for use at the graduate level to teach introductory courses in optimization and game theory and MBA courses in decision theory. Because of its content, the book would appeal to anyone who thinks seriously about making good decisions. Thus the material in this book is useful to the business manager, the policymaker, and the budding entrepreneur as well as the serious undergraduate student in economics or business who aspires to acquire a graduate degree.

In writing the book our objective was to introduce some of the central ideas of decision theory and game theory without trying to treat either subject exhaustively, which we think cannot be done adequately in a single text. Therefore, we tried to be eclectic. Whether we succeeded in this effort is for the reader to judge. There is a pattern we follow, which the careful reader may discern. We start with the most elementary decision-making problem—that of the single decision maker—move on to progressively more complex decision problems, and complete the decision making with a discussion on sequential rationality. We then use this material to study topics of more immediate interest like auctions and bargaining.

A special feature of the book is that it treats decision theory and game theory as part of the same body of knowledge. This feature separates it from the texts that are devoted to only game theory or deal solely with decision theory. In this book, single-person decision theory is used as the building block of game theory. This is the essential theme underlying the book. It highlights the interplay that exists between single-person decision problems and multiperson decision problems.

The text leaves out important elements from both decision theory as well as game theory. We never discuss dynamic programming, though hints of the theory are present when we discuss backward induction. Our treatment of multivariate decision problems is at best cursory. Large chunks of game theory are also not discussed. There is a huge literature on the refinements of Nash equilibrium that we haven't even touched, and we totally bypassed the extensive work on repeated games. We are well aware of all these omissions and many more that we have not mentioned. Our excuse is that we did this to avoid writing an incredibly formidable manuscript that would intimidate the student. We wanted to write a text that would serve as a solid introduction to some of the basic issues and techniques of modern decision making and games.

We have made every effort to make the book as self-contained as possible. Thus, although some of the material in the later chapters requires some extra knowledge of mathematics, the necessary material is developed as an integral part of the text. The book is written with some thought to the sequence in which topics are introduced. Each chapter builds on the material presented in the earlier chapters. For instance, the chapters on sequential games build on the chapter of sequential decision making. We paid special attention to this because much of game theory is technical, and, as a result, it becomes unduly difficult if the ideas are not presented in their proper order.

In the first chapter we develop classical optimization theory using elementary calculus. The material in this chapter is similar to that usually found in texts written for courses in mathematics for economists. The first chapter thus is a condensed version of the chapters on optimization in a book like *Mathematics for Economic Analysis* [23] by Sydsaeter and Hammond or a book like *Fundamental Methods of Mathematical Economics* [2] by Chiang. The novelty in the first chapter is in the way we introduce the material. Using problems from economics, business, operations research, and so forth, we demonstrate how to use the first- and second-order conditions of calculus to find optimal solutions to optimization problems. In this motivational chapter we show how to use mathematics in a variety of useful and interesting ways.

While Chapter 1 deals with classical optimization theory with a single decision maker, Chapter 2 introduces the fundamentals of modern game theory. Chapter 2 builds on the techniques developed in Chapter 1, and focuses on game theory, while at the same time drawing extensively from the material in Chapter 1. In the second chapter, we develop the theory of strategic form games and their solutions. We also present applications from markets, voting, auctions, resource extraction, and so forth. In Chapter 3, we study sequential decision making and introduce the language of trees and graphs to define sequential games. Thus we avoid the usual questions about graphs and trees that inevitably arise when one starts to define sequential games. In Chapters 4 and 5 we discuss sequential games using the techniques of Chapter 3 as building blocks. We deal with the concepts of subgame perfection and sequential rationality in some detail.

Chapter 6 is devoted to a discussion of auctions. We study various types of auctions and the possible outcomes. Our discussion of auctions is done within the framework of game theory. We view an auction as a game and examine the equilibrium outcome of the game. Chapter 7 is concerned with bargaining. We treat both the axiomatic approach to bargaining as well as the analysis of bargaining problems using sequential games. Thus Chapter 7 investigates the Nash bargaining solution, the Shapley value, and the core. It also deals with sequential bargaining. Chapters 6 and 7 are, in fact, applications of the principles developed in the earlier chapters.

We take this opportunity to thank the principal investigators of the project, Professors Bart Ng of IUPUI and Dan Maki of Indiana University, for providing us with summer support to develop the course. We also thank Robert Sandy, the Chairman of the Department of Economics, IUPUI, for his support. Finally, we would like to acknowledge the patient understanding of our wives—Bernadette and Tuhina—who allowed us to spend many hours away from our families and our children Claire, Dionissi, Anisha, Devika, and Sharmistha.

C. D. Aliprantis and S. K. Chakrabarti
Indianapolis, Indiana

GAMES AND
DECISION MAKING

CHOICES

Individuals as well as groups have to make decisions in many different contexts. As individuals, we have to make decisions about how to divide our income among different goals and objectives. A firm has to decide among the different things it needs to do in order to compete effectively in the marketplace. Governments need to make decisions about their foreign policy, domestic policy, fiscal policy, and monetary policy. Students need to decide among courses they need to take every semester. The list of situations in which individuals have to make a decision is indeed very impressive.

When we are faced with decisions, we wonder as to which decision would be best. Sometimes we spend enormous amounts of time and energy agonizing about what to do. Faced with the same alternatives, two individuals may choose quite differently. Is one individual then wrong and the other right? Has one individual made a good decision and the other a bad one? Obviously, the answer to these questions lies in the criteria used to evaluate decisions. As is well known, individuals have different objectives and diverse interests that may affect their decision making.

As a decision problem usually has an objective to be attained and a set of alternative choices with which to achieve it, a *decision problem* or an *optimization problem* has an *objective function* (the goal to be achieved) and a *feasible set* or a *choice set* (the alternative choices). The issue is then which choice will best achieve the specified objective or goal.

In this chapter, we sketch some of the main principles of the mathematical theory of optimization. The intention is not to overwhelm the reader with technical details but rather to present some of the major results in the area. We also indicate how the techniques of optimization might be used not only to get accuracy in decision making but also, more important, to indicate how to start thinking about formulating and modeling these decision problems.

1.1 FUNCTIONS

One of the basic concepts of mathematics is that of a function. The notion of a function is essential for the study of mathematics as well as its applications. It is also going to be of fundamental importance here.

In calculus, we usually teach that a function is a "formula" $y = f(x)$, which relates two variables, x and y. The variable x is called the *independent variable* and y the *dependent*. For instance,

$$y = x^2, \quad y = \sqrt{x - 2}, \quad \text{and} \quad y = \frac{x + 1}{x - 1}$$

are all functions. The collection of all values of x for which the formula $f(x)$ "makes algebraic sense" is called the *domain* of the function. For instance, the domain of the function $y = x^2$ is the set $\mathbb{R}$ of all real numbers,[1] and the domain of $f(x) = \sqrt{x - 2}$ consists of all real numbers x for which $x - 2 \geq 0$, that is, $[2, \infty)$.

The concept of a function is much more general than the one discussed above and is closely related to that of a set. Recall that a *set* can be naively defined as a collection of objects (or elements) viewed as a single entity—as usual, we shall denote sets by capital letters. A *function* f is usually defined as a "rule" that assigns to every element x from a set X a *unique* element $y = f(x)$ in another set Y. The object x is called the *input*, and the element $f(x)$ is called the *output*. Schematically, the function f is denoted by $f : X \rightarrow Y$, and its geometrical interpretation is shown in Figure 1.0. The set X is now called the *domain* of the function. If $Y = \mathbb{R}$, then f is called a *real function*.

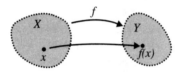

Figure 1.0

Here are a few general examples of functions.

- Define the real function $f : \mathbb{R} \rightarrow \mathbb{R}$ via the formula $f(x) = 3x$. That is, the rule f informs us that if x is a real number, then in order to find the output $f(x)$ we must multiply x by 3. For instance, $f(2) = 6$, $f(-3) = -9$, and $f(0) = 0$.
- Let X denote the collection of all books in your library and let $\mathbb{N} = \{1, 2, 3, \ldots\}$ (the set of *natural numbers*). Define a function $f : X \rightarrow \mathbb{N}$ via the rule:

  $f(x) =$ the number of pages of the book x .

  For instance, if book b has 235 pages, then $f(b) = 235$.
- Let A denote the collection of all cars in your city and let B denote the set of all possible colors. Then we can consider the function c that assigns to each car its color. That is, $c : A \rightarrow B$ is the rule that for a given car x, $c(x)$ is its color. For instance, if car a has yellow color, then $c(a) =$ yellow, and if x is a red car, then $c(x) =$ red.
- Let B be the set of all birds in a forest and let T denote the set of all trees in the forest. You can define a function $f : B \rightarrow T$ via the rule: if b is a bird, then $f(b)$ is the tree where the bird b has its nest.

[1]Throughout this book the symbol $\mathbb{R}$ will denote the set of *real numbers*.

- Assume that P denotes the set of all persons living in the United States and let C be the collection of all U.S. Congressional representatives. We can define a function $f : P \to C$ by letting $f(a)$ be the congressional representative of the district where person a lives.

Can you think of other examples of functions from everyday life?

1. Find the domain of the function $f(x) = \frac{x+1}{x-1}$.

2. Consider the set P of all persons living in your city at present. Determine which rules from the ones below define functions.
   - *a.* For each person x, let $f(x)$ be the father of person x.
   - *b.* For each person x, let $g(x)$ be the son of person x.
   - *c.* For each person x, let $h(x)$ be the height of person x.
   - *d.* For each person x, let $w(x)$ be the weight of person x.

3. Consider the set of natural numbers $X = \{1789, 1790, 1791, \ldots, 1996\}$ and let $\mathcal{P}$ denote the set of all U.S. Presidents. Define the function $f : X \to \mathcal{P}$ via

   $$f(x) = \text{the President of the United States on December 1 of the year } x .$$

   For instance, $f(1826) = $ J. Q. Adams, $f(1863) = $ A. Lincoln, $f(1962) = $ J. F. Kennedy, and $f(1971) = $ R. M. Nixon. What are the values $f(1789)$, $f(1900)$, $f(1947)$, and $f(1988)$?

4. Consider X and $\mathcal{P}$ as in the previous exercise and for each year x in X let

   $$f(x) = \text{the President of the United States on November 22 of the year } x .$$

   Does this rule f define a function from X to $\mathcal{P}$?

5. Let B denote the collection of all books in your library and for each book x let $f(x)$ be the author of the book x.

   Does this rule define a function? If not, then what modification can you make to the rule in order to make it a function?

1.2 THE OPTIMIZATION PROBLEM

It is not an overstatement to say that every time we make a decision, we face an optimization problem. When we enter a store, like Walmart, we have a list of things that we want to buy. But whatever we want to buy presents us with a decision. Should we buy the cheaper brand? Or should we go with the more expensive brand, which probably has the higher quality? Or maybe the issue is whether we really need that extra pair of trousers or that additional skirt? A family looking to buy a house has to decide whether it wants more space or a smaller house in the right location. Every year the federal government has to pass a budget after deciding which program gets what funds. In economics, a central feature of consumer theory is about the choice that a consumer makes. In the theory of the firm, a firm decides how to maximize profits and minimize costs.

All these decision problems have a feature in common. There is a set of alternatives Ω from which the decision maker has to choose. If the individual who walks into Walmart needs to buy a pair of trousers, then he or she may have half a dozen of choices from which to select. In the case of the family that has decided to buy a house given the price range (that is, given its budget), there might be many different models available in various locations. These different models of houses then define the set Ω for the family. As we shall see shortly, a consumer, in the theory of consumer behavior, has a choice set—as does the firm in the theory of the firm.

The other common feature of all decisions is that the decision maker needs to devise some criterion of choosing between alternatives. In other words, the decision maker must have some ranking over the different alternatives in the choice set. This ranking is expressed by a real-valued function $f: \Omega \to \mathbb{R}$, where the higher value of an alternative implies that it has a higher rank than an alternative with a lower value.

The concepts of a set and a function that were introduced in the previous section are the basic tools used to describe an optimization problem. In its abstract form, an optimization problem consists of a set Ω (called the *choice set* or the *opportunity set*[2]) and a function $f: \Omega \to \mathbb{R}$ (called the *objective function*). The goal is to select an alternative from the set Ω that maximizes or minimizes the value of the objective function f. That is, the decision maker either solves

1. Maximize $f(\omega)$ subject to $\omega \in \Omega$, or
2. Minimize $f(\omega)$ subject to $\omega \in \Omega$.

Since minimizing $f(\omega)$ subject to $\omega \in \Omega$ is equivalent to maximizing $-f(\omega)$ subject to $\omega \in \Omega$, the above problems can be combined into the following general optimization[3] problem.

The Optimization Problem

Maximize $f(\omega)$

such that $\omega \in \Omega$.

Any choice $\omega^* \in \Omega$ that yields the maximum value of the objective function f is known as a *maximizer* (or as an *optimizer*) of f over the choice set Ω.

We now illustrate the idea of the optimization problem with some examples of common interest.

---

[2]The choice set is also referred to as the *constraint set* or the *feasible set*.

[3]The word *optimization* is derived from the Latin word "optimum" which means the "best."

Example 1.1

Assume that a consumer entering a supermarket wishes to buy apples and oranges at a cost that will not exceed his available amount of $12. Apples cost $1 per pound and oranges $2 per pound.

The consumer not only wishes to purchase the largest possible "bundle" of apples and oranges but he also wishes to get the most "satisfaction." In practice, the satisfaction (or taste) of a consumer is expressed in terms of a function—known as the *utility function* of the consumer. In this case, let us assume that the utility function is given by

$$u(x, y) = xy.$$

The pair (x, y) represents a possible "bundle" of apples and oranges that can be purchased by the consumer. Since $u(2, 3) = 6 > 4 = u(4, 1)$, the consumer prefers the bundle $(2, 3)$ (two pounds of apples and three pounds of oranges) to the bundle $(4, 1)$ (four pounds of apples and one pound of oranges).

The cost of a bundle (x, y) is simply the number $x + 2y$. The constraint that the consumer should not spend more than $12 is expressed by saying that his allowable bundles (x, y) are the ones that satisfy $x + 2y \leq 12$. In other words, the choice set Ω of the consumer is the set

$$\Omega = \{(x, y) \colon \ x \geq 0, \ y \geq 0, \ \text{and} \ x + 2y \leq 12\}.$$

Now we can write the choice problem of the consumer as: Maximize $u(x, y) = xy$ subject to $(x, y) \in \Omega$.

Example 1.2

A promoter of social events wishes to determine the ticket price of an upcoming event that will maximize her revenue. From past experience she knows that if the ticket price is $12 per person, then the attendance is approximately 1,200 people. Her experience also tells her that for every $1 increase in the price she will lose 150 people, while a $1 drop in the price will attract 150 additional people to the event. In addition, she knows that every person will spend on average $6 on concessions. The promoter's problem is now the following: *What should be the admission price in order to maximize the total revenue?*

To set up the problem as an optimization problem, we proceed as follows. We denote by x the increase in dollars of the $12 ticket ($x < 0$ means a decrease in price). That is, the price per ticket is $12 + x$ dollars. Then the attendance will be $1200 - 150x$ people and the concessions will bring a revenue of $6(1200 - 150x)$ dollars. If $R(x)$ denotes the revenue obtained after the increase of the price by x dollars, then we have:

$$
\begin{aligned}
R(x) &= \text{revenue from tickets} + \text{revenue from concessions} \\
&= (\text{\# of people}) \times (\text{price per ticket}) + 6 \times (\text{\# of people}) \\
&= (1200 - 150x)(12 + x) + 6(1200 - 150x) \\
&= (1200 - 150x)(18 + x) \\
&= -150x^2 - 1,500x + 21,600
\end{aligned}
$$

Thus the promoter's problem here is to maximize

$$R(x) = -150x^2 - 1,500x + 21,600$$

subject to $x > -12$, or $x \in (-12, \infty)$.

Example 1.3

Experimental evidence suggests that the concentration of a drug in the bloodstream (measured in milligrams per liter) t hours after its injection into the human body is given by

$$C(t) = \frac{t}{t^2 + 9}.$$

When does the maximum concentration take place?

That is, how many hours t after its injection into the body does the drug have its largest concentration? In the language of optimization theory we must solve the problem: Maximize $C(t)$ subject to $t \geq 0$.

Example 1.4

Assume that the price per bushel of wheat is \$4 and the price of fertilizer per pound is \$0.25. A farmer has observed that when he uses n pounds of fertilizer per acre, his land yields $\sqrt{n + 30}$ bushels of wheat per acre. *How many pounds of fertilizer per acre will maximize the farmer's profit?*

From the formula profit = revenue − cost, it is easy to see that the profit per acre is:

$$P(n) = 4\sqrt{n + 30} - 0.25n.$$

The farmer has to maximize $P(n)$ subject to $n \geq 0$.

Example 1.5

A car dealership owner sells 200 cars a year. To keep a car in storage costs \$100 a year. The cost of ordering new cars from the manufacturer involves a fixed cost of \$100 plus \$80 per car. *How many times per year should he order cars, and in what lot size, in order to minimize his annual cost?*

To set up this problem in our optimization form, we start by assuming that x is the lot size of the order—of course, $x > 0$. Then the number of orders per year will be $\frac{200}{x}$. Since the cost of ordering x cars is $100 + 80x$, the cost per year for ordering the 200 cars is

$$(100 + 80x)\frac{200}{x} = \frac{20,000}{x} + 16,000$$

dollars. On the other hand, assuming that out of the x cars an average of $\frac{x}{2}$ are held in storage, the yearly inventory cost is

$$100 \times \tfrac{x}{2} = 50x$$

dollars. Therefore, the total annual cost for the car dealership owner is

$$C(x) = 50x + \tfrac{20,000}{x} + 16,000$$

dollars.

To solve our problem we now have to minimize the function $C(x)$ subject to $x > 0$.

EXERCISES

1. A company knows from empirical evidence that the demand for a certain product is given by the function

$$D(p) = 120 - 2\sqrt{p},$$

where p denotes the price of the product in dollars. Set up an optimization problem for maximizing the revenue of the company in terms of the price p of the product. [Answer: $R(p) = 120p - 2p^{\frac{3}{2}}$.]

2. A television manufacturer determines that in order to sell x television sets, the price must be

$$p = 1200 - x.$$

The cost of the manufacturer for producing x television sets is

$$C(x) = 4,000 + 30x.$$

Set up an optimization problem that will maximize the profit of the manufacturer. [Answer: $P(x) = -x^2 + 1170x - 4,000$.]

3. You walk into a floral shop with $20 in your pocket, and you wish to spend all the money purchasing a bouquet of carnations and roses. Carnations are $1 a stem (a piece) and roses are $3 a stem. If your satisfaction is described by the utility function $u(x, y) = x^2 y^3$ (where x is the number of carnations and y the number of roses in the bouquet), what maximization problem if solved will offer you the most satisfactory bouquet for your money?

4. An electronics store owner expects to sell 6000 calculator batteries each year. The cost of each battery is $0.25. The ordering fee for each new shipment is $20, and it costs $0.96 to store a battery for a year. Assume that the store owner places n orders per year with a lot size x per order—where, of course, $n = \tfrac{6000}{x}$. Set up an optimization problem in terms of the lot size that minimizes the owner's annual cost. [Answer: The owner must minimize the cost function $C(x) = 0.48x + \tfrac{120,000}{x} + 1,500$.]

1.3 FIRST-ORDER CONDITIONS

The solution to an optimization problem is closely related to the *rate of change* of the objective function. The rate of change of a function is known in mathematics as the *derivative* of the function. The *derivative* of a function $f: (a, b) \to \mathbb{R}$ at a point c is the limit (if it exists)

$$f'(c) = \lim_{x \to c} \frac{f(x) - f(c)}{x - c} .$$

If the function has derivative at every point c, then it is said to be *differentiable*. As mentioned at the beginning, the derivative $f'(c)$ represents the rate of change of $f(x)$ at the point c relative to the change of x. Constant functions have zero rates of change, and so their derivatives are also zero.

We list below the basic rules for computing derivatives. Details can be found in any elementary calculus text; see, for instance, Reference 23 in the bibliography at the end of the book.

The Rules for Computing Derivatives

- The Power Rule: $(x^p)' = px^{p-1}$
- The Product Rule: $(fg)' = f'g + fg'$
- The Quotient Rule: $\left(\frac{f}{g}\right)' = \frac{f'g - fg'}{g^2}$
- The Chain Rule: $[f(g(x))]' = f'(g(x))g'(x)$

We are now ready to present the following basic result regarding optimization of functions of one variable defined on an open interval of the set of real numbers. A point (i.e., a real number) c is said to be a *critical point* or a *stationary point* for a function f if its derivative $f'(c)$ at c is zero, that is, if $f'(c) = 0$.

The First-Order Test for Optima

Let $f: (a, b) \to \mathbb{R}$ be a differentiable function and assume that f has a unique stationary point $c \in (a, b)$; that is, c is the only point in (a, b) with $f'(c) = 0$.

- If $f'(x) > 0$ for some $a < x < c$ and $f'(x) < 0$ for some $c < x < b$, then f attains its maximum at $x = c$ and c is the unique maximizer of the function f over (a, b).

- If $f'(x) < 0$ for some $a < x < c$ and $f'(x) > 0$ for some $c < x < b$, then f attains its minimum at $x = c$ and c is the unique minimizer of the function f over (a, b).

The preceding result is called the *first-order test* since it involves only the first derivative of the function. The geometric meaning of the maximum and minimum of a function defined on an open interval (a, b) is shown in Figure 1.1.

When the objective function has a second derivative, we can use the following *second-order test* to find the nature of stationary points.

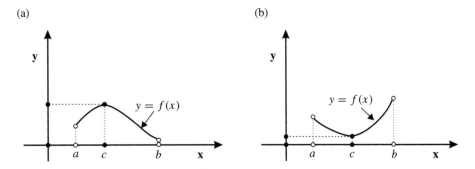

Figure 1.1   (a) A function having a maximum value at a point c. (b) A function having a minimum value at a point c.

The Second-Order Test for Optima

Let $f : (a, b) \rightarrow \mathbb{R}$ be a twice-differentiable function and assume that f has a unique stationary point $c \in (a, b)$; that is, c is the only point in (a, b) with $f'(c) = 0$.

- If $f''(c) < 0$, then f attains its maximum at $x = c$ and c is the unique maximizer of the function f over (a, b).

- If $f''(c) > 0$, then f attains its minimum at $x = c$ and c is the unique minimizer of the function f over (a, b).

Let us use the first-order test to solve the optimization problems stated in the examples of the previous section.

Solution to the optimization problem of Example 1.1   The set Ω is shown in Figure 1.2. It is usually called the *budget set* of the consumer. The line $x + 2y = 12$ is known as the *budget line*.

Notice that an increase in the bundles x and y will strictly increase the value of the utility function $u = xy$. This guarantees that the maximizers of $u(x, y)$ must lie on the budget line $x + 2y = 12$. (Why?) Now observe that

$$u = u(x, y) = xy = (12 - 2y)y = -2y^2 + 12y$$

and $0 \leq y \leq 6$. Therefore, we must maximize $u(y) = -2y^2 + 12y$ subject to $0 \leq y \leq 6$.

Taking the derivative, we get $u'(y) = -4y + 12 = -4(y - 3)$. Letting $u'(y) = 0$ yields $y = 3$, and so the only critical point is $y = 3$. Now it is easy to observe that $u'(y) > 0$ if $y < 3$ and $u'(y) < 0$ if $y > 3$. The latter, in connection with the first-order test, guarantees that u be maximized at $y = 3$. But then $x = 12 - 2y = 12 - 2 \times 3 = 6$.

Thus the bundle $(6, 3)$ maximizes the utility function $u(x, y) = xy$ over the set Ω.

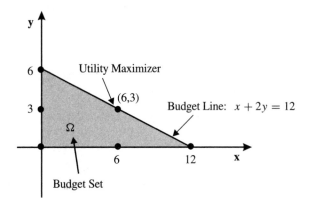

Figure 1.2

Solution to the optimization problem of Example 1.2 We must maximize the function

$$R(x) = -150x^2 - 1,500x + 21,600$$

subject to $x \in (-12, \infty)$. Factoring, we can rewrite $R(x)$ as

$$R(x) = 150(-x^2 - 10x + 144).$$

Differentiating, we obtain $R'(x) = 150(-2x - 10) = -300(x + 5)$. This easily implies that $x = -5$ is the only stationary point of R. Moreover, we have

$$R'(x) > 0 \text{ for } x < -5 \quad \text{and} \quad R'(x) < 0 \text{ for } x > -5.$$

By the first-order test, we see that R attains a maximum value at $x = -5$. That is, a decrease of \$5 in the ticket price will yield the maximum revenue $R(-5) = \$25,351$. In other words, the admission ticket price of $\$12 - \$5 = \$7$ will maximize the revenue. The graph of the function $R(x)$ is shown in Figure 1.3(a).

Solution to the optimization problem of Example 1.3 Differentiating the function $C(t) = \frac{t}{t^2+9}$ using the quotient rule, we get

$$C'(t) = \frac{(t)'(t^2 + 9) - t(t^2 + 9)'}{(t^2 + 9)^2} = \frac{1 \times (t^2 + 9) - t \times (2t)}{(t^2 + 9)^2} = \frac{9 - t^2}{(t^2 + 9)^2}.$$

To find the critical points of $C(t)$, we must solve the equation $C'(t) = 0$. In our case, this means that we must solve the equation $9 - t^2 = 0$. Solving, we get $t = \pm 3$. Since we are optimizing over the interval $[0, \infty)$, we must consider only the critical point $t = 3$.

Now notice that $C'(t) > 0$ for $0 \le t < 3$ and $C'(t) < 0$ for all $3 < t < \infty$. By the first-order test, we see that $C(t)$ attains its maximum at $t = 3$. Consequently, the maximum concentration of the drug is

$$C(3) = \frac{3}{3^2 + 9} = \frac{3}{18} = \frac{1}{6} = 0.1666 \text{ milligrams per liter},$$

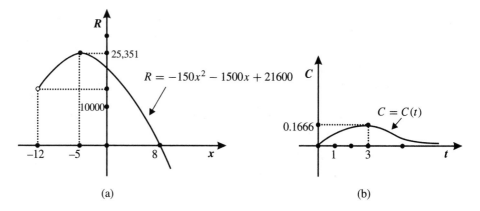

Figure 1.3

and takes place 3 hours after its injection into the human body. The graph of the function $C(t)$ is shown in Figure 1.3(b).

Solution to the optimization problem of Example 1.4 In this case we must optimize the function

$$P(n) = 4\sqrt{n+30} - \tfrac{1}{4}n = 4(n+30)^{\frac{1}{2}} - \tfrac{1}{4}n$$

subject to $n \in [0, \infty)$. Differentiating, we get

$$P'(n) = 4 \times \tfrac{1}{2}(n+30)^{-\frac{1}{2}} - \tfrac{1}{4} = \frac{4}{2\sqrt{n+30}} - \frac{1}{4} = \frac{8 - \sqrt{n+30}}{4\sqrt{n+30}}.$$

For the critical points of $P(n)$ we must solve the equation $P'(n) = 0$ or $8 - \sqrt{n+30} = 0$. The latter equation can be written as $\sqrt{n+30} = 8$. Squaring both sides, we get $n+30 = 64$, or $n = 34$.

It is easy to see that $P'(n) > 0$ for $0 \le n < 34$ and $P'(n) < 0$ for all $34 < n < \infty$. By the first-order test, we see that $P(n)$ attains its maximum at $n = 34$. Thus the farmer must use 34 pounds of fertilizer per acre in order to maximize his profit. The maximum profit per acre is

$$P(34) = 4\sqrt{34+30} - \frac{34}{4} = 4 \times 8 - 8.5 = 23.5.$$

Solution to the optimization problem of Example 1.5 Differentiating the cost function $C(x) = 50x + \frac{20,000}{x} + 16,000$, we get

$$C'(x) = 50 - \frac{20,000}{x^2} = \frac{50(x^2 - 400)}{x^2} = \frac{50(x - 20)(x + 20)}{x^2}.$$

It is easy to see that $C'(x) < 0$ for $0 < x < 20$, $C'(x) > 0$ for $x > 20$, and $C'(20) = 0$. So, by the first-order test, $x = 20$ is the minimizer of $C(x)$ over the open interval $(0, \infty)$.

In other words, the owner of the car dealership must order $\frac{200}{20} = 10$ times a year at a lot size of 20 cars in order to minimize his inventory cost.

1. The cost function of a manufacturer for producing x units of a commodity is $C(x) = 2x^2 + 40x + 5000$. The selling price of the commodity in the market is $1000 per unit. How many units should the manufacturer produce in order to maximize his profit? Also, what is the maximum profit? [Answer: 240 units will bring the maximum profit of $110,200.]

2. The temperature T (measured in degrees Fahrenheit) during a person's illness at time t (measured in days after the beginning of the illness) is given by

$$T(t) = -0.3t^2 + 1.2t + 98.6.$$

What is the highest temperature of the person, and at what time does it take place? [Answer: The temperature has its highest value of 99.8 degrees on the second day of the illness.]

3. A television manufacturer determines that in order to sell x units of a new television, the price per television set must be

$$p = 960 - x.$$

The total cost of producing x television sets is given by the cost function

$$C(x) = 4000 + 30x.$$

How many television sets must the manufacturer produce and sell in order to maximize his profit? [Answer: 465.]

4. The owner of an 80-unit motel knows that all units are occupied when he charges $60 a day per unit. Each occupied room costs $4 for service and maintenance a day. From experience the owner also knows that for every x dollars increase in the daily rate of $60 there will be x units vacant. What daily price per unit will maximize the owner's profit? [Answer: $72.]

5. A cable television firm serves 20,000 households and charges $30 per month. A marketing survey reveals that each decrease of $1 in the monthly charge will result in 500 new customers—and, of course, an increase of $1 will result in a loss of 500 customers. What increase or decrease will maximize the monthly revenue, and what is the largest possible monthly revenue? [Answer: An increase of $5 will bring the largest possible revenue of $612,500.]

6. An appliance store sells 810 television sets per year. It costs $12 to store a set for a year. To reorder new television sets from the manufacturer, there is a fixed cost of $60 plus $10 for each set. How many times per year should the store reorder, and in what lot size in order to minimize inventory costs? [Answer: 9 times a year with a lot size of 90 television sets.]

7. A tree that is planted at time $t = 0$ has a current value at time t years after it was planted given by the function $P(t) = 2t - 10$. Assume that the interest rate is 5% per

year discounted continuously. When should the tree be cut down in order to maximize its present discounted value? [Hint: The present discounted value of the tree is $Q(t) = (2t - 10)e^{-0.05t}$.]

1.4 OPTIMIZING USING THE LAGRANGE METHOD

In the preceding two sections we discussed the technique of finding the optimum when the choice set is an interval. In many situations, however, we need to find the optimum when the choice set is quite explicitly described by a set of equations. Here we discuss the case in which the choice set is a subset of the xy plane desribed by an equation $g(x, y) = c$. That is, our choice set is given by

$$\Omega = \left\{(x, y) \in \mathbb{R}^2 : g(x, y) = c\right\}.$$

The *constraint function* $g(x, y)$ as well as the objective functions are usually assumed to have continuous partial derivatives on an open set O containing Ω. In this case, our optimization problem is formulated as:

> Maximize $u(x, y)$ subject to $g(x, y) = c$.

The geometrical meaning of the constraint $g(x, y) = c$ is shown in Figure 1.4. Our optimization problem here has a nice physical interpretation. We can think of the equation $g(x, y) = c$ as representing the shape of a wire and $u(x, y)$ as measuring the temperature (or the mass density) of the wire at the location (x, y). A solution to our optimization problem will then give the location on the wire with the highest temperature (or the highest mass density).

To solve this type of optimization problem, we must employ a technique known as *Lagrange's method*. This method uses partial derivatives. Recall that if $f(x, y)$ is a function of two variables, then the *partial derivative* $\frac{\partial f}{\partial x}$ with respect to x is the derivative of $f(x, y)$ with respect to x, treating the variable y as a constant. And similarly, the partial derivative

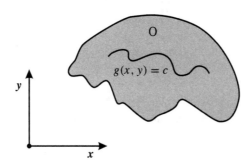

Figure 1.4

$\frac{\partial f}{\partial y}$ is the derivative of $f(x, y)$ with respect to y if we treat x as a constant. For instance, if $f(x, y) = x^2 + 2xy^3 + y^2$, then

$$\frac{\partial f}{\partial x} = 2x + 2y^3 \quad \text{and} \quad \frac{\partial f}{\partial y} = 6xy^2 + 2y.$$

We can also take partial derivatives of functions having more than two variables. When we compute the partial derivative with respect to a variable, we must remember during the differentiation process to treat all other variables as constants. For instance, consider the functions

$$f(x, y, z) = x^2 + 2x\sqrt{y} + xz^2 \quad \text{and} \quad g(x, y, z, v) = xy + zv^2 - \cos v.$$

Their partial derivatives are

$$\frac{\partial f}{\partial y} = \frac{x}{\sqrt{y}}, \quad \frac{\partial f}{\partial z} = 2xz, \quad \frac{\partial g}{\partial z} = v^2, \quad \text{and} \quad \frac{\partial g}{\partial v} = 2zv + \sin v.$$

The basic steps involved in using Lagrange's method can be described as follows. With the functions u and g we associate a new function $\mathcal{L}$, known as the *Lagrangian*, defined by the formula

$$\mathcal{L}(x, y, \lambda) = u(x, y) + \lambda\big[c - g(x, y)\big].$$

In analogy with the first-order test, the solution to our optimization problem takes place when all partial derivatives of the Lagrangian $\mathcal{L}$ are zero, that is, when $\frac{\partial \mathcal{L}}{\partial x} = \frac{\partial \mathcal{L}}{\partial y} = \frac{\partial \mathcal{L}}{\partial \lambda} = 0$. The guidelines for applying Lagrange's method are summarized as follows:

Guidelines for Lagrange's Method

To solve the optimization problem

"*Maximize (or minimize) $u(x, y)$ subject to $g(x, y) = c$*"

we must solve the system of equations

$$\frac{\partial \mathcal{L}}{\partial x} = 0, \quad \frac{\partial \mathcal{L}}{\partial y} = 0, \quad \text{and} \quad \frac{\partial \mathcal{L}}{\partial \lambda} = 0$$

or, more explicitly, we must solve the system of equations

$$\frac{\partial u}{\partial x} = \lambda \frac{\partial g}{\partial x}$$

$$\frac{\partial u}{\partial y} = \lambda \frac{\partial g}{\partial y}$$

$$g(x, y) = c$$

for the three unknowns x, y, and λ.

Then all maximizers and minimizers of the objective function $u(x, y)$ are among the pairs (x, y) that appear in the solutions of the above system.

The examples to follow are used to illustrate Lagrange's method.

Example 1.6

A company has two factories, each manufacturing the same product. Factory A produces x units of the product at a cost of $2x^2 + 50,000$ dollars, and factory B can produce y units at a cost of $y^2 + 40,000$. *If an order for 1200 units is to be filled, how should the production be distributed among the two factories in order to minimize the total production cost? Also, what is the minimum cost?*

To solve this problem, we calculate first the cost function $C(x, y)$ for producing x units from factory A and y units from factory B. Clearly,

$$C(x, y) = (2x^2 + 50,000) + (y^2 + 40,000) = 2x^2 + y^2 + 90,000.$$

If we are filling an order of 1200 units, then we have the constraint $g(x, y) = x + y = 1,200$. So, by the Lagrangian method, we must solve the system of equations

$$\frac{\partial C}{\partial x} = \lambda \frac{\partial g}{\partial x}, \quad \frac{\partial C}{\partial y} = \lambda \frac{\partial g}{\partial x}, \quad g(x, y) = 1200.$$

Computing the derivatives, we get:

$$4x = \lambda \tag{1.1}$$

$$2y = \lambda \tag{1.2}$$

$$x + y = 1200. \tag{1.3}$$

From (1.1) and (1.2), we get $2y = 4x$, or $y = 2x$. Substituting this value into (1.3), we get $x + 2x = 1200$ or $3x = 1200$. This implies $x = 400$ and $y = 1200 - 400 = 800$.

Thus the total production cost will be minimized if factory A produces 400 units and factory B produces 800 units. The total cost of the production is

$$C(400, 800) = 2 \times 400^2 + 800^2 + 90,000 = 1,050,000$$

dollars.

Example 1.7

A manufacturer uses an amount of capital K and L hours of labor to produce Q units of a product according to the production function

$$Q(K, L) = 60K^{\frac{1}{2}}L^{\frac{1}{3}}.$$

The price of capital is $20 per unit and labor costs $15 per hour.

What are the cost minimizing values of K and L that will produce a quantity of 4200 units of the product? Also, what is the minimum cost of producing the 4200 units?

The cost function for K units of capital and L hours of labor is

$$C(K, L) = 20K + 15L.$$

So our problem can be formulated in optimizing terms as follows:

$$\text{minimize } C(K, L) = 20K + 15L$$

$$\text{subject to } Q(K, L) = 60K^{\frac{1}{2}}L^{\frac{1}{3}} = 4200.$$

We shall solve this problem using Lagrange's method. First, we compute the derivatives $\frac{\partial Q}{\partial K}$ and $\frac{\partial Q}{\partial L}$. We have

$$\frac{\partial Q}{\partial K} = \frac{60}{2}K^{\frac{1}{2}-1}L^{\frac{1}{3}} = \frac{Q}{2K} \quad \text{and} \quad \frac{\partial Q}{\partial L} = \frac{60}{3}K^{\frac{1}{2}}L^{\frac{1}{3}-1} = \frac{Q}{3L}.$$

Now the Lagrange method requires one to solve the system

$$\frac{\partial C}{\partial K} = \lambda \frac{\partial Q}{\partial K}, \quad \frac{\partial C}{\partial L} = \lambda \frac{\partial Q}{\partial L}, \quad 60K^{\frac{1}{2}}L^{\frac{1}{3}} = 4200.$$

Substituting the derivatives, we obtain the system:

$$20 = \lambda \frac{Q}{2K} \tag{1.4}$$

$$15 = \lambda \frac{Q}{3L} \tag{1.5}$$

$$60K^{\frac{1}{2}}L^{\frac{1}{3}} = 4200 \tag{1.6}$$

Dividing (1.4) by (1.5), we get $\frac{20}{15} = \frac{3L}{2K}$, or $\frac{4}{3} = \frac{3L}{2K}$. This implies

$$L = \frac{8}{9}K. \tag{1.7}$$

Substituting this value into (1.6), we get $60K^{\frac{1}{2}}(\sqrt[3]{8}/\sqrt[3]{9})K^{\frac{1}{3}} = 4200$, from which it follows $K^{\frac{1}{2}+\frac{1}{3}} = 4200 \times \sqrt[3]{9}/120 = 72.8$. Thus $K^{\frac{5}{6}} = 72.8$ and so

$$K = (72.8)^{\frac{6}{5}} = 72.8^{1.2} = 171.62.$$

Now using (1.7), we get $L = 8 \times 171.62/9 = 152.55$.

In other words, a capital of 171.62 units and a labor of 152.55 hours will produce the 4200 units of the product at the minimal cost of $20 \times 171.62 + 15 \times 152.55 = \$5721$.

The next example uses the Lagrangian method to address a central issue in the theory of consumer behavior. The basic problem is to find the commodity basket that maximizes the consumer's utility subject to his income constraint.

Example 1.8 (Utility Maximization)

The budget set of the consumer is

$$\Omega = \{(x, y): x \geq 0, \ y \geq 0, \ \text{and } p_1 x + p_2 y \leq m\},$$

where p_1 and p_2 are prices and m is the income.

We use the Lagrangian method to present another technique of solving the problem posed in Example 1.1. We must solve the following optimization problem:

$$\text{Maximize } u(x, y) = xy \text{ s.t. } x \geq 0, \ y \geq 0, \ \text{and } x + 2y \leq 12.$$

It is easy to convince ourselves that the maximum takes place on the "budget line" $x + 2y = 12$. Hence we solve the optimization problem:

Maximize $u(x, y) = xy$ s.t. $x \geq 0$, $y \geq 0$, $x + 2y = 12$.

The Lagrangian method requires us to solve the system

$$\frac{\partial u}{\partial x} = \lambda \frac{\partial(x+2y)}{\partial x}, \quad \frac{\partial u}{\partial y} = \lambda \frac{\partial(x+2y)}{\partial y}, \quad x + 2y = 12$$

or

$$y = \lambda \tag{1.8}$$

$$x = 2\lambda \tag{1.9}$$

$$x + 2y = 12. \tag{1.10}$$

Substituting the values of x and y from (1.8) and (1.9) into (1.10), we get $2\lambda + 2\lambda = 12$. This implies $\lambda = 3$. Hence $x = 6$ and $y = 3$. That is, the maximizer is $(6, 3)$.

EXERCISES

1. Solve Problem 3 of Section 1.2. [Answer: A bouquet of 8 carnations and 4 roses will give the best satisfaction.]

2. A producer has $\$10,000$ to spend on the development and promotion of a new product. From experience he knows that if x thousand dollars are used for development and y thousand dollars on advertisement, sales will be approximately $Q(x, y) = 100x^{\frac{3}{2}}y^{\frac{1}{2}}$ units. How many thousands of dollars should the producer spend on development and how many on advertisement in order to maximize sales? What is the maximum number of units that the producer can sell? [Answer: $x = 7.5$; $y = 2.5$; maximum # of units 3248.]

3. Maximize the utility function $u(x, y) = x^3 y^2$ over the budget set

$$\Omega = \left\{ (x, y) : x \geq 0, \ y \geq 0 \text{ and } 3x + 5y = 15 \right\}.$$

4. There are 80 yards of fencing available to enclose a rectangular field. What are the dimensions (i.e., the length and the width) of the enclosed rectangle with the largest possible area? What is the largest area? [Answer: length $=$ width $= 20$ yd.]

5. A cylindrical can is to hold 4π cubic inches of apple juice. The cost per square inch of constructing the metal top and bottom is twice the cost per square inch of constructing the cardboard side. What are the dimensions of the least expensive can? [Answer: radius $= 1$ in.; height $= 4$ in.]

1.5 UNCERTAINTY AND CHANCE

It has been said that the only two certain things in this world are death and taxes. Everything else is governed by randomness and uncertainty. To understand random phenomena in a systematic way, mathematicians developed the *theory of probability*.[4] It is based on the fundamental concept of a probability space.

[4]A delightful history of this can be found in Peter L. Bernstein's book *Against the Gods: The Remarkable Story of Risk*, John Wiley and Sons, New York, 1996.

A *probability space* is a pair (S, P), where S is a finite set, called the *sample space*, and P is a function that assigns to every subset A of S a real number $P(A)$ between 0 and 1. If we let $S = \{s_1, s_2, \ldots, s_n\}$ and $p_i = P(\{s_i\})$ (the probability of the singleton $\{s_i\}$), then the function P satisfies the following properties:

1. $p_i \geq 0$ for each i and $\sum_{i=1}^{n} p_i = 1$.
2. If A is a subset of S, then $P(A) = \sum_{s_i \in A} p_i$.

In particular, we have

$$P(\emptyset) = 0 \quad \text{and} \quad P(S) = 1 .^5$$

The subsets of the sample space S are called *events*. If A is an event, then $P(A)$ is the probability of the event A, that is, the chance of the occurrence of A. The sample space S can be an infinite set. However, in this case, the probability function P is a special set function (called a *probability measure*) defined on a specific collection of subsets of S (the events).

Events can be thought of as representing the random outcomes of chance experiments. For example, in tossing a coin, the outcomes are "heads" or "tails." In this situation, our sample space is the set $S = \{H, T\}$. For the coin to be fair (or unbiased), we assign the probabilities $P(H) = P(T) = \frac{1}{2}$. However, if we think that the coin is not fair, then we can assign other probabilities to the events H and T; for instance, we can put $P(H) = \frac{1}{3}$ and $P(T) = \frac{2}{3}$.

In the chance experiment of throwing dice, the sample space is the set $S = \{1, 2, 3, 4, 5, 6\}$, where each number i represents the event: *After throwing the die the number i appears on the top face*. If we think that the die is fair, then we assign the probabilities $p_i = \frac{1}{6}$ for each i.

A very useful way of understanding the outcomes of random events is by means of the random variables. To discuss this concept, we start with a probability space (S, P).

A *random variable* is a function $X: S \to \mathbb{R}$ (from the sample space into the real numbers). With the random variable X, we can associate several events in the sample space. If A is a subset of $\mathbb{R}$ (the set of real numbers), then we denote by $X \in A$ the event of the sample space $\{s \in S: X(s) \in A\}$. That is, we have

$$X \in A = \{s \in S: X(s) \in A\}.$$

For instance, if x is an arbitrary real number, then

$$X \leq x = \{s \in S: X(s) \leq x\}.$$

DEFINITION 1.9 (The Distribution of a Random Variable)   If $X: S \to \mathbb{R}$ is a random variable, then the *distribution function* of X is the function $F: \mathbb{R} \to \mathbb{R}$ defined by

$$F(x) = P(X \leq x)$$

for each real number x.

---

[5]The symbol $\emptyset$ denotes, as usual, the *empty set*—the set without any elements.

We present two examples to illustrate the concept of distribution function of a random variable.

Example 1.10

Consider the chance experiment of tossing a coin. We mentioned before that the sample space is $S = \{H, T\}$ and (assuming that we are tossing an unbiased coin) the probabilities are $P(H) = P(T) = \frac{1}{2}$.

Consider the random variable $X: S \to \mathbb{R}$ defined by $X(H) = 1$ and $X(T) = 2$. Then it is easy to see that

$$X \leq x = \begin{cases} \emptyset & \text{if } x < 1, \\ \{H\} & \text{if } 1 \leq x < 2, \\ \{H, T\} & \text{if } x \geq 2. \end{cases}$$

This gives the following distribution function

$$F(x) = P(X \leq x) = \begin{cases} 0 & \text{if } x < 1, \\ \frac{1}{2} & \text{if } 1 \leq x < 2, \\ 1 & \text{if } x \geq 2. \end{cases}$$

Its graph is shown in Figure 1.5(a).

Example 1.11

Here we consider the chance experiment of tossing a fair die. The sample space is $S = \{1, 2, 3, 4, 5, 6\}$ and $p_i = \frac{1}{6}$ for each i. The random variable $X: S \to \mathbb{R}$ is defined by $X(i) = i$. It is easy to see that the distribution function F of X is defined as follows: If k_x denotes the number of integers among $1, 2, 3, 4, 5, 6$ that are less than or equal to x, then

$$F(x) = \frac{k_x}{6}.$$

The graph of $F(x)$ is shown in Figure 1.5(b).

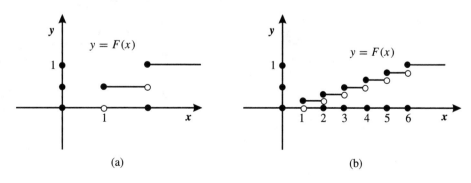

(a)   (b)

Figure 1.5

The shapes of the graphs of the distribution functions shown in Figure 1.5 depict the fundamental properties of all distribution functions. They are described in the next theorem.

Theorem 1.12 (Properties of Distributions)   If $F: \mathbb{R} \rightarrow \mathbb{R}$ is the distribution function of a random variable X, then:

- **i.** $0 \le F(x) \le 1$ for each x.
- **ii.** F is increasing; that is, $F(x) \le F(y)$ if $x < y$.
- **iii.** $\lim_{x \to -\infty} F(x) = 0$ and $\lim_{x \to \infty} F(x) = 1$.
- **iv.** $P(a < X \le b) = F(b) - F(a)$ if $a < b$.
- **v.** $P(X = a) = $ the jump of the distribution function $F(x)$ at $x = a$.

A typical example of a distribution function is shown in Figure 1.6. There are three important numbers associated with random variables. They are known as the *expectation*, the *variance*, and the *standard deviation*. They are defined as follows.

DEFINITION 1.13   If $X: S \rightarrow \mathbb{R}$ is a random variable, then:

1. The *expectation* or the *expected value* $E(X)$ of X is the real number

$$E(X) = \sum_{i=1}^{n} p_i X(s_i).$$

2. The *variance* $\text{Var}(X)$ of X is the non-negative real number

$$\text{Var}(X) = \sum_{i=1}^{n} p_i \left[X(s_i) - E(X) \right]^2.$$

3. The *standard deviation* σ of X is the positive square root of $\text{Var}(X)$, that is,

$$\sigma = \sqrt{\text{Var}(X)}.$$

We illustrate the preceding notions using Examples 1.10 and 1.11. For Example 1.10, we have

$$E(X) = \tfrac{1}{2} \times 1 + \tfrac{1}{2} \times 2 = \tfrac{3}{2}$$

$$\text{Var}(X) = \tfrac{1}{2}\left(1 - \tfrac{3}{2}\right)^2 + \tfrac{1}{2}\left(2 - \tfrac{3}{2}\right)^2 = \tfrac{1}{4}$$

$$\sigma = \sqrt{\text{Var}(X)} = \sqrt{\tfrac{1}{4}} = \tfrac{1}{2}.$$

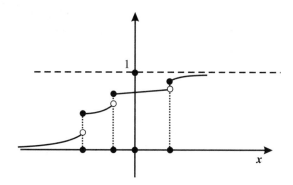

Figure 1.6 The graph of a typical distribution.

For Example 1.11, we have

$$E(X) = \tfrac{1}{6} \times 1 + \tfrac{1}{6} \times 2 + \tfrac{1}{6} \times 3 + \tfrac{1}{6} \times 4 + \tfrac{1}{6} \times 5 + \tfrac{1}{6} \times 6 = \tfrac{21}{6} = \tfrac{7}{2}$$

$$\mathrm{Var}(X) = \tfrac{1}{6} \sum_{i=1}^{6} \left(i - \tfrac{7}{2}\right)^2 = \tfrac{35}{12}$$

$$\sigma = \sqrt{\mathrm{Var}(X)} = \sqrt{\tfrac{35}{12}} = 1.708 \,.$$

In many situations of randomness and uncertainty the distribution function of a random variable is good enough to provide all information regarding the chance experiment. For this reason, in applications the sample space (and even the random variable) are relegated to the background, and they are replaced by the distribution function of the random variable. Certain distributions are very common and appear in many problems. As a matter of fact, in a variety of applications the distributions are also continuous functions and can be expressed in terms of a density function as follows.

DEFINITION 1.14   A distribution function F of a random variable is said to have a *density function* if there exists a non-negative function $f: \mathbb{R} \rightarrow \mathbb{R}$ (called the *density function*) such that

$$F(x) = \int_{-\infty}^{x} f(t)\, dt$$

holds for all x.

The density function f, besides being positive, also satisfies the property $\int_{-\infty}^{\infty} f(t)\, dt = 1$. The density function allows us to compute the probabilities of the random variable X in terms of integrals. We have

$$P(a \leq X \leq b) = \int_{a}^{b} f(t)\, dt$$

for all reals $a < b$. In terms of the density function, the expected value and the variance of a random variable can be computed from the following formulas.

$$E(X) = \int_{-\infty}^{\infty} t f(t)\, dt$$

$$\text{Var}(X) = \int_{-\infty}^{\infty} \left[t - E(X)\right]^2 f(t)\, dt$$

We close the section by presenting two important examples of distribution functions that are very common in practical problems.

Example 1.15 (The Uniform Distribution)

A random variable X is said to have a *uniform distribution function F* over a finite closed interval $[a, b]$ if F has the density function

$$f(x) = \begin{cases} \frac{1}{b-a}, & \text{if } a < x < b \\ 0, & \text{if } x \le a \text{ or } x \ge b. \end{cases}$$

The distribution function F is now given by

$$F(x) = \int_{-\infty}^{x} f(t)\, dt = \begin{cases} 0, & \text{if } x \le a \\ \frac{x-a}{b-a}, & \text{if } a < x < b \\ 1, & \text{if } x \ge b. \end{cases}$$

The graphs of the density and distribution functions of a uniformly distributed random variable are shown in Figure 1.7.

Computing the expectation, variance, and standard deviation of a uniformly distributed random variable X, we find that:

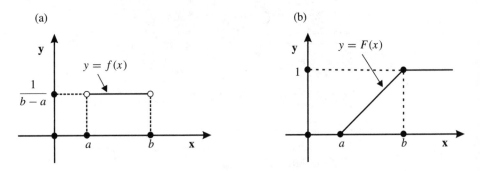

Figure 1.7   (a) The density function of the uniform distribution. (b) The uniform distribution.

$$E(X) = \int_{-\infty}^{\infty} t f(t)\, dt = \frac{1}{b-a} \int_a^b t\, dt = \frac{b^2-a^2}{2(b-a)} = \frac{a+b}{2}$$

$$\mathrm{Var}(X) = \frac{1}{b-a} \int_a^b \left(t - \frac{a+b}{2}\right)^2 dt = \frac{(b-a)^2}{12}$$

$$\sigma = \sqrt{\mathrm{Var}(X)} = \sqrt{\frac{(b-a)^2}{12}} = \frac{(b-a)\sqrt{3}}{6}\,.$$

Example 1.16 (The Normal Distribution)

A random variable is said to have a *normal distribution* with parameters m and σ^2 if its distribution has the density function

$$f(x) = \frac{1}{\sigma\sqrt{2\pi}} e^{-\frac{(x-m)^2}{2\sigma^2}}\,.$$

That is, the distribution function of a normally distributed random variable X with the parameters m and σ^2 is given by the formula

$$\Phi_X(x) = \frac{1}{\sigma\sqrt{2\pi}} \int_{-\infty}^x e^{-\frac{(t-m)^2}{2\sigma^2}}\, dt\,.$$

The graph of the density function $f(x)$ is a bell-shaped curve that is symmetric with respect to the line $x = m$. The graphs of the functions $f(x)$ and $\Phi_X(x)$ are shown in Figure 1.8.

It turns out that the expectation and variance of a normally distributed random variable X with the parameters m and σ^2 are given by

$$E(X) = m \quad \text{and} \quad \mathrm{Var}(X) = \sigma^2\,.$$

A random variable that is normally distributed with parameters $m = 0$ and $\sigma = 1$ is said to have the *standard normal distribution*. The standard normal distribution function Φ is given by

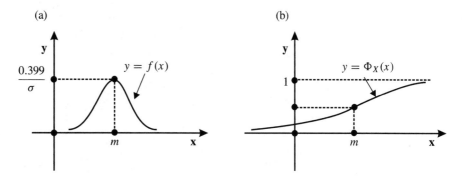

Figure 1.8   (a) The density of a normal distribution. (b) The distribution of a normal random variable.

$$\Phi(x) = \frac{1}{\sqrt{2\pi}} \int_{-\infty}^{x} e^{-\frac{t^2}{2}} \, dt \,.$$

The values of Φ are shown in Table 1.1. For negative values of x the value of Φ can be computed from the formula

$$\Phi(-x) = 1 - \Phi(x) \,.$$

In general, if X is a normally distributed random variable with parameters m and σ^2, then its distribution Φ_X is related to the standard distribution via the formula

$$\Phi_X(x) = \Phi\left(\frac{x-m}{\sigma}\right). \tag{1.11}$$

Equation (1.11) together with Table 1.1 allow us to compute the values of any normal distribution Φ_x.

TABLE 1.1
Values of $\Phi(x)$

x	0.00	0.01	0.02	0.03	0.04	0.05	0.06	0.07	0.08	0.09
0.0	0.5000	0.5040	0.5080	0.5120	0.5160	0.5199	0.5239	0.5279	0.5319	0.5359
0.1	0.5398	0.5438	0.5478	0.5517	0.5557	0.5596	0.5636	0.5675	0.5714	0.5753
0.2	0.5793	0.5832	0.5871	0.5910	0.5948	0.5987	0.6026	0.6064	0.6103	0.6141
0.3	0.6179	0.6217	0.6255	0.6293	0.6331	0.6368	0.6406	0.6443	0.6480	0.6517
0.4	0.6554	0.6591	0.6628	0.6664	0.6700	0.6736	0.6772	0.6808	0.6844	0.6879
0.5	0.6915	0.6950	0.6985	0.7019	0.7054	0.7088	0.7123	0.7157	0.7190	0.7224
0.6	0.7257	0.7291	0.7324	0.7357	0.7398	0.7422	0.7454	0.7486	0.7517	0.7549
0.7	0.7580	0.7611	0.7642	0.7673	0.7704	0.7734	0.7764	0.7794	0.7823	0.7852
0.8	0.7881	0.7910	0.7939	0.7967	0.7995	0.8023	0.8051	0.8078	0.8106	0.8133
0.9	0.8159	0.8186	0.8212	0.8238	0.8264	0.8289	0.8315	0.8340	0.8365	0.8389
1.0	0.8413	0.8438	0.8461	0.8485	0.8508	0.8531	0.8554	0.8577	0.8599	0.8621
1.1	0.8643	0.8665	0.8686	0.8708	0.8729	0.8749	0.8770	0.8790	0.8810	0.8830
1.2	0.8849	0.8869	0.8888	0.8907	0.8925	0.8944	0.8962	0.8980	0.8997	0.9015
1.3	0.9032	0.9049	0.9066	0.9082	0.9099	0.9115	0.9131	0.9147	0.9162	0.9177
1.4	0.9192	0.9207	0.9222	0.9236	0.9251	0.9265	0.9279	0.9292	0.9306	0.9319
1.5	0.9332	0.9345	0.9357	0.9370	0.9382	0.9394	0.9406	0.9418	0.9429	0.9441
1.6	0.9452	0.9463	0.9474	0.9484	0.9495	0.9505	0.9515	0.9525	0.9535	0.9545
1.7	0.9554	0.9564	0.9573	0.9582	0.9591	0.9599	0.9608	0.9616	0.9625	0.9633
1.8	0.9641	0.9649	0.9656	0.9664	0.9671	0.9678	0.9686	0.9693	0.9699	0.9706
1.9	0.9713	0.9719	0.9726	0.9732	0.9738	0.9744	0.9750	0.9756	0.9761	0.9767
2.0	0.9772	0.9778	0.9783	0.9788	0.9793	0.9798	0.9803	0.9808	0.9812	0.9817
2.1	0.9821	0.9826	0.9830	0.9834	0.9838	0.9842	0.9846	0.9850	0.9854	0.9857
2.2	0.9861	0.9864	0.9868	0.9871	0.9875	0.9878	0.9881	0.9884	0.9887	0.9890
2.3	0.9893	0.9896	0.9898	0.9901	0.9904	0.9906	0.9909	0.9911	0.9913	0.9916
2.4	0.9918	0.9920	0.9922	0.9925	0.9927	0.9929	0.9931	0.9932	0.9934	0.9936
2.5	0.9938	0.9940	0.9941	0.9943	0.9945	0.9946	0.9948	0.9949	0.9951	0.9952

TABLE 1.1
Values of Φ(x) Continued

x	0.00	0.01	0.02	0.03	0.04	0.05	0.06	0.07	0.08	0.09
2.6	0.9953	0.9955	0.9956	0.9957	0.9959	0.9960	0.9961	0.9962	0.9963	0.9964
2.7	0.9965	0.9966	0.9967	0.9968	0.9969	0.9970	0.9971	0.9972	0.9973	0.9974
2.8	0.9974	0.9975	0.9976	0.9977	0.9977	0.9978	0.9979	0.9929	0.9980	0.9981
2.9	0.9981	0.9982	0.9982	0.9983	0.9984	0.9984	0.9985	0.9985	0.9986	0.9986
3.0	0.9987	0.9987	0.9987	0.9988	0.9988	0.9989	0.9989	0.9989	0.9990	0.9990
3.1	0.9990	0.9991	0.9991	0.9991	0.9992	0.9992	0.9992	0.9992	0.9993	0.9993
3.2	0.9993	0.9993	0.9994	0.9994	0.9994	0.9994	0.9995	0.9995	0.9995	0.9995
3.3	0.9995	0.9995	0.9995	0.9996	0.9996	0.9996	0.9996	0.9996	0.9996	0.9997
3.4	0.9997	0.9997	0.9997	0.9997	0.9997	0.9997	0.9997	0.9997	0.9997	0.9998

EXERCISES

1. Sketch the distribution function of the random variable of Example 1.10 with probabilities $P(H) = \frac{1}{3}$ and $P(T) = \frac{2}{3}$. Also compute its expectation, variance, and standard deviation. [Answers: $E(X) = \frac{5}{3}$; $\mathrm{Var}(X) = \frac{2}{9}$.]

2. The return of a stock can be viewed as a random variable X. Sketch the distribution of the "return random variable" X for a stock that has a return of 3% with a probability of $\frac{1}{3}$, 6% with a probability of $\frac{1}{3}$, and 10% with a probability of $\frac{1}{3}$. What is the sample space of the random variable X?

3. A bus company schedules a southbound train every 30 minutes at a certain station. A woman enters the station at a random time. Let X be the random variable that counts the number of minutes she has to wait for the next bus.

   Assume that the statement "she enters the station at random time" means that X has a uniform distribution at the interval $[0, 30]$. Draw the graph of the distribution and compute the probability that she has to wait at most 21 minutes for the next train. [Answer: 70%.]

4. Let X be the random variable that counts the number of typographical errors on a page of this book. If X has a uniform distribution on the interval $[0, 1.1]$, what is the probability that there is at least one typographical error on this page? [Answer: 9.1%.]

5. The annual rainfall (in inches) in a certain location is a random variable X. Assume that X is normally distributed with parameters $m = 30$ and $\sigma = 5$. What is the probability that this location will have over 35 inches of rain in any given year? [Answer: 15.87%.]

6. Let X be a random variable measuring the number of miles that a car can run before its battery wears out. Assume that the distribution of X is given by

$$F(x) = \begin{cases} 1 - e^{-0.0001x}, & \text{if } x \geq 0 \\ 0, & \text{if } x < 0. \end{cases}$$

If a person takes a 5000-mile trip, what is the probability that the person will be able to complete the trip without replacing the car battery? [Answer: $e^{-0.5} \approx 60.65\%$.]

7. The lifetime in years of a certain electronic tube can be described by a random variable X whose distribution has the density function

$$f(x) = \begin{cases} xe^{-x}, & \text{if } x \geq 0 \\ 0, & \text{if } x < 0. \end{cases}$$

What is the expected life of such a tube? [Answer: 2 years.]

8. A certain brand of cereal claims that the mean number of raisins in each box is 80 with a standard deviation of 6. If the raisins are normally distributed, what are the chances that an arbitrary box has (a) fewer than 70 raisins and (b) more than 90 raisins?
What should be your answers if the raisins are uniformly distributed?

1.6 DECISION MAKING UNDER UNCERTAINTY

In many situations the outcome of a decision depends on chance. When an individual buys a stock or a bond, the individual does not know precisely the future value of his investment. When a farmer decides on the kind of crop to plant, he does not know what price the crop will fetch when it is harvested. Similarly, when an individual buys a lottery ticket, the individual is very uncertain about winning the lottery. Nonetheless, decisions have to be made under such conditions of uncertainty, and the question then is whether there is a consistent way in which to think about how to make decisions under these conditions. Here we explore the fundamentals of a theory of decision making under uncertainty known as *expected utility theory*.

To motivate the discussion, let us assume, for the sake of simplicity, that an individual has to decide how to invest $100. The choices are:

1. To buy a bond that returns 6% with certainty, or
2. To invest in a stock that returns 3% with a probability of $\frac{1}{3}$, 6% with a probability of $\frac{1}{3}$, and 10% with a probability of $\frac{1}{3}$.

Clearly, investing in the stock is risky, as there is a chance that one may end up with the smaller return of 3%. But then again, there is also a good chance that one may end up with the higher return of 10%. What choice will the individual make in this situation? Obviously, the answer will depend on the risk-taking propensities of the individual. If the individual is willing to take some risk, she will compute the *expected returns* from the two investments. In the case of the bond the expected return is 6%. In the case of the stock, the expected return is a little more complex and is computed as

$$\frac{1}{3} \times 3\% + \frac{1}{3} \times 6\% + \frac{1}{3} \times 10\% = 6.33\%.$$

Therefore, the expected return from the stock is higher than the expected return of 6% of the bonds. One should note that, in terms of the language of probability theory, the expected return is none other than the expected value of the random variable, which gives us the value of the different possible returns from the stock.

In decision making under uncertainty, the different outcomes that can result, in general, lead to different levels of wealth. Wealth can usually be translated into consumption and, hence, utility. We can, therefore, speak of the utility generated by wealth w and write it as $u(w)$. In the more abstract and formal language of mathematics, we would say that if a decision d leads to one of the alternative levels of wealth w_1, w_2, and w_3, then the decision will result in one of three alternative levels of utility $u(w_1)$, $u(w_2)$, and $u(w_3)$. If the probabilities with which these three outcomes can occur are known to be p_1, p_2, and p_3, then the *expected utility of the decision d* is given by

$$Eu(d) = p_1 u(w_1) + p_2 u(w_2) + p_3 u(w_3).$$

The function $u(w)$, which is called the *utility function over wealth* or the *von Neumann–Morgenstern utility function*, is intrinsic to the individual and represents his preferences over different levels of wealth. For our purposes, a *utility function over wealth* is any strictly increasing function $u: [0, \infty) \to \mathbb{R}$. In the discussion that follows we ignore the case of negative wealth, since bankruptcy laws prevent individuals from having negative levels of wealth.[6]

Now every decision made under uncertainty can be viewed as having chosen a lottery L over alternative levels of wealth w_i, where each level of wealth w_i can be assigned a probability p_i. The probability p_i is the probability of receiving wealth w_i when the decision is made or the lottery is played. Therefore, we can denote a lottery L by the collection of pairs $L = \{(w_i, p_i): i = 1, \ldots, n\}$, when the lottery has n possible alternative outcomes and each outcome i occurs with probability p_i. Indeed, the proper way to think of decision making under uncertainty is to think of it as involving making choices over alternative lotteries. Thus an individual given a choice between two lotteries L_1 and L_2 would either prefer L_1 to L_2 or L_2 to L_1 or be indifferent between the two lotteries.

Now assume that two lotteries with the same set of alternatives are given, say, as

$$L_1 = \left\{(w_i, p_i): i = 1, \ldots, n\right\} \quad \text{and} \quad L_2 = \left\{(w_i', p_i'): i = 1, \ldots, n\right\}.$$

Then every probability p (i.e., $0 \le p \le 1$) gives rise to a new lottery

$$pL_1 + (1 - p)L_2 = \left\{(pw_i + (1 - p)w_i', pp_i + (1 - p)p_i'): i = 1, \ldots, n\right\}.$$

If the lotteries L_1 and L_2 do not have the same set of alternatives, then we can take the union A of all possible alternatives of both lotteries and consider that L_1 and L_2 have alternatives A. Notice, of course, that an alternative in A that is not an alternative of L_1 is assumed to have probability zero for the lottery L_1, and an alternative of A that is not an alternative of L_2 has probability zero for the lottery L_2. Thus for any probability p the lottery $pL_1 + (1 - p)L_2$ is well defined. Any lottery of the form $pL_1 + (1 - p)L_2$ is called a *compound lottery*.

Now suppose that an individual prefers the lottery L_1 to the lottery L_2. It is reasonable to expect that the ranking of L_1 and L_2 should remain unchanged if we mix a third lottery L_3 with both L_1 and L_2. This reasoning leads to the following axiom.

---

[6]In some cases, the utility when $w = 0$ is taken to be $-\infty$, i.e., $u(0) = -\infty$. In principle, it is possible to define a utility function on $(-\infty, \infty)$, but this often leads to problems with interpretation of the utility function. Note, however, that the utility function u can take negative values.

DEFINITION 1.17 (The Independence Axiom)   An individual's choice over lotteries satisfies the *independence axiom* whenever a lottery L_1 is preferred to another lottery L_2, then for each $0 < p < 1$ the compound lottery $pL_1 + (1-p)L_3$ is preferred to the compound lottery $pL_2 + (1-p)L_3$ for all lotteries L_3.

Another property of choice over lotteries that is used is that of continuity.

DEFINITION 1.18 (The Continuity Axiom)   An individual's choice over lotteries satisfies the *continuity axiom* whenever a sequence $\{p_n\}$ of probabilities (i.e., $0 \le p_n \le 1$ holds for each n) converges to p, that is, $p_n \to p$, and the lottery $p_n L_1 + (1 - p_n)L_2$ is preferred to a lottery L_3 for all n, then $pL_1 + (1-p)L_2$ is preferred to L_3.

Intuitively, the above definition means that an individual's choice over lotteries satisfies the continuity axiom if small changes in the probabilities with which the lotteries are chosen changes the rank over the lotteries only slightly.

Let $\mathcal{L}$ denote the set of all lotteries. Then an individual's choice over lotteries is simply a utility function $U: \mathcal{L} \to \mathbb{R}$. If an individual's choice over lotteries satisfies the axioms of independence and continuity, then the individual's choice has a particularly nice representation in terms of expected utilities. This result, which is central in the theory of decision making under uncertainty, is known as the "Expected Utility Theorem"[7]:

Theorem 1.19 (Expected Utility Theorem)   If an individual's utility function $U: \mathcal{L} \to \mathbb{R}$ over the set of lotteries satisfies independence and continuity, then there is a von Neumann–Morgenstern utility function u over wealth such that

$$U(L) = \sum_{i=1}^{n} p_i u(w_i)$$

for every lottery $L = \{(w_i, p_i): i = 1, \ldots, n\}$.

One may now argue, of course, that the utility of the decision, which is the utility from the lottery, is different from the expected utility computed above. This is indeed a reasonable point that the expected utility may possibly give us an erroneous notion of the

[7]For further details about the Expected Utility Theorem see the books by H. L. Varian [24, p. 156], D. M. Kreps [9, Proposition 3.1, p. 76], and A. Mas-Colell, M. D. Whinston, and J. R. Green [12, Chapter 6].

true utility of the decision. However, if the utility profiles over lotteries are consistent with the axioms of independence and continuity, one can invoke the expected utility theorem to argue that if the utility profile over wealth is properly chosen, then one can use expected utilities to correctly compute the true utility profile over the lotteries. In such cases, since the objective of the decision maker is to choose the lottery that gives him the highest utility, the Expected Utility Theorem guarantees that this can be achieved by finding the lottery that maximizes the expected utility over wealth.

Quite often the expected return of a lottery L is described by a continuous "return" distribution with a density function $f(r)$ over the rate of return r. In this case, if an individual has a utility function $u(w)$ over wealth and invests $\$W$ in the lottery, then his expected utility of the lottery L is given by the formula

$$Eu(L) = \int_{-1}^{\infty} u((1+r)W) f(r) \, dr \, .$$

Observe that $f(r)$ is defined over the interval $[-1, \infty)$, where $r = -1$ is the value for which the individual's wealth has been driven down to zero.

We now present some examples to illustrate the Expected Utility Theorem.

Example 1.20

Suppose an individual is offered two gambles. In the first gamble he has to pay $\$100$ in order to win $\$500$ with a probability of $\frac{1}{2}$ or win $\$100$ otherwise. The individual's utility over wealth, that is, his von Neumann–Morgenstern utility function, is $u(w) = \sqrt{w}$. The expected utility of the first gamble is:

$$\tfrac{1}{2}\sqrt{500 - 100} + \tfrac{1}{2}\sqrt{100 - 100} = \tfrac{1}{2}\sqrt{400} = \tfrac{20}{2} = 10 \, .$$

In the second gamble the individual pays $\$100$ for the chance of winning $\$325$ with a probability of $\frac{1}{2}$ and $\$136$ also with a probability of $\frac{1}{2}$. The expected utility of the second gamble is

$$\tfrac{1}{2}\sqrt{225} + \tfrac{1}{2}\sqrt{36} = \tfrac{1}{2} \times 15 + \tfrac{1}{2} \times 6 = \tfrac{21}{2} = 10.5 \, .$$

The individual, therefore, prefers the second gamble even though in the first gamble he stands to win a larger sum. Now if the same gamble is offered to an individual whose utility of wealth is given by $u(w) = w$, then the expected utility of the first gamble for the second individual is

$$\tfrac{1}{2} \times 400 = 200 \, ,$$

while the expected utility of the second gamble is

$$\tfrac{1}{2} \times 225 + \tfrac{1}{2} \times 36 = 130.5 \, .$$

The second individual prefers the first gamble.

The example illustrates an important fact about decision making under uncertainty, namely, that different individuals have quite different tolerance for *risk*. In the example, the first individual is not very comfortable taking risks, while the second individual seems to tolerate it quite well. Indeed, this element is so important in the theory of choice under uncertainty that in the literature one distinguishes between three types of individuals: those who are *risk averse*, those who are *risk neutral*, and those who are *risk seeking*.

It is worth noticing in the example that the *expected value* of the gambles (to be distinguished from the *expected utility*) is $200 and $130.5, respectively. The second individual evidently ranks lotteries according to expected value. *An individual who ranks gambles according to their expected value is said to be risk neutral.* The first individual, however, does not rank according to expected value. Indeed, if the first individual is offered a choice between the first gamble and a sure win of $200, the individual would choose the sure win over the gamble, as the expected utility of the sure win of $200 is $\sqrt{200} = 14.14$, which is greater than 10; the expected utility of the gamble. Such *individuals who prefer the sure thing to gambles with the same expected value are said to be risk averse.* Likewise, a *risk seeking* individual prefers the gamble to a sure thing with the same expected value.

In general, we can characterize an individual's risk-taking propensities by the nature of their utility function $u: [0, \infty) \to \mathbb{R}$. If the utility function is *linear* in wealth, that is, the utility function u is of the form

$$u(w) = aw + b$$

the individual is *risk neutral*. If the utility function u is strictly concave, the individual is *risk averse*, and finally, if the utility function is strictly convex, the individual is *risk seeking*. The graphs in Figure 1.9 illustrate utility functions with the three different risk-taking propensities.

Let us recall the definitions of concave and convex functions. A function $u: I \to \mathbb{R}$, where I is an interval, is said to be:

- **convex**, whenever

$$u(\alpha x_1 + (1 - \alpha)x_2) \le \alpha u(x_1) + (1 - \alpha)u(x_2)$$

holds for all $x_1, x_2 \in I$ with $x_1 \ne x_2$ and each $0 < \alpha < 1$, and

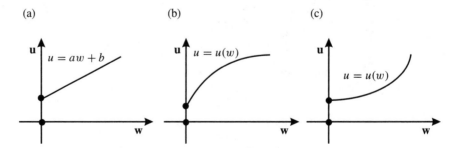

Figure 1.9   (a) Linear utility: risk neutral. (b) Concave utility: risk averse. (c) Convex utility: risk seeking.

- **concave**, whenever

$$u(\alpha x_1 + (1 - \alpha)x_2) \geq \alpha u(x_1) + (1 - \alpha)u(x_2)$$

holds for all $x_1, x_2 \in I$ with $x_1 \neq x_2$ and each $0 < \alpha < 1$.

If the above inequalities are strict, then f is called *strictly convex*, respectively, *strictly concave*. In terms of derivatives, it is well known that if a function u satisfies $u''(w) > 0$ [resp. $u''(w) < 0$] for each w, then u is strictly convex (resp., strictly concave).

Typical examples of risk-averse utility functions are provided by the functions $u(w) = \sqrt[n]{w}$, and typical examples of risk-seeking utility functions are the functions $u(w) = w^n$, where n is a natural number.

Example 1.21 (Application to Insurance)

Suppose an individual owns a house worth \$W. There is a possibility that the house may be destroyed by flood or fire with probability p. Assume also that the individual can buy \$1 amount of coverage for \$x. Here x is the *insurance premium*. How much coverage will the individual buy?

An individual will, in general, buy enough coverage that is compatible with his or her tolerance for risk [i.e., compatible with the individual's utility function $u(w)$] and the cost of the coverage. We expect the individual to choose just the right (optimal) amount of coverage.

Formally, we express this as an expected utility-maximizing choice. The reason for doing this is the *Expected Utility Theorem*. Hence the amount of coverage q purchased by an individual would maximize the expected utility

$$E(q) = pu(q - xq) + (1 - p)u(W - xq). \tag{1.12}$$

This formula is justified as follows. If the house is destroyed, then the owner will receive the amount q of the coverage minus the amount xq paid to purchase this coverage, a total of $q - xq$. Since the probability of destruction of the house is p, this implies that the expected utility from destruction of the house is $pu(q - xq)$. On the other hand, with probability $1 - p$ the house will not be destroyed, in which case its value is $W - xq$ and therefore its expected utility is $(1 - p)u(W - xq)$.

Next, notice that since u is not defined for negative wealth, it follows from (1.12) that $W - xq \geq 0$ or $q \leq \frac{W}{x}$. This guarantees that the domain of the expected utility function $E(q)$ is the closed interval $[0, \frac{W}{x}]$.

Now assume that $W = \$100,000$, $p = 0.01$, and $x = 0.02$. As we shall see next, the method of maximizing $E(q)$ depends upon the type of individual. We analyze the situation by distinguishing between the following three cases.

CASE I.
The individual is risk averse with utility function over wealth $u(w) = \sqrt{w}$.

In this case, it follows from (1.12) that

$$E(q) = p\sqrt{(1-x)q} + (1-p)\sqrt{W - xq}$$
$$= 0.01\sqrt{0.98q} + 0.99\sqrt{W - 0.02q}$$
$$= 0.01\left(\sqrt{0.98q} + 99\sqrt{W - 0.02q}\right).$$

The graph of $E(q)$ is shown in Figure 1.10(a). Taking the derivative, we get

$$E'(q) = 0.01\left(\frac{0.98}{2\sqrt{0.98q}} - \frac{99 \times 0.02}{2\sqrt{W - 0.02q}}\right)$$
$$= 0.005\left(\sqrt{\frac{0.98}{q}} - \frac{1.98}{\sqrt{W - 0.02q}}\right).$$

Letting $E'(q) = 0$, we get $\sqrt{0.98/q} = 1.98/\sqrt{W - 0.02q}$ and by squaring both sides we see that $0.98/q = (1.98)^2/(W - 0.02q)$ or $0.98(W - 0.02q) = 3.9204q$. Letting $W = 100,000$ and multiplying, we obtain $98,000 - 0.0196q = 3.9204q$ or $98,000 = 3.94q$. This implies

$$q = \frac{98,000}{3.94} = \$24,873.10.$$

CASE II.
The individual is risk seeking with utility function over wealth $u(w) = w^2$.

Computing the expected utility from (1.12), we get

$$E(q) = 0.01(0.98q)^2 + 0.99(W - 0.02q)^2$$
$$= 0.01\left[0.9604q^2 + 99(W^2 - 0.04Wq + 0.0004q^2)\right]$$
$$= 0.01\left(q^2 - 3.96Wq + 99W^2\right).$$

The graph of this function is shown in Figure 1.10(b). Notice that $q = 0$ is the maximizer of $E(q)$, which means that this risk-seeking individual will not purchase any insurance.

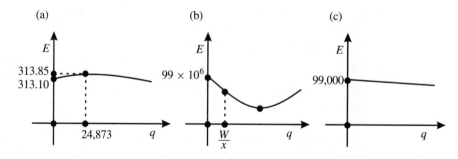

Figure 1.10 (a) Risk-averse individual. (b) Risk-seeking individual. (c) Risk-neutral individual.

CASE III.
The individual is risk neutral with utility function over wealth $u(w) = w$.

Here the expected utility is

$$E(q) = p(1 - x)q + (1 - p)(W - xq)$$
$$= [p(1 - x) - (1 - p)x]q + (1 - p)W$$
$$= (p - x)q + (1 - p)W$$
$$= -0.01q + 99,000.$$

This is a linear function (see Figure 1.10(c)) and is maximized when $q = 0$.

In other words, if the premium is 2 cents for every dollar of coverage, a house that is currently valued at $100,000 and that has a chance of 1 in 100 of being destroyed by a flood or a fire would be insured up to $24,873$ by a risk averse individual with utility function $u(w) = \sqrt{w}$ and will not be insured neither by a risk seeking individual with utility function $u(w) = w^2$ nor by a risk neutral individual with utility function $u(w) = w$.

The next three examples indicate how to choose an optimal portfolio given several investment choices.

Example 1.22 (Choosing the Optimal Portfolio)

Suppose an individual has $10,000 to invest between a stock and a bond. The stock is a financial asset that has a return rate 2% with a probability of 37% and a return rate of 10% with a probability of 63%. The bond returns 7% with certainty. The individual is risk averse and her utility function over wealth is given by $u(w) = \sqrt{w}$.

Faced with a choice between putting her money in the stock or the bond, this individual will choose a portfolio that makes her the most comfortable. *Is there some way in which we can find out which portfolio the individual is most likely to choose?* Given her utility function over wealth, a reasonable prediction would be that she would choose the portfolio that *maximizes her expected utility*.

Let s be the proportion of the $10,000 invested in the stock, where, of course, $0 \le s \le 1$. The investor has a chance of 37% of getting the amount

$$10,000s \times 1.02 + 10,000(1 - s) \times 1.07 = 10,000(1.07 - 0.05s),$$

and a chance of 63% of getting the amount

$$10,000s \times 1.1 + 10,000(1 - s) \times 1.07 = 10,000(1.07 + 0.03s).$$

The investor's expected utility $E(s) = Eu(s)$ is then given by

$$E(s) = 0.37\sqrt{10,000(1.07 - 0.05s)} + 0.63\sqrt{10,000(1.07 + 0.03s)}$$
$$= 37\sqrt{1.07 - 0.05s} + 63\sqrt{1.07 + 0.03s}$$
$$= 37(1.07 - 0.05s)^{\frac{1}{2}} + 63(1.07 + 0.03s)^{\frac{1}{2}}.$$

Now the rational investor should choose the value of s that maximizes the expected utility $E(s)$. Differentiating, we get

$$E'(s) = = -37 \times \tfrac{1}{2} \times 0.05(1.07 - 0.05s)^{-\frac{1}{2}} + 63 \times \tfrac{1}{2} \times 0.03(1.07 + 0.03s)^{-\frac{1}{2}}$$

$$= 0.945(1.07 + 0.03s)^{-\frac{1}{2}} - 0.925(1.07 - 0.05s)^{-\frac{1}{2}},$$

and

$$E''(s) = -\left[0.014175(1.07 + 0.03s)^{-\frac{3}{2}} + 0.023125(1.07 - 0.05s)^{-\frac{3}{2}}\right] < 0.$$

The first-order test gives

$$E'(s) = 0.945(1.07 + 0.03s)^{-\frac{1}{2}} - 0.925(1.07 - 0.05s)^{-\frac{1}{2}} = 0,$$

or

$$0.945\sqrt{1.07 - 0.05s} = 0.925\sqrt{1.07 + 0.03s}.$$

Squaring both sides we get $0.89302(1.07 - 0.05s) = 0.8556(1.07 + 0.03s)$, which after deleting the parentheses yields

$$0.9555 - 0.0446s = 0.9155 + 0.0257s,$$

or $0.04 = 0.0703s$. Thus,

$$s = \frac{0.04}{0.0703} = 0.56899 \approx 56.9\%.$$

This shows that this investor will put only 56.9% of her $10,000 in the stocks the rest (43.1%) she will invest in the bond.

Example 1.23 (Risk Reduction and Portfolio Choice)

Suppose an individual has $10,000 to invest in two stocks, namely the stock of a company called Service Inc. (S) and the stock of a company called Manufacturing Inc. (M). Both stocks are risky assets in the sense that each has some chance of giving either a high return or a low return. The return on the stocks are, however, not independent and the joint distribution on the returns is shown on the Table 1.2.

The joint distribution of the returns on the two assets show that the returns on the stocks are such that the probability of one stock giving a higher return when the

TABLE 1.2
The Returns from Stocks S and M

		Return From Stock M	
		20%	5%
Return From Stock S	5%	0.4	0.1
	20%	0.1	0.4

other stock gives a low return are high, whereas the probabilities that both stocks give a high return or a low return at the same time are very low. The individual who is contemplating investing the $10, 000 is risk averse and has a utility over wealth given by $u(w) = \sqrt{w}$.

As in the previous example, given her utility function over wealth, the individual will choose the portfolio that *maximizes her expected utility*. Let s be the proportion of the $10, 000 that is invested in the stock S so that $1 - s$ is the proportion of the wealth invested in the stock M. Therefore, $0 \leq s \leq 1$. The investor's expected utility is then given by

$$E(s) = 0.4\sqrt{10^4 \times 1.05s + 10^4 \times 1.20(1 - s)} + 0.1\sqrt{10^4 \times 1.05}$$
$$+ \ 0.4\sqrt{10^4 \times 1.20s + 10^4 \times 1.05(1 - s)} + 0.1\sqrt{10^4 \times 1.20}$$
$$= 40\sqrt{1.20 - 0.15s} + 40\sqrt{1.05 + 0.15s} + 10\sqrt{1.05} + 10\sqrt{1.20}$$

The first-order test $E'(s) = 0$ for a maximum gives

$$E'(s) = \frac{40(-0.15)}{\sqrt{1.20 - 0.15s}} + \frac{40(0.15)}{\sqrt{1.05 + 0.15s}} = 0.$$

This gives

$$1.05 + 0.15s = 1.20 - 0.15s$$

which reduces to $0.3s = 0.15$, so that

$$s = \frac{0.15}{0.3} = 0.5 = 50\%.$$

This shows that the investor will put exactly 50% of her $10, 000 in the stock S and the other 50% in the stock M.

When we take a closer look at the distribution of the returns it becomes quite clear as to why the investor would want to hold substantial amounts of both stocks, even though the probability of a high return or a low return from both stocks seem to be quite similar. When stock S gets a high return, stock M gets a low return, and when the return from the stock M is high, the return from the stock S is low. That is, the return from the two stocks move in opposite directions or are *negatively correlated*. It thus reduces the risk considerably, when both stocks are part of the investor's portfolio, as a low return from one stock would be offset by a high return from the other stock.

Example 1.24 (Choosing the Optimal Portfolio)

Suppose an individual has $10,000 to invest between a stock and a bond. The stock is a financial asset which has a variable return that is *uniformly distributed* with an average return of 8.525% and a standard deviation of 3.767%. The bond returns 8.5% with certainty. The individual is risk averse and her utility function over wealth is given by $u(w) = \sqrt{w}$.

The investor, as in the previous examples, faced with a choice between putting her money in the stock or the bond will choose the portfolio that *maximizes her expected utility*. Let s be the proportion of the $10,000 invested in the stock, where, of course, $0 \leq s \leq 1$. In this case, the investor's expected utility is given by

$$E(s) = \tfrac{1}{b-a} \int_a^b \sqrt{10,000s(1+r) + 10,000(1-s) \times 1.085} \, dr$$

$$= 100 \left[\tfrac{1}{b-a} \int_a^b \sqrt{(r - 0.085)s + 1.085} \, dr \right],$$

where $[a, b]$ is the interval which gives the possible returns from the stock and r represents the return from the stock.

Since the distribution is uniform and the mean is 0.0825 and the standard deviation is 0.03767, it follows from Example 1.15 that

$$\frac{a+b}{2} = 0.08525 \quad \text{and} \quad \frac{(b-a)\sqrt{3}}{6} = 0.03767 \, .$$

This gives $a + b = 0.1705$ and $b - a = \frac{6 \times 0.03767}{\sqrt{3}} = 0.1305$. Solving the system, we get $a = 0.02$ and $b = 0.1505$. Therefore,

$$E(s) = 766.28 \int_{0.02}^{0.1505} \sqrt{(r - 0.085)s + 1.085} \, dr \, .$$

Making the substitution $u = r - 0.085$, we get

$$E(s) = 766.28 \int_{-0.065}^{0.0655} (us + 1.085)^{\frac{1}{2}} \, du = \tfrac{2}{3} \times \tfrac{766.28}{s} (us + 1.085)^{\frac{3}{2}} \Big|_{u=-0.065}^{u=0.0655}$$

$$= 510.85 \frac{(0.0655s + 1.085)^{\frac{3}{2}} - (1.085 - 0.065s)^{\frac{3}{2}}}{s} \, .$$

Differentiating with respect to s yields

$$E'(s) = 510.85 \frac{0.09825(0.0655s+1.085)^{\frac{1}{2}} + 0.0975s(1.085-0.065s)^{\frac{1}{2}} - (0.0655s+1.085)^{\frac{3}{2}} + (1.085-0.065s)^{\frac{3}{2}}}{s^2} \, .$$

Now we must solve the First-Order Condition: $E'(s) = 0$. This is a very complicated equation, and we must employ some computer program to solve it. However, even with a calculator we can verify that $E'(s) = 0$ implies

$$s \approx 0.9996 = 99.96\% \, .$$

This shows that this investor will put 99.96% of her $10,000 (which is basically the entire amount) in stocks, the rest (0.04%) she will invest in bonds.

We have presented "expected utility theory" as a theory of behavior under uncertainty. However, this theory sometimes fails to describe how individuals actually make decisions. Indeed, if individuals were risk averse or risk neutral, expected utility theory would not be able to explain why lotteries would ever make any money, as the expected return from a lottery is usually negative, or why gambling houses are such profitable enterprises, when the odds are usually stacked against the customer. For instance, if we examine a power ball lottery ticket whose jackpot is worth $7,000,000, the odds of winning it is 1 in 85, 000, 000, and the ticket costs \$1, then we will find that its expected value is:

$$7,000,000 \times \frac{1}{85,000,000} + (-1) \times \frac{84,999,999}{85,000,000} = -0.917647.$$

The expected value of a power ball lottery ticket is usually negative. Therefore, according to expected utility theory, even a risk-neutral individual will not buy such a lottery ticket. But individuals who, otherwise, behave in a risk averse way often do buy lottery tickets.

This apparently anomalous behavior has also been observed in experiments involving lotteries. The first such experiment, due to Maurice Allais, [8] is now known as the *Allais Paradox* and shows how individuals can behave in ways that violate expected utility theory. Consider the following lotteries:

- *Lottery 1*: Receive 2 million dollars with certainty.
- *Lottery 2*: Receive 10 million dollars with a probability of 0.15, 2 million dollars with a probability of 0.75, and nothing with a probability of 0.1.
- *Lottery 3*: Receive 2 million dollars with a probability of 0.25 and nothing with a probability of 0.75.
- *Lottery 4*: Receive 10 million dollars with a probability of 0.15 and nothing with a probability of 0.85.

Given a choice between lotteries 1 and 2 and lotteries 3 and 4, individuals will often choose lottery 1 over lottery 2, and lottery 4 over lottery 3. But as we demonstrate, this sequence of choices violates the theory of expected utility. If an individual chooses lottery 1 over lottery 2, then according to expected utility theory,

$$u(2) > 0.15u(10) + 0.75u(2) + 0.1u(0),$$

or

$$0.25u(2) > 0.15u(10) + 0.1u(0).$$

But by adding 0.75u(0) to both sides of the preceding inequality, we get

$$0.25u(2) + 0.75u(0) > 0.15u(10) + 0.85u(0).$$

This last inequality shows that the individual should choose lottery 3 over lottery 4. Thus, the individual who chooses lottery 4 over lottery 3 does not behave according to the postulates of expected utility theory. This phenomenon, which is called *preference reversal* in the literature, has been observed subsequently in many other instances. This also explains why individuals who buy lotteries would behave in a highly risk-averse manner in other situations. A lottery is typically a situation in which by paying a small amount one has a slight chance of winning a very large amount, so individuals often ignore the negative

[8]M. Allais, Le compottement de l'homme rationnel devant le risque, critique des postulats et axiomes de l'école Américaine, *Econometrica* **21** (1953), 503–546. This work of Maurice Allais contributed towards his receiving the Nobel prize in economics in 1993.

expected value of lotteries, as the loss is usually very small. But if the potential loss is larger, then the same individual may choose very differently.

Such violations of the expected utility theory are quite common. Therefore, one should be careful in using the theory of expected utility as predicting behavior under uncertainty. The theory should rather be considered as providing the guidelines for completely rational behavior under uncertainty. Thus, an individual who fully understands the implications of all the axioms of expected utility theory, would always want to use expected utility theory as the most reasonable method for making careful decisions under uncertainty.

EXERCISES

1. An individual with utility function $u(w) = w$ over wealth invests $ W in a lottery that has a continuous return distribution over the rate r. What should be his expected utility? [Answer: $(1 + m)W$, where m is the expected value of the distribution.]

2. An individual has a von Neumann–Morgenstern utility function of the form $u(w) = \sqrt{w}$. What would the individual be willing to pay for a lottery that pays $ $1, 000, 000$ with a probability of 0.0015 and zero otherwise?

3. You are a risk-neutral individual whose net worth is $ $10, 000$ and you are thinking of opening a Donut Franchise. To open the franchise you must invest $5,000. If you buy the franchise, the probability is $\frac{1}{3}$ that you will make $500,000, $\frac{1}{3}$ that you break even, and $\frac{1}{3}$ that you lose the entire investment. What would be your decision? In general, at what probabilities would you change your decision?

4. In Exercise 3 what would your answer be if $u(w) = \ln w$?

5. In certain casinos the "expected values of all gambles are negative." Which of the three risk types of individuals would you expect to see in these casinos?

6. In Example 1.21 we discussed how much insurance an individual would buy. Now suppose an individual, if he buys insurance, will have to buy coverage that is 80% of the value of the house. What premium x is the individual willing to pay for a house that is worth $100,000 if $u(w) = \sqrt{w}$?

7. What would be the answer to the preceding exercise if the utility function is $u(w) = w$?

8. Suppose an individual has $10,000 to invest between a stock and a bond. The stock is a financial asset which has a rate of return of 5% with probability 79.5% and a rate of return of 15% with probability 20.5%. The bond returns 7% with certainty. The individual is risk averse and her utility function over wealth is given by $u(w) = \sqrt{w}$.
    What portfolio should this individual choose? [Answer: Stock 67.5%; Bond 32.5%]

9. Refer to Example 1.24 and consider a risk-seeking investor having the utility function over wealth $u(w) = w^2$. Show that:

    a. The expected utility is given by the formula

$$Eu(s) = \frac{10^8}{0.1305} \int_{0.02}^{0.1505} \left[(r - 0.085)s + 1.085 \right]^2 dr$$

$$= 10^4(14.1925s^2 + 5.425s + 11,772.25),$$

where $0 \leq s \leq 1$ is the proportion of the $10,000 invested in the stock.

b. $Eu(s)$ is maximized when $s = 1$. That is, show that a risk-seeking investor will put all her money in the stock.

10. Again refer to Example 1.24 and consider a risk-neutral investor having the utility function over wealth $u(w) = w$. Show that:

a. The expected utility is given by the formula

$$Eu(s) = \frac{10^4}{0.1305} \int_{0.02}^{0.1505} \left[(r - 0.085)s + 1.085\right] dr$$

$$= 2.5s + 10,850,$$

where $0 \leq s \leq 1$ is the proportion of the $10,000 invested in the stock.

b. $Eu(s)$ is maximized when $s = 1$. That is, show that this risk-neutral investor will put all her money in the stock.

11. Consider the insurance problem of Example 1.21 with parameters W, p, and x. What amount of coverage q will a risk averse investor with utility function over wealth $u(w) = 1 - e^{-w}$ buy? Express q in terms of the parameters W, p and x. [Answer: $q = W + \ln(\frac{p(1-x)}{x(1-p)})$.]

DECISIONS AND GAMES

In the previous chapter, we discussed how one can identify the best choice from a set of alternative choices. In every context that we discussed there, the decision maker, by choosing the right alternative could unambiguously influence the outcome and, therefore, the utility or satisfaction that he or she received. This is not always true. In many cases, the well being of an individual depends not only on what he or she does but on what outcome results from the choices that other individuals make. In some instances, this element of *mutual interdependence* is so great that it must be explicitly taken into account in describing the situation.

For example, in discussing the phenomenon of *global warming* it would be ludicrous to suggest that any one country could, by changing its policies, affect this in a significant way. Global warming is precisely that: a global phenomenon. Therefore, in any analysis of global warming we have to allow for this. But then this raises questions about what is the right strategy[1] to use in tackling the problem. How should any one country respond? What will be the reaction of the other countries? and so on. Clearly, this is quite different from the situations analyzed in the preceding chapter. Here strategic play is important, and it is not as clear as to what is an optimal strategy.

Let us take a look at another situation in which strategic play is important. The following excerpt taken from the *New York Times*[2] reported on a settlement made by airlines on a price-fixing lawsuit.

- Major airlines agreed to pay $40 million in discounts to state and local governments to settle a price-fixing lawsuit. The price-fixing claims centered on an airline practice of announcing price changes in advance through the reservations systems. If competitors did not go along with the price change, it could be rescinded before it was to take effect.

It seemed that the airlines were trying to coordinate price increases by using a signaling scheme. If the other airlines did not go along with the change, the price increase would not

---

[1]The word *strategy* is the Greek word $\sigma\tau\rho\alpha\tau\eta\gamma\iota\kappa\acute{\eta}$, which means a plan, a method, or an approach.
[2]Source: "Suit Settled by Airlines," New York Times, p. D8, October 12, 1994.

take effect. Why would an airline be interested in knowing how the other airlines would respond? Why were the airlines so wary about changing prices unilaterally? The reasons are not immediately obvious. Some of the incentives for doing what the airlines were doing can be surmised from the following description of the situation.

Example 2.1

Suppose USAir and American Airlines (AA) are thinking about pricing a round-trip airfare from Chicago to New York. If both airlines charge a price of $500, the profit of USAir would be $50 million, and the profit of AA would be $100 million. If USAir charges $500 and AA charges $200, then the profit of AA is $200 million and USAir makes a loss of $100 million. If, however, USAir sets a price of $200 and AA charges $500, then USAir makes a profit of $150 million, while AA loses $200 million. If both charge a price of $200 then both airlines end up with losses of $10 million each. This information can be depicted in the form of Table 2.1.

TABLE 2.1
The Fare-Setting Game

		American Airlines	
	Fare	$500	$200
USAir	$500	(50,100)	(−100,200)
	$200	(150,−200)	(−10,−10)

The example is illustrative of what was happening in the airline industry. It is worth noting that it would be best for both airlines to coordinate price changes because without such coordination the airlines would end up making fairly serious losses. In situations of this kind the following three elements always seem to be present:

1. There are two or more participants,
2. Each participant has a set of alternative choices, and
3. For each outcome there is a payoff that each participant gets.

These are the essential ingredients that constitute what is called a game in strategic form. In more formal language, a *strategic form game* consists of a *set of players*, for each player there is a *strategy set*, and for each *outcome* (or strategy combination) of the game there is a *payoff* for each player.

It would be nice if we could find certain central principles that would allow us to analyze the solution to games, in the same way that we were able to find general principles for solving optimization problems, as we did in the preceding chapter. One might start by asking what is most likely to happen in a game once the players are completely informed about the game they are playing. In other words, given a situation that can be modeled as a game, what guiding principles should we use in deciding the most plausible outcome of the game?

We proceed by first analyzing two-person games in which the strategy sets are small and finite. Some of the more interesting elements of games start to emerge even in this most elementary construct. We take a look at dominant strategies and solutions obtained through the elimination of dominated strategies. The concept of a Nash equilibrium is then introduced. The *Prisoner's Dilemma*, a two-person matrix game, is analyzed, as are a few other matrix games.

The chapter then discusses *n*-person games, reintroducing the concepts of dominant strategies and Nash equilibrium in a more general context. It then moves on to the applications. The Cournot duopoly shows how two firms competing to sell the same product find the output they should produce. The median voter model illustrates the use of game theory in understanding ideological shifts in the position of candidates. The example on the extraction of common property resources shows how useful game theory can be in understanding the existence of sometimes perverse incentives. The last example deals with second-price auctions in which the highest bidder wins and pays the second-highest bid. The remarkable fact that emerges is that every bidder should bid their true valuation of the product.

The chapter ends with a discussion of how to solve games using mixed strategies. We discuss the difference between *pure* strategies and *mixed* strategies using examples like the *game of matching pennies*.

2.1 TWO-PERSON MATRIX GAMES

The most elementary depiction of a game is the one featured in the fare-setting game. In that example, we gave a description of the payoffs or the profits that the airlines would make for every possible outcome of the game using a table. We can use such a *matrix* format for many interesting games. We start our discussion with one of the most well-known matrix games, called the Prisoner's Dilemma. The game illustrates a social phenomenon that is best understood using game-theoretic ideas. It describes a situation in which the players would do better by cooperating but nevertheless seem to have an incentive not to do so!

Example 2.2 (The Prisoner's Dilemma)

This game—which perhaps has been the most widely analyzed game—is given by the matrix in Table 2.2. The matrix game shown is best described as a situation where two individuals who have committed a crime have a choice of either confessing the crime or keeping silent. In case one of them confesses and the other keeps silent, then the one who has confessed does not go to jail, whereas the one who has not confessed gets a sentence of ten years. In case both confess, then each gets a sentence of five years. If both do not confess, then both get off fairly lightly with sentences of one year each.

The matrix game shows clearly that there are two players and the strategy set of each player is {Mum, Fink}. The payoffs are given by the pairs (a, b) for each outcome, with a being player 1's payoff and b player 2's payoff; here, of course, $-a$ and $-b$ represent years in jail. The matrix completely describes a game in strategic form. In examining the game, one notices the following features:

TABLE 2.2
The Prisoner's Dilemma Game

		Player 2	
	Strategy	Mum	Fink
Player 1	Mum	$(-1,-1)$	$(-10,0)$
	Fink	$(0,-10)$	$(-5,-5)$

1. Both players have a stake in keeping mum, as they both get a sentence of one year each, and
2. Given that a player is going to keep mum, the other player has an incentive to fink.

These are precisely the sort of paradoxes that are so inherent in playing games. The central issue is not only about the choice that a player makes but also about the choices of the other players.

A close examination of the game shows that if player 1 uses the "confess" (Fink) strategy, then he gets a better payoff for each choice that player 2 makes. To see this, let $u_1(\cdot, \cdot)$ denote the utility function of player 1 and note that if player 2 plays "Mum," then

$$u_1(\text{Fink, Mum}) = 0 > -1 = u_1(\text{Mum, Mum}),$$

while if player 2 plays "Fink," then

$$u_1(\text{Fink, Fink}) = -5 > -10 = u_1(\text{Mum, Fink}).$$

That is, *no matter what the choice of player 2, it is best for player 1 to play the strategy Fink*. We say that the strategy *fink* is a *strictly dominant* strategy of player 1. A similar examination of player 2's strategies reveals that the strategy *Fink* is a strictly dominant strategy for player 2.

In the absence of any communication or any coordination scheme, rational players are expected to play their strictly dominant strategies, since a strictly dominant strategy gives a player an unequivocally higher payoff. A solution to the "Prisoner's Dilemma," could, therefore, end up being (Fink, Fink). This is the solution using *strictly dominant strategies*.

We note that the solution using strictly dominant strategies will give each player a sentence of five years, which, of course, is a worse outcome than if each prisoner could trust the other to keep mum. This conflict between playing noncooperatively, in which case the strictly dominant strategy solution seems so persuasive, and playing so as to coordinate to get the better payoff is what makes predicting the outcome of a game difficult.

Going back to the fare-setting game, we notice that setting the fare of $200 is a strictly dominant strategy for both airlines. Hence, the strictly dominant strategy solution causes both airlines to make a loss of $10 million. This then provides airlines with an incentive to try to reach some form of a price-fixing agreement.

The two games that we have discussed so far are examples of matrix games. They are formally defined as follows.

DEFINITION 2.3 (Matrix Game)   A *matrix game* is a two-player game such that:

1. Player 1 has a finite strategy set S_1 with m elements,
2. Player 2 has a finite strategy set S_2 with n elements, and
3. The payoffs of the players are functions $u_1(s_1, s_2)$ and $u_2(s_1, s_2)$ of the outcomes $(s_1, s_2) \in S_1 \times S_2$.

The matrix game is played as follows: At a certain time player 1 chooses a strategy $s_1 \in S_1$ and simultaneously player 2 chooses a strategy $s_2 \in S_2$, and once this is done each player i receives the payoff $u_i(s_1, s_2)$. If $S_1 = \{s_1^1, s_2^1, \ldots, s_m^1\}$, $S_2 = \{s_1^2, s_2^2, \ldots, s_n^2\}$, and we put

$$a_{ij} = u_1(s_i^1, s_j^2) \quad \text{and} \quad b_{ij} = u_2(s_i^1, s_j^2),$$

then the payoffs can be arranged in the form of the $m \times n$ matrix shown in Table 2.3.

The "fare-setting game" and the "prisoner's dilemma" are matrix games, and we have seen that both have a solution in strictly dominant strategies. In both cases the strategy sets are made up of two elements so that if a strategy dominates another strategy, then a player knows which strategy he or she has to play. The concepts of dominance and strict dominance are fairly general concepts and can be defined for every matrix game as follows.

DEFINITION 2.4   A strategy s_i of player 1 in a matrix game is said to:

a. *dominate* another strategy s_j of player 1 if

$$u_1(s_i, s) \geq u_1(s_j, s)$$

for each strategy s of player 2, and
b. *strictly dominate* another strategy s_j of player 1 if

$$u_1(s_i, s) > u_1(s_j, s)$$

for each strategy s of player 2.

The dominating and strictly dominating strategies for player 2 are defined in a similar manner. In other words, a strategy s_i of player 1 that strictly dominates a strategy s_j gives

TABLE 2.3
The Two-Person Matrix Game

			Player 2		
	Strategy	s_1^2	s_2^2	$\cdots$	s_n^2
Player 1	s_1^1	(a_{11}, b_{11})	(a_{12}, b_{12})	$\cdots$	(a_{1n}, b_{1n})
	s_2^1	(a_{21}, b_{21})	(a_{22}, b_{22})	$\cdots$	(a_{2n}, b_{2n})
	$\vdots$	$\vdots$	$\vdots$	$\ddots$	$\vdots$
	s_m^1	(a_{m1}, b_{m1})	(a_{m2}, b_{m2})	$\cdots$	(a_{mn}, b_{mn})

player 1 a higher payoff for every choice that player 2 could make. Hence, there is no reason for player 1 to play a strictly dominated strategy s_j. This presents us with the possibility that strictly dominated strategies will never be used and, hence, can be dropped from consideration. Thus in playing a game players may progressively throw out strictly dominated strategies. This process of eliminating strictly dominated strategies sometimes leads us to a solution of a matrix game. Such a method of solving games is referred to as the *method of iterated elimination of strictly dominated strategies*.

The following matrix game can be solved using iterated elimination of strictly dominated strategies.

		Player 2		
	Strategy	L	C	R
Player 1	T	(1,0)	(1,3)	(3,0)
	M	(0,2)	(0,1)	(3,0)
	B	(0,2)	(2,4)	(5,3)

In examining the game one notices that *C* strictly dominates *R* for player 2. Therefore, player 2 eliminates the strategy *R*, and the game is reduced to:

		Player 2	
	Strategy	L	C
Player 1	T	(1,0)	(1,3)
	M	(0,2)	(0,1)
	B	(0,2)	(2,4)

In this reduced game we notice that *T* strictly dominates *M* for player 1; so player 1 eliminates *M*, and the game reduces to:

	Player 2		
	Strategy	L	C
Player 1	T	(1,0)	(1,3)
	B	(0,2)	(2,4)

The resulting game is a 2×2 matrix game in which player 2 has the strictly dominant strategy C so that L is now eliminated. Player 1 can now choose between T and B, and he will clearly choose B. The solution using iterated elimination of strictly dominated strategies is, therefore, (B, C).

Unfortunately, this method of solving a matrix game cannot be used for many games. For instance, the matrix game

	Player 2		
	Strategy	L	R
Player 1	T	(1,1)	(0,0)
	B	(0,0)	(1,1)

has no strictly dominated strategies. This game is a variant of the game called the *battle of the sexes*. The story told about the battle of the sexes goes as follows. A couple, one a male the other a female, want to go to the "Opera" or the "Bullfight." The female prefers the opera to the bullfight, while the male prefers to go to the bullfight; but they also want to spend time together. The resulting game can be written as:

	Female Player		
	Strategy	Opera	Bullfight
Male Player	Opera	(1,2)	(0,0)
	Bullfight	(0,0)	(2,1)

This game too has no strictly dominated strategies.

If one pauses at this point to think a little, he will realize that the requirement for a strategy to be strictly dominant is rather stringent. Therefore, it would be nice if one could say something about the solution of games that do not have strictly dominated strategies. The *Nash equilibrium* concept, which we define below, gives us such a solution.

DEFINITION 2.5   A pair of strategies $(s_1^*, s_2^*) \in S_1 \times S_2$ is a *Nash equilibrium*[3] of a matrix game if

1. $u_1(s_1^*, s_2^*) \geq u_1(s, s_2^*)$ for each $s \in S_1$, and
2. $u_2(s_1^*, s_2^*) \geq u_2(s_1^*, s)$ for each $s \in S_2$.

In other words, a Nash equilibrium is an outcome (i.e., a pair of strategies) of the game from which none of the players has an incentive to deviate, as, given what the other player is doing, it is optimal for a player to play the Nash equilibrium strategy. In this sense, a Nash equilibrium has the property that it is *self-enforcing*. That is, if both players knew that everyone has agreed to play a Nash equilibrium, then everyone would indeed want to play his Nash equilibrium strategy for the simple reason that it is optimal to do so.

The Nash equilibrium has been widely used in applications of game theory. Perhaps a reason for this popularity of the Nash equilibrium is that when one looks at an outcome that is *not* a Nash equilibrium, then there is at least one player who is better off playing some other strategy if that outcome is proposed. An outcome that is not a Nash equilibrium is, therefore, not going to be self-enforcing.

Notice that the game

		Player 2	
	Strategy	L	R
Player 1	T	(1,1)	(0,0)
	B	(0,0)	(1,1)

which does not have strictly dominated strategies, has two Nash equilibria, namely (T, L) and (B, R). It is also worth noting that if we look at an outcome that is not a Nash equilibrium, then one player will want to deviate from playing that outcome. For instance, if we take the strategy (T, R), then player 2 is better off playing L if he knows that player 1 is going to play T. One should further notice at this point that: *If a game can be solved using iterated elimination of strictly dominated strategies, then the game has a unique Nash equilibrium that is precisely the strategy pair found through eliminating strictly dominated strategies.*

A question that arises now is whether every matrix game has a Nash equilibrium. The answer, briefly, is no. For instance, it is easy to see that the matrix game

[3]This equilibrium concept was introduced by John Nash in 1951; see Ref. [16] in the bibliography list. For this and related work Professor Nash was awarded the Nobel Prize in Economics in 1994.

		Player 2	
	Strategy	L	R
Player 1	T	(0,3)	(3,0)
	B	(2,1)	(1,2)

does not have a Nash equilibrium. Games without Nash equilibria in pure strategies can often be solved by using *mixed strategies*. In the last section of this chapter we discuss mixed strategies in some detail.

EXERCISES

1. Find the Nash equilibria of the Fare Setting Game of Example 2.1.

2. Find the Nash equilibrium of the Prisoner's Dilemma Game of Example 2.2. Also find a strategy profile that gives a higher payoff than the payoff the players get in the Nash equilibrium.

3. Show that if a matrix game can be solved by using iterated elimination of dominated strategies, then the solution is a Nash equilibrium.

4. Consider the matrix game:

		Player 2	
	Strategy	L	R
Player 1	T	(1,0)	(0,0)
	B	(0,0)	(0,1)

Using the method of iterated elimination of dominated strategies, verify that the strategies TL, TR, and BR are all Nash equilibria.

5. Give an example of a matrix game having at least two Nash equilibria one of which can be obtained by the method of elimination of dominated strategies and the other of which cannot be obtained by the method of elimination of dominated strategies.

6. Verify that if a matrix game can be solved by using iterated elimination of strictly dominated strategies, then the game has a unique Nash equilibrium that is precisely the strategy pair found through eliminating strictly dominated strategies.

7. A *zero-sum game* is a matrix game such that $u_1(s_1, s_2) = -u_2(s_1, s_2)$ for each strategy profile $(s_1, s_2) \in S_1 \times S_2$. In other words, a zero-sum game is a matrix game such that the payoffs of the players are negatives of each other (or else they sum up to zero) for every strategy profile. For zero-sum games, we need only the payoff matrix A of one of the players—the payoff matrix of the other player is $-A$. Thus, in a way, every $m \times n$ matrix can be thought of as the payoff matrix of one of the players in a zero-sum game.

An $m \times n$ matrix $A = [a_{ij}]$ has a *saddle point* at a location (i, j) if

$$a_{ij} = \max_{1 \le k \le m} a_{kj} = \min_{1 \le r \le n} a_{ir} .$$

That is, the matrix A has a saddle point at a location (i, j) if a_{ij} is the largest element in its column and the smallest element in its row.

a. Determine the saddle points of the matrices

$$\begin{bmatrix} -1 & 0 & 2 \\ 3 & 1 & 1 \\ 0 & 1 & 2 \end{bmatrix} \quad \text{and} \quad \begin{bmatrix} -4 & 0 & 3 & 4 \\ -6 & 1 & 2 & 3 \\ -3 & 0 & -1 & -2 \end{bmatrix} .$$

b. Show that a matrix $A = [a_{ij}]$ has a saddle point at (i, j) if and only if the strategy (i, j) is a Nash equilibrium for the zero-sum game determined by the matrix A.

2.2 STRATEGIC FORM GAMES

We saw that a game between two players can be written as a matrix game. We also saw how to analyze matrix games. In many applications the games are often played among more than two players. Also the strategy sets of the players may be such that the games do not have a nice matrix representation. Fortunately, however, most of the ideas about how to solve games that we introduced for matrix games can be easily extended to a more general class of games—the class of strategic form games. We start by defining strategic form games in a more formal way.

DEFINITION 2.6   A *strategic form game* (or a *game in normal form*) is simply a set of n persons labeled $1, 2, \ldots, n$ (and referred to as the *players* of the game) such that each player i has:

1. A choice set S_i (also known as the *strategy set* of player i; its elements are called the *strategies* of player i), and
2. A *payoff function* $u_i \colon S_1 \times S_2 \times \cdots \times S_n \to \mathbb{R}$.

The game is played as follows: Each player k chooses simultaneously a strategy $s_k \in S_k$, and once this is done each player i receives the payoff $u_i(s_1, s_2, \ldots, s_n)$. A strategic form game with n players, strategy sets $S_1, \ldots, S_n$, and payoff functions $u_1, \ldots, u_n$ will be denoted by

$$G = \left\{ S_1, \ldots, S_n, u_1, \ldots, u_n \right\} .$$

So, in order to describe a strategic form game G, we need the strategy sets and the payoff functions of the players.

You should notice immediately that each payoff function u_i is a real-function of the n variables $s_1, s_2, \ldots, s_n$ [i.e., $u_i(s_1, s_2, \ldots, s_n)$], where each variable s_k runs over the strategy set of player k. The value $u_i(s_1, s_2, \ldots, s_n)$ is interpreted as the *payoff* of player i if each player k plays the strategy s_k.

The Cartesian product $S_1 \times S_2 \times \cdots \times S_n$ of the strategy sets is known as the *strategy profile set* or the *set of outcomes* of the game, and its elements $(s_1, s_2, \ldots, s_n)$ are called *strategy profiles* or *strategy combinations*. Of course, the payoff $u_i(s_1, s_2, \ldots, s_n)$ for a player i might represent a monetary gain or loss or any other type of "satisfaction" that is of importance to the player.

We present here an example of a strategic form game.

Example 2.7 (A Strategic Form Game)

This is a strategic form game with three players 1, 2, 3. The strategy sets of the players are

$$S_1 = S_2 = S_3 = [0, 1].$$

Their payoff functions are given by

$$u_1(x, y, z) = x + y - z, \quad u_2(x, y, z) = x - yz, \quad \text{and} \quad u_3(x, y, z) = xy - z,$$

where for simplicity we let $s_1 = x$, $s_2 = y$, and $s_3 = z$.

If the players announce the strategies $x = \frac{1}{2}$, $y = 0$, and $z = \frac{1}{4}$, then their payoffs will be

$$u_1\left(\tfrac{1}{2}, 0, \tfrac{1}{4}\right) = \tfrac{1}{4}, \quad u_2\left(\tfrac{1}{2}, 0, \tfrac{1}{4}\right) = \tfrac{1}{2} \quad \text{and} \quad u_3\left(\tfrac{1}{2}, 0, \tfrac{1}{4}\right) = -\tfrac{1}{4}.$$

Notice that the strategy profile $(1, 1, 0)$ gives a better payoff to each player.

When a strategic form game is played, a player's objective is to maximize her payoff. However, since the payoff of a player depends not just on what she chooses but also on the choices of the other players, the issue of optimizing one's payoff is a lot more subtle here than in the case of the simpler decision problem when there is just one decision maker. An individual player may, if she or he knows the choices of the other players, choose to maximize her payoff given the others' choices. But then, all the other players would want to do the same. Indeed, it seems quite natural to look for an outcome that results from the simultaneous maximization of individual payoffs. Such a strategy profile is usually called—as in the case of matrix games—a Nash equilibrium and is defined as follows.

DEFINITION 2.8   A *Nash equilibrium* of a strategic form game

$$G = \left\{ S_1, \ldots, S_n, u_i, \ldots, u_n \right\}$$

is a strategy profile $(s_1^*, s_2^*, \ldots, s_n^*)$ such that for each player i we have

$$u_i(s_1^*, \ldots, s_{i-1}^*, s_i^*, s_{i+1}^*, \ldots, s_n^*) \geq u_i(s_1^*, \ldots, s_{i-1}^*, s, s_{i+1}^*, \ldots, s_n^*)$$

for all $s \in S_i$.

While the Nash equilibrium seems to be reasonable as the proposed solution to a strategic form game, it is in the interest of a player to play a Nash equilibrium strategy only if the player is quite certain that the others are going to play the Nash equilibrium. Often this requires that each player knows this, every player knows that every player knows this, and so on ad infinitum. In other words, it must be *common knowledge* that the players are going to play the Nash equilibrium. In fact, this simply means that *every player knows* that the particular Nash equilibrium is to be played. The appeal of Nash equilibrium stems from the fact that if a Nash equilibrium is common knowledge, then every player would indeed play the Nash equilibrium strategy, thereby resulting in the Nash equilibrium being played. In other words, a Nash equilibrium strategy profile is *self-enforcing*. Hence, if the players are searching for outcomes or solutions from which no player will have an incentive to deviate, then the only strategy profiles that satisfy such a requirement are the Nash equilibria.

There is a useful criterion for finding the Nash equilibrium of a strategic form game when the strategy sets are open intervals of real numbers. It is easy to see that if, in such a case, a strategy profile $(s_1^*, \ldots, s_n^*)$ is the Nash equilibrium of the game, then it must be a solution of the system of equations

$$\frac{\partial u_i(s_1^*, \ldots, s_n^*)}{\partial s_i} = 0, \quad i = 1, 2, \ldots, n. \tag{2.1}$$

Therefore, the Nash equilibria are among the solutions of the system (2.1). When the system (2.1) has a unique solution, then it is the only Nash equilibrium of the game. This is essentially the test for determining the Nash equilibrium in strategic form games whose strategy sets are open intervals. In precise mathematical terms this is formulated as follows.

A Nash Equilibrium Test

Let G be a strategic form game whose strategy sets are open intervals and with twice differentiable payoff functions. Assume that a strategy profile $(s_1^*, \ldots, s_2^*)$ satisfies:

1. $\dfrac{\partial u_i(s_1^*, \ldots, s_n^*)}{\partial s_i} = 0$ for each player i,

2. Each s_i^* is the only stationary point of the function

$$u_i(s_1^*, \ldots, s_{i-1}^*, s, s_{i+1}, \ldots, s_n^*), \quad s \in S_i,$$

and

3. $\dfrac{\partial^2 u_i(s_1^*, \ldots, s_n^*)}{\partial^2 s_i} < 0$ for each i.

Then $(s_1^*, \ldots, s_n^*)$ is a Nash equlibrium of the game G.

In practice, we usually find the solution of the system (2.1) and then use other economic considerations to verify that the solution is the Nash equilibrium of the game.

Here is an example illustrating the Nash Equilibrium Test.

Example 2.9

Consider a three-person strategic form game in which each player has a strategy set equal to the open interval $(0, \infty)$. The payoff functions of the players are given by

$$u_1(x, y, z) = 2xz - x^2 y$$
$$u_2(x, y, z) = \sqrt{12(x + y + z)} - y$$
$$u_3(x, y, z) = 2z - xyz^2 .$$

To find the Nash equilibrium of the game, we must solve the system of equations

$$\frac{\partial u_1}{\partial x} = 0, \quad \frac{\partial u_2}{\partial y} = 0, \quad \text{and} \quad \frac{\partial u_3}{\partial z} = 0 .$$

Taking derivatives, we get

$$\frac{\partial u_1}{\partial x} = 2z - 2xy, \quad \frac{\partial u_2}{\partial y} = \sqrt{\frac{3}{x + y + z}} - 1, \quad \text{and} \quad \frac{\partial u_3}{\partial z} = 2 - 2xyz .$$

So we must solve the system of equations

$$2z - 2xy = 0, \quad \sqrt{\frac{3}{x + y + z}} - 1 = 0, \quad \text{and} \quad 2 - 2xyz = 0 ,$$

or, by simplifying the equations,

$$z = xy \tag{2.2}$$
$$x + y + z = 3 \tag{2.3}$$
$$xyz = 1 . \tag{2.4}$$

Substituting the value of xy from (2.2) to (2.4) yields $z^2 = 1$, and (in view of $z > 0$) we get $z = 1$. Now substituting the value $z = 1$ in (2.2) and (2.3), we get the system

$$xy = 1 \quad \text{and} \quad x + y = 2 .$$

Solving this system, we obtain $x = y = 1$. Thus the only solution of the system of equations (2.2), (2.3) and (2.4) is $x = y = z = 1$.

Computing the second derivatives, we get

$$\frac{\partial^2 u_1}{\partial x^2} = -2y < 0$$

$$\frac{\partial^2 u_2}{\partial y^2} = -\frac{\sqrt{3}}{2}(x + y + z)^{-\frac{3}{2}} < 0$$

$$\frac{\partial^2 u_3}{\partial z^2} = -2xy < 0$$

for all choices $x > 0$, $y > 0$, and $z > 0$. The Nash Equilibrium Test guarantees that $(1, 1, 1)$ is the only Nash equilibrium of the game.

1. Prove that the strategy profiles $(1, \alpha, 0)$ (where $0 \leq \alpha \leq 1$) are the only Nash equilibria of the game presented in Example 2.7.

2. Consider the game of Example 2.7. Assume that the players have the same payoff functions but their strategy sets are now $S_1 = S_2 = S_3 = (0, 1)$. Does this game have a Nash equilibrium? (Compare your conclusion with the answers in the preceding exercise.)

3. Verify that $(1, 1, 1)$ is the only Nash equilibrium of the game in Example 2.9.

4. Consider a two-person strategic form game such that $S_1 = S_2 = \mathbb{R}$. The utility functions of the two players are

$$u_1(x, y) = xy^2 - x^2 \quad \text{and} \quad u_2(x, y) = 8y - xy^2.$$

Find the Nash equilibrium of the game. [Answer: $(2, 2)$.]

5. Find the Nash equilibrium of a two-person strategic form game with strategy sets $S_1 = S_2 = \mathbb{R}$ and utility functions

$$u_1(x, y) = y^2 - xy - x^2 - 2x + y \quad \text{and} \quad u_2(x, y) = 2x^2 - xy - 3y^2 - 3x + 7y.$$

[Answer: $(-\frac{19}{11}, \frac{16}{11})$.]

6. Consider a two-person strategic form game with $S_1 = S_2 = \mathbb{R}$ and utility functions

$$u_1(x, y) = x^2 - 2xy \quad \text{and} \quad u_2(x, y) = xy - y^2.$$

Verify that this game does not have a Nash equilibrium.

7. Let $\{\alpha_1, \ldots, \alpha_n\}$ and $\{\beta_1, \ldots, \beta_n\}$ be two sets each consisting of n distinct positive real numbers. We consider the two-person strategic form game with the following characteristics.

   a. The strategy set S_1 of player 1 consists of all n-dimensional vectors $s = (s_1, \ldots, s_n)$, where $(s_1, \ldots, s_n)$ is a permutation of the positive real numbers $\{\alpha_1, \ldots, \alpha_n\}$. (So S_1 has $n!$ elements—all possible permutations of $\{\alpha_1, \ldots, \alpha_n\}$.) Similarly, S_2 consists of all n-dimensional vectors $t = (t_1, \ldots, t_n)$ whose components form a permutation of the real numbers $\beta_1, \ldots, \beta_n$; again, S_2 consists of $n!$ elements.

   b. The payoff functions of the players are given by

$$\pi_1(s, t) = \sum_{i=1}^{n} s_i t_i \quad \text{and} \quad \pi_2(s, t) = \sum_{i=1}^{n} s_i t_i^2.$$

If $s^* = (s_1^*, \ldots, s_n^*)$ and $t^* = (t_1^*, \ldots, t_n^*)$ satisfy

$$s_1^* < s_2^* < \cdots < s_n^* \quad \text{and} \quad t_1^* < t_2^* < \cdots < t_n^*,$$

then show that the strategy profile (s^*, t^*) is a Nash equilibrium. [Hint: Note that if an arbitrary strategy profile $s = (s_1, \ldots, s_n)$ satisfies $s_{k+1} < s_k$ for some k, then

$$s_{k+1}t_k^* + s_k t_{k+1}^* - (s_k t_k^* + s_{k+1} t_{k+1}^*) = (t_{k+1}^* - t_k^*)(s_k - s_{k+1}) > 0.]$$

2.3 APPLICATIONS

We now look at examples of strategic form games from economics and political science. One of the first games analyzed in economics was by the eighteenth century French mathematician *Augustin Cournot*.[4] His solution to the two-person game anticipated the Nash equilibrium by almost a century.

The Cournot duopoly model describes how two firms selling exactly identical products decide on their individual output levels. The model as presented is in many ways simplistic, but it captures some of the essential features of competition between firms and has become a foundation stone of the *theory of industrial organization*. Variants of the model would include the case in which there are n firms rather than two firms, or the firms may compete in prices rather than in quantities (the *Bertrand Model*).

Example 2.10 (The Cournot Duopoly Model)

This is a strategic form game played between two firms; we will call them firm 1 and firm 2. The two firms produce identical products, with firm 1 producing an amount of q_1 units and firm 2 producing an amount of q_2 units. The total production by both firms will be denoted by q; that is, $q = q_1 + q_2$.

Let $p(q) = A - q$ be the price per unit of the product in the market, where A is a fixed number. Assume that the total cost to firm i of producing the output q_i is $c_i q_i$, where the c_i are positive constants.

This economic model may be written as a strategic form game in which:

- There are two players: the two firms.

- The strategy set of each player is the set of positive quantities that a firm can choose. That is, the strategy set of each player is $(0, \infty)$.

- The payoff function of firm i is simply its profit function

$$\pi_i(q_1, q_2) = (A - q_1 - q_2)q_i - c_i q_i.$$

The problem faced by the firms is how to determine how much each one of them should produce in order to maximize profit—notice that the profit of each firm depends on the output of the other firm. Since we will assume that the firms choose their production quantities independently and simultaneously, it is reasonable to think of the Nash equilibrium as the solution.

We shall find the Nash equilibrium of the game using the Nash Equilibrium Test. To this end, note first that

[4]Antoine-Augustin Cournot (1801–1877) was a French mathematician and philosopher of science. With the publication of his famous book *Recherches sur les Principes Mathématiques de la Théorie des Richesses* (Paris, 1838), he was the first to formulate the problem of price formation in a market with two firms. He is considered by many as one of the founders of modern mathematical economics.

$$\pi_1(q_1, q_2) = (A - q_1 - q_2)q_1 - c_1q_1$$
$$= -(q_1)^2 + (-q_2 + A - c_1)q_1$$

and

$$\pi_2(q_1, q_2) = (A - q_1 - q_2)q_2 - c_2q_2$$
$$= -(q_2)^2 + (-q_1 + A - c_2)q_2 \,.$$

So, according to the Nash Equilibrium Test, the Nash equilibrium (q_1^*, q_2^*) is the solution of the system

$$\frac{\partial \pi_1(q_1, q_2)}{\partial q_1} = -2q_1 - q_2 + A - c_1 = 0$$

$$\frac{\partial \pi_2(q_1, q_2)}{\partial q_2} = -q_1 - 2q_2 + A - c_2 = 0 \,,$$

or, after rearranging,

$$2q_1 + q_2 = A - c_1$$
$$q_1 + 2q_2 = A - c_2 \,.$$

Solving the above linear system, we get

$$q_1^* = \frac{A + c_2 - 2c_1}{3} \quad \text{and} \quad q_2^* = \frac{A + c_1 - 2c_2}{3} \,.$$

Finally, notice that if $A > c_1 + c_2$, then we find that the two firms produce a positive output at the Nash equilibrium.

It is instructive to pause here a little and think about the Nash equilibrium of the Cournot duopoly game. Since the Cournot duopoly is really a market, it could be argued that what we should really want to find is the market equilibrium. Therefore, if possible we should find a pair $(\hat{q}_1, \hat{q}_2)$ and a price $\hat{p}$ that satisfy the *market equilibrium conditions*:

1. The quantity demanded $q(\hat{p})$ at the price $\hat{p}$ is exactly $\hat{q}_1 + \hat{q}_2$, and
2. $(\hat{q}_1, \hat{q}_2)$ is the output that the firms will want to supply at the price $\hat{p}$.

The claim is that the Nash equilbrium output pair (q_1^*, q_2^*) is precisely what gives us the market equilibrium output. Indeed, the price that is realized in the duopoly market when the firms produce q_1^* and q_2^*, respectively, is

$$p^* = A - q_1^* - q_2^* = A - \frac{A + c_2 - 2c_1}{3} - \frac{A + c_1 - 2c_2}{3} = \frac{A + c_1 + c_2}{3} \,.$$

The quantity demanded at this price p^* is

$$q(p^*) = A - p^* = \frac{2A - c_1 - c_2}{3} \,.$$

But

$$q_1^* + q_2^* = \frac{A + c_2 - 2c_1}{3} + \frac{A + c_1 - 2c_1}{3} = \frac{2A - c_1 - c_2}{3}.$$

This shows that

$$q(p^*) = q_1^* + q_2^*,$$

so that the quantity demanded at p^* is indeed what the firms produce in a Nash equilibrium. But would the firms want to produce their Nash equilibrium output at this price? The answer is yes, of course, as at this price the Nash equilibrium output of the firm is the firm's profit maximizing output.

We have just made a significant observation.

- The Nash equilibrium of the Cournot duopoly game gives us exactly what we want for the duopoly, namely, the market equilibrium of the duopoly.

The next example looks at the nature of election platforms. While again one may argue as to how rich in institutional details the model is, it provides us with a fairly deep insight into some of the rationale that candidates have for choosing election platforms. The choice of an election platform is seldom independent of the platform of the other candidates, and the reason for running as a candidate always has something to do with the desire to win. Therefore, given that winning is important to a candidate, it is of interest to ask how this would influence a candidate's choice of position in the ideological spectrum.

Example 2.11 (The Median Voter Model)

Consider an electorate that is distributed uniformly along the ideological spectrum from the left $a = 0$ to the right $a = 1$. There are two candidates, say, 1 and 2, and the candidate with the most votes wins. Each voter casts his vote for the candidate that is closest to his ideological position. The candidates know this and care only about winning. If there is a tie, then the winner is decided by, say, the toss of a coin. *Given such a scenario, is it possible to make a prediction about the ideological position that the two candidates would choose?*

We first note that we can view the situation as a strategic form game played between two players—the two candidates. The strategy of each player i is to choose an ideological position $a_i \in [0, 1]$. In other words, the strategy set of each player is $[0, 1]$. The payoff function $u_i(a_1, a_2)$ of player i is the percentage of the vote obtained by him if the strategy profile (a_1, a_2) is adopted by the players. It turns out that

$$u_1(a_1, a_2) = \begin{cases} \frac{a_1 + a_2}{2} & \text{if } a_1 < a_2 \\ 0.50 & \text{if } a_1 = a_2 \\ 1 - \frac{a_1 + a_2}{2} & \text{if } a_1 > a_2, \end{cases}$$

and

$$u_2(a_1, a_2) = \begin{cases} 1 - \frac{a_1 + a_2}{2} & \text{if } a_1 < a_2 \\ 0.50 & \text{if } a_1 = a_2 \\ \frac{a_1 + a_2}{2} & \text{if } a_1 > a_2. \end{cases}$$

To verify the validity of these formulas, consider the case of a strategy profile (a_1, a_2) with $a_1 < a_2$; see Figure 2.1. Then the ideologies closer to a_1 rather than to a_2 are represented by the interval $\left[0, \frac{a_1+a_2}{2}\right]$. This means that the percentage of people voting for candidate 1 is $\frac{a_1+a_2}{2}$, that is, $u_1(a_1, a_2) = \frac{a_1+a_2}{2}$. Similarly, the interval $\left[\frac{a_1+a_2}{2}, 1\right]$ represents the ideologies closer to a_2 rather than to a_1, and so $u_2(a_1, a_2) = 1 - \frac{a_1+a_2}{2}$.

It is reasonable to argue that a Nash equilibrium of this game may be the most likely outcome, as each candidate would vie for the largest number of votes given the position of his rival. As a matter of fact, we claim that:

- The only Nash equilibrium of this game is $\left(\frac{1}{2}, \frac{1}{2}\right)$.

We shall establish the above claim in steps. To do this, we fix a Nash equilibrium (s_1, s_2).

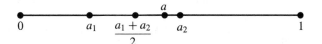

Figure 2.1

STEP I: $s_1 = s_2$.

Assume by way of contradiction that $s_1 \neq s_2$. By the symmetry of the situation, we can assume $s_1 < s_2$. In this case, it is easy to see that any strategy a for candidate 2 between $\frac{s_1+s_2}{2}$ and s_2 satisfies $u_2(s_1, a) > u_2(s_1, s_2)$; see Figure 2.2. The latter shows that (s_1, s_2) is not a Nash equilibrium, which is a contradiction. Hence, $s_1 = s_2$.

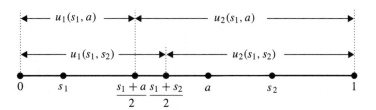

Figure 2.2

STEP II: $s_1 = s_2 = \frac{1}{2}$.

To verify this, assume by way of contradiction $s_1 = s_2 \neq \frac{1}{2}$. Again, by the symmetry of the situation, we can suppose that $s_1 = s_2 < \frac{1}{2}$. If candidate 2 chooses any strategy a such that $s_1 < a < 0.5$, then it should be clear that $u_2(s_1, a) > u_2(s_1, s_2) = 0.5$; see Figure 2.3. This clearly contradicts the fact that (s_1, s_2) is a Nash equilibrium, and so $s_1 = s_2 = \frac{1}{2}$ must be true.

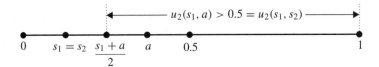

Figure 2.3

The preceding two steps show that the strategy profile $(s_1, s_2) = \left(\frac{1}{2}, \frac{1}{2}\right)$ is the only possible candidate for a Nash equilibrium of the game. To complete the argument, we shall show that $\left(\frac{1}{2}, \frac{1}{2}\right)$ is indeed a Nash equilibrium.

STEP III: The strategy profile $\left(\frac{1}{2}, \frac{1}{2}\right)$ is a Nash equilibrium.

From Figure 2.4 it should be clear that if candidate 2 keeps the strategy $\frac{1}{2}$, then candidate 1 cannot improve his utility $u_1\left(\frac{1}{2}, \frac{1}{2}\right) = 0.5$ by choosing any strategy $a \neq 0.5$.

This model's prediction is, therefore, that each candidate will seek to appeal to the *median voter*, the voter who is exactly in the middle of the distribution of the ideological spectrum. For a generalization of this model, see Exercise 11 at the end of this section.

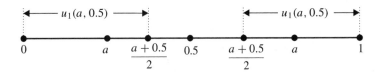

Figure 2.4

The next example is in some ways perhaps one of the more interesting applications of game theory. It shows how perverse incentives can sometimes work against what is in the common interest. While the example focuses on the exploitation of a commonly owned resource, like the world's fishing grounds, a little re-examination of the example shows that it has implications for global warming and the exploitation of the world's rain forests, to mention just a few of the situations that would fit into this general mold. It brings to the surface an element that is present in many games, including the prisoner's dilemma: the Nash equilibrium, which describes what happens when the players play *noncooperatively*, may lead to an outcome in which each player gets less than what they could get by adhering to a cooperative agreement, like treaties among countries on fishing rights.

Example 2.12 (Use of Common Property Resources)

Suppose that there are n countries that have access to fishing grounds in open seas. It is widely accepted that the fishing grounds of the world, which may be viewed as common property resources, have been overfished; that is, the amount of fishing has been so intensive that there is a sense that in the near future the fish population will reach levels so low that some species may be in danger of extinction.

One of the major achievements of game theory—from a practical standpoint—has been to show why such common property resources will always be exploited beyond the point that is most desirable from the collective viewpoint. The argument, which we make in some detail here, is that the Nash equilibrium of the game that is played between the consumers of the resource will always lead to an outcome that is worse than the socially most desirable.

We do this by using a simple model of a strategic form game. Let there be n players with player i using r_i amount of the resource. The total resource used is then $R = \sum_{i=1}^{n} r_i$. The following now describes the chief features of the game.

1. The cost to player i of getting r_i units of the resource depends not only on the amount r_i used by the player but also on the amount $R - r_i = \sum_{j \neq i} r_j$ used by the other players. This cost is denoted by $C(r_i, R - r_i)$. We shall assume that the cost function $C: (0, \infty) \times (0, \infty) \rightarrow (0, \infty)$ satisfies the following properties:

   a. $\frac{\partial C(r,R)}{\partial r} > 0$, $\frac{\partial C(r,R)}{\partial R} > 0$, $\frac{\partial^2 C(r,R)}{\partial r^2} > 0$, and $\frac{\partial^2 C(r,R)}{\partial R^2} > 0$ for all $r > 0$ and $R > 0$. That is, the marginal cost of using a resource increases with the total amount of the resource used.[5] Hence, as the countries catch more, the marginal cost of catching additional fish goes up.

   b. The marginal cost function satisfies

   $$\lim_{r \to \infty} \frac{\partial C(r,R)}{\partial r} = \infty \quad \text{and} \quad \lim_{R \to \infty} \frac{\partial C(r,R)}{\partial R} = \infty.$$

   Indeed, it is not unreasonable to assume that the marginal cost starting from some small number greater than zero increases monotonically without bound. These properties of the cost function are consistent with the intuition that as more fish are caught, the harder it becomes to catch additional amounts.

   c. To simplify matters, the cost function C will be taken to be a *separable function* of the form $C(r, R) = \kappa(r) + K(R)$. In this case, the properties in part (a) can be written as

   $$\kappa'(r) > 0, \quad \kappa''(r) > 0, \quad K'(R) > 0, \quad \text{and} \quad K''(R) > 0$$

   for all $r > 0$ and $R > 0$. An example of a separable cost function of the above type is given by $C(r, R) = r^2 + R^2$.

2. The utility that a player receives from r_i units of the resource is $u(r_i)$. We suppose that the function $u: (0, \infty) \rightarrow (0, \infty)$ satisfies $u'(r) > 0$ and $u''(r) < 0$ for each $r > 0$. This simply means that, as the amount of r consumed increases, the value of an additional unit of r falls. (In mathematical terms, u is a strictly increasing and strictly concave function.)

   We also assume that the marginal utility at zero is greater than the marginal cost at zero; that is,

---

[5]Recall that the *marginal cost* of a cost function $C(x)$ is the derivative $C'(x)$. As usual, $C'(x)$ is interpreted as the cost of producing an additional unit of the product when x units have already been produced.

$$\lim_{r \to 0^+} u'(r) > \lim_{r \to 0^+} \kappa'(r).$$

The situation we have just described can be written as an n-person game in strategic form as follows.

- There are n players.

- The strategy set of player i is $(0, \infty)$, the open interval of all positive real numbers. [In fact, $S_i = (0, R_{max})$, where R_{max} is a certain maximum amount of the resource.]

- The payoff of player i is

$$\pi_i(r_1, r_2, \ldots, r_n) = u_i(r_i) - C(r_i, R - r_i)$$
$$= u(r_i) - [\kappa(r_i) + K(R - r_i)].$$

By the Nash equilibrium test, the Nash equilibria of the game are the solutions $(r_1^*, \ldots, r_n^*)$ of the system

$$\frac{\partial \pi_i(r_1, r_2, \ldots, r_n)}{\partial r_i} = 0, \quad i = 1, 2, \ldots, n,$$

subject to $\frac{\partial^2 \pi_i(r_1, \ldots, r_n)}{\partial r_i^2} < 0$ for each $i = 1, \ldots, n$. Taking into account that $R = \sum_{j=1}^{n} r_j$ and $R - r_i = \sum_{j \neq i} r_j$, a direct computation of the partial derivatives gives

$$\frac{\partial \pi_i(r_1, r_2, \ldots, r_n)}{\partial r_i} = u'(r_i) - \kappa'(r_i) = 0, \quad i = 1, 2, \ldots, n,$$

and $\frac{\partial^2 \pi_i(r_1, \ldots, r_n)}{\partial r_i^2} = u''(r_i) - \kappa''(r_i) < 0$ for each $i = 1, \ldots, n$. [For this conclusion, we use the fact that $u''(r) < 0$ and $\kappa''(r) > 0$ for each $r > 0$.]

The geometry of the situation guarantees $r_1 = r_2 = \cdots = r_n = \rho^*$.[6] That is, at a Nash equilibrium $(r_1^*, \ldots, r_n^*)$ each player consumes exactly the same amount of the resource

$$r_1^* = r_2^* = \cdots = r_n^* = \rho^* = \frac{R^*}{n},$$

where $R^* = r_1^* + r_2^* + \cdots + r_n^* = n\rho^*$. So, $\left(\frac{R^*}{n}, \ldots, \frac{R^*}{n}\right)$ is the only Nash equilibrium of the game; see also Exercise 7 at the end of the section. Hence the amount R^* of the resource consumed at the Nash equilibrium is the unique solution of the equation

$$u'\left(\frac{R^*}{n}\right) = \kappa'\left(\frac{R^*}{n}\right). \tag{2.5}$$

---

[6]Since $u''(r) < 0$ for each $r > 0$, we know that u' is a strictly decreasing function. Since $\kappa''(r) > 0$ for each $r > 0$, the function κ' is strictly increasing. So $u'(r) = \kappa'(r)$ has a unique solution ρ^*; see Figure 2.5. For more about this, see Exercise 7 at the end of this section.

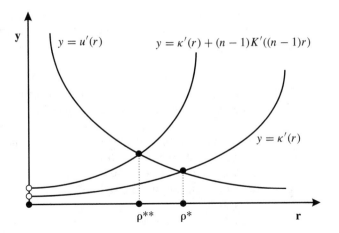

Figure 2.5

In contrast to the condition for a Nash equilibrium given above, the social optimum[7] R^{**} solves

$$\max_{R>0} \left\{ n\left[u\left(\tfrac{R}{n}\right) - \left[\kappa\left(\tfrac{R}{n}\right) + K\left(R - \tfrac{R}{n}\right)\right]\right]\right\}.$$

That is, the social optimum R^{**} is chosen to maximize the total payoff to all the members of society. The first-order test for this gives

$$n\left\{ \tfrac{1}{n}u'\left(\tfrac{R^{**}}{n}\right) - \left[\tfrac{1}{n}\kappa'\left(\tfrac{R^{**}}{n}\right) + \left(1 - \tfrac{1}{n}\right)K'\left(R^{**} - \tfrac{R^{**}}{n}\right)\right]\right\} = 0,$$

which, after some algebraic simplifications, yields

$$u'\left(\tfrac{R^{**}}{n}\right) = \kappa'\left(\tfrac{R^{**}}{n}\right) + (n-1)K'\left(\tfrac{n-1}{n}R^{**}\right). \tag{2.6}$$

Again, we leave it as an exercise for the reader to verify that (6) has a unique solution $R^{**} = n\rho^{**}$; see Exercise 7 at the end of the section and Figure 2.5. From examining (2.5), (2.6), and Figure 2.5, we see that $R^* > R^{**}$.

Clearly, the amount of resource R^* that is used in a Nash equilibrium is *strictly greater* than the amount R^{**} of consumption of the resource that is best for the common good. One wonders at this point about the intuition behind this rather remarkable result. A moment's thought shows that if the game is played independently by the players, then the private incentives are to use the resource as much as is justified by the cost of consuming the resource to the individual player. In a Nash equilibrium, a player is concerned about the impact of his consumption of the resource only on his cost, and ignores the cost imposed on the others. The cost to the individual, however, is a lot less than the cost imposed on society collectively. For the socially optimum amount

---

[7]The *social optimum* is the amount that leads to the maximum *joint payoff*. Hence, if society is made up of the players in the game, then the social optimum gives us the amount that would lead to the most desirable outcome from the social viewpoint.

of consumption of the resource, however, the cost imposed on everyone is taken into consideration, and as a result the amount of consumption justified by the overall cost to society is less.

The next example is based on a model of a "second-price auction." The issue here is the amount that an individual at the auction should bid in order to maximize her surplus from the auction. Obviously, an immediate complication is that the surplus that a bidder receives depends on whether she has the winning bid. Since whether an individual wins depends on the bids that the others make, we see that the payoff of an individual depends on the entire array of bids. Auctions, therefore, can be written as n-person strategic form games. We see in this example that thinking of auctions in the form of a game can lead us to very interesting and sharp insights.

Example 2.13 (Second-Price Auction)

A seller has an expensive painting to sell at an auction that is valued at some amount by n potential buyers. Each buyer k has his own valuation $v_k > 0$ of the painting. The buyers must simultaneously bid an amount; we denote the bid of buyer i by $b_i \in (0, \infty)$. In a second-price auction the highest bidder gets the painting and pays the second-highest bid. If there is more than one buyer with the highest bid, the winner is decided by a drawing among the highest bidders, and she pays the highest bid. The rest receive a payoff of zero.

We can formulate this auction as a strategic form game in which there are:

1. n players (the n buyers; the auctioneer is not considered a player),
2. The strategy set of each player is $(0, \infty)$, and
3. The payoff of a player k is the following expected utility function

$$\pi_k(b_1, \ldots, b_n) = \begin{cases} v_k - s, & \text{if } b_k > s \\ 0, & \text{if } b_k < s \\ \frac{1}{r}(v_k - s), & \text{if } k \text{ is among } r \text{ buyers with highest bid}, \end{cases}$$

where s designates the second highest bid.[8]

We claim that the strategy profile $(v_1, v_2, \ldots, v_n)$ is a Nash equilibrium for this game. We shall establish this in two steps.

- *A player i never gains by bidding $b_i > v_i$.*

To see this, assume $b_i > v_i$ and let $b_{-i} = \max_{j \neq i} b_j$. We distinguish five cases.

CASE I.
$b_{-i} > b_i$

In this case, some other bidder has the highest bid and so player i gets zero, which he could get by bidding v_i.

---

[8]Note that if player k is the only buyer with the highest bid, then $s = \max_{i \neq k} b_i$.

CASE II.

$v_i < b_{-i} < b_i$

In this case, bidder i wins and gets $v_i - b_{-i} < 0$. However, had he bid v_i, then his payoff would have been zero—a higher payoff than that received by bidding b_i.

CASE III.

$b_{-i} = b_i$

Here bidder i is one among r buyers with the highest bid, and he receives $\frac{v_i - b_{-i}}{r} <$ 0. But by bidding v_i, he can get 0, a higher payoff.

CASE IV.

$b_{-i} < v_i$

In this case bidder i gets $v_i - b_{-i}$, which he could get by bidding v_i.

CASE V.

$b_{-i} = v_i$

Here again bidder i is one among r buyers with the highest bid, and he receives $\frac{v_i - b_{-i}}{r} = 0$. But by bidding v_i, he can also get 0.

- *A player i never gains by bidding $b_i < v_i$.*

If $b_{-i} > v_i$, then bidder i would have a zero payoff, which is the same as the payoff she would get if she bid v_i. On the other hand, we leave it as an exercise for the reader to verify that if $b_{-i} \leq v_i$, then player i would do at least as well if she bid v_i.

We have thus shown the following:

- *The strategy profile $(v_1, v_2, \ldots, v_n)$ is a Nash equilibrium.*

Therefore, it is reasonable to expect that every bidder will bid their true valuation of the painting and the bidder with the highest valuation wins. Note that this is true even if the bidders do not know the valuation of the other bidders.

EXERCISES

1. Two firms (call them 1 and 2) produce exactly identical products. Firm 1 produces q_1 units of the product, and firm 2 produces q_2 units so that the total number of units of the product in the market is $q = q_1 + q_2$. We assume that:
   a. The market price of the product is $p(q) = 100 - 2\sqrt{q}$,
   b. The production cost of producing q_1 units by firm 1 is $C_1(q_1) = q_1 + 10$, and
   c. The production cost of producing q_2 units by firm 2 is $C_2(q_2) = 2q_2 + 5$.
   Set up a strategic form game with two players (as in Example 2.10) whose payoffs functions are the profit functions of the firms. Determine the following.
   (i) The profit functions $\pi_1(q_1, q_2)$ and $\pi_2(q_1, q_2)$ of the firms.

(ii) The Nash equilibrium of the game.

(iii) The market price of the product at the Nash equilibrium.

(iv) The profits of the firms at the Nash equilibrium.

Hints: (i) $\pi_1(q_1, q_2) = (99 - 2\sqrt{q_1 + q_2})q_1 - 10$ and

$$\pi_2(q_1, q_2) = (98 - 2\sqrt{q_1 + q_2})q_2 - 5$$

(ii) The Nash equilibrium can be found by solving the system

$$\frac{\partial \pi_1(q_1, q_2)}{\partial q_1} = 0 \quad \text{and} \quad \frac{\partial \pi_2(q_1, q_2)}{\partial q_2} = 0,$$

or (after computing derivatives and simplifying)

$$3q_1 + 2q_2 = 99\sqrt{q_1 + q_2} \tag{2.7}$$

$$2q_1 + 3q_2 = 98\sqrt{q_1 + q_2} . \tag{2.8}$$

Dividing (2.7) and (2.8) and simplifying yields $q_2 = \frac{96}{101}q_1$. Substituting this value in (2.7) and working the algebra, we get $q_1 = 795.88$. This implies $q_2 = 756.48$. So, the Nash equilibrium is $(q_1^*, q_2^*) = (795.88, 756.48)$.

(iii) The market price is $p = 21.2$.

(iv) $\pi_1(795.88, 756.48) = 16,066.78$; $\pi_2(795.88, 756.48) = 14,519.42$.

2. Consider a strategic form game with two players. A *best-response* (or a *reaction*) function for a player 1 is a function $r_1: S_2 \to S_1$ such that

$$u_1(r_1(s_2), s_2) = \max_{s_1 \in S_1} u_1(s_1, s_2) .$$

A best-response function of the second player is defined analogously.

Find the response functions of the players in the Cournot duopoly model of Example 2.10. [Answers: $r_1(q_2) = \frac{A - q_2 - c_1}{2}$ and $r_2(q_1) = \frac{A - q_1 - c_2}{2}$.]

3. Consider the Cournot duopoly model as described in Example 2.10. Compute the profits of the firms at the Nash equilibrium. [Answer: If (q_1^*, q_2^*) is the Nash equilibrium, then

$$\pi_1(q_1^*, q_2^*) = \frac{(A + c_2 - 2c_1)^2}{9} \quad \text{and} \quad \pi_2(q_1^*, q_2^*) = \frac{(A + c_1 - 2c_2)^2}{9},$$

where $A + c_2 - 2c_1 \geq 0$ and $A + c_1 - 2c_2 \geq 0$.]

4. Consider the Cournot duopoly model discussed in Example 2.10. If the market has three firms instead of two firms, can you find the Nash equilibrium? What if you have n firms? What do you think happens as $n \to \infty$?

5. (*The Bertrand model*) Consider a market with two firms that produce identical products. The capacity of each firm is fixed so that the firms choose prices instead of quantities. Let $q = A - p$ be the total quantity sold when the price is p. If both firms charge the same price, then each sells one-half of the total. If the firms charge different prices, then the firm with the lower price sells everything. Assume that each firm has enough capacity to produce the entire amount of the output for the market at any price. The

marginal cost of firm i is c_i. The positive parameters c_1, c_2, and A satisfy $c_1 \neq c_2$ and $2 \max\{c_1, c_2\} < A + \min\{c_1, c_2\}$.

    a. Write down the strategic form game with the price p_i being the strategy of the firm i.

    b. Show that

$$\pi_i(p_1, p_2) = \begin{cases} p_i(A - p_i) - c_i(A - p_i), & \text{if } p_i < p_j \\ \frac{1}{2}[p(A - p) - c_i(A - p)], & \text{if } p_i = p_j = p \geq c_i \\ 0, & \text{if } p_j < p_i. \end{cases}$$

    c. Show that the game does not have a Nash equilibrium.

    d. We say that a strategy combination $(s_1^*, s_2^*, \ldots, s_n^*)$ for an n-person strategic form game is an ϵ-*Nash equilibrium* (where $\epsilon > 0$) if for each player i we have

$$u_i(s_1^*, \ldots, s_{i-1}^*, s_i^*, s_{i+1}^*, \ldots, s_n^*)$$
$$\geq u_i(s_1^*, \ldots, s_{i-1}^*, s_i, s_{i+1}^*, \ldots, s_n^*) - \epsilon$$

for each strategy $s_i \in S_i$ of player i.

Show that for each $\epsilon > 0$ the game has an ϵ-Nash equilibrium.

6. Suppose in the Bertrand model of the previous exercise the amount sold by each firm when $p_1 = p_2 = p \geq c$ is not one-half of the market but some pair (q_1, q_2) such that $q_1 + q_2 = A - p$. That is, the payoff functions are now given by

$$\pi_1(p_1, p_2, q_1, q_2) = \begin{cases} 0, & \text{if } p_1 > p_2 \\ (p - c_1)q_1, & \text{if } p_1 = p_2 = p \\ (A - p_1)(p_1 - c_1), & \text{if } p_1 < p_2 \end{cases}$$

and

$$\pi_2(p_1, p_2, q_1, q_2) = \begin{cases} 0, & \text{if } p_2 > p_1 \\ (p - c_2)q_2, & \text{if } p_1 = p_2 = p \\ (A - p_2)(p_2 - c_2), & \text{if } p_2 < p_1. \end{cases}$$

Show that in this case there is a Nash equilibrium.

7. In this exercise, we shall fill in some of the mathematical details regarding the use of common property resources encountered in Example 2.12. Assume that the functions C and u satisfy the properties stated in Example 2.12.

    a. Establish that the equation $u'(r) = \kappa'(r)$ has a unique solution ρ^*, which gives the Nash equilibrium of the game $R^* = n\rho^*$. [Hint: Since u' is strictly decreasing and κ' is strictly increasing, the equation cannot have more than one solution. Now use $\lim_{r \to 0+}[u'(r) - \kappa'(r)] > 0$ and $\lim_{r \to \infty}[u'(r) - \kappa'(r)] = -\infty$ to conclude that the equation has indeed a unique solution ρ^*; see Figure 2.5.]

    b. Show that the "common property resources" problem of Example 2.12 has a unique social optimum R^{**}, by showing that $u'(r) = \kappa'(r) + (n-1)K'((n-1)r)$ has a unique solution ρ^{**}. [Hint: Notice that the function $f(r) = u'(r)$ is strictly decreasing and the function $g(r) = \kappa'(r) + (n-1)K'((n-1)r)$ is strictly increasing. Now argue as in the previous part; see also Figure 2.5.]

    c. Show that $R^{**} < R^*$. What happens if $n \to \infty$?

8. Consider the "common property resources" problem of Example 2.12 with functions $u(r) = \sqrt{r}$, $\kappa(r) = 2r^2$, and $K(R) = R^2$. Show that these functions satisfy the required properties and compute the Nash equilibrium R^* and the social optimum R^{**}. [Answers: $R^* = \frac{n}{4}$ and $R^{**} = \dfrac{n}{\sqrt[3]{4[4+2(n-1)^2]^2}}$.]

9. Consider the functions u, κ, $K : (0, \infty) \to (0, \infty)$ defined by

$$u(r) = r + 1 - e^{-2r}, \quad \kappa(r) = r + e^{-r} - 1, \quad \text{and} \quad K(R) = R^2.$$

Show that:

    a. $u'(r) > 0$ and $u''(r) < 0$ for each $r > 0$ and $\lim_{r \to 0^+} u'(r) = 3 > 0$.

    b. $\kappa'(r) > 0$ and $\kappa''(r) > 0$ for each $r > 0$, $\lim_{r \to 0^+} \kappa'(r) = 0$, and $\lim_{r \to \infty} \kappa'(r) = 1$.

    c. $K'(R) > 0$ and $K''(R) > 0$ for each $R > 0$, $\lim_{R \to 0^+} K'(R) = 0$, and $\lim_{R \to \infty} K'(R) = \infty$.

    d. With these functions, the "common property resources" problem as stated in Example 2.12 does not have a Nash equilibrium. Why doesn't this contradict the conclusion of Example 2.12?

    e. With these functions, the "common property resources" problem as stated in Example 2.12 has a social optimum.

10. (*Global warming*) Suppose there are n countries that produce goods that cause the emission of carbon dioxide. Let $B(x)$ denote the benefit from the production of x amounts of the goods lumped together. Assume that $B'(x) > 0$ and $B''(x) < 0$. Also assume that the total cost of producing x_i units by each country i is $\kappa(x_i) + K(X - x_i)$, where $X = \sum_{i=1}^{n} x_i$. The functions κ, $K : (0, \infty) \to (0, \infty)$ satisfy $\kappa'(x) > 0$, $\kappa''(x) > 0$, $K'(X) > 0$ and $K''(X) > 0$ for each $x > 0$ and $X > 0$. In addition, the marginal benefit for each country at zero is assumed to be larger than the marginal cost at zero.

    a. Write this as an n-person strategic form game (where the players are the countries).

    b. Find the condition for the Nash equilibrium of the game.

    c. Find the condition for the socially optimum amount.

    d. Compare the conditions and draw the conclusion.

11. (*Generalized voter model*) This exercise is an extension of the "voter model" presented in Example 2.11. We consider an electorate that is distributed along the ideological spectrum from the left $a = 0$ and the right $a = 1$ according to an *ideological density function* $\delta : [0, 1] \to \mathbb{R}$. This means that the function δ is continuous, satisfying $\delta(x) > 0$ for each $0 \le x \le 1$ and $\int_0^1 \delta(x)\, dx = 1$. We interpret the integral $\int_a^b \delta(x)\, dx$, where $0 \le a < b \le 1$, as the percentage of voters whose ideological preferences are between a and b. A typical ideological density function δ is shown in Figure 2.6.

    As in Example 2.11, we assume that there are two candidates, say, 1 and 2, each voter casts his vote for the candidate who is closest to his ideological position, and the candidate with the most votes wins.

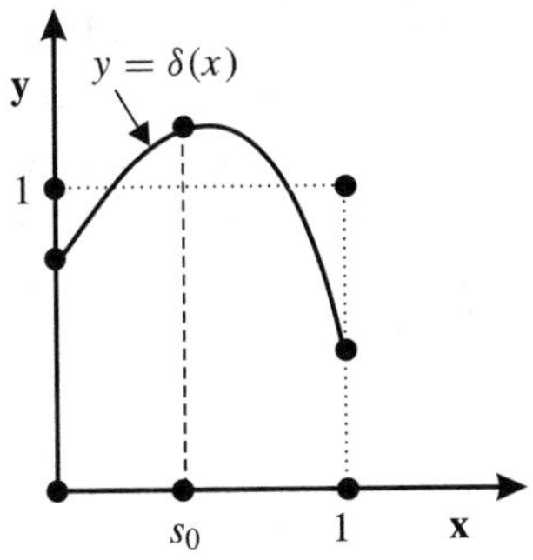

Figure 2.6.   An ideological density function.

a. Determine the ideological density function for the voter model described in Example 2.11.

b. Show that the utility functions of the two candidates are given by

$$u_1(a_1, a_2) = \begin{cases} \int_0^{\frac{a_1+a_2}{2}} \delta(x)\,dx, & \text{if } a_1 < a_2 \\ 0.50, & \text{if } a_1 = a_2 \\ \int_{\frac{a_1+a_2}{2}}^1 \delta(x)\,dx, & \text{if } a_1 > a_2 \end{cases}$$

and

$$u_2(a_1, a_2) = \begin{cases} \int_{\frac{a_1+a_2}{2}}^1 \delta(x)\,dx, & \text{if } a_1 < a_2 \\ 0.50, & \text{if } a_1 = a_2 \\ \int_0^{\frac{a_1+a_2}{2}} \delta(x)\,dx, & \text{if } a_1 > a_2. \end{cases}$$

c. Show that there exists a unique $s_0 \in (0, 1)$ such that $\int_0^{s_0} \delta(x)\,dx = \frac{1}{2}$.

d. Establish that (s_0, s_0) is the only Nash equilibrium of the strategic form game with two candidates.

12. The ideological density (see the previous exercise) of the electorate of the State of Indiana is given by $\delta(x) = -1.23x^2 + 2x + 0.41$.

a. Sketch the graph of the density.

b. Compute the unique real number $s_0 \in (0, 1)$ such that $\int_0^{s_0} \delta(x)\,dx = \frac{1}{2}$. [Answer: $s_0 \approx 0.585$.]

c. In 1988, after many years of Republican governors, Evan Bayh, a Democrat, was elected governor of the State of Indiana. Can you guess (and justify) the ideological direction of Evan Bayh's political campaign?

13. Consider the voting model (discussed in Example 2.11) when the number of candidates is three.

a. Write down the payoff function of candidate i.

b. Show that there is a strategy combination with distinct ideological positions that gives each candidate $\frac{1}{3}$ of the votes.

c. Show that there is no Nash equilibrium.

d. Do the candidates still appeal to the median voter?

2.4 SOLVING MATRIX GAMES WITH MIXED STRATEGIES

We have mentioned before that not every matrix game has an equilibrium. This then raises substantive issues about the solution of these games. The question is important, as it relates to a fairly large class of games. In searching for a solution for games without a Nash equilibrium it could be instructive to examine the problem within the context of an example. If we look at the matrix game

A Game without a Nash Equilibrium

	Strategy	Player 2	
		L	R
Player 1	T	(0,3)	(3,0)
	B	(3,0)	(0,3)

then we notice that if player 1 plays T, then player 2 will want to play L, but in that case player 1 will want to play B, in which case player 2 will want to play R, and so on. We, therefore, have this cycle of players wanting to change strategies. Indeed, if we think about what player 1 should do, we realize that the player should be very careful in revealing his strategy to player 2, for if player 2 has any idea of what strategy player 1 is going to play, then player 2's choice will result in the worst possible payoff for player 1. For instance, if player 2 knows that player 1 is going to play T, then he will play L, and player 1's payoff is then 0, the worst possible.

Clearly, player 1 should make every attempt to keep player 2 guessing about whether he intends to play T or B. One way to do this is by using a randomizing device to choose between the strategies. The randomizing device in this case could be a coin or some other device that gives us a random selection of T or B.

Of course, since the situation is similar for player 2, she will want to do the same. The result is then that both players use some random scheme to choose their strategies when they play the game. Such random schemes that choose between strategies are called *mixed strategies*, and we discuss them next.

We have seen so far that a matrix game can be described by an $m \times n$ matrix of the form

	Strategy	Player 2			
		s_1^2	s_2^2	$\cdots$	s_n^2
Player 1	s_1^1	(a_{11}, b_{11})	(a_{12}, b_{12})	$\cdots$	(a_{1n}, b_{1n})
	s_2^1	(a_{21}, b_{21})	(a_{22}, b_{22})	$\cdots$	(a_{2n}, b_{2n})
	$\vdots$	$\vdots$	$\vdots$	$\ddots$	$\vdots$
	s_m^1	(a_{m1}, b_{m1})	(a_{m2}, b_{m2})	$\cdots$	(a_{mn}, b_{mn})

,

where a_{ij} and b_{ij} are the payoffs of player 1 and player 2, respectively. In fact, we can split the above matrix into the two payoff matrices

$$A = \begin{bmatrix} a_{11} & a_{12} & \cdots & a_{1n} \\ a_{21} & a_{22} & \cdots & a_{2n} \\ \vdots & \vdots & \ddots & \vdots \\ a_{m1} & a_{m2} & \cdots & a_{mn} \end{bmatrix} \quad \text{and} \quad B = \begin{bmatrix} b_{11} & a_{12} & \cdots & b_{1n} \\ b_{21} & b_{22} & \cdots & b_{2n} \\ \vdots & \vdots & \ddots & \vdots \\ b_{m1} & b_{m2} & \cdots & b_{mn} \end{bmatrix}.$$

This shows that a matrix game is completely determined by its pair of payoff matrices A and B. When we present a matrix game by the pair (A, B) of its payoff matrices, we shall say that the game is in its *bimatrix form*. It is a standard terminology to call player 1 the *row player* and player 2 the *column player*. Consequently, the strategies of the row player are denoted by the index i $(i = 1, \ldots, m)$ and the strategies of the column player by the index j $(j = 1, \ldots, n)$.

With this notation, we can describe a strategy profile as a pair (i, j) and a Nash equilibrium (or simply an *equilibrium*) as a strategy profile (i, j) such that

1. a_{ij} is the largest element in column j of the matrix A; that is, $a_{ij} = \max_{1 \le k \le m} a_{kj}$; and
2. b_{ij} is the largest element in row i of the matrix B; that is, $b_{ij} = \max_{1 \le r \le m} a_{ir}$.

A *mixed strategy* (or a *probability profile*) for the row player is simply any vector $\mathbf{p} = (p_1, p_2, \ldots, p_m)$ such that $p_i \ge 0$ for each strategy i and $\sum_{i=1}^{m} p_i = 1$. Similarly, a mixed strategy for the column player is a vector $\mathbf{q} = (q_1, q_2, \ldots, q_n)$ such that $q_j \ge 0$ for each strategy j and $\sum_{j=1}^{n} q_j = 1$. A mixed strategy $\mathbf{p}$ for the row player is said to be a *pure strategy* if for some strategy i we have $p_i = 1$ and $p_k = 0$ for $k \ne i$. That is, the pure strategy i for the row player is the strategy according to which the row player plays her original strategy i with probability 1 and every other strategy with probability 0. In other words, the pure strategies of player 1 are the strategies of the form

$$\mathbf{p} = (0, 0, \ldots, 0, 1, 0, \ldots, 0),$$

where the 1 appears once. Clearly, the row player has exactly m pure strategies, which we usually identify with her original strategies.

Similarly, any strategy of the form

$$\mathbf{q} = (0, 0, \ldots, 0, 1, 0, \ldots, 0),$$

where the 1 appears once, is called a pure strategy for the column player. Notice again that the column player has exactly n pure strategies, which we identify with his original strategies.

Suppose now that each player (in order to confuse the other player) chooses his or her strategy according to some probability profile—the row player plays according to a mixed strategy $\mathbf{p}$ and the column player according to a mixed strategy $\mathbf{q}$. If this is the case, then each player has no way of predicting the strategy of the other player and the only hope he or she has is to maximize his or her expected payoff. *How do we compute the expected payoff of the row player if the players play according to the mixed strategies* $\mathbf{p}$ *and* $\mathbf{q}$?

Notice first that if the column player plays the strategy j, then the row player, playing with probability profile $\mathbf{p}$, can expect a payoff of $\sum_{i=1}^{m} p_i a_{ij}$. Now taking into account the fact that the column player also plays his strategies according to the probability profile $\mathbf{q}$, it follows that the row player can expect a payoff of $q_j \sum_{i=1}^{m} p_i a_{ij}$ from the column player playing strategy j. This implies that the cumulative expected payoff of the row player is

$$\pi_1(\mathbf{p}, \mathbf{q}) = \sum_{i=1}^{m} \sum_{j=1}^{n} p_i q_j a_{ij} .$$

Similarly, the expected payoff of the column player is

$$\pi_2(\mathbf{p}, \mathbf{q}) = \sum_{i=1}^{m} \sum_{j=1}^{n} p_i q_j b_{ij} .$$

We now have a strategic form game in which the strategy sets of the players have been replaced by the sets of probability profiles over strategies. Such a game is referred to as the game in mixed strategies. *Does the matrix game have a Nash equilibrium in mixed strategies?* The answer is yes! And this is a celebrated result in game theory. We state it below as a theorem; for details see Ref. [18], Chapter VII.

Theorem 2.14   Every matrix game has a Nash equilibrium in mixed strategies.[9]

It is not difficult to see that the Nash equilibria in pure strategies (when they exist) of a matrix game can be identified with the mixed strategies equilibria $(\mathbf{p},\mathbf{q})$, in which the strategies $\mathbf{p}$ and $\mathbf{q}$ are of the form

$$\mathbf{p} = (0, \ldots, 0, 1, 0, \ldots, 0) \quad \text{and} \quad \mathbf{q} = (0, \ldots, 0, 1, 0, \ldots 0) .$$

Theorem 2.15   A strategy profile (i, j) for a matrix game is a Nash equilibrium if and only if the pure strategy (i, j) is also a Nash equilibrium for the game in mixed strategies.

In other words, every Nash equilibrium in pure strategies is also a Nash equilibrium of the game in mixed strategies. That is, if Nash equilibria exist, then they are also (as Theorem 2.15 asserts) equilibria for the game in mixed strategies. However, the big difference is that while the game might not have an equilibrium in pure strategies, it always has (according to Theorem 2.14) a mixed strategies equilibrium! We now present some guidelines for finding mixed strategies equilibria.

---

[9] A generalized version of this result was proved by John Nash for n-player games in 1951; see Ref. [16] in the bibliography.

Guidelines for Computing Mixed Strategies Equilibria

To compute mixed strategies equilibria in a matrix game we use the following four steps.

1. Write the matrix game in its bimatrix form $A = [a_{ij}]$, $B = [b_{ij}]$.

2. Compute the two payoff functions

$$\pi_1(\mathbf{p}, \mathbf{q}) = \sum_{i=1}^{m} \sum_{j=1}^{n} p_i q_j a_{ij} \quad \text{and} \quad \pi_2(\mathbf{p}, \mathbf{q}) = \sum_{i=1}^{m} \sum_{j=1}^{n} p_i q_j b_{ij}$$

3. Replace $p_m = 1 - \sum_{i=1}^{m-1} p_i$ and $q_n = 1 - \sum_{j=1}^{n-1} q_j$ in the payoff formulas and express (after the computations) the payoff functions π_1 and π_2 as functions of the variables $p_1, \ldots, p_{m-1}, q_1, \ldots, q_{n-1}$.

4. Compute the partial derivatives $\frac{\partial \pi_1}{\partial p_i}$ and $\frac{\partial \pi_2}{\partial q_j}$ and consider the system

$$\frac{\partial \pi_1}{\partial p_i} = 0 \; (i = 1, \ldots, m-1) \quad \text{and} \quad \frac{\partial \pi_2}{\partial q_j} = 0 \; (j = 1, \ldots, n-1).$$

Any solution of this system $p_1, \ldots, p_{m-1}, q_1, \ldots, q_{n-1}$ with $p_i \geq 0$ and $q_j \geq 0$ for all i and j, $\sum_{i=1}^{m-1} p_i \leq 1$ and $\sum_{j=1}^{n-1} q_j \leq 1$ is a mixed strategies equilibrium.

An equilibrium $(\mathbf{p}, \mathbf{q})$ is said to be an *interior equilibrium* if $p_i > 0$ and $q_j > 0$ for all i and j. The interior equilibria of the game correspond precisely to the solutions $p_1, \ldots, p_{m-1}, q_1, \ldots, q_{n-1}$ of the system

$$\frac{\partial \pi_1}{\partial p_i} = 0 \; (i = 1, \ldots, m-1) \quad \text{and} \quad \frac{\partial \pi_2}{\partial q_j} = 0 \; (j = 1, \ldots, n-1)$$

with $p_i > 0$ and $q_j > 0$ for all i and j, $\sum_{i=1}^{m-1} p_i < 1$ and $\sum_{j=1}^{n-1} q_j < 1$.

Let us illustrate the guidelines for finding mixed strategies equilibria with an example.

Example 2.16

It is easy to see that the matrix game

$$A = \begin{bmatrix} 0 & 3 \\ 2 & 1 \end{bmatrix} \quad \text{and} \quad B = \begin{bmatrix} 3 & 0 \\ 1 & 2 \end{bmatrix},$$

has no Nash equilibrium in pure strategies. We shall use the guidelines presented above to compute a mixed strategies equilibrium for this game.

We start by computing the expected payoff functions of the players. We have

$$\pi_1 = 3p_1 q_2 + 2p_2 q_1 + p_2 q_2$$
$$= 3p_1(1 - q_1) + 2(1 - p_1)q_1 + (1 - p_1)(1 - q_1)$$
$$= -4p_1 q_1 + 2p_1 + q_1 + 1$$

and

$$\pi_2 = 3p_1q_1 + p_2q_1 + 2p_2q_2$$
$$= 3p_1q_1 + (1 - p_1)q_1 + 2(1 - p_1)(1 - q_1)$$
$$= 4p_1q_1 - q_1 - 2p_1 + 2.$$

Differentiating, we get the system

$$\frac{\partial \pi_1}{\partial p_1} = -4q_1 + 2 = 0 \quad \text{and} \quad \frac{\partial \pi_2}{\partial q_1} = 4p_1 - 1 = 0$$

which yields $p_1 = \frac{1}{4}$ and $q_1 = \frac{1}{2}$. This implies $p_2 = 1 - p_1 = \frac{3}{4}$ and $q_2 = 1 - q_1 = \frac{1}{2}$. Therefore, $\left(\left(\frac{1}{4}, \frac{3}{4}\right), \left(\frac{1}{2}, \frac{1}{2}\right)\right)$ is a mixed strategies equilibrium—which is also an interior equilibrium.

EXERCISES

1. Prove Theorem 2.15.

2. Verify directly that the probability profile $\left(\left(\frac{1}{4}, \frac{3}{4}\right), \left(\frac{1}{2}, \frac{1}{2}\right)\right)$ is a mixed strategies Nash equilibrium for the matrix game

$$A = \begin{bmatrix} 0 & 3 \\ 2 & 1 \end{bmatrix} \quad \text{and} \quad B = \begin{bmatrix} 3 & 0 \\ 1 & 2 \end{bmatrix}.$$

3. Consider the matrix game in the bimatrix form

$$A = \begin{bmatrix} 3 & 0 \\ 0 & 1 \end{bmatrix} \quad \text{and} \quad B = \begin{bmatrix} 1 & 0 \\ 0 & 4 \end{bmatrix}.$$

   a. Find the Nash equilibria of the game. [Answers: (first row, first column) and (second row, second column).]
   b. Compute the expected payoff functions of the two players.
      [Answer: $\pi_1 = 4p_1q_1 - p_1 - q_1 + 1$; $\pi_2 = 5p_1q_1 - 4p_1 - 4q_1 + 4$.]
   c. Find all mixed strategies equilibria of the game.
      [Answer: $((1, 0), (1, 0))$, $((0, 1), (0, 1))$, and $\left(\left(\frac{4}{5}, \frac{1}{5}\right), \left(\frac{1}{4}, \frac{3}{4}\right)\right)$.]

4. (*The matching coins game*) Consider the following simple game—known as the *matching coins game*—played between two players as follows. Each player conceals either a penny or a nickel in her hand without the other player knowing it. The players open their hands simultaneously, and if they hold the same coins, then player 2 receives one dollar from player 1. If the coins are different, then player 2 pays one dollar to player 1. This game has the following matrix form:

		Player 2	
	Strategy	P	N
Player 1	P	(−1,1)	(1,−1)
	N	(1,−1)	(−1,1)

a. Show that this game does not have a Nash equilibrium.
b. Compute the expected payoff functions of the players.
   [Answer: $\pi_1 = -4p_1q_1 + 2p_1 + 2q_1 - 1$; $\pi_2 = 4p_1q_1 - 2p_1 - 2q_1 + 1$.]
c. Find the mixed strategies Nash equilibria of the game.
   [Answer: $((\frac{1}{2}, \frac{1}{2}), (\frac{1}{2}, \frac{1}{2}))$.]
d. What is the highest expected payoff of each player?
   [Answer: The highest expected payoff of each player is zero!]

5. Consider the Prisoner's Dilemma game (as presented in Example 2.2) in its bimatrix form

$$A = \begin{bmatrix} -1 & -10 \\ 0 & -5 \end{bmatrix} \quad \text{and} \quad B = \begin{bmatrix} -1 & 0 \\ -10 & -5 \end{bmatrix}.$$

a. Show that the game has a unique Nash equilibrium.
b. Compute the expected payoff functions of the two players.
   [Answer: $\pi_1 = 4p_1q_1 - 5p_1 + 5q_1 - 5$; $\pi_2 = 4p_1q_1 - 5q_1 + 5p_1 - 5$.]
c. Show that the pure strategy (second row, second column) is the only mixed
   strategies equilibrium of the game.

THREE | SEQUENTIAL DECISIONS

In all that we have seen so far, decisions had to be taken once, and the decision makers then received the rewards. In many contexts, however, decisions have to be taken sequentially, and the rewards are received only after an entire sequence of decisions has been taken. For instance, in manufacturing, the product usually has to go through a sequence of steps before it is finished, and at each step the manufacturer has to decide which of several alternative processes to use. Before becoming established in one's career or profession, an individual has to take a sequence of decisions that leads to a final outcome. Similarly, financial planning over a lifetime is done via a sequence of decisions taken at various points of an individual's life span.

By now we have a fairly good grasp of how optimal decisions are made when a decision has to be made once. Sequential decision making is different because the decision-making process is more involved. A choice made initially has an impact on what choices can be made later. For instance, in choosing a career, if an individual decided not to go to college, then the choice of a career is limited to those that require only a high school education. Similarly, if one chooses not to save very much in the early years of his life, then the choice of how much to accumulate for retirement in the later years is much more constrained. This fact, that choices made in the initial stages affect the alternatives available in the later stages, is an element of decision making that is central to sequential decision making.

In this chapter, we start by laying the analytical foundation to sequential decisions by discussing graphs and trees. We then discuss sequential decisions under certainty as well as under uncertainty. In the section in which we discuss decision making under uncertainty, we introduce the technique of using *Bayes's theorem* as a method of using information in updating beliefs.

3.1 GRAPHS AND TREES

Sequential decisions are better understood in terms of "graph diagrams." For this reason, the notion of a graph will play an essential role in our study and will be discussed in this section. We start with the definition of a directed graph.

DEFINITION 3.1   A *directed graph* is a pair $G = (V, E)$, where V is a finite set of points (called the *nodes* or the *vertices* of the graph) and E is a set of pairs of V (called the *edges* of the graph).

A directed graph is easily illustrated by its diagram. The *diagram of a directed graph* consists of its vertices (drawn as points of a plane) together with several oriented line segments corresponding to the pairs of the edges. For instance, if (u, v) is an edge, then in the diagram of the directed graph we draw the line segment uv with an arrowhead at the point v. The diagram shown in Figure 3.1(a) is the diagram of the directed graph with vertices

$$V = \{u, v, w, x, y\}$$

and edges

$$E = \{(u, v), (v, u), (v, w), (v, x), (w, y), (y, x)\}.$$

On the other hand, the directed graph with vertices $\{1, 2, 3, 4, 5, 6\}$ and edges $\{(1, 2), (6, 2), (6, 3), (3, 6), (3, 4), (4, 5)\}$ is shown in Figure 3.1(b). It is customary (and very instructive) to identify a directed graph with its diagram.

If (u, v) is an edge of a directed graph, then we usually say that u is a *predecessor* of v or that v is a *successor* of u. For instance, in the directed graph shown in Figure 3.1(a), v is a predecessor of x and w, and in the directed graph shown in Figure 3.1(b) the nodes 2 and 3 are both successors of the node 6.

We shall say that in a graph there is a *path* from a node u to another node v if there exist nodes $w_1, w_2, \ldots, w_k$ such that the pairs

$$(u, w_1), (w_1, w_2), (w_2, w_3), \ldots, (w_{k-1}, w_k), (w_k, v) \tag{3.1}$$

are all edges of the directed graph. The collection of edges in (3.1) is also called a *path* of the graph from node u to node v. In other words, a path from a vertex u to another vertex v describes how the node v can be reached from u following the edges of the directed graph.

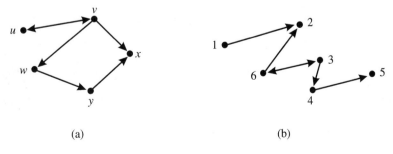

(a)   (b)

Figure 3.1

If there is a path from u to v, it is common to say that we can *join* u with v. The *length* of a path is the number of its edges. The path in (3.1) will also be denoted by

$$u \rightarrow w_1 \rightarrow w_2 \rightarrow w_3 \rightarrow \cdots \rightarrow w_{k-1} \rightarrow w_k \rightarrow v .$$

For instance, in Figure 3.1(b) there exists a path from vertex 6 to vertex 5 (the path $6 \rightarrow 3 \rightarrow 4 \rightarrow 5$) but not a path from vertex 3 to vertex 1. In the directed graph of Figure 3.1(a) there are two paths from vertex u to vertex x.

A *terminal node* for a directed graph is a node with no edge starting from it. For instance, in the directed graph of Figure 3.1(a) the node x is a terminal node. In Figure 3.1(b), the nodes 2 and 5 are the only terminal nodes of the directed graph.

With every directed graph $G = (V, E)$ there is another natural directed graph associated with it—called the *backward graph* of G. It is the directed graph whose nodes are the nodes of G, and its edges are the edges of G with the opposite orientation. That is, the backward graph (V, E') of G is the graph with nodes V and edges $E' = \{(u, v): (v, u) \in E\}$. It is important to notice that the paths of the backward graph are precisely the paths of the original directed graph oriented in the opposite direction. The directed graphs in Figure 3.1 and their backward graphs (drawn with dotted edges) are shown in Figure 3.2.

Now we come to the important notion of a tree.

DEFINITION 3.2   A directed graph T is said to be a *tree* if

1. There exists a distinguished node R (called the *root* of the tree) that has no edges going into it, and
2. For every other node u of the graph there exists exactly one path from the root R to u.

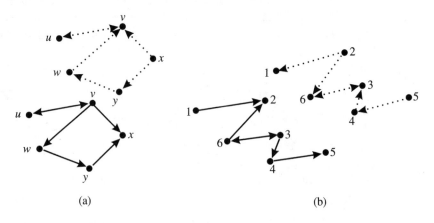

(a)   (b)

Figure 3.2

It is easy to see that the directed graphs in Figure 3.2 are not trees. An example of a tree is shown in Figure 3.3. There is a certain terminology about trees that is very convenient and easy to adopt.

- If (u, v) is an edge of a tree, then u is called the *parent* of the node v, and node v is referred to as a *child* of u.
- If there is a path from node u to node v, then u is called an *ancestor* of v, and node v is known as a *descendant* of u.

With the above terminology in place, the root R is an ancestor of every node, and every node is a descendant of the root R.

Here are some other basic properties of trees; we leave the verification of these properties as an exercise for the reader.

Theorem 3.3   In any tree:

1. There is at most one path from a node u to another node v;
2. If there is a path from u to v, then there is no path from v to u;
3. Every node other than the root has a unique parent; and
4. Every nonterminal node has at least one terminal descendant node.

The unique path joining a node u to another node v in a tree will be denoted by $P(u, v)$. For instance, in the tree of Figure 3.3, we have $P(u, 4) = u \rightarrow 1 \rightarrow 3 \rightarrow 4$. Notice that the path $P(u, v)$ is itself a tree having root u and terminal node v.

A *branch* of a tree T is a directed graph having nodes starting at a node u and containing all its descendants together with their original edges. We shall denote by T_u the branch starting at u. It should not be difficult to see that T_u is itself a tree whose root is u. The branch T_u using the directed graph of Figure 3.3 is shown in Figure 3.4.

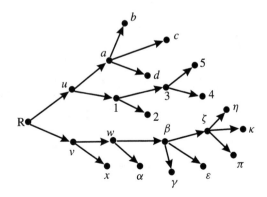

Figure 3.3

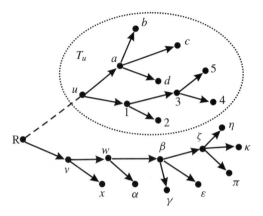

Figure 3.4

We close our discussion with the definition of a subtree.

> **DEFINITION 3.4**   A tree S is called a *subtree* of a tree T if:
>
> **1.** The nodes of S form a subset of the nodes of T;
> **2.** The edges between the nodes of S are precisely the same edges joining the nodes when considered as nodes of the tree T;
> **3.** The terminal nodes of S form a subset of the terminal nodes of T; and
> **4.** The root of S is the same as the root of the tree T.

In Figure 3.4, the directed graph having nodes $\{R, v, w, \beta, \epsilon, \zeta, \pi, \kappa\}$ together with their original edges is a subtree.

EXERCISES

1. Consider the tree shown in Figure 3.3.
   a. Describe the branches T_u and T_v.
   b. Find the terminal nodes of the tree.
   c. Describe the paths $P(R, \kappa)$ and $P(R, 5)$.
   d. Draw the backward graph of this tree.

2. Consider the directed graph shown in Figure 3.5.
   a. Describe the directed graph in set notation.
   b. Find the paths (and their lengths) from vertex 1 to 6.
   c. Find the paths from vertex 3 to vertex 4.
   d. Draw the backward graph.

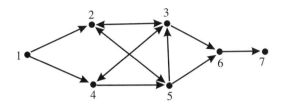

Figure 3.5

3. Verify the properties listed in Theorem 3.3.

4. Show that any path $P(u, v)$ of a tree is itself a tree with root u and terminal node v. In particular, show that every path from the root of a tree to a terminal node is a subtree.

5. Verify that every branch T_u of a tree is itself a tree having root u.

6. Verify that the remaining part of a tree T after removing all the descendants of a node is a subtree of T.

7. Determine all subtrees of the tree in Figure 3.3.

8. Show that if a tree has n edges and k vertices, then $n = k - 1$.

3.2 SINGLE-PERSON DECISIONS

A decision maker may often face a situation in which a series of decisions have to be made in a sequential manner—one after the other. For instance, a firm that produces a certain product starts by choosing the initial process and then has to choose among several intermediate processes before the final stage is reached. Many decisions of a very personal nature also involve sequential decision making.

One of the best ways to describe sequential decision processes is by means of some special directed graphs. These directed graphs are called *decision graphs*, and they are defined as follows.

DEFINITION 3.5   A *decision graph* is any directed graph having a unique root R, in the sense that:

1. R is the only node with no edge ending into it;
2. For every node N other than R, there is at least one path from R to N;
3. There is at least one terminal node; and
4. From every nonterminal node N there is at least one path from N to a terminal node.

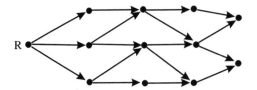

Figure 3.6   A decision graph.

Every tree is a decision graph, but a decision graph need not be a tree. An example of a decision graph is shown in Figure 3.6.

A decision graph is interpreted as describing a sequential decision process in the following manner. The root R represents the beginning of the sequential decision process taken by an individual, the nodes represent the various stages of the decision process, and the edges represent the decisions taken by the individual. The terminal nodes are the terminal stages of the decision process, and they are usually accompanied with their payoffs. That is, the payoff at any particular terminal node is the "reward" (which might appear in many forms) received by the individual after his sequence of decisions led him to that particular terminal node. In other words, a *single-person decision process* consists of a decision graph together with an assignment of payoff values at each terminal node of the decision graph.

Let us illustrate the single-person decision process with an example.

Example 3.6

A high school graduate after leaving school has to decide whether to go to college. If the choice is "not to go to college," then should she go to a technical school to learn a trade or should she start to work? The consequences in terms of lifetime earnings will be different in the two cases. If, however, the decision is to go to college, then after graduation (provided she graduates) she has to decide whether to earn a professional degree, to go to graduate school, or to enter the labor market and find a job. Notice that each decision involves different costs and benefits. The sequential decision problem that we have just outlined can be represented by a decision tree. In Figure 3.7 we have written down the payoffs for a hypothetical high school graduate. The payoffs for different decisions will be different across high school graduates, and as a result we will see a variety of decisions, none of which can be summarily dismissed as irrational.

The problem that is now a central issue in the decision process is to choose an *optimal decision path*. An *optimal decision path* is—as its name suggests—a decision path that leads the decision maker to a terminal node with the "best" possible payoff. If we have a decision tree, then there is usually one optimal decision path—unless there are two or more terminal nodes with the same best possible payoff. It is not difficult to see that $A \to B_1 \to C_3$ is the optimal decision path for the high school graduate with the decision tree shown in Figure 3.7.

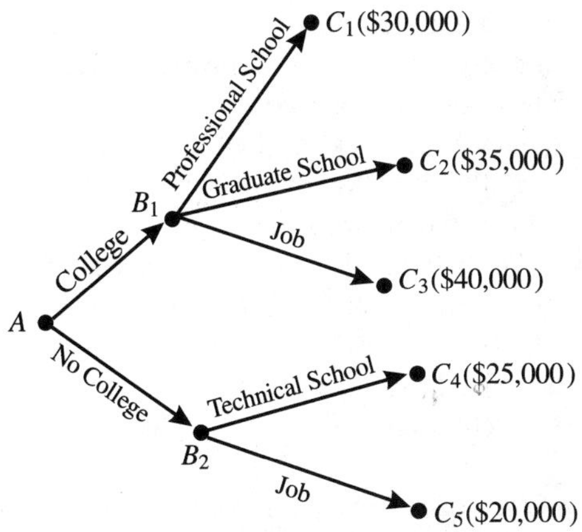

Figure 3.7   The career decision tree.

Instead of listing the payoffs at each terminal node of a decision graph, it is common practice to list the payoffs of individual decisions along the edges of the graph. In this case, the payoff of a given path $N \to N_1 \to N_2 \to \cdots \to N_{k-1} \to N_k$ (from node N to node N_k) is simply the sum of the payoffs of the edges

$$NN_1, N_1N_2, \ldots, N_{k-1}N_k.$$

A method of finding the optimal paths in a decision tree that has been extensively used in applications is the so-called *backward induction method*. It is based upon the following simple property.

Theorem 3.7   If in a decision graph a path

$$N_1 \to N_2 \to \cdots \to N_k \to N_{k+1} \to \cdots \to N_\ell \to \cdots \to N_m$$

is optimal, then the path $N_k \to N_{k+1} \to \cdots \to N_\ell$ is also an optimal path from N_k to N_ℓ.

Here we describe the *backward induction method* for decision trees[1] in great detail. The method consists of going backward by steps starting from the terminal nodes of the decision tree and proceeding a step at a time until we reach the root. The precise procedure of the "backward steps" is described as follows.

In the first step, we select all predecessors of the terminal nodes whose *children are all terminal nodes* (i.e., all nodes whose edges end at terminal nodes); let us call these nodes the nodes of Step 1 or Stage 1. We then assign to each node of Step 1 the payoff that can be obtained by reaching the best possible terminal node from the given node. (We remark here that since we work with a decision tree rather than a general decision graph, there always

---

[1]For general decision graphs the method of backward induction is not always applicable; see Exercise 1 at the end of the section.

exist nodes whose children are all terminal nodes. The latter is false for general decision graphs; see Exercise 1 at the end of the section.) Next we delete the children of the nodes of Step 1 and obtain the truncated tree of Step 1.

The second step repeats this process by looking at the predecessors of the nodes of Step 1 whose children are all terminal nodes of the truncated tree of Step 1. That is, the nodes of Step 2 are all nodes having *all their edges* ending at the terminal nodes of the truncated tree of Step 1. We shall call these nodes the nodes of Step 2. In each node N of Step 2, we find an edge that leads to a node of Step 1 with the highest possible total payoff, and we assign this total payoff to the node N. (Clearly, this represents the best payoff that the individual can get starting from node N and ending at a terminal node.) We delete from the truncated tree the children of the nodes of Step 2 and obtain the truncated tree of Step 2.

The predecessors of the nodes in Step 2 having all their edges ending at the nodes of the truncated tree of Step 2 are now the nodes of Step 3. As before, at each node N of Step 3, we find an edge that leads to a node of Step 2 with the highest possible total payoff, and we assign this total payoff to node N. (Again, this payoff represents the best payoff an individual can get starting from N and ending at some terminal node.) The truncated tree of Step 3 is obtained by deleting from the truncated tree of Step 2 the children of the nodes of Step 3.

We continue this backward process until we arrive at a stage where all predecessors of the nodes of that step consist precisely of the root R. A path from the root R to a node of that step that yields the best total payoff is the beginning of an optimal decision path that can be traced out now in the opposite direction.

Let us illustrate the backward induction method using the decision graph of Example 3.6 shown in Figure 3.7. We start by observing that the collection of terminal nodes of the decision graph shown in Figure 3.7 is the set $\{C_1, C_2, C_3, C_4, C_5\}$. According to the backward induction method, in the first step of the process we select all predecessors of the set of terminal nodes whose children are all terminal nodes; here it is the set of nodes $\{B_1, B_2\}$. At each node B_1 and B_2, we assign the best payoff the high school graduate can get by reaching the terminal nodes. We see that the best payoff at B_1 is $\$40,000$ and the best payoff at B_2 is $\$25,000$. This is indicated in the "truncated decision tree" of Figure 3.8. In the truncated version of the original decision tree the optimal edge is the one that leads to the node B_1. The optimal decision path in this case is, $A \rightarrow B_1 \rightarrow C_3$, that is, to go to college and then to enter the labor market.

Here is another example illustrating the backward induction method.

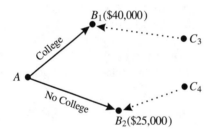

$B_1(\$40,000)$

College

A

No College

$B_2(\$25,000)$

C_3

C_4

Figure 3.8   The truncated decision tree.

Example 3.8

Consider the single-person decision tree shown in Figure 3.9. The numbers along the edges represent cost. So the optimal path is the one that minimizes the cost.

At Step 1, we find the nodes having all their edges ending at terminal nodes. An inspection shows that this set is $\{D, T, G\}$. The best edge going from D to the terminal nodes is DL at the minimum cost of 1; we keep this edge and delete the other one and indicate this minimum cost at node D by writing $D(1)$. Similarly, we have the edges TN and GS; see Figure 3.9.

Next, we find the nodes of Step 2. They are precisely the nodes having all their edges ending at the terminal nodes of the truncated tree of Step 1. An easy inspection shows that this is the set $\{A, B, C\}$; see Figure 3.9. At node A we find the edge with the minimum cost to the terminal nodes, and we do the same thing for the other nodes B and C. The new truncated tree is shown in Figure 3.9 (Step 2). Notice that the numbers in parentheses indicate the minimum cost for reaching the terminal nodes of the original decision tree from that node. For instance, $C(3)$ indicates the fact that from the node C we can reach the terminal nodes of the original decision tree with the minimum cost of 3.

The nodes of Step 3 now consist of the root R alone. Clearly, the edge that gives the mimimum cost from R to the nodes A, B, and C is RC. This completes the backward induction and yields the optimal path $R \rightarrow C \rightarrow G \rightarrow S$.

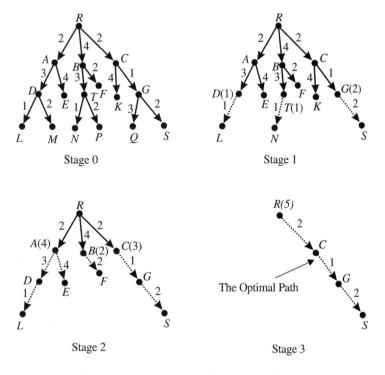

Figure 3.9   The backward induction method.

Let us illustrate the backward induction method once more by looking at another example of a sequential decision tree.

Example 3.9

Suppose a manufacturer produces a product that goes through four separate steps, from an initial step A to its final step D. In going from one step to another the manufacturer has a choice of several different processes. In going from step A to step B, the manufacturer has the option of four separate processes. In going from step B to step C, the choice of processes depends on the choice made earlier and, similarly, for going from step C to the final step D. The manufacturer would obviously want to use a combination of processes that would produce the product at the least possible cost.

The problem is one that involves making sequential decisions, as at every step a process has to be chosen conditioned on what choices were made in the earlier steps. We can describe the problem best by drawing the decision graph, which is shown in Figure 3.10. The objective is to find the path that gives the smallest total cost. The graph shows the cost per unit of using each process. For instance, if the manufacturer uses process $A \rightarrow B_1$, then the cost per unit of production is $\$7$ for going from step (node) A to step (node) B_1. Next we shall determine the optimal decision path by backward induction—shown graphically in Figure 3.11.

From the terminal node D we go backward and select all nodes N whose edges (starting from N) terminate at D; here, we have only the edge ND. The collection of these nodes form the set of nodes of step 1: clearly $\{C_1, C_2, C_3, C_4\}$. The minimum cost for reaching D from a node C_i is shown on the top diagram of Figure 3.11. This completes the first step of backward induction.

For the second step of the induction process we look at the set of nodes whose edges terminate at the nodes $\{C_1, C_2, C_3, C_4\}$. These are the nodes of the set $\{B_1, B_2, B_3, B_4\}$. At each node B_i we add (in parentheses) the total minimum cost needed to reach the nodes of step 1 from B_i. This is shown on the second from the top diagram of Figure 3.11. The next step brings us to the root A. We see that the edge AB_1 will yield the total minimum cost from A to any node among B_1, B_2, B_3, B_4.

Therefore, the path

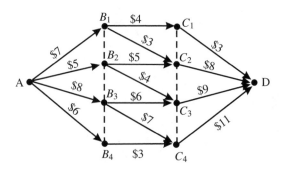

Figure 3.10

$$D \to C_1 \to B_1 \to A$$

is the backward optimizer. Reversing the direction of this path yields the optimal decision path $A \to B_1 \to C_1 \to D$; see Figure 3.11.

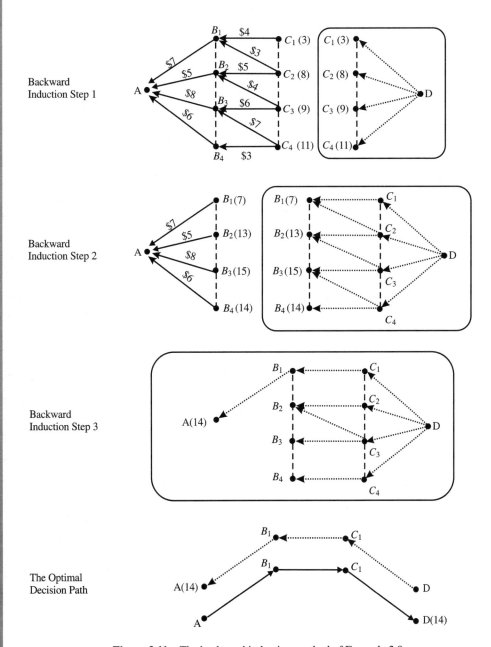

Figure 3.11 The backward induction method of Example 3.9.

1. This exercise shows that (in general) the backward induction method cannot be applied to find the optimal decision path when the decision process is described by a decision graph that is not a tree. Consider the decision process described by the decision graph shown in Figure 3.12.

    a. Find the optimal decision path. [Answer: $R \to B \to C \to E \to A \to D \to G$.]

    b. Show that the backward induction method (as described in this section) is not applicable in this case.

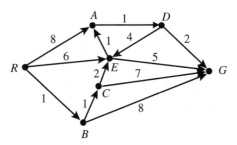

Figure 3.12

2. The graph in Figure 3.13 describes a sequential decision process. The numbers along the edges represent the cost of taking the corresponding decisions. The decision process starts at R and ends in one of the terminal nodes L, M, N, P, Q, S.

    a. Show that the decision graph is not a tree.

    b. Verify that in this case the backward induction method is applicable and use it to find the optimal path and the minimum cost from R to the terminal nodes. [Answers: $R \to C \to E \to H \to K \to S$ and $R \to C \to F \to H \to K \to S$.]

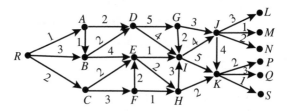

Figure 3.13

3. Prove Theorem 3.7.

4. Show that every tree has at least one terminal node N such that the children of the parent M of N (i.e., N's "brothers" and "sisters") are all terminal nodes. (This conclusion is essential for the applicability of the backward induction method.)

5. Show that every single-person decision process has an optimal path.

6. The American Airlines pilots struck work on February 17, 1997, demanding better contract terms.

    a. Draw up a decision tree indicating the decision problem faced by the pilots before their decision to strike.

    b. What payoffs in the decision tree are consistent with the decision to strike?

7. In the career choice decision problem of Example 3.6, the payoffs are the income stream net of expenditure on training. In the example, the optimal choice for the individual is to go to college and then enter the job market.

    a. Suppose the individual received a scholarship to go to a professional school. Would this change the decision?

    b. Now consider another individual whose preference for graduate school implies that he is willing to receive a lower income stream in order to go to graduate school. How would this change the payoffs? Indicate this in the decision tree.

8. An investor faces a decision about whether to buy a firm that is up for a bid. After buying the firm (if he buys the firm) he can break it up and resell it, or run it under new management. He could then choose to sell it in the near future or retain it.

    a. Construct the decision tree of the investor.

    b. Write down payoffs over the terminal nodes and solve for the optimal path. Explain your reasons for the payoffs and the solution.

9. A venture capitalist is thinking of financing two alternative ventures. One is a proposal to market a generic brand of a drug whose patent expires shortly. The other project would require investing in developing a commercial application of a gene splicing technique.

    a. Draw a decision tree for the venture capitalist. [Hint: Notice that the second project will fetch high returns only in the second stage if it is marketed.]

    b. What option will the venture capitalist choose? [Hint: Write down the profits from following each option and analyze the optimal path.]

10. A wine producer has a choice of producing and selling a generic variety of wine or an exclusive brand. The decision process is sequential and is given by the decision tree shown in Figure 3.14. The decision tree shows the cost per bottle at every stage of a decision (M means "marketing" and A means "advertising"). The terminal nodes give the price per bottle.

a. Find the decision path that maximizes the profit per bottle.
b. Will this decision path provide the wine producer with the optimal decision? Why or why not? [Hint: The general brand bottles may sell in larger quantities.]

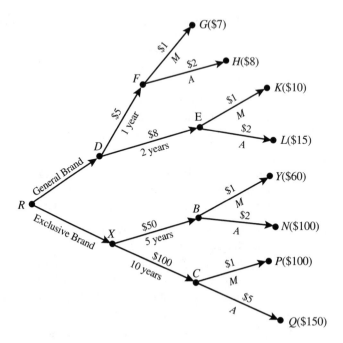

Figure 3.14

3.3 UNCERTAINTY AND SINGLE-PERSON DECISIONS

In the previous section, while discussing sequential decision problems, we glossed over the fact that a choice at any stage may have uncertain consequences. It is quite possible that in the career choice problem, if one decides to become an actor after graduating from high school, then there is a small chance that the individual may end up with a very high lifetime income and a high probability that the individual will make a more modest income. Similarly, in the decision problem involving the manufacturer's choice of processes, the choice of a process may be associated with a higher or a lower chance of having a defective product. In other words, while decisions are made in a sequential process, the consequences, during the implementation of some of these decisions, for the success or failure of the final outcome are uncertain.

Uncertainty of this kind is introduced in sequential decision problems by adding nodes at which nature chooses. The following examples indicate how uncertainty can be handled in sequential decision problems.

Example 3.10

A pharmaceutical firm X faces a decision concerning the introduction of a new drug. Of course, this means that there is an initial decision about how much to spend on research and development, the possibility that the drug may fail to be developed on schedule, and the fact that the drug may not be quite successful in the market. At each stage of this decision-making process, we notice the presence of uncertainty. A decision tree of this problem is shown in Figure 3.15.

At the initial stage firm X has to decide whether to spend a large amount "Hi" or a small amount "Lo" on research and development. The result of this investment could either lead to success S or failure F, with the probability p of success being higher in the case of Hi expenditure on research and development. Even when the drug is successfully produced, the firm may decide not to market it. The uncertainty about whether the drug can be produced or not is handled here by introducing the nodes "Nature" at which nature chooses. The edges M and DM stand for "Market" and "Do not Market" the produced drug.

We can solve this decision problem by using backward induction. In the present case, with the payoffs as shown in Figure 3.15, the firm has to decide at the nodes of the first stage of the backward induction whether to market (M) or not to market (DM) the drug. The firm always chooses to market the drug. But then this leads to the truncated version of the decision tree shown in Figure 3.16, in which case the payoffs are expressed in the form of expected payoffs.

The firm now has to compare two lotteries involving a Hi expenditure choice and a Lo expenditure choice. If the firm is risk neutral, the choice, of course, is the lottery with the highest expected value; otherwise, the choice would depend on the von Neumann–Morgenstern utility function of the firm. If the firm is risk neutral and the expected profits are negative, then the firm will not proceed with the marketing of the product.

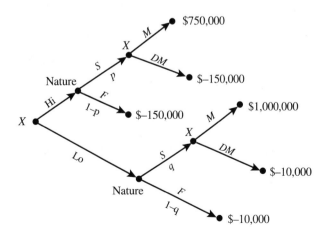

Figure 3.15

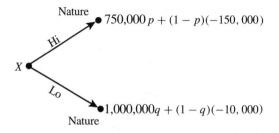

Figure 3.16

The firm can, however, face a slightly more complex problem if the firm is unsure about how successful the drug will be once it is marketed. Firms will often want to resolve such uncertainty by trying to gather some information about the marketability of their products, and on the basis of this information would revise their estimates of how well their products will do in the market. The processing of such information into the decision-making process is of great importance to any firm. To illustrate this we go back to our previous example.

Example 3.11

We consider the same pharmaceutical firm X as in Example 3.10. However, we now expand the original decision tree so as to include the event that the drug once marketed may not do very well. This decision tree is now shown in Figure 3.17.

The two added edges G (good) and B (bad) at the nodes where "Nature" interferes allow for the possibility (with probability s) for the produced drug to be a real money maker and also for the possibility (with probability $1-s$) to be a complete failure.

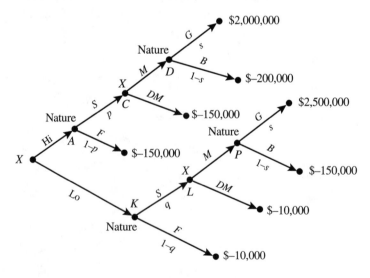

Figure 3.17

The *prior probability* that the drug will do well in the market is given by s. It is interesting to observe that after the firm gathers information about the market, this prior probability is revised to a *posterior probability*. This is usually done by using Bayes's formula from probability theory which we describe below.

We now proceed to discuss Bayes's formula—one of the most famous and useful formulas in probability theory. The formula provides an answer to the following important question: *If an event B is known to have occurred what is the probability that another event A will happen?*

Theorem 3.12 (Bayes's formula)   If A and B are two events in a probability space (S, P), then

$$P(A/B) = \frac{P(B/A)P(A)}{P(B/A)P(A) + P(B/A^c)P(A^c)}.^2$$

As usual, the event A^c is the complementary event of A; that is,

$$A^c = X \setminus A = \{x \in S: x \notin A\}$$

and so $P(A^c) = 1 - P(A)$. The non-negative numbers $P(U/V)$ appearing in Bayes's formula are known as conditional probabilities. We say that $P(U/V)$ is the *conditional probability* of the event U given the event V and define it by

$$P(U/V) = \frac{P(U \cap V)}{P(V)},$$

provided that $P(V) > 0$. Therefore, a useful way to interpret Bayes's formula is to think of it as the conditional probability of event A given that event B is observed.

Bayes's formula is useful whenever agents need to revise or update their probabilistic beliefs about events. The following example provides an illustration of Baye's formula and indicates its usefulness and wide applicability.

Example 3.13

It is known that a certain disease is fatal 40% of the time. At present a special radiation treatment is the only method for curing the disease. Statistical records show that 45% of the people cured took the radiation treatment and that 20% of the people who did not survive took the treatment. *What is the chance that a person suffering from the disease is cured after undergoing the radiation treatment?*

---

[2] The theorem is essentially due to Thomas Bayes (1702–1761), an English theologian and mathematician. This famous formula that immortalized Bayes was included in his article *Essays towards Solving a Problem in the Doctrine of Chances*. It was published posthumously in the *Philosophical Transactions of the Royal Society of London* **53** (1763), 370–418.

We set up the problem as follows: First, in the sample space of all persons suffering from the disease, we consider the two events

A = The person is cured from the disease; and

B = The person is taking the radiation treatment.

Our problem is confined to finding $P(A/B)$.

Notice that A^c = the person did not survive. To apply Bayes's formula, we need to compute a few probabilities. From the given information, we have:

$$P(A) = 0.6,$$

$$P(B/A) = 0.45,$$

$$P(A^c) = 0.4, \text{ and}$$

$$P(B/A^c) = 0.20.$$

Consequently, according to Bayes's formula, the desired probability is

$$P(A/B) = \frac{P(B/A)P(A)}{P(B/A)P(A) + P(B/A^c)P(A^c)}$$

$$= \frac{0.45 \times 0.6}{0.45 \times 0.6 + 0.2 \times 0.4} = 0.7714.$$

In other words, a person having the disease has a 77.14% chance of being cured after undergoing the radiation treatment.

Example 3.14 (Revising the Prior Probability)

Going back to the decision problem of the pharmaceutical firm X (Example 3.11), the *prior probability* that the drug will do well in the market (i.e., the good outcome G occurs) is given by $P(G) = s$. The firm, in order to find out more about how the market will receive the drug, may perform a test I, for instance, study what a sample of potential buyers think of the drug.

Based on this study the firm may want to revise its probability $P(G)$. If the test is successful, then the firm infers that the market condition is better than originally thought and would want to revise $P(G)$ accordingly. However, if it is not successful, then the inference should go the other way. Bayes's formula provides the tool for revising this prior probability $P(G)$ conditioned on the new information I obtained from the test. The *posterior probability*, as the revised probability is called, is given by Bayes's formula

$$P(G/I) = \frac{P(I/G)P(G)}{P(I/G)P(G) + P(I/B)P(B)},$$

where $P(I/G)$ is the probability that the test indicates success if indeed the market situation is G, and $P(I/B)$ is the probability that the test indicates success when the market situation is B.

It is of interest to note that if the new information is good and reliable, then the posterior (or revised) probability should predict the state of the market with a high degree of accuracy, which usually means that the revised probability would be close to zero or one depending on the state of the market. Bayes's formula is, therefore, a nice way of using relevant information to "update beliefs about events."

Now suppose that $P(I/G) = 0.9$ and $P(I/B) = 0.2$. If $s = 0.6$ then after a test of the market that gave a positive result, the revised posterior probability is

$$P(G/I) = \frac{0.9 \times 0.6}{0.9 \times 0.6 + 0.2 \times 0.4} = 0.87.$$

This is a lot higher than the prior probability of 0.6. The firm, therefore, revises its belief about the state of the market being good after observing a positive result from the test. The information from the test is used to revise the probability upward. In the decision tree this will have consequences as the expected payoff from marketing the drug changes drastically.

EXERCISES

1. You know that one child in a family of two children is a boy. What is the probability that the other child is a girl? [Hint: The sample space is $\{(b, b), (b, g), (g, g), (g, b)\}$.]

2. Find the optimal decision path of the firm in Example 3.10 in terms of the values of p and q. [Answer: The firm will choose "Hi" if $90p > 101q + 14$ and $p > \frac{1}{6}$.]

3. Consider the decision problem in Example 3.11 assuming that the firm is risk neutral.
   a. Solve the firm's decision problem.
   b. Express the solution in terms of p, q, and s.
   c. What happens if $p = 0.9$ and $q = 0.4$?
   d. At what value for s will the firm decide to market the drug? Does this depend on p and q?

4. Consider Example 3.14 and the values given there for the conditional probabilities. Assume also that the firm is risk neutral.
   a. Solve the firm's decision problem in terms of p and q.
   b. What happens if $p = 0.9$ and $q = 0.5$?
   c. If the test costs $50, 000$, will the firm want to pay for it?
   d. What is the maximum amount the firm will pay for the test?

5. Estimates show that 0.3% of the U.S. population is carrying the sexually transmitted HIV virus—which is known to cause the deadly disease AIDS. In order to study the spread of the HIV virus in the population, it was suggested that the U.S. Congress pass a law requiring that couples applying for a marriage licence should take the blood test for the HIV virus. The HIV blood test is considered very "effective," since:
   a. A person with the HIV virus has a 95% chance to test positive, and
   b. An HIV virus free person has a 4% chance to test positive.

After several lengthy discussions, it was decided that the HIV blood test was ineffective for determining the spread of the AIDS disease, and its implementation was abandoned.

Can you figure out what argument persuaded the legislators of the ineffectiveness of the HIV virus test for determining the spread of the AIDS disease? [Hint: Consider the events "$A =$ a person taking the HIV virus test has the disease" and "$B =$ the test is positive." Using Bayes's formula determine that $P(A/B) \approx 6.67\%$!]

6. Prove Bayes's formula. [Hint: By definition we have $P(U/V) = \frac{P(U \cap V)}{P(V)}$, provided that $P(V) > 0$. Now note that $P(V) = P(V \cap U) + P(V \cap U^c)$.]

FOUR

SEQUENTIAL GAMES

In the previous chapter we discussed sequential decisions made by a single individual. In every situation that we encountered, the payoff to the individual depended on the sequence of decisions made by the individual. In many other contexts, however, the payoff to the individual may depend not just on what the individual does but also on the sequence of decisions made by other individuals.

Thus we may have a game that is being played by a number of individuals, but instead of taking decisions simultaneously, the players may have to play the game sequentially. For instance, if an investor makes a takeover bid, then the bid has to be made before the management of the firm can respond to the bid. Such a situation is best analyzed as a game in which the investor makes his move in the first stage and the management then responds in the second stage. Obviously, the players in this game are not moving simultaneously, but rather in two stages. Games that are played in stages are variously called *multistage games*, *games in extensive form,* or *sequential games*. In our case, we will use the term *sequential game* for any game in which moves by more than one player are made in a sequence.

Sequential games provide a rich framework to study situations where decisions have to be made in a sequence of stages and in which different individuals have to choose. Sequential games thus have the elements of both sequential decision making as well as games. As with sequential decisions, the issue of how much a player knows at the time he or she has to choose is an important issue and leads to the fundamental classification of sequential games into games with *perfect information* and games with *imperfect information*. Also, like sequential decisions, the idea of sequential rationality plays a crucial role.

In this chapter, we discuss sequential games. In the first section we introduce the concept of a *game tree*. We then proceed to define *information sets*, give the formal definition of a sequential or an extensive form game, and introduce the concept of a strategy in such games. In the subsequent sections we discuss games with perfect information and the concept of an equilibrium. We then illustrate the concepts by discussing a few applications. Two sections are devoted to discussing games with imperfect information. In the first one we introduce the notion of a *subgame*, and in the other we deal with the slightly more complex question of *sequential rationality*.

4.1 THE STRUCTURE OF SEQUENTIAL GAMES

Sequential games are closely associated with trees. As a matter of fact, as we shall see, every tree can be viewed as a "game tree" in many ways. We start by defining an n-player game tree.

> **DEFINITION 4.1**   A tree T is said to be an n-player (or n-person) *game tree* (or a *game tree* for n players $P_1, \ldots, P_n$) if
>
> **a.** Each nonterminal node of the tree is "owned" by exactly one of the players, and
> **b.** At each terminal node v of the tree an n-dimensional "payoff" vector
>
> $$p(v) = \big(p_1(v), p_2(v), \ldots, p_n(v)\big)$$
>
> is assigned.

We emphasize immediately the following two things regarding game trees:

1. *No* terminal node is owned by any player, and
2. There is no guarantee that each player "owns" at least one non-terminal node of the tree. That is, in an n-person game there might be players who do not own any nonterminal node!

A node N owned by a player P is also expressed by saying that the node N *belongs to* player P. The nonterminal nodes of a game tree are called *decision nodes*. A three-person game tree is shown in Figure 4.1.

An n-person game tree represents a sequential process of decisions made by the players starting from the root of the game tree and ending at a terminal node. The game

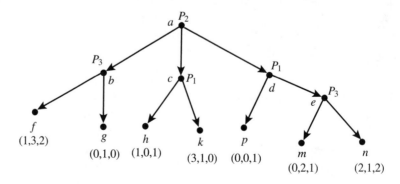

Figure 4.1

starts as follows. The player who owns the root starts the game by making a decision (i.e., he or she chooses an edge) that brings the decision process to another node. If the node is not terminal, it is owned by a player who in turn chooses his or her own edge. Again, if the node is not terminal, it is owned by a player who is next in line to choose an edge. This sequential decision process is continued until a terminal node is reached.

For instance, in the three-person game shown in Figure 4.1 the node a belongs to player 2, who must start the game. Suppose that he chooses the edge (ad) and so his decision reaches the node d, which belongs to player 1. Player 1 must make the next decision by choosing an edge; suppose that he or she selects the edge (de), that is, the decision of player 1 brings the decision process to node e. Node e is owned by player 3, who must make the next decision; suppose that the decision of player 3 is the edge (en). Since n is a terminal node, the game ends at node n. In this case, the decision path chosen by the players is $a \to d \to e \to n$. The payoff vector of the terminal node n is $(2, 1, 2)$, which means that player 1 gets a payoff of 2, player 2 a payoff of 1, and player 3 a payoff of 2.

Two nodes N_1 and N_2 of a game tree owned by a player P are said to be *equivalent* for player P if

  1. There is the same number of edges, say, k, starting from N_1 and N_2; and
  2. The edges from N_1 and N_2 given by

$$\{e_1^1, e_2^1, \ldots, e_k^1\} \quad \text{and} \quad \{e_1^2, e_2^2, \ldots, e_k^2\}$$

can be rearranged in such a way that for each i the edges e_i^1 and e_i^2 are viewed as identical by the player P; we shall indicate this equivalence by $e_i^1 \approx e_i^2$.

This leads us naturally to the concept of an information set.

DEFINITION 4.2   In a game tree, a set of nodes $I = \{N_1, \ldots, N_\ell\}$ is called an *information set* for a player P if:

  1. All nodes of I are nonterminal and belong to player P;
  2. No node of I is related to any other node of I; that is, if N_i and N_j are nodes in I, then N_i is neither an ancestor nor a successor of N_j; and
  3. All nodes of I are equivalent for player P; that is, there is a rearrangement $\{e_1^i, e_2^i, \ldots, e_k^i\}$ of the k edges starting from each node N_i such that $e_r^i \approx e_r^j$ for all i, j, and r.

The intuition behind the notion of an information set I is the following. Assume that at some stage of the decision process in an n-person game, a player P must make the "next decision." Suppose also that, due to his lack of information of the "history" of the game, he knows that the place where he must make the decision is a node of an information set I, but he does not know which one. Moreover, to player P the same number of choices (say k) at each node of I look identical—that is, at each node of I, player P understands that there are k identical choices labeled $1, 2, \ldots, k$. This forces player P to make a decision among $1, 2, \ldots, k$ based only on the k choices and not on the actual location of the node where the decision is taken.

An example of an information set is shown in Figure 4.2. Notice that the information set $I = \{N_1, N_2, N_3\}$ belongs to player P_2. The fact that N_1, N_2 and N_3 belong to the same information set is indicated by joining these nodes by the dotted line. Note also that at each node of I player P_2 has three choices—labeled 1, 2, and 3.

A sequential game is now defined as follows.

DEFINITION 4.3   A *sequential game* or an *extensive form game* is an n-player game tree such that the decision nodes have been partitioned into information sets that belong to the players.

Unlike the case of a game in strategic form, the concept of a strategy in a sequential game is a little more involved. To understand and define strategies in sequential games, we need to introduce a few new concepts.

A *choice* for a player owning a node N in a game tree is simply an edge starting from the node N. In a game tree, a *choice function* for a player owning the set of nodes $\mathcal{N}$ is a function $f: \mathcal{N} \to V$, where V denotes the set of nodes of the tree, such that $f(N)$ is a child of N for each node N of $\mathcal{N}$. Since a child C of a node N is determined completely by the edge NC, it is also customary to identify $f(N)$ with an edge of the tree starting at the node N. It is also quite common to denote a choice function f by a set of edges, where the set f contains exactly one edge originating from each node of $\mathcal{N}$.

A choice function f of a player P is said to *respect an information set* I of P if $f(N_1) \approx f(N_2)$ for each pair of nodes $N_1, N_2 \in I$. That is, the choices at the nodes that belong to the same information set are identical.

Now we define the concept of a strategy.

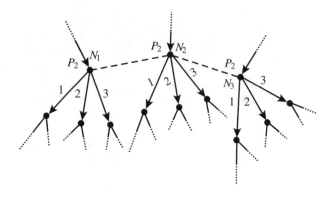

Figure 4.2

DEFINITION 4.4   Let $\mathcal{N}$ denote the set of nodes owned by a player P in a game tree and assume that $\mathcal{N}$ is partitioned into information sets for P. Then a choice function $s: \mathcal{N} \to V$ is a *strategy* for player P if it respects each information set.

A strategy in a "sequential" game thus seems to be a fairly subtle concept. Briefly, a strategy for a player in a sequential game describes the choices that the player is going to make at each of his information sets. Therefore, a strategy for a player in a sequential game is a *complete plan* of how to play the game and prescribes his choices at every information set. In other words, a player's strategy will indicate the choices that the player has planned to make a priori (i.e., before the game starts) in case his information sets are reached during the course of playing the game. A *strategy profile* for an n-person sequential game is then simply an n-tuple $(s_1, s_2, \ldots, s_n)$, where each s_i is a strategy for player i.

It is useful to note here that once a strategy profile $(s_1, \ldots, s_n)$ is given in a sequential game, a terminal node of the game tree will be reached automatically. In other words, as mentioned before, a sequential game is understood to be played as follows. The player (say P_j) who owns the root R chooses a node according to his selected strategy s_j; here he chooses the node $s_j(R)$. Then the player who owns the node $s_j(R)$ chooses according to his strategy, and the game continues in this fashion until a terminal node v is reached and the game ends. Subsequently, each player i gets the payoff $p_i(v)$. Notice that the strategy profile $(s_1, s_2, \ldots, s_n)$ uniquely determines the terminal node v that is reached. Hence the payoff (or utility) of each player is a function u_i of the strategy profile $(s_1, s_2, \ldots, s_n)$. That is, we usually write

$$u_i(s_1, s_2, \ldots, s_n) = p_i(v).$$

Thus, in sum, a sequential game is represented by a game tree with players moving sequentially. At each information set the player who needs to choose has determined a priori a choice (i.e., an edge) at each of the nodes in the information set, which is exactly the same for each node in the same information set. After the players have chosen their actions at their information sets a terminal node is reached and the outcome of the game is realized.

Here is an example of a business decision process that can be translated into a two-person sequential game.

Example 4.5 (The Takeover Game)

An investor, whom we will refer to as player I, is considering bidding for a company called Fortune F. Currently, the shares of F are valued at \$100. If I can take over the company, it is known that F would be worth \$110 per share under the new management. The investor I can make a bid of $b \, (> 100)$ dollars per share in order to take over the company by buying 50% of the total shares of F. *How much should I offer? After I makes an offer what should the shareholders of F do?*

We have just described a two-player game in which at stage 1 player I makes a bid for F and at stage 2 player F decides whether to take the bid or reject it. Schematically, the situation can be described by the two-person sequential game shown in Figure 4.3.

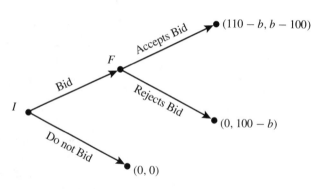

Figure 4.3

The payoffs of the game are to be understood as follows. If the investor makes a bid of b dollars per share, then either fortune F can accept the bid and sell the shares to the investor at b dollars per share or reject the bid by buying back its shares at b dollars per share. If it accepts the bid, fortune F makes a profit of $b - 100$ dollars per share. The investor, however, makes $110 - b$ dollars per share after the value of the shares increases to \$110 per share under the new management. If fortune F rejects the bid, then it has to buy back the shares at b dollars per share and loses $b - 100$ dollars per share. The investor in this case gets zero.

In the takeover game of Example 4.5, each player knows precisely the node at which she has to make her choices. Many sequential games satisfy this condition. In such games each player knows all the relevant past information necessary to identify the node at which she has to make her choice. Sequential games with this special feature are called *games of perfect information*. Sequential games that do not meet this condition are called *games of imperfect information*. Their precise definition is as follows.

DEFINITION 4.6   A sequential game is a game of *perfect information* if every information set is a singleton. Otherwise, it is a game with *imperfect information*.

A sequential game of perfect information, therefore, is a sequential game in which a player knows exactly what choices have been made in the game at the time she has to make a choice. While this is not going to be true in every situation, it is true in many situations.

On the other hand, sequential games of imperfect information are games in which players either cannot observe some of the choices made in the preceding stages of the game or players who play in the earlier stages prefer not to reveal the information to players in the succeeding stages. Games of imperfect information as well as games of perfect information arise quite naturally in many contexts. We have already seen an example (Example 4.5) of a sequential game of perfect information. The next example demonstrates how easy it is for a sequential game with perfect information to become a sequential game with imperfect information.

Example 4.7

We modify the takeover game described in Example 4.5. Fortune F is now known to have a project P under development that if successful could increase the price of F's shares to \$125 under current management and \$140 under I's management. At the time the investor I makes his bid b, only F knows whether the project is successful. Thus there is imperfect information, as I does not know at the time he makes his decision the fate of the project. A way to describe the new situation in the takeover game is by the three-player sequential game shown in Figure 4.4.

Notice that I's information set at the time that I decides on whether to bid consists of two nodes, depending on what nature N decided about the project P. Therefore, player I, given his information, is unable to distinguish between the two nodes. Note, however, at the time F decides whether to accept the bid b or reject it, F knows the outcome of the project. Because I's information set consists of more than one node, this game is an example of a game with imperfect information.

In this game, which is an extension of the sequential game shown in Figure 4.3, if the project succeeds and the investor I makes a bid of b dollars per share and if fortune F accepts the bid, then fortune F makes $b - 125$ dollars per share, whereas the investor I makes $140 - b$ dollars per share. If fortune F rejects the bid, then it has to buy back the shares at b dollars per share and loses $125 - b$ dollars per share. The investor in this

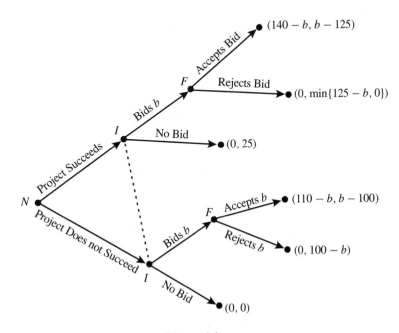

Figure 4.4

case makes nothing. If, on the other hand, the project does not succeed, the investor I bids b dollars, and fortune F accepts the bid, then fortune F gets $b - 100$ dollars per share. If fortune F rejects the bid, then the investor gets zero and fortune F ends up losing $b - 100$ dollars per share.

Sequential games with perfect and imperfect information will be discussed in detail in the next sections.

We close this section with a remark concerning the classification of information sets. An information set I of a player P is said to be an *information set with recall* if it has the following property:

- Whenever the player P owns a node N that is a predecessor of all nodes of the information set I, then all nodes in the information set I are the descendants of the same child of N.

The distinction between information sets with recall and general information sets is illustrated in the games shown in Figure 4.5. This distinction allows us to differentiate between cases in which players remember all the moves observed in the past and situations in which some players forget some past moves.

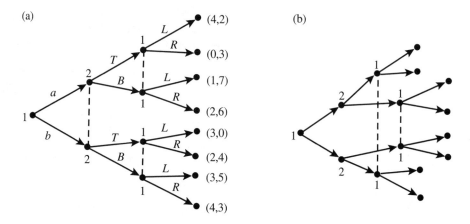

Figure 4.5 (a) A game having information sets with recall. (b) A game having information sets without recall.

EXERCISES

1. Show that in a perfect information sequential game there are as many strategies for a player as there are choice functions for that player.

2. Consider the game trees shown in Figure 4.6.

   a. Verify that the game tree of Figure 4.6(a) describes a perfect information sequential game and that the game tree of Figure 4.6(b) describes an imperfect information sequential game.

   b. Describe the strategies of the players in each game.

   c. Describe the utility functions $u_i(s_1, s_2, s_3)$ $(i = 1, 2, 3)$ of the players in each game.

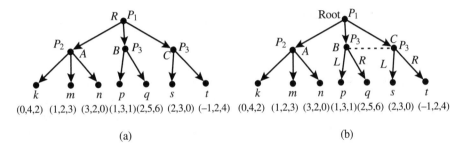

Figure 4.6

3. Verify that the Prisoner's Dilemma game can be expressed as a sequential game whose game tree is shown in Figure 4.7. Describe the strategies of each player.

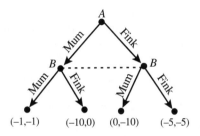

Figure 4.7

4. Consider the sequential game outlined in Figure 4.8.

   a. Find the subtrees in the game tree.
   b. Compute the optimal choice of every player in every subtree of the game.
   c. Given the position of the players in the game tree, what choice will player P_2 make?

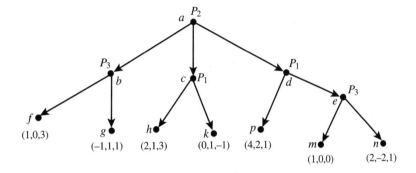

Figure 4.8

5. Consider the takeover game discussed in Example 4.5. What should be the smallest and highest values of the bid b that a rational investor would make to the company Fortune? (Justify your answers.)

6. Consider the takeover game of Example 4.7. Assume that the project P if successful will increase the price of F's shares to \$140 under the current management and \$125 under I's management. Under these conditions what should be the payoff vectors in the game tree shown in Figure 4.4?

4.2 SEQUENTIAL GAMES WITH PERFECT INFORMATION

As defined in the previous section (see Definition 4.6), in the class of sequential games with perfect information, every player knows exactly the moves that players have made in the earlier stages of the game. The takeover game that we discussed in Example 4.5 belongs to this class of games, as player F knows exactly the bid that player I made in the first stage. The question that arises at this point is about ways of "solving" sequential games. Before discussing how to solve sequential games, we need to explain the rationale behind the "solution concept" for such games.

Suppose that we have an n-player sequential game. We shall denote by S_i the set of all strategies of player i. As usual, a *strategy profile* is an n-tuple $(s_1, s_2, \ldots, s_n)$, where $s_i \in S_i$ (i.e., each s_i is a strategy for the player i). Every strategy profile $(s_1, s_2, \ldots, s_n)$ determines a unique terminal node v (the outcome of the game if each player plays with the strategy s_i). At the terminal node v we have the payoff vector $p(v) = (p_1(v), \ldots, p_n(v))$. Translating this into the terminology of utility functions, we see that the utility function $u_i \colon S_1 \times S_2 \times \cdots \times S_n \to \mathbb{R}$ of player i is defined by

$$u_i(s_1, s_2, \ldots, s_n) = p_i(v),$$

where again $p(v) = (p_1(v), \ldots, p_n(v))$ is the payoff vector at the node v determined (uniquely) by the strategy profile $(s_1, s_2, \ldots, s_n)$.

As in the case of strategic form games, a *solution* of a sequential game is understood to be a Nash equilibrium, and is defined as follows.

DEFINITION 4.8   In an n-player sequential game (with perfect or imperfect information) a strategy profile $(s_1^*, s_2^*, \ldots, s_n^*)$ is said to be a *Nash equilibrium* (or simply an *equilibrium*) if for each player i we have

$$u_i(s_1^*, \ldots, s_{i-1}^*, s_i^*, s_{i+1}^*, \ldots, s_n^*) = \max_{s \in S_i} u_i(s_1^*, \ldots, s_{i-1}^*, s, s_{i+1}^*, \ldots, s_n^*).$$

In other words, as in the previous cases, a Nash equilibrium is a strategy profile $(s_1^*, s_2^*, \ldots, s_n^*)$ such that no player can improve his payoff by changing his strategy if the other players do not change theirs.

We now proceed to discuss Nash equilibrium strategy profiles for sequential games. Let us recall that for every terminal node N of a tree T there exists a unique path starting from the root R and ending at N. So, if T is also the game tree of a sequential game, then every strategy profile $(s_1, s_2, \ldots, s_n)$ determines a unique path from the root to some terminal node of the tree. We shall call this unique path the path *supported by the strategy profile* $(s_1, s_2, \ldots, s_n)$. A path supported by a Nash equilibrium will be called an *equilibrium path*. We remark that:

1. Two different strategy profiles can have the same path (see, for instance, Example 4.9), and
2. Every path from the root to a terminal node is supported by at least one strategy profile.

Let us illustrate the preceding discussion with an example.

Example 4.9

Consider the following simple two-person sequential game with perfect information whose game tree is shown in Figure 4.9. If player 1 plays L, then node B is reached and player 2 will play R', in which case player 1 gets zero. If player 1 plays R, then node C is reached and player 2 plays L'' (and player 1 gets 4). The solution path is, therefore, $A \rightarrow C \rightarrow F$, which leads to the terminal node F at which the payoff vector is (4, 1).

Now if we think of the strategies that the players use, we find that player 1 has choices at one node (the node A) at which he can choose either R or L. Player 2, however, has to choose at the two different nodes B and C. Player 2's strategy is, therefore, a function from $\{B, C\}$ to $\{L', R', L'', R''\}$ with the feasibility restriction that from node B one can only choose R' or L' and a similar restriction on choices from node C. *What strategies are then equilibrium strategies?*

The reader should verify that the two strategy profiles $\big(\{R\}, \{R', L''\}\big)$ and $\big(\{R\}, \{L', L''\}\big)$ are the only Nash equilibria of the game. They both support the equilibrium path $A \rightarrow C \rightarrow F$.

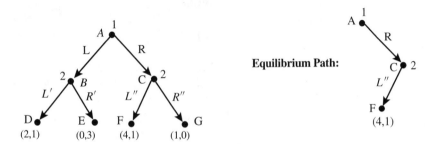

Figure 4.9

Do sequential games have equilibria? The answer is "Yes" if the sequential game is of perfect information. This important result was proved by H. W. Kuhn.[1]

Theorem 4.10 (Kuhn)   Every sequential game with perfect information has a Nash equilibrium.

To prove Theorem 4.10 one can employ our familiar *backward induction method*, which can be described (as we saw before) by the following steps.

In the first step, we select all predecessors of the terminal nodes whose *children are all terminal nodes* (i.e., all nodes whose edges end at terminal nodes); let us call these nodes the nodes of Stage 1 or Step 1. We then assign to each node N of Stage 1 the payoff vector of a terminal node, say M, that offers the best possible return to the player owning the node N from N to all possible terminal nodes. Subsequently, we delete the children of the nodes of Stage 1, and the remaining tree is the truncated game tree of Stage 1.

The second step repeats this process by looking at the predecessors of the nodes of Stage 1 whose children are all terminal nodes of the truncated tree of Stage 1. That is, the nodes of Stage 2 are all nodes having *all their edges* ending at the terminal nodes of the truncated tree of Stage 1. We shall call these nodes the nodes of Stage 2. In each node N of Stage 2, we associate a child of N, say Q, with the best payoff for the player owning the node N from N to all possible terminal nodes. We then assign the payoff vector of node Q to node N. (Clearly, if the node N is owned by the kth player, then the kth coordinate of this payoff vector represents the best payoff that player k can get starting from node N and ending at any terminal node of the original tree.) We delete from the truncated tree the children of the nodes of Stage 2 and obtain the truncated tree of Stage 2.

The predecessors of the nodes in Stage 2 having all their edges ending at the terminal nodes of the truncated tree of Stage 2 are now the nodes of Stage 3. As before, at each node N of Stage 3, we find an edge that leads to a node of Stage 2, say, S, with the highest possible payoff for the player owning N, and we assign the payoff vector of the node S to the node N. (Again, if node N belongs to the kth player, then the kth coordinate of this payoff vector represents the best payoff that player k can get starting from N and ending at the terminal nodes of the original tree.) The truncated tree of Stage 3 is obtained by deleting from the truncated tree of Stage 2 the children of the nodes of Stage 3.

We continue this backward process until we arrive at a stage where the predecessors of the nodes of that step consist precisely of the root R. A path from the root R to a node of that step that yields the best total payoff for the player owning the root is the beginning of an optimal decision path that can be traced out now in the opposite direction.

---

[1]Harold W. Kuhn is Professor Emeritus of Mathematical Economics at Princeton University. He made many contributions to Game Theory.

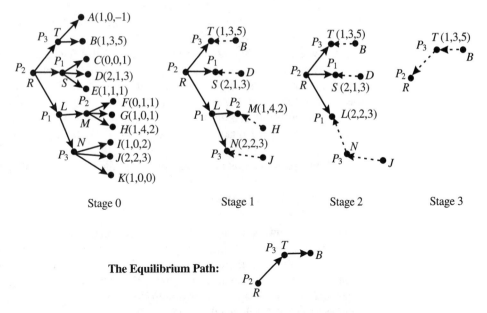

Stage 0   Stage 1   Stage 2   Stage 3

The Equilibrium Path:

Figure 4.10   The backward induction method.

The backward induction method is illustrated in the sequential game shown in Figure 4.10. Notice that the backward induction method gives the path $B \to T \to R$. Reversing it, we see that a solution path is $R \to T \to B$. This guarantees, for instance, that the strategy

$$\big(\{LN, SC\}, \{RT\}, \{TB, NI\}\big)$$

is a Nash equilibrium supporting the equilibrium path $R \to T \to B$.

We would like to emphasize the following fact regarding the backward induction method.

- While the backward induction method when applicable in a given sequential game always produces an equilibrium path, it need not give us all the equilibrium paths!

For an example illustrating this, see Exercise 4 at the end of this section.

Let us now go back to the takeover game of Example 4.5 and find a Nash equilibrium by using the backward induction method just outlined.

In the takeover game player I knows that if the bid b is less than 100 dollars per share, then player F will reject the bid, as player F knows that she can do better. Knowing this, if player I is serious about the bid, he should bid at least 100 dollars per share. In this case it is not in player F's interest to reject the bid. If player I has bid b dollars per share and b is greater than 100, then player F accepts the bid, and player I realizes a net profit of $110 - b$ per share. It is clear that player I will bid at least b dollars per share, but how much is b? Player I in order to maximize his profit will bid exactly 100 per share, in which case he makes a profit of 10. We have just found a solution to the takeover game. Player I bids a little bit over 100 per share, and player F accepts. Under this condition, the backward induction method applied to the game tree of Figure 4.3 yields the following Nash equilibrium: (Bid, Accepts Bid)

It is worth analyzing the method we used to solve the takeover game. We noted that when player I made his bid, he thought seriously about how player F will react to the bid. Taking player F's possible reactions to bids into account, player I bid what he thought was optimal for player I. A slightly different way of doing this is to find out player F's optimal response for each bid that player I could make and take that as the consequence of the bid that player I makes. Then find out what is optimal for player I for this modified decision problem.

We now present a few more examples of sequential games with perfect information.

Example 4.11 (Nuclear Deterrence)

Two nuclear powers are engaged in an arms race in which each power stockpiles nuclear weapons. At issue is the rationality of such a strategy on the part of both powers.

Let us examine the question by looking at a stylized version of the game that the two powers are engaged in. Country 1 moves in the first stage and may choose between nuclear weapons N or nonproliferation (NP). Country 2 in stage 2 of the game observes the choice that country 1 has made and chooses between N and NP. A representative game tree of the situation is shown in Figure 4.11.

According to the payoffs shown in Figure 4.11, country 2 likes the option N whether country 1 chooses NP or N. If country 1 chooses NP, then country 2 by choosing N guarantees for itself a very powerful position vis-a-vis country 1. If country 1 chooses N, then country 2 would like to choose N, as this allows it a credible deterrence against a possible nuclear attack by country 1.

Knowing country 2's thinking on this issue, country 1 knows that it is optimal for it to choose N. It is easy to see that the backward induction solution of this game is the following.

- Country 2 chooses N irrespective of whether country 1 chooses N or NP.
- Country 1 chooses N.

In other words, the path $a \rightarrow c \rightarrow d$ is the only Nash equilibrium path of the game.

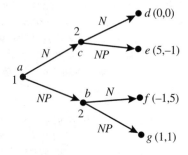

Figure 4.11

While the example is quite clearly highly stylized, it brings to the fore the incentives that countries have in engaging in arms races. In the game, it is clearly rational for the two countries to build up their nuclear arsenal. And left to themselves the countries would do exactly what the model predicts.

It is also clear that both countries would be better off without having to spend on an arms race, but the equilibrium solution predicts differently. This is precisely why arms races are so prevalent and why it is so difficult to dissuade countries from pursuing other strategies.[2]

The next example is very well known in economics. We revisit the scenario of the duopoly game of Example 2.10, but instead of having the firms move simultaneously, we now have one firm making its move before the other firm. That is, one of the firms sets its quantity before the other firm. This, of course, changes the entire game. The game has now become a sequential game with perfect information, as the quantity choice of the firm that sets its quantity first is known to the second firm when the second firm decides what quantity to produce. This duopoly model was first analyzed by von Stackelberg.

Example 4.12 (The Stackelberg Duopoly Model)

The Stackelberg duopoly game is played as follows. There are two firms producing identical products: firm 1 and firm 2. Firm 1 chooses a quantity $q_1 \geq 0$, and firm 2 observes q_1 and then chooses q_2. The resulting payoff or profit of firm i is

$$\pi_i(q_1, q_2) = q_i \big[\, p(q) - c_i \,\big],$$

where $q = q_1 + q_2$, $p(q) = A - q$ is the market clearing price when the total output in the market is q, and c_i is the marginal cost of production of the product by firm i. That is, the profit of each firm i is

$$\pi_i(q_1, q_2) = q_i \big(A - q_1 - q_2 - c_i\big).$$

Note that the game is a two-person sequential game with two stages and with perfect information. If we use the backward induction method to solve the game, we must first find the reaction of firm 2 to every output choice of firm 1. Hence we must find the output q_2^* of firm 2 that maximizes firm 2's profit given the output q_1 of firm 1. That is, $q_2^* = q_2^*(q_1)$ solves

$$\pi_2(q_1, q_2^*) = \max_{q_2 \geq 0} \pi_2(q_1, q_2)$$

$$= \max_{q_2 \geq 0} q_2 \big(A - q_1 - q_2 - c_2\big).$$

Since $\pi_2(q_1, q_2) = -(q_2)^2 + (A - q_1 - c_2)q_2$, taking the first and second derivatives with respect to q_2, we get

$$\frac{\partial \pi_2}{\partial q_2} = -2q_2 + A - q_1 - c_2 \quad \text{and} \quad \frac{\partial^2 \pi_2}{\partial q_2^2} = -2 < 0.$$

---

[2]This example was written a year prior to the nuclear explosions in India and Pakistan!

So, according to the first- and second-order tests, the maximizer q_2^* is the solution of the equation $\frac{\partial \pi_2}{\partial q_2} = -2q_2 + A - q_1 - c_2 = 0$. Solving for q_2, we get

$$q_2^* = q_2^*(q_1) = \frac{A - q_1 - c_2}{2}, \tag{4.1}$$

provided $q_1 < A - c_2$.

Firm 1 should now anticipate that firm 2 will choose q_2^* if firm 1 chooses q_1. Therefore, firm 1 will want to choose q_1 to maximize the function

$$\pi_1(q_1, q_2^*) = q_1\big(A - q_1 - q_2^* - c_1\big)$$
$$= q_1\Big(A - q_1 - \frac{A - q_1 - c_2}{2} - c_1\Big)$$
$$= \tfrac{1}{2}\big[-(q_1)^2 + (A + c_2 - 2c_1)q_1\big]$$

subject to $q_1 \geq 0$. Using again the first- and second-order tests, we get

$$\frac{\partial \pi(q_1, q_2^*)}{\partial q_1} = -q_1 + \frac{A + c_2 - 2c_1}{2} \quad \text{and} \quad \frac{\partial^2 \pi(q_1, q_2^*)}{\partial q_1^2} = -1 < 0.$$

Therefore, the maximizer of $\pi(q_1, q_2^*)$ is $q_1^* = \frac{A+c_2-2c_1}{2}$. Substituting this value in (4.1), we get $q_2^* = \frac{A+2c_1-3c_2}{4}$.

This is the backward induction solution of the Stackelberg game. The equilibrium strategy of firm 1 is $q_1^* = \frac{A+c_2-2c_1}{2}$, while the equilibrium strategy of firm 2 is $q_2^* = \frac{A+2c_1-3c_2}{4}$.

One should compare this with the results obtained for the Cournot duopoly game of Example 2.10, which is the simultaneous move version of the duopoly game. In doing so, one will notice that the profit of firm 1 is greater in the Stackelberg duopoly game than in the Cournot duopoly game, whereas the profit of firm 2 is lower in the Stackelberg duopoly game than in the Cournot duopoly game; see Exercise 8 at the end of the section.

From the point of view of playing strategically, it would seem that moving first gives firm 1 a certain advantage. This is a fact that often holds in sequential games and has been dubbed *the first mover advantage*. The intuition behind the phenomenon could be that firm 2 reacts to *a commitment that firm* 1 *makes*, and firm 1, by moving first, commits to a strategy that is the most advantageous to itself, thereby giving itself an edge. We will see more of this power of commitment in other situations.

Example 4.13 (A Partnership Game)

Two partners are interested in financing a project. If the project is financed, then each receives W dollars; otherwise each receives zero. The total cost of financing the project is A dollars, and the two partners must come up with this total. Partner 1 makes the first move by committing c_1 dollars to the project. Partner 2 then decides whether he would want to make up the difference by contributing c_2 dollars to the project. If $c_1 + c_2 = A$, then the project is completed; otherwise each partner receives zero.

The opportunity cost of contributing c dollars to the project is c^2 dollars to each partner.[3] Partner 1, who makes the initial contribution in period one, discounts the payoff in the second period (the period when partner 2 makes his contribution) by the discount factor δ. Now it should be clear that the utility functions of the partners are

$$u_1(c_1, c_2) = \delta\left(W - c_1^2\right) \quad \text{and} \quad u_2(c_1, c_2) = W - c_2^2.$$

The situation we have just described can immediately be recognized as a two-stage game of perfect information. Partner 1 makes his contribution first, and partner 2 then responds with his share of the cost. If we solve this game using the backward induction method, we must first solve the decision problem of partner 2 given the contribution c_1 of the first partner. Partner 2 will contribute $c_2 = A - c_1$ as long as

$$A - c_1 \geq 0 \quad \text{and} \quad W - c_2^2 = W - (A - c_1)^2 \geq 0, \tag{4.2}$$

otherwise $c_2 = 0$. Solving (4.2) for c_1, we get

$$A - \sqrt{W} \leq c_1 \leq A. \tag{4.3}$$

Now partner 1 knowing this should decide to contribute an amount c_1 such that $A - \sqrt{W} \leq c_1 \leq A$. However, this might not always be profitable for partner 1. To be profitable for partner 1, we must also have $W - c_1^2 \geq 0$ or $c_1 \leq \sqrt{W}$. In this case, the parameters A and W must satisfy $A - \sqrt{W} \leq \sqrt{W}$ or $A \leq 2\sqrt{W}$. Therefore, the profit of partner 1 depends upon the parameters A and W, which in turn can be considered determined by Nature N. The game tree of this sequential game is shown in Figure 4.12.

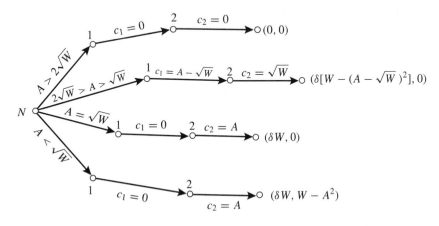

Figure 4.12

---

[3]Recall that in economics the *opportunity cost* of a particular action is the gain that one could get from the next best alternative source of investment. Thus the cost to a partner may grow by more than the actual dollar amount.

In case $A < \sqrt{W}$, we see that $c_1 = 0$ and $c_2 = A$. But in this case, the second partner can finance the entire project on his own and would want to discontinue the partnership. Notice also that the payoff of the second partner in this case is $2W - A$.

Note here again that the partner who moves first has a decisive advantage. By making the first move and thereby committing himself to the move, he lets the second partner make up the difference in the amount of the contribution. As in the Stackelberg duopoly game, we see that the first mover has a certain advantage. In committing himself to the amount he is willing to contribute, he forces the second partner to come up with the difference as long as it is profitable for the second partner to do so. But in deciding the amount that he wants to commit to the project, the first partner makes an optimal decision. The commitment that we, therefore, see in the backward induction solution is an *optimal commitment*.

Example 4.14 (Optimal Contracts: The Perfect Information Case)

This example is at the heart of the literature on *moral hazard* in economics. In the way we formulate it here there is no moral hazard, but we can use a version of the same model to illustrate the basic results in that literature.[4]

This is a two-player sequential game in which the *Principal P* is considering the possibility of contracting out some work to an *Agent A*. The agent has a choice of either accepting the contract offered or rejecting it. If the agent accepts the contract, then the agent can either work hard (H) or be lazy (L); we assume that H and L are measured in dollars. If the agent works hard, the project is worth \$100 to the principal with a probability of 0.9 or worth just \$10 with a probability of 0.1. If the agent is lazy, the principal receives the high value of \$100 with a probabiltity of 0.1 and the low value of \$10 with a probability of 0.9. In this game, we assume that the principal can observe whether the agent works hard or is lazy. Thus the game is a game with perfect information.

The principal can offer a contract that is conditioned on whether the agent works hard or is lazy; so we denote the contract that is offered by the wage function $W(\cdot)$, where this function takes two values, $W(H)$ and $W(L)$. The resulting *Principal-Agent* game is shown in Figure 4.13. The payoff to the principal, in case the worker works hard and the high value occurs, is \$100 $- W(H)$, and the agent receives $W(H) - H$. We will assume here that

$$H > L.$$

Clearly, the payoffs to the principal and the agent depend on the contract that the principal offers. The principal knows this and will offer a contract that he knows the worker will take. The principal, however, has to offer a contract that will either induce the worker to work hard or be lazy.

---

[4]The literature on *moral hazard* in economics deals with issues in which there is the possibility that agents might take actions that are undesirable. For instance, a worker may choose to be lazy or shirk rather than work hard.

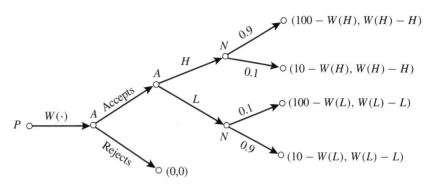

Figure 4.13

If the principal wants the worker to work hard, then the contract must satisfy the following conditions:

$$W(H) - H \geq W(L) - L \quad \text{and} \quad W(H) - H \geq 0 \,.$$

The condition $W(H) - H \geq W(L) - L$ guarantees that the worker will choose to work hard, as he derives a higher payoff from doing so.[5] The other condition makes certain that the worker is better off accepting the contract. One contract that does this is the following:

$$W(H) > H, \ \ W(H) \cong H, \quad \text{and} \quad W(L) = L \,,$$

where the symbol $W(H) \cong H$ means that $W(H)$ is very close to being equal to H.

The contract just described is actually a contract that induces the agent to work hard. One can compute the (approximate) expected payoff of the principal as

$$0.9 \times [100 - W(H)] + 0.1 \times [10 - W(H)] = 91 - W(H) \,. \tag{4.4}$$

The agent in this case gets a small amount—which is almost equal to zero. This contract induces the agent to work hard, and the principal gets the maximum conditioned on the fact that the agent works hard.

The other contract of interest is the one where the principal can induce the worker to be lazy. In this case the contract must satisfy the conditions

$$W(L) - L \geq W(H) - H \quad \text{and} \quad W(L) - L \geq 0 \,.$$

As before, these conditions guarantee that the worker gets a higher payoff by being lazy and will choose to accept the contract. A contract that does this is the contract $W(H) = H$ and $W(L) = L$. The expected payoff of the principal is

$$0.1 \times [100 - W(L)] + 0.9 \times [10 - W(L)] = 19 - W(L) \,. \tag{4.5}$$

---

[5]Note that if $W(H) - H = W(L) - L$ occurs, then the agent is indifferent between working hard and being lazy. In this case, one might guess that the agent will prefer to be lazy, but the possibility of working hard cannot be exluded!

This is the maximum that the principal can anticipate in getting if the worker is lazy. Thus the principal prefers the agent to work hard if $91 - H > 19 - L$, or

$$H - L < 72.$$

Otherwise, the principal will want the worker to be lazy.

Thus, assuming $0 < H - L < 72$, the backward induction method to this sequential game yields the following solution:

1. The principal offers the contract $W(H) > H, W(H) \cong H$, and $W(L) = L$, and
2. The agent "accepts and works hard."

In case $H - L > 72$ and $L = W(L) < 19$, the principal will offer the contract $W(H) = H$ and $W(L) = L$ in which case the worker accepts the contract and he is lazy.

1. Show that in a sequential game any path from the root to a terminal node is supported by at least one strategy profile. Give an example of a sequential game and two different strategies supporting the same path.

2. Show that the strategy profiles $(\{R\}, \{R', L''\})$ and $(\{R\}, \{L', L''\})$ are the only Nash equilibria of the sequential game of Example 4.9. Also show that they both support the unique equilibrium path $A \to C \to F$.

3. Verify that the path $a \to c \to d$ is the only Nash equilibrium path of the game in Example 4.11. Also find all the Nash equilibrium strategy profiles that support the path $a \to c \to d$.

4. Consider the two-person sequential game shown in Figure 4.14.
   a. Show that the only equilibrium path given by the backward induction method is the path $A \to B \to D$.
   b. Show that the path $A \to C \to F$ is an equilibrium path supported by the Nash equilibrium $(\{AC\}, \{CF, BE\})$.

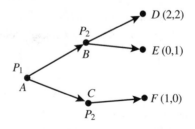

Figure 4.14

5. Consider the Partnership Game of Example 4.13. Assume now that the partners choose c_1 and c_2 simultaneously; that is, we consider the game in its strategic form. Find the Nash equilibria of the game.

6. Consider an n-player extensive form game having terminal nodes $v^1, \ldots, v^k$ and payoff vector at each v^i given by

$$p(v^i) = (p_1(v^i), p_2(v^i), \ldots, p_n(v^i)) .$$

Assume that at some terminal node v^ℓ we have $p_i(v^\ell) = \max_{1 \leq r \leq k} p_i(v^r)$ for each $1 \leq i \leq n$. That is, assume that the largest payoff that can be obtained by each player i is at the node v^ℓ.

Show that the (unique) path from the root to v^ℓ is the path of a Nash equilibrium.

7. Describe all the Nash equilibria that can be obtained using the backward induction method in the sequential game shown in Figure 4.15.

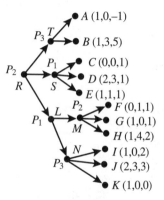

Figure 4.15

8. This exercise illustrates the *first mover advantage* for the Cournot and Stackelberg duopoly models as described in Examples 2.10 and 4.12, respectively.

   a. Compute the profits π_1^s and π_2^s of the firms in the Stackelberg duopoly model for the Nash equilibrium (q_1^*, q_2^*) obtained in Example 4.12. [Answer:

   $$\pi_1^s = \frac{(A + c_2 - 2c_1)^2}{8} \quad \text{and} \quad \pi_2^s = \frac{(A + 2c_1 - 3c_2)^2}{16} .]$$

   b. If π_1^c and π_2^c are the profits of the firms at the Nash equilibrium in the Cournot duopoly model obtained in Example 2.10, then show that

   $$\pi_1^s \geq \pi_1^c \quad \text{and} \quad \pi_2^s \leq \pi_2^c .$$

   [Hint: Invoke the values of π_1^c and π_2^c from Exercise 3 of Section 4.12.]

9. Verify that the equilibrium paths of the partnership game described in Example 4.13 are as shown in Figure 4.12.

10. Consider the game described in Example 4.14 with the parameters H and L satisfying $H - L > 72$ and $L < 19$. Show that the principal will offer the contract $W(H) = H$ and $W(L) = L$, in which case the worker accepts the contract and he is lazy.

11. Establish that the backward induction method can be used to prove Theorem 4.10. That is, show that in a sequential game with perfect information every equilibrium path obtained by the backward induction method is always a Nash equilibrium path.

4.3 SEQUENTIAL GAMES WITH IMPERFECT INFORMATION

We have seen quite a few examples of games with perfect information. The analysis of sequential games with imperfect information runs along similar lines. However, there are a few differences. Recall that a sequential game with imperfect information is a game in which the information set of at least one player has more than one node. To study games with imperfect information, we need to introduce the notion of a subgame. Subgames can be understood in terms of the concept of a branch[6] of the tree. A subgame of a sequential game is an extensive form game whose game tree is a branch of the original game tree with the same information sets and the same payoff vectors as the original game. Here is its formal definition.

> **DEFINITION 4.15**   A *subgame* of an n-player extensive form game is another extensive form n-player game such that:
>
> 1. Its game tree is a branch of the original game tree,
> 2. The information sets in the branch coincide with the information sets of the original game and cannot include nodes that are outside the branch, and
> 3. The payoff vectors of the terminal nodes of the branch are precisely the same as the payoff vectors of the original game at these terminal nodes.

Note that Condition 2 of the definition implies that the information sets of a subgame *cannot* intersect information sets of the original game not included in the branch. In particular, the root of a subgame (i.e., the root of the branch defining the subgame) must be a node of the original tree that is the only node in its information set. Since every tree can itself be considered as a branch, every extensive form game is automatically a subgame—called the *trivial subgame*.

---

[6]Recall that a *branch* T_u of a tree T is the directed graph having nodes starting at the node u and including all its descendants together with their original edges. Clearly, T_u is itself a tree having u as its root.

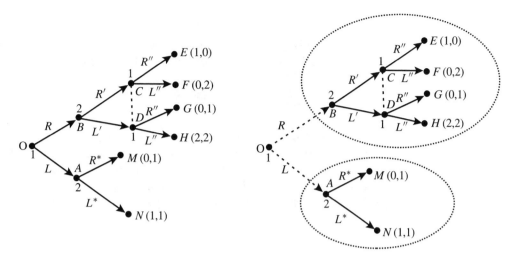

Figure 4.16

The game shown in Figure 4.16 is an extensive form game with imperfect information as nodes C and D form an information set for player 1. It is not difficult to see that this sequential game has two (proper) subgames, the first having its branch starting at A and the second having its branch starting at B; see again Figure 4.16.

Recall that a strategy for a player is a function defined on the nodes owned by the player, to the children of these nodes, which respects the information sets. Since a subgame is itself a sequential game, a strategy in a subgame is also a function defined on the nodes owned by a player, to the children of these nodes, which respects the information sets in the subgame. Since the information sets in a subgame are also information sets of the original game, it is easy to see that every strategy profile of a sequential game gives rise automatically to a strategy profile for any subgame. Conversely, it should be easy to see (from the definition of the subgame again) that every strategy profile of a subgame can be extended to a strategy profile of the game. In other words, we have the following important property:

- The strategy profiles of a subgame are precisely the restrictions of the strategy profiles of the game to the subgame.

And now we come to the concept of *a subgame perfect equilibrium*. It was introduced by R. Selten.[7]

---

[7]Reinhard Selten is Professor of Economics at the University of Bonn, Germany. Together with John Nash and John C. Harsanyi he shared the 1994 Nobel Prize in Economics. He was the first to recognize the importance of subgame perfection and developed the concept in his seminal work "Reexamination of the Perfectness Concept for Equilibrium Points in Extensive Games" [*International Journal of Game Theory* **4** (1975), 25–55].

DEFINITION 4.16 (Selten)   A strategy profile of a sequential game is a *subgame perfect equilibrium* if it is a Nash equilibrium for every subgame of the original game.

We emphasize immediately that, since every game can be considered as a subgame, a subgame perfect equilibrium is automatically a Nash equilibrium of the original game. In other words, a strategy profile is a subgame perfect equilibrium if, besides being a Nash equilibrium, it is in addition a Nash equilibrium on every subgame.

Let us illustrate the concept of subgame perfect equilibrium with an example.

Example 4.17

We consider the extensive form game shown in Figure 4.16. A direct verification shows that this sequential game with imperfect information has two equilibrium paths. Namely,

$$O \to B \to D \to H \qquad \text{and} \qquad O \to A \to N .$$

The equilibrium path $O \to B \to D \to H$ is supported by the Nash equilibrium strategy profile $(\{R, L''\}, \{L^*, L'\})$. That is,

1. Player 1 plays R at O and L'' at C or D, and
2. Player 2 plays L^* at A and L' at B.

We claim that the strategy profile $(\{R, L''\}, \{L^*, L'\})$ is a subgame perfect equilibrium. Indeed, on one hand, on the subgame starting at A, this strategy profile reduces to L^*, which is obviously a Nash equilibrium for the subgame starting at A (a subgame in which player 1 is inactive). On the other hand, the strategy profile $(\{R, L''\}, \{L^*, L'\})$ for the subgame starting at B reduces to the strategy profile (L'', L'), which is also a Nash equilibrium (why?).

Now the equilibrium path $O \to A \to N$ is supported by the Nash equilibrium strategy profile $(\{L, R''\}, \{L^*, R'\})$. That is,

1. Player 1 plays L at O and R'' at C or D, and
2. Player 2 plays L^* at A and R' at B.

We claim that the strategy profile $(\{L, R''\}, \{L^*, R'\})$ is not a subgame perfect equilibrium. Indeed, this strategy profile restricted to the branch starting at node B reduces to (R'', R'), which, as is easily seen, is not a Nash equilibrium for this subgame.

The subgame perfect equilibrium concept is, therefore, a refinement of the concept of a Nash equilibrium. By imposing the condition that a Nash equilibrium must also be an equilibrium on every subgame, one rules out equilibria that often behave very "strangely" or "unresonably" on certain subgames, namely, on the subgames that are not in the "path" of the strategy profile.

Let us see this in the context of Example 4.17, which we have just analyzed. Notice that the Nash equilibrium strategy profile $(\{L, R''\}, \{L^*, R'\})$ (whose path is $O \to A \to N$) restricted to the subgame starting at B is the strategy profile (R'', R'). However, this is not "self-enforcing" or a Nash equilibrium. Indeed, if player 2 changes his play from R' to L' at B while player 1 keeps playing R'' at his information set, then player 2 improves himself. This means that player 2's choice to play R' at B is not rational or (by employing modern game-theoretic terminology) *noncredible*.

A Nash equilibrium that fails to be subgame perfect is also known as a Nash equilibrium supported by *noncredible behavior*. The issue, then, is why does such noncredible behavior happen in a Nash equilibrium? The answer is, of course, that the part of the game tree for which the noncredible behavior is specified is never reached while playing the Nash equilibrium!

The standard method of finding subgame perfect equilibrium strategies in sequential games is by using the backward induction method on the subgames of the original games. This was exactly what was done in Example 4.17. The first equilibrium strategy was found by first looking at the equilibrium strategies of the smallest subgame at the end of the tree, and then we worked backwards. Starting at node B, the Nash equilibrium strategy profile of the subgame starting at node B is (L', L''), with the payoff vector $(2, 2)$. Assuming, therefore, that if node B is reached the players will play an equilibrium, the original game may be viewed as the game shown in Figure 4.17. We now have a game in which the Nash equilibrium strategy profile requires that

1. Player 1 plays R at O, and
2. Player 2 plays L^* or R^* at A.

This strategy combination, together with the equilibrium strategy profile already obtained in the subgame, constitutes the subgame perfect equilibrium of the game.

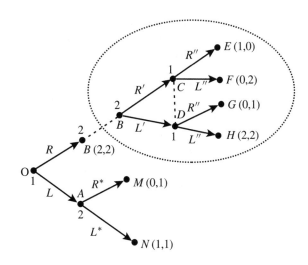

Figure 4.17

Not all sequential games have subgames. For instance, in the game shown in Figure 4.16 (or in Figure 4.17), the branch starting at B does not have any (nontrivial) subgames. The game shown in Figure 4.18 also does not have any subgame, since every branch of the game tree will violate condition 2 of the definition of a subgame.

For sequential games that do not have (nontrivial) subgames, the concept of subgame perfect equilibrium has no "bite," as every Nash equilibrium is also subgame perfect by default. When a sequential game has a subgame, the concept of subgame perfect equilibrium can give us reasonable answers ruling out the more unreasonable Nash equilibria. Let us see how we can do this by means of the following example.

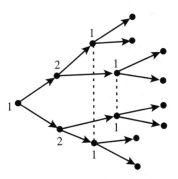

Figure 4.18

Example 4.18

An employer has hired a worker who has been given a certain task to complete. The employer can choose to monitor the worker, or choose not to do so. We will assume that monitoring is costly and that the worker knows whether or not he is being monitored.

The worker can choose to put in high effort in completing the task or be lazy. In case the employer monitors the worker, the effort level of the worker is observed by the employer, otherwise the employer does not observe the effort level. The employer then pays a high wage or a low wage when the worker reports that the task is complete. The situation that we have just described can be cast as a sequential game with imperfect information, which is shown in Figure 4.19.

In stage 1, the employer (player 1) chooses whether to monitor or not to monitor. In stage 2, the employee (player 2) chooses whether to work hard (h) or be lazy (z). In the following stage, player 1 (the employer) decides whether to pay a high wage (w_h) or a low wage (w_z).

We denote by m the cost of monitoring to the employer and by e the cost of the effort put in by the employee. We assume that $20 < m < 30$ and $0 < e < 10$.

Then the equilibrium in the subgame starting at node A is (w_z, z), and the equilibrium in the subgame starting at node B is h', that is, work hard. The subgame perfect equilibrium of this game is

$$(\{\text{Don't Monitor}, w_z\}, \{z, h'\}).$$

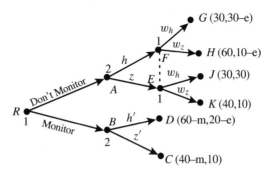

Figure 4.19

The path of the subgame perfect equilibrium is thus

$$R \to A \to E \to K .$$

Notice, though, that the strategy profile $(\{\text{Monitor}, w_h\}, \{h, h'\})$ is a Nash equilibrium; this Nash equilbrium fails to be an equilibrium when restricted to the subgame starting at node A. This is so, as it would be unreasonable to expect player 2 to work hard and player 1 to pay a high wage, as player 2 is clearly better off being lazy and player 1 is clearly better off paying the low wage. The requirement that a Nash equilibrium satisfy the condition that it be subgame perfect rules out this second unreasonable Nash equilibrium.

We now go back to the game on optimal contracts introduced in Example 4.14. In that example, a principal P and an agent A played a game in which the principal was able to observe whether the worker worked hard or was lazy. In any real-world situation, this is either too costly to do, or it may simply be impossible to observe the effort level. Consequently, the contract that the principal is willing to offer must be conditioned on what the principal observes. The details are included in the next example.

Example 4.19 (Optimal Contracts: The Imperfect Information Case)

We consider again the general setting of the game in Example 4.14. Here we will assume that the principal is able to observe the outcome only and not the effort level of the agent. The game that is now played by the principal and the agent is a game of imperfect information. Its game tree is shown in Figure 4.20.

In this case, since the principal cannot observe the effort level of the agent, the wage contract $W(\cdot)$ depends on the level of output observed by the principal. Therefore, $W(\cdot)$ is now a function of the level of output rather than the level of effort. We let

$$w_1 = W(\text{high output}) \quad \text{and} \quad w_2 = W(\text{low output}),$$

and note that a wage contract offered by the principal is simply a pair (w_1, w_2) with $w_1 \geq 0$ and $w_2 \geq 0$.

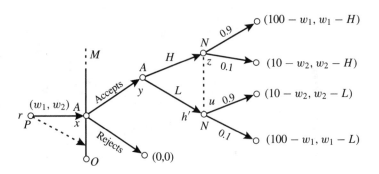

Figure 4.20

In this game a strategy of the principal consists of making a wage offer (w_1, w_2), and a strategy of the agent consists of a plan of action of whether to accept the wage contract or to reject it at node x, and whether to work hard or be lazy, when the contract has been acccepted at node y. It is important to note that the node x which is reached after a wage offer (w_1^0, w_2^0), is different from the node x that is reached after a wage offer $(w_1^1, w_2^1) \neq (w_1^0, w_2^0)$. Therefore, we denote the node that is reached after a wage offer of (w_1, w_2) as $x(w_1, w_2)$. This means that (unlike all games discussed so far) we have infinitely many possibilities for the node x. The set of alternatives for the node x is shown in Figure 4.20 by means of the points on the half-line OM. In other words, once the node $x = x(w_1, w_2)$ is reached, then the rest of the game (starting at x) is as shown in Figure 4.20.

We now recall that a strategy of a player in a sequential game is a function from the nodes that belong to a player, to the children of those nodes. Hence a strategy of the agent is a function $s(w_1, w_2) = \big(X(w_1, w_2), Y\big)$, where $X(w_1, w_2)$ is the choice of the agent at node $x(w_1, w_2)$ and Y is her choice at node y. Clearly, $X(w_1, w_2)$ is either A (accepts) or R (rejects) and Y is either H or L. Computing the expected payoffs π_p and π_a for the principal and the agent, we get:

$$\pi_p\big((w_1, w_2), s\big) = \begin{cases} 91 - 0.1(9w_1 + w_2), & \text{if } s(w_1, w_2) = (A, H) \\ 19 - 0.1(w_1 + 9w_2), & \text{if } s(w_1, w_2) = (A, L) \\ 0, & \text{if } s(w_1, w_2) = (R, \dagger) \end{cases}$$

and

$$\pi_a\big((w_1, w_2), s\big) = \begin{cases} 0.1(9w_1 + w_2 - 10H), & \text{if } s(w_1, w_2) = (A, H) \\ 0.1(w_1 + 9w_2 - 10L), & \text{if } s(w_1, w_2) = (A, L) \\ 0, & \text{if } s(w_1, w_2) = (R, \dagger) \end{cases}$$

The symbol $\dagger$ represents an arbitrary choice of the agent at the node y. So a Nash equilibrium in this game is a pair of strategy profiles $\big((w_1^*, w_2^*), s^*\big)$ such that

$$\pi_p\big((w_1, w_2), s^*\big) \leq \pi_p\big((w_1^*, w_2^*), s^*\big)$$

for all wage offers (w_1, w_2) and

$$\pi_a\big((w_1^*, w_2^*), s\big) \leq \pi_a\big((w_1^*, w_2^*), s^*\big)$$

for all strategies s of the agent. Recall also that a subgame perfect equilibrium is a Nash equilibrium strategy profile that is a Nash equilibrium on every subgame.

Once the contract (w_1, w_2) has been offered, that is, when node x is reached, the agent (who is assumed to be rational) will choose a strategy $s(w_1, w_2)$ so that she achieves her maximum expected payoff

$$\max\{0.1(9w_1 + w_2 - 10H), 0.1(w_1 + 9w_2 - 10L), 0\}.$$

Let $s^* = s^*(w_1, w_2)$ be a best choice of the agent given the contract (w_1, w_2). That is, s^* satisfies

$$\pi_a((w_1, w_2), s^*) = \max\{0.1(9w_1 + w_2 - 10), 0.1(w_1 + 9w_2 - 10L), 0\}$$
$$= \begin{cases} 0.1(9w_1 + w_2 - 10H), & \text{if } 9w_1 + w_2 - 10H \geq \max\{w_1 + 9w_2 - 10L, 0\} \\ 0.1(w_1 + 9w_2 - 10L), & \text{if } w_1 + 9w_2 - 10L > \max\{9w_1 + w_2 - 10H, 0\} \\ 0, & \text{if } \max\{9w_1 + w_2 - 10H, w_1 + 9w_2 - 10L\} < 0 \end{cases}$$

In other words, we have

$$s^*(w_1, w_2) = \begin{cases} (A, H), & \text{if } 9w_1 + w_2 - 10H \geq \max\{w_1 + 9w_2 - 10L, 0\} \\ (A, L), & \text{if } w_1 + 9w_2 - 10L > \max\{9w_1 + w_2 - 10H, 0\} \\ (R, \dagger), & \text{if } \max\{9w_1 + w_2 - 10H, w_1 + 9w_2 - 10L\} < 0. \end{cases}$$

To make the problem more tractable, from now on we shall assume that the parameters H and L satisfy the following inequalities:

$$H > L \quad \text{and} \quad 9L \geq H.$$

Given these inequalities, the reader should verify that the wage offers for which the agent chooses (A, H) and (A, L) are shown in the darkened regions of Figures 4.21 and 4.22, respectively. That is, the agent will choose (A, H) if the offer (w_1, w_2) lies in the darkened region R_1 of Figure 4.21 defined by the inequalities:

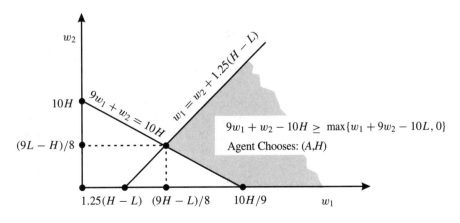

Figure 4.21

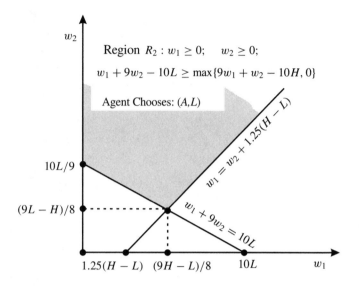

w_2

Region $R_2 : w_1 \geq 0; \quad w_2 \geq 0;$

$w_1 + 9w_2 - 10L \geq \max\{9w_1 + w_2 - 10H, 0\}$

Agent Chooses: (A,L)

$w_1 = w_2 + 1.25(H - L)$

$10L/9$

$(9L - H)/8$

$w_1 + 9w_2 = 10L$

$1.25(H - L) \quad (9H - L)/8 \quad 10L \quad w_1$

Figure 4.22

$$w_1 - w_2 \geq 1.25(H - L), \quad 9w_1 + w_2 \geq 10H, \quad w_1 \geq 0, \text{ and } w_2 \geq 0.$$

Similarly, the agent will choose (A, L) if the offer (w_1, w_2) lies in the darkened region R_2 of Figure 4.22 defined by the inequalities:

$$w_2 - w_1 \geq 1.25(L - H), \quad w_1 + 9w_2 \geq 10L, \quad w_1 \geq 0, \text{ and } w_2 \geq 0.$$

The principal, being also rational, will choose a contract (w_1, w_2) to maximize his expected payoff. In order for the principal to induce the agent to choose (A, H), he must solve the following maximization problem:

$$\text{Maximize}: \ 91 - 0.9w_1 - 0.1w_2 \text{ such that } (w_1, w_2) \in R_1,$$

or

$$\text{Maximize}: \ 91 - 0.9w_1 - 0.1w_2 = 91 - 0.1(9w_1 + w_2)$$

$$\text{Subject to}: \qquad\qquad w_1 - w_2 \geq 1.25(H - L)$$

$$9w_1 + w_2 \geq 10H, w_1 \geq 0, \text{ and } w_2 \geq 0.$$

Notice that the principal in deciding on the optimal wage offers has to consider the response of the agent. He does this by including the two constraints in his optimization problem. The first constraint guarantees that the agent (given that she decides to accept the offer) makes the right choice between H and L. In the literature, this constraint is called the *incentive constraint*. The second constraint, which is called the *individual rationality constraint*, guarantees that the agent will choose the contract. It should be clear that in this case, the expected payoff of the principal will achieve its maximum value $91 - H$ when the contract (w_1, w_2) satisfies the conditions $9w_1 + w_2 = 10H$ and $0 \leq w_1 \leq \frac{9H - L}{8}$.

Similarly, from Figure 4.22, we see that if the principal wants to induce the agent to choose (A, L), then he must make her an offer (w_1, w_2) such that $w_1 + 9w_2 = 10L$, where $0 \leq w_1 \leq \frac{9H-L}{8}$. In this case, the expected payoff of the principal is $19 - L$.

Now the principal in deciding between these two wage contracts compares $91 - H$ and $19 - L$. If $91 - H \geq 19 - L$, then he chooses the first wage contract, otherwise he chooses the second. That is, the *optimal* wage contract (w_1^*, w_2^*) is described as follows:

- If $72 + L \geq H$, then $0 \leq w_1^* \leq \frac{9H-L}{8}$ and $9w_1^* + w_2^* = 10H$ [in which case the agent's strategy is $s^*(w_1^*, w_2^*) = (A, H)$].

- If $72 + L < H$, then $0 \leq w_1^* \leq \frac{9H-L}{8}$ and $w_1^* + 9w_2^* = 10L$ [in which case the agent's strategy is $s^*(w_1^*, w_2^*) = (A, L)$].

It is important to note that the above wage contract (w_1^*, w_2^*), offered by the principal, is such that in each case the wage offer maximizes the principal's expected payoff given the strategy of the agent. Similarly, given the wage offer, the strategy chosen by the agent maximizes her expected payoff. This means that the strategy profile $\big((w_1^*, w_2^*), s^*(w_1^*, w_2^*)\big)$ is a Nash equilibrium of this game. It should be also noticed that once the wage offer (w_1^*, w_2^*) has been made, the agent selects her optimal strategy on the two possible subgames with origins at the nodes $x(w_1^*, w_2^*)$ and y. Hence the optimal wage contract is a subgame perfect equilibrium of the game. This is true of each of the optimal wage contracts described above. It is also worth noting at this point that the best response of the agent to a wage contract $w_1 = 0$ and $w_2 = 0$ is to choose $s(w_1, w_2) = (R, L)$. Therefore, a wage offer of $w_1 = 0$ and $w_2 = 0$ is a Nash equilibrium of the game that leads to a payoff of zero for both the principal and the agent. But this is a Nash equilibrium of the game that the principal will choose not to play for the obvious reasons.

EXERCISES

1. Verify that the strategies of a player P in a subgame are precisely the restrictions of the strategies of the player P on the whole game.

2. Find all the Nash equilibria strategy profiles that support the two equilibrium paths

$$O \rightarrow B \rightarrow D \rightarrow H \qquad \text{and} \qquad O \rightarrow A \rightarrow N$$

of the sequential game with imperfect information shown in Figure 4.16.

3. Consider the extensive form game shown in Figure 4.16. Show in detail that the Nash equilibrium $(\{R, L''\}, \{L^*, L'\})$ is a subgame perfect equilibrium, while the Nash equilibrium $(\{L, R''\}, \{L^*, R'\})$ is not a subgame perfect equilibrium.

4. Consider the game of Example 4.18 shown in Figure 4.19. Verify that if $0 < M < 20$:

   a. The strategy profile $(\{\text{Don't Monitor}, w_z\}, \{z, h'\})$ is a subgame perfect equilibrium, and

   b. The strategy profile $(\{\text{Monitor}, w_h\}, \{F, h'\})$ is a Nash equilibrium but not a subgame perfect equilibrium.

5. Consider the game of Example 4.18. If the cost of monitoring is zero (i.e., $m = 0$) and the cost of putting in effort e satisfies $20 < e < 30$, then find all Nash and subgame perfect equilibria.

6. Again consider the game of Example 4.18. Assume now that the worker does not know whether or not he is being monitored. Describe the sequential game and find its Nash equilibria.

7. Consider the sequential games shown in Figure 4.23.

   a. Show that the strategy profile $(\{\pi, \epsilon\}, \{\alpha, \delta\})$ is a subgame perfect equilibrium for the game shown in Figure 4.23(a).

   b. Show that the strategy profile $(\{\sigma, \epsilon\}, \{\beta, \delta\})$ is a Nash equilibrium for the game shown in Figure 4.23(a) but not a subgame perfect equilibrium.

   c. Find the Nash and subgame perfect equilibria of the game shown in Figure 4.23(b).

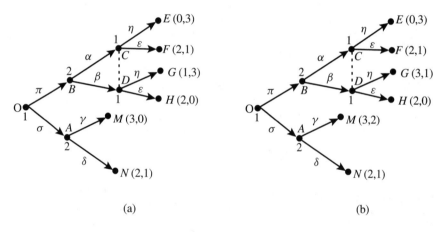

(a)   (b)

Figure 4.23

8. Consider the game described in Example 4.19. Assume that the principal offers a contract (w_1, w_2) to the agent satisfying $w_1 - w_2 < 1.25(H - L)$. Make a thorough analysis (in terms of the parameters H and L) of the Nash equilibria and describe the expected payoffs of the players.

9. In the game of Example 4.19, the utility function of the agent was given by $u(w, e) = w - e$, where w is the wage received and e is the effort level of the agent. Now suppose the utility function of the agent is given by

$$u(w, e) = \ln(\tfrac{w}{e}).$$

Assume as in Example 4.19 that the principal does not observe the effort level, and the parameters and contracts satisfy $0 < 2L = H < 85$ and $w_1 \geq 2^{1.25} w_2$.

    a. Draw the game tree with the new utility function of the agent.

    b. What is the optimizing problem that the principal now needs to solve?

    c. Solve the problem of the principal that you described in (b).

    d. What is the optimal contract offered by the principal?

10. Find the optimal wage contract in Example 4.19 when the parameters satisfy the inequality $9L < H$.

SEQUENTIAL RATIONALITY

The concept of subgame perfection that we discussed in the previous chapter is a concept that surfaces specifically in the context of sequential games. One way to think of subgame perfection is to view it as a Nash equilibrium that satisfies a criterion for sequential rationality. That is, as a sequential game is played, subgame perfection ensures that the players continue to play rationally as the game progresses.

Subgame perfection, however, does not give us any clue about sequential rationality in sequential games that do not have subgames. This is a fairly major problem, as many important classes of sequential games do not have subgames. For instance, it is very common for sequential games arising from situations in which the players have differential information not to have any subgames. Thus there arises the issue of what we understand by sequential rationality in such cases.

The issue is important because unlike a Nash equilibrium strategy profile in a strategic form game, not every Nash equilibrium of a sequential game provides a convincing solution of the game. We observed this to be true in the case of sequential games with subgames. And this observation then raises the same concerns about Nash equilibrium in sequential games without subgames. The subgame perfect Nash equilibrium seems to be a reasonable solution, as it satisfies the condition that while the game is played, given the node of the game tree that has been reached, it remains a solution for the remainder of the game. We can thus say that a subgame perfect equilibrium strategy profile satisfies *sequential rationality*, since as play progresses, it is rational to keep playing the subgame perfect equilibrium strategy profile. But this now begs the question about what it would mean for a Nash equilibrium to be sequentially rational in sequential games that do not have subgames. In this chapter we provide an answer to this question by discussing *sequential equilibrium* and, in the process, describing one way in which a Nash equilibrium may be sequentially rational.

We start with the example of the market for lemons as a way of motivating the rest of the chapter, as this is a sequential game that does not have a proper subgame. We then discuss strategies and beliefs, consistency of beliefs, expected payoffs, and finally define sequential equilibrium. We end the chapter with several applications of sequential equilibrium.

5.1 THE MARKET FOR LEMONS

This is an example of a two-player game in which one of the players has more information than the other. The example is a highly stylized version of the market for lemons.[1] In this market there are two types of cars: good-quality cars and bad-quality cars, which are found in equal proportions. In such a market the seller usually has a *reservation price* p_h for a good-quality car (the lowest price he is willing to accept for a high-quality car), and a reservation price p_ℓ for a low-quality car (the lowest price he is willing to accept for a low-quality car). On the other hand, the buyer has his own reservation prices: a reservation price of H dollars for a high-quality car (the highest price he is willing to pay for a high-quality car) and a reservation price of L dollars for a low-quality car (the highest price he is willing to pay for a low-quality car). For the viability of market transactions, we shall assume that $H > p_h$ and $L > p_\ell$. We also assume that the reservation prices H, L, p_h, and p_ℓ are known to all players; it is also assumed that $p_\ell < p_h$ and $L < H$. In this market the seller of a used car typically has more information than the buyer.

Now let us look at the sequential game that results when a seller puts a used car in the market. Nature reveals the quality of the car (G for good and B for bad) to the seller (player 1), who then decides whether he should ask a high price p_h, or a low price p_ℓ, for the used car. The buyer (player 2) does not know the quality of the car, but sees the price p announced by the seller. Player 2 then has to decide whether to buy the car. This sequential process is described in the game shown in Figure 5.1.

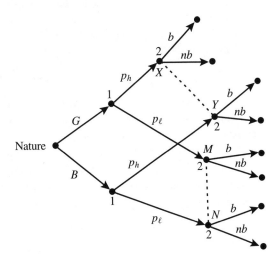

Figure 5.1

[1]The lemons game is a version of the lemons market analyzed by George Akerlof in his seminal piece: "The Market for Lemons: Quality Uncertainty and the Market Mechanism," *Quarterly Journal of Economics* **89** (1970), 488–500.

Clearly, this sequential game with imperfect information does not have any subgames, so that any Nash equilibrium would at first seem to be sequentially rational. However, once an information set of player 2 is reached, it is unclear what player 2 will do (or what is rational for player 2 to do), as he does not know whether the car is of good quality or bad quality. If player 2 has beliefs about the quality of the car, then the player will decide what to do on the basis of these beliefs. The question that arises now is: *What beliefs should a rational player have at player 2's information sets?*

Whatever beliefs player 2 has at the information sets, the beliefs should be "rational." One way to examine whether the players' beliefs are rational is to check whether the beliefs are consistent with the choices that the players would make. In the lemons game it may "seem" sensible to believe that:

- If player 2 (the buyer) observes the listed price p to be close to p_h, then he should believe that the car is of high quality, and

- If he observes the price p to be close to p_ℓ, then he should believe that the car is of low quality.

But if player 1 knows this, should player 1 (the seller) charge a high price for a high-quality car and a low price for a low-quality car? The answer is, of course, to charge a high price for every car! We see that the beliefs of player 2 are not consistent with the choices that player 1 would make given player's 2 beliefs.

Moreover, some careful thinking reveals that seeing a high price should not lead player 2 to believe that the seller only offers the high-quality car at the high price. Hence player 2 should believe that the car offered at the high price is *equally likely* to be of high or of low quality. In such a case, the buyer (acting rationally) would buy a car only if the expected value of buying a car exceeds the expected value of not buying. That is, the buyer will buy the car only if $\frac{1}{2}(H - p) + \frac{1}{2}(L - p) \geq 0$, or

$$p \leq \tfrac{1}{2}(H + L).$$

If the seller sets the price p any higher, the (rational) buyer who believes that the car is equally likely to be worth H or L will not buy the car. Thus, in this sequential game, if the price p is such that $p \geq p_h$, then the buyer believes that the car can be worth H with probability $\frac{1}{2}$ and L with probability $\frac{1}{2}$, as both high- and low-quality cars will be offered at this price. That is, the buyer (player 2) believes that he is at node X with probability $\frac{1}{2}$ and at node Y with probability $\frac{1}{2}$; see Figure 5.1. In this case, "sensible beliefs" by player 2 are given by

$$P(\{X\}) = P(\{Y\}) = \tfrac{1}{2}$$

at the nodes that belong to the information set $I_1 = \{X, Y\}$.

If, however, $p_h > p \geq p_\ell$, then the buyer knows that the high quality cars are not offered for sale, and only the low-quality cars are in the market. Thus when the buyer sees a price p less than p_h, he should believe that he is at node N with certainty. In this case, the sensible beliefs of player 2 are given by

$$P(\{M\}) = 0 \quad \text{and} \quad P(\{N\}) = 1$$

at the nodes that belong to the information set $I_2 = \{M, N\}$.

We now note that two cases can arise.

CASE I.

$\frac{1}{2}(H + L) \geq p_h$.

In this case, since the price $p = \frac{1}{2}(H + L)$ is greater than or equal to the reservation price p_h of the seller for the high-quality car, the seller would offer both types of cars at this price. The buyer would believe that both types of cars were offered, and both types of cars are then offered and purchased at the price p; the buyer's expected value. Since, in this case, the expected payoff of the buyer is zero, the buyer will buy the car at this price.

CASE II.

$p_h > \frac{1}{2}(H + L)$.

In this case, if $p = \frac{1}{2}(H + L)$ is proposed as a price, the seller with the high-quality cars will not offer those cars for sale. Thus only the low-quality cars are offered for sale. Here the buyer knows that node N has been reached, and thus offers to pay at most L dollars. Therefore, in this case only the low-quality cars are bought and sold, and the price settles somewhere between p_ℓ and L.

In the preceding sequential game, we saw that the beliefs of the players play a critical role. It is also important to note that the beliefs somehow have to make sense. In other words, given the price p,

1. The beliefs of the buyer are consistent with the incentives the seller has, and
2. The strategy of the buyer is optimal given his beliefs about the seller's optimal strategy.

We thus seem to have ended up, in each case, with an "equilibrium" that is driven by a system of consistent beliefs—beliefs that are consistent with the optimal strategies of the buyer and seller. In fact, we have just given a heuristic description of the concept of a *sequential equilibrium* for the lemons game. In the next sections, we shall fully describe this concept.

We now proceed to demonstrate that the intuitive equilibrium described above is indeed a Nash equilibrium for the lemons game.

Example 5.1 (The Lemons Game)

If we want to verify that the above process leads to a Nash equilibrium, we must redraw the game tree of the lemons game. As a matter of fact, since the price $p \geq 0$ can take an infinite number of non-negative values ($0 \leq p < \infty$), this game tree has in actuality infinitely many nodes. To see this, notice again that the game starts with nature revealing the quality of the car to the seller (player 1): B (for bad) and G (for good). Once this is done, the seller sets up the price p for the car. In case the car is good, then this brings the game to node X, and to node Y in case the car is bad. This game tree

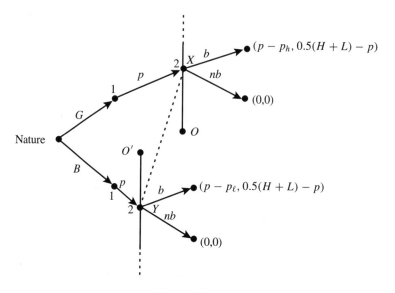

Figure 5.2

is shown in Figure 5.2. Thus the set $\{X, Y\}$ is an information set for player 2. Clearly, the nodes X and Y have infinitely many possibilities—the points of the half-lines OX and $O'Y$.

We now discuss the strategies of each player. A strategy for the seller is simply any price $p \geq 0$ (the listed price for the car). A strategy s for the buyer is a function of the nodes X and Y, which takes the values b (buy) or nb (not buy). Since the nodes X and Y are completely determined by the price p, we can also think of the strategy s as a function $s: [0, \infty) \to \{n, nb\}$. As before, we distinguish two cases.

CASE I.
$\frac{1}{2}(H + L) \geq p_h$.

It is easy to see that the payoff functions of the players are given by

$$u_1(p, s) = \begin{cases} p - p_h, & \text{if } s(X) = b \\ p - p_\ell, & \text{if } s(Y) = b \\ 0, & \text{if } s(X) = nb \\ 0, & \text{if } s(Y) = nb, \end{cases} \text{ and}$$

$$u_2(p, s) = \begin{cases} \frac{1}{2}(H + L) - p, & \text{if } s = b \\ 0, & \text{if } s = nb. \end{cases}$$

In this case, the strategy profile (p^*, s^*) defined by

$$p^* = \frac{1}{2}(H + L) \quad \text{and} \quad s^*(p) = \begin{cases} b, & \text{if } \frac{1}{2}(H + L) \geq p \\ nb, & \text{if } \frac{1}{2}(H + L) < p \end{cases}$$

is a Nash equilibrium.

CASE II.

$p_h > \frac{1}{2}(H + L)$.

Here the seller knows that the buyer will never buy a car at a price greater than $\frac{1}{2}(H + L)$, and so only the low-quality cars will be in the market. This means that the players have the following payoff functions:

$$u_1(p, s) = \begin{cases} p - p_\ell, & \text{if } s = b \\ 0, & \text{if } s = nb \end{cases} \quad \text{and} \quad u_2(p, s) = \begin{cases} \frac{1}{2}(H + L) - p, & \text{if } s = b \\ 0, & \text{if } s = nb. \end{cases}$$

In this case, the strategy profile (p^*, s^*) defined by

$$p^* = L \quad \text{and} \quad s^*(p) = \begin{cases} b & \text{if } L \geq p \\ nb & \text{if } L < p, \end{cases}$$

is a Nash equilibrium.

We leave it as an exercise for the reader to verify that the above strategy profiles are indeed Nash equilibria for the lemons game.

The lemons example is instructive in at least two ways. First, it is an example of a sequential game that does not have proper subgames. Second, in arriving at an equilibrium solution, the role of beliefs was critical. Both issues are important for games with imperfect information, and it is important that we explicitly take these facts into account when solving for equilibria. Of course, it should be clear that not every belief can be justified. For instance, the belief that a seller with a low-quality car will announce this fact to a buyer is hardly credible. The concept of a sequential equilibrium is designed to handle just such issues.

EXERCISES

1. Does the game shown in Figure 5.1 have any subgames?

2. Verify that the strategy profiles described in Example 5.1 are indeed Nash equilibria for the lemons game.

3. Find an equilibrium in the lemons game when two-thirds of the cars in the market are of bad quality.

4. In the lemons game if players could get sellers to certify the quality of the cars, how would you modify the game?

5.2 BELIEFS AND STRATEGIES

In the preceding section we saw that beliefs played a very important role in finding solutions. We also noted that reasonable beliefs have to be consistent with the way the game is to be played. In this section, we develop a rigorous method of describing a system of beliefs. Later, we will see that such systems of beliefs play a crucial role in the definition of sequential equilbrium.

- A *system of beliefs* μ for a player P is a function that assigns a probability distribution to the nodes in the information sets of the player. That is, if $I = \{N_1, \ldots, N_k\}$ is an information set for the player P, then μ assigns a probability distribution $\mu_I : I \to [0, 1]$ [which means, of course, that $\sum_{i=1}^{k} \mu_I(N_i) = 1$]. The number $\mu_I(N_i)$ is interpreted as the *belief* (probability) of the player that node N_i has been reached. In Figure 5.3(a) a system of beliefs is shown for a player owning the information set $\{N_1, N_2, N_3\}$.

- A *belief system* for an n-person sequential game with imperfect information is an n-tuple $\mu = (\mu_1, \ldots, \mu_n)$, where μ_i is a system of beliefs for player i.

The next concept is that of a behavior strategy of a player that extends the concept of a strategy profile to the framework of sequential games.

- A *behavior strategy* π for a player P is a function that assigns a probability distribution to the edges of every node owned by the player P that respects his information sets. That is, if $I = \{N_1, \ldots, N_k\}$ is an information set of the player P, and the set of edges at each node N_i of I can be identified with the set $E = \{1, 2, \ldots, m\}$, then π assigns the probability distribution $\pi_E : E \to [0, 1]$. The number $\pi_E(i)$ is the probability that player P will choose the edge i when he or she reaches the information set I. In Figure 5.3(b) the reader will find two examples of behavior strategies for the players P_1 and P_2.

- A *behavior strategy profile* is an n-tuple $\pi = (\pi_1, \ldots, \pi_n)$, where π_i is the behavior strategy for player i.

- A behavior strategy profile π is said to be *completely mixed* if every choice at every node is taken with positive probability.

Assume now that a behavior strategy profile $\pi = (\pi_1, \ldots, \pi_n)$ for an n-player game has been determined, and let $N_k N_\ell$ be an edge owned by a player i. For ease of notation, we shall denote the probability of moving from N_k to N_ℓ by $\pi(N_k N_\ell)$ instead of by $\pi_i(N_k N_\ell)$,

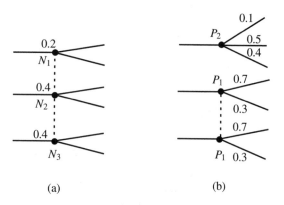

(a)   (b)

Figure 5.3

though that is the probability assigned by player i to the edge $N_k N_\ell$ in the behavior strategy π. Similarly, we define the probability of moving from a node N_1 to another node N_m by

$$\pi(N_1 N_m) = \pi(N_1 N_2)\pi(N_2 N_3) \cdots \pi(N_k N_m),$$

where $N_1 \rightarrow N_2 \rightarrow N_3 \rightarrow \cdots \rightarrow N_k \rightarrow N_m$ is the unique path joining N_1 with N_m. If there is no path joining N_1 to N_m, then $\pi(N_1 N_m) = 0$.

If N is an arbitrary node, we shall denote $\pi(RN)$, where R is the root of the game tree, by $\pi(N)$; that is, $\pi(N) = \pi(RN)$. The number $\pi(N)$ represents the *probability of reaching the node N* starting from the root.

With the assignments of these probabilities, the alert reader will notice that once a completely mixed strategy profile is made known to the players, it automatically leads to the creation of a system of beliefs in a natural way. We show this in the example below.

Example 5.2

Consider the sequential game shown in Figure 5.4. In this game a completely mixed strategy profile π is given by:

1. Player 1 plays a with probability 0.1 and b with probability 0.9,
2. Player 2 makes the following choices at his information set: T with probability 0.1 and B with probability 0.9, and finally
3. Player 1 on reaching his information set plays L and L' with probability 0.1 and R and R' with probability 0.9.

If this is the behavior strategy profile, then the question is: *What beliefs should rational players have about which nodes have been reached at their information sets?* Clearly, player 2 should believe that the probability is 0.1 that he is at the top node X in his information set. What should player 1's belief be once he reaches his information

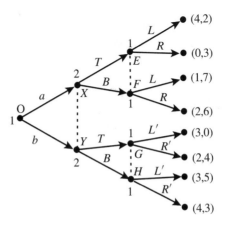

Figure 5.4

sets after player 2 has chosen? In particular, what should player 1's beliefs be at the information sets $I_1 = \{E, F\}$ and $I_2 = \{G, H\}$?

If player 1 reaches his information set I_1, then it must have been the case that he chose a at the initial node. The information that he is at the information set I_1 must then be used to form beliefs about which node has been reached. One way of doing this is to use the familiar Bayes formula in the way we used it in studying sequential decisions.

Therefore, if $\pi(E)$ is the probability that node E is reached starting from the root, and $\pi(E/I_1)$ is the conditional probability that node E is reached given that the information set I_1 is reached, then this probability according to Bayes's formula is:

$$\pi(E/I_1) = \frac{\pi(I_1/E)\pi(E)}{\pi(I_1/E)\pi(E) + \pi(I_1/F)\pi(F)}$$

$$= \frac{\pi(E)}{\pi(E) + \pi(F)}.$$

Thus, in this case,

$$\pi(E/I_1) = \frac{1 \times 0.01}{1 \times 0.01 + 1 \times 0.09} = 0.1.$$

In other words, player 1, after updating his beliefs from the information provided by the behavior strategy π, now finds that the probability of being at node E is 0.1, though at the start of the game the probability of reaching node E at the information set I_1 is 0.01.

Player 1 has thus used the new information about what has happened in the game to revise the original probabilities. This is expressed by saying that player 1 is updating beliefs in a *sequentially rational* way. If player 1 does this for every node in his information sets, then his beliefs are:

$$\pi(E/I_1) = 0.1, \quad \pi(F/I_1) = 0.9,$$

$$\pi(G/I_2) = 0.1, \quad \pi(H/I_2) = 0.9.$$

Clearly, these beliefs are the only ones that are consistent with the behavior strategy profile π and thus the only ones that seem reasonable given the behavior strategy profile.

Assume now that π is a completely mixed strategy profile for an n-person sequential game and that $I = \{N_1, N_2, \ldots, N_k\}$ is an information set. Then it is easy to see that

$$P(N_j/I) = \frac{\pi(N_j)}{\sum_{i=1}^{k} \pi(N_i)}$$

holds true for each $j = 1, \ldots, k$. Moreover, the formula

$$\mu^{\pi}(N_j) = P(N_j/I) = \frac{\pi(N_j)}{\sum_{i=1}^{k} \pi(N_i)}$$

defines a belief system, which is called the *belief system generated* by π.

1. Verify that if π is a behavior strategy profile for an n-person sequential game and $I = \{N_1, N_2, \ldots, N_k\}$ is an information set, then

$$P(N_j/I) = \frac{\pi(N_j)}{\sum_{i=1}^{k} \pi(N_i)}$$

holds true for each $j = 1, \ldots, k$.

2. Consider the game shown in Figure 5.5. Show that the belief at the information set $\{E, F\}$ is determined only by the behavior strategy of player 2 at the information set $\{X\}$. What determines the belief at the information set $\{G, H\}$?

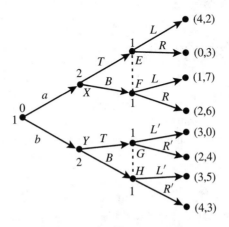

Figure 5.5

3. Consider the sequential game shown in Figure 5.6.

   a. Compute the probabilities $\pi(F)$, $\pi(D)$, $\pi(A)$, and $\pi(XB)$.
   b. If $I_1 = \{X, Y\}$ and $I_2 = \{E, F, G, H\}$, compute $P(X/I_1)$, $P(E/I_2)$, and $P(G/I_2)$.

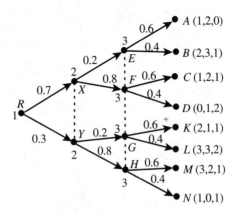

Figure 5.6

4. Consider the Lemons Game of Figure 5.1. Suppose that player 1 chooses p_h with probability 0.9 if G is chosen by nature, and p_h with probability 0.1 if B is chosen by nature. Assuming that G and B have equal chance to be chosen by nature, describe the values of the belief system generated by this completely mixed behavior strategy profile at the nodes of the information sets.

5. Verify that every behavior strategy profile restricted to any subgame is a behavior strategy profile for the subgame. Verify a similar claim for a belief system.

6. Let π be a behavior strategy profile for an n-person sequential game. If $X_1, X_2, \ldots, X_k$ are the terminal nodes of the game tree, then show that

$$\pi(X_1) + \pi(X_2) + \cdots + \pi(X_k) = 1.$$

[Hint: Use Exercise 4 of Section 3.2.]

5.3 CONSISTENCY OF BELIEFS

In this section, we provide a precise definition of reasonable beliefs that will play a crucial role in formalizing the notion of sequential rationality. We start with the following definition.

> **DEFINITION 5.3**   A system of beliefs μ is said to be *Bayes consistent* with respect to a completely mixed behavior strategy profile π if μ is generated by π, that is, if $\mu = \mu^{\pi}$.

Suppose that in Example 5.2 the completely mixed behavior strategy profile is changed in a sequential manner so that the probability of 0.1 is made smaller and smaller, and consequently the choices made with probability 0.9 are made with probabilities that get closer and closer to 1. The system of beliefs consistent with this sequence of completely mixed behavior strategy profiles will also change at each step of the sequence, and the question then is: *What happens at the limit?*

It is not difficult to see that the "limiting belief system" μ for each player is described as follows.

1. At player 1's information set: $\mu(E/I_1) = \mu(G/I_2) = 0$ and $\mu(F/I_1) = \mu(H/I_2) = 1$, and

2. At player 2's information set: $\mu(X) = 0$ and $\mu(Y) = 1$.

This system of beliefs—which cannot be directly obtained by using Bayes's formula from the strategy profile—yields the path

$$O \to Y \to H \to (4, 3)$$

that can be supported by the strategy profile $\big((b, R, R'\}, B\big)$. What makes the system of beliefs and the strategy profile consistent is the fact that they are the limit of a sequence of Bayes consistent belief systems and strategy profiles. This defining characteristic of "consistency" is formalized as follows.

DEFINITION 5.4   A strategy profile π and a belief system μ are said to be *consistent* if there is a sequence of completely mixed behavior strategy profiles $\{\pi^n\}$ such that the sequence (π^n, μ^{π^n}), where each μ^{π^n} is the system of beliefs that is Bayes consistent with $\{\pi^n\}$, converges to the pair (π, μ) in the sense that:

1. $\pi^n(N_i N_j) \to \pi(N_i N_j)$ for each edge $N_i N_j$, and
2. $\mu^{\pi^n}(N) \to \mu(N)$ for each node N.

It should be clear now that any equilibrium notion for a sequential game with imperfect information should incorporate the notion of consistent beliefs and strategy profiles, as this concept seems to be an essential feature for any reasonable formulation of "sequential rationality." Unfortunately, as the following example shows, although the consistency notion seems to be an important ingredient for any concept of sequentially rationality, it is not enough to characterize it.

Example 5.5

Consider the sequential game shown in Figure 5.7. In examining this game we find that there are two Nash equilibria in the game, namely, (a, R) and (b, L). The issue now is which of the two seems to be most reasonable.

Clearly, we cannot use the criterion of subgame perfection to delete one or the other equilibrium, as the game has no (proper) subgames. One can argue in this case that the Nash equilibrium in which the first player has the greater payoff will prevail, as he has the first move and can dictate the play of the game. An even more compelling

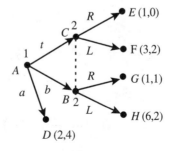

Figure 5.7

argument for deleting the Nash equilibrium (a, R) is the observation that if player 2's information set is ever reached, then there is no reason to suppose that player 2 will choose R, as irrespective of what player 2's assessment about where he is, player 2 is better off playing L. Moreover, it can be checked that the strategy profile (b, L) is consistent with the belief system μ, defined by $\mu(C) = 0$ and $\mu(B) = 1$.

For the other Nash equilibrium (a, R), it can be checked that any belief system is consistent with the strategy profile (a, R); see Exercise 2 at the end of this section. However, no matter what beliefs player 2 has at the information set $\{B, C\}$, he should never play R if play ever reaches this information set. This is because he gets a higher payoff if he plays L, no matter what he believes about which node has been reached. This Nash equilibrium is thus quite hard to defend as a "reasonable" solution of the game. The only acceptable equilibrium in this game seems to be the strategy profile (b, L).

The example we have just discussed teaches us a couple of important lessons. First, a consistent system of beliefs seems to be only one step towards a reasonable solution of a sequential game. Second, a Nash equilibrium strategy profile does not necessarily include the optimal action at every information set. The choice of R at the information set $\{B, C\}$ is clearly not optimal. One would hope that given the system of beliefs, choosing the optimal action would be a requirement of a solution of a sequential game. In the next two sections we shall examine exactly how we go about finding an equilibrium with precisely these properties.

EXERCISES

1. Describe the system of beliefs μ which is Bayes consistent with the completely mixed behavior strategy profile shown on the game tree of the sequential game of Figure 5.6.

2. Consider the sequential game shown in Figure 5.7.

   a. Show that the strategy profiles (b, L) and (a, R) are both Nash equilibria.

   b. The Nash equilibrium (a, R) is supported by the strategy profile $\pi = (\pi_1, \pi_2)$ given by

   $$\pi(t) = \pi(b) = \pi(L) = 0 \quad \text{and} \quad \pi(a) = \pi(R) = 1.$$

   Show that every belief system μ is consistent with the strategy profile π. [Hint: If $\mu(C) = p$ and $\mu(B) = 1 - p$, where $0 < p < 1$, consider the sequence $\{\pi^n\}$ of strategy profiles given by

   $$\pi^n(t) = \frac{p}{2n}, \quad \pi^n(b) = \frac{1-p}{2n}, \quad \pi^n(a) = 1 - \frac{1}{2n},$$

   $$\pi^n(R) = 1 - \frac{1}{2n}, \quad \text{and} \quad \pi^n(L) = \frac{1}{2n}.$$

   When $\mu(C) = 1$ and $\mu(B) = 0$, consider the sequence $\{\pi^n\}$ of strategy profiles given by

   $$\pi^n(t) = \frac{1}{2n}, \quad \pi^n(b) = \frac{1}{4n^2}, \quad \pi^n(a) = 1 - \frac{1}{2n} - \frac{1}{4n^2},$$

   $$\pi^n(R) = 1 - \frac{1}{2n}, \quad \text{and} \quad \pi^n(L) = \frac{1}{2n}.]$$

c. Show that the strategy profile π that supports the Nash equilibrium (b, L), given by

$$\pi(a) = \pi(t) = \pi(R) = 0 \text{ and } \pi(b) = \pi(L) = 1,$$

is consistent with the belief system μ given by $\mu(B) = 1$ and $\mu(C) = 0$.

5.4 EXPECTED PAYOFF

In this section, we describe how to compute the payoff of a player starting from an information set. We do this by first discussing how to compute the payoffs that the players receive from playing a behavior strategy profile. A behavior strategy combination can be either pure or mixed. Recall that a strategy profile that selects edges with a probability of zero or one is called a *pure strategy profile*. Analogous to the concept of mixed strategies that we already encountered in Section 2.4, a strategy profile that chooses edges with probabilities other than zero or one is called a *mixed strategy profile*. Accordingly, from now on, a strategy profile that is an equilibrium will be understood to be in mixed strategies. If a behavior strategy combination is pure, then the play will lead to a specific terminal node of the game. Otherwise, terminal nodes will be reached with some positive probability, not necessarily one. For these cases we need to describe the resulting payoffs.

Consider an n-person sequential game having terminal nodes $X_1, \ldots, X_k$ with the n-dimensional payoff vectors

$$u(X_i) = \big(u_1(X_i), u_2(X_i), \ldots, u_n(X_i)\big)$$

at these terminal nodes. Also, suppose that a behavior strategy profile π and a belief system μ have been assigned to this n-person game. If N is a node of this game tree, then the *expected payoff* (or *utility*) of the game starting at node N is the n-dimensional vector defined by

$$E(N, \pi) = \sum_{i=1}^{k} \pi(NX_i)u(X_i).$$

In particular, the expected utility of player j starting at node N is given by

$$E_j(N, \pi) = \sum_{i=1}^{k} \pi(NX_i)u_j(X_i).$$

If now $I = \{N_1, \ldots, N_m\}$ is an information set for the n-person game, then the *expected payoff of I* relative to the pair (π, μ) is the n-dimensional vector defined by

$$E(I, \pi, \mu) = \sum_{r=1}^{m} \mu(N_r)E(N_r, \pi) = \sum_{r=1}^{m} \mu(N_r) \sum_{i=1}^{k} \pi(N_rX_i)u(X_i).$$

This means that the expected payoff of a player j, given that the information set I has been reached, is given by

$$E_j(I, \pi, \mu) = \sum_{r=1}^{m} \mu(N_r) E_j(N_r, \pi) = \sum_{r=1}^{m} \mu(N_r) \sum_{i=1}^{k} \pi(N_r X_i) u_j(X_i).$$

We illustrate the various expected utility concepts with the next example.

Example 5.6

Consider the two-person game shown in Figure 5.8. The behavior strategy profile π is also described in Figure 5.8.

Notice that

$$E(N, \pi) = 0.6(4, 2) + 0.4(0, 3) = (2.4, 2.4),$$

$$E(F, \pi) = 0.6(1, 7) + 0.4(2, 6) = (1.4, 6.6),$$

$$E(G, \pi) = 0.9(3, 0) + 0.1(2, 4) = (2.9, 0.4),$$

$$E(H, \pi) = 0.9(3, 5) + 0.1(4, 3) = (3.1, 4.8),$$

$$E(X, \pi) = 0.3E(N, \pi) + 0.7E(F, \pi) = (1.7, 5.34),$$

$$E(Y, \pi) = 0.3E(G, \pi) + 0.7E(H, \pi) = (3.04, 3.48),$$

$$E(O, \pi) = 0.5E(X, \pi) + 0.5E(Y, \pi) = (2.37, 4.41).$$

Now assume that the following belief system μ has been assigned: $\mu(X) = \mu(Y) = 0.5$, $\mu(E) = 0.2$, $\mu(F) = 0.8$, $\mu(G) = 0.15$, and $\mu(H) = 0.85$.

If $I_1 = \{X, Y\}$, $I_2 = \{E, F\}$, and $I_3 = \{G, H\}$, then note that

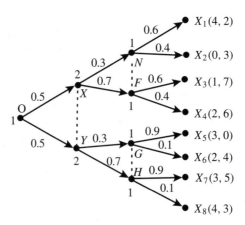

Figure 5.8

$$E(I_1, \pi, \mu) = \mu(X)E(X, \pi) + \mu(Y)E(Y, \pi)$$
$$= 0.5(1.7, 5.34) + 0.5(3.04, 3.48) = (2.37, 4.41),$$
$$E(I_2, \pi, \mu) = \mu(E)E(N, \pi) + \mu(F)E(F, \pi)$$
$$= 0.2(2.4, 2.4) + 0.8(1.4, 6.6) = (1.6, 5.76), \text{ and}$$
$$E(I_3, \pi, \mu) = \mu(G)E(G, \pi) + \mu(H)E(H, \pi)$$
$$= 0.15(2.9, 0.4) + 0.85(3.1, 4.8) = (3.07, 4.14).$$

This completes the computation of the expected utilities.

EXERCISES

1. Consider the sequential game with imperfect information shown in Figure 5.7. Assume that the following behavior strategy profile π and system of beliefs μ have been assigned:

$$\pi(t) = \pi(b) = 0.25, \quad \pi(a) = 0.5, \quad \pi(R) = 0.3, \quad \text{and} \quad \pi(L) = 0.7$$
$$\mu(C) = 0.8 \quad \text{and} \quad \mu(B) = 0.2.$$

Compute the expected payoff at every information set of the game.

2. Consider the sequential game with imperfect information shown in Figure 5.6. The set $I_1 = \{X, Y\}$ is an information set for player 2 and $I_2 = \{E, F, G, H\}$ for player 3. If π denotes the strategy profile shown on the game tree, and μ is the system of beliefs that is Bayes consistent with π, compute the expected payoffs $E(I_1, \pi, \mu)$ and $E(I_2, \pi, \mu)$.

3. Consider the sequential game shown in Figure 5.7 and let $\pi = (\pi_1, \pi_2)$ be the strategy profile given by

$$\pi(a) = \pi(t) = 0, \quad \pi(b) = 1, \quad \pi(R) = q, \quad \text{and} \quad \pi(L) = 1 - q.$$

Also consider the system of beliefs $\mu = (\mu_1, \mu_2)$ given by $\mu(C) = p$ and $\mu(B) = 1 - p$.

   a. Compute the expected payoff vector $E(A, \pi)$.
   b. If $I = \{B, C\}$, compute the expected payoff vector $E(I, \pi, \mu)$. [Answer: $E(I, \pi, \mu) = (6 - 3p - 5q + 3pq, 2 - q - pq)$.]
   c. Show that if $0 < q \leq 1$, then player 2 can increase his expected payoff by changing his behavior strategy.
   d. Establish that the maximum expected payoff for player 2 is when $q = 0$, that is, when player 2 plays R with probability 0 and L with probability 1.

5.5 SEQUENTIAL EQUILIBRIUM

Now assume that an n-person sequential game is played according to a given behavior strategy profile $\pi = (\pi_1, \pi_2, \ldots, \pi_n)$. With this knowledge at hand, the only meaningful information for a player about the outcome of the game is his expected payoff. As a matter of fact, as we have just seen, at any node N of the game, each player j knows exactly his or her expected payoff

$$E_j(N, \pi) = E_j(N, \pi_1, \pi_2, \ldots, \pi_n) \, .$$

Since the objective of each player is to maximize his or her expected payoff, it is to the benefit of a player to change his behavior strategy at some node, if that change (given that the other players do not change theirs) results in a higher expected payoff. We shall say that a player can *gain* during the play of the game if by changing his behavior strategy at some of his information sets he can improve his expected payoff, provided that no other player changes his behavior strategy.

It now seems natural to say that "rational" players will play a behavior strategy profile $\pi = (\pi_1, \pi_2, \ldots, \pi_n)$ such that no player can improve his expected payoff at any information set by changing his behavior strategy at that information set, when the other players still play π everywhere else. Notice that this is our old concept of Nash equilibrium modified to fit the framework of a sequential game. We now, finally, introduce the notion of a sequential equilibrium.

DEFINITION 5.7   A *sequential equilibrium* for an n-person sequential game is a pair (π, μ), where π is a behavior strategy profile and μ is a system of beliefs consistent with π, such that no player can gain by deviating from π at any of her information set.

Thus a behavior strategy profile and a belief system is a sequential equilibrium of a sequential game, if, starting from any information set of the game, the strategy profile continues to be an equilibrium strategy profile given the system of beliefs with which it is consistent. A sequential equilibrium, therefore, is a solution that embodies in it a strong concept of sequential rationality. We can now say that the players in a sequential game are *sequentially rational* if they play a sequential equilibrium.

Since beliefs in a sequential equilibrium are consistent with the strategy profile, beliefs are consistently updated as the game is played. Given these updated beliefs and the strategy profile, the behavior strategies used by a player maximizes her expected payoff at each of her information sets. Thus, as the game is played, a player has no incentive to deviate from her strategy at any of her information sets. This should immediately remind one of the definition of a subgame perfect equilibrium as one can think of a subgame perfect equilibrium as having a similar property, but only for the singleton information sets that are the initial starting nodes of subgames. Indeed, one should notice that the concept of sequential equilibrium generalizes the notion of subgame perfection to general sequential games that do not have proper subgames.

It is interesting to note that sequential equilibria are always subgame perfect equilibria. This is an important result.

Theorem 5.8   Every sequential equilibrium is a subgame perfect sequential equilibrium.

Do sequential equilibria exist? The answer is yes, and this is due to D. Kreps and R. Wilson.[2]

Theorem 5.9 (Kreps–Wilson)   Every sequential game with imperfect information has a sequential equilibrium.

In the example that follows, we illustrate Theorem 5.9 by presenting a sequential equilibrium of the game shown in Figure 5.9 that neither has any proper subgames nor any Nash equilibria in pure strategies.

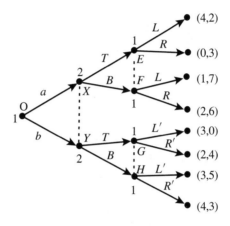

Figure 5.9

Example 5.10

Consider the sequential game with imperfect information shown in Figure 5.9. The reader should verify that this game does not have a Nash equilibrium in pure strategies; see Exercise 1 at the end of the section. We now find a Nash equilibrium in mixed strategies that we will show to be also a sequential equilibrium.

We consider the behavior strategy profile $\pi = (\pi_1, \pi_2)$ given by

$$\pi_1(b) = 1, \quad \pi_1(a) = 0, \quad \pi_1(L) = 1, \quad \pi_1(R) = 0, \quad \pi_1(L') = \tfrac{1}{6}, \quad \pi_1(R') = \tfrac{5}{6}$$

and

$$\pi_2(T) = \pi_2(B) = \tfrac{1}{2}.$$

We first claim that the belief system μ that is consistent with this strategy profile is given by

[2]The result is to be found in the work of D. Kreps and R. Wilson, "Sequential Equilibrium" [*Econometrica* **50** (1982), 863–894], in which they also define for the first time the concept of sequential equilibrium and discuss its properties.

$$\mu_2(X) = 0, \quad \mu_2(Y) = 1 \quad \text{at the information set } \{X, Y\}$$

$$\mu_1(G) = \tfrac{1}{2}, \quad \mu_1(H) = \tfrac{1}{2} \quad \text{at the information set } \{G, H\}$$

$$\mu_1(E) = \tfrac{1}{2}, \quad \mu_1(F) = \tfrac{1}{2} \quad \text{at the information set } \{E, F\}.$$

This can be checked by observing that if we take the sequence of completely mixed behavior strategy profiles $\{\pi_n\} = \{(\pi_1^n, \pi_2^n)\}$, given by

$$\pi_1^n(b) = 1 - \tfrac{1}{2n}, \quad \pi_1^n(a) = \tfrac{1}{2n}$$

$$\pi_1^n(L') = \tfrac{1}{6}, \quad \pi_1^n(R') = \tfrac{5}{6}$$

$$\pi_1^n(L) = 1 - \tfrac{1}{2n}, \quad \pi_1^n(R) = \tfrac{1}{2n}$$

$$\pi_2^n(T) = \tfrac{1}{2} - \tfrac{1}{2n}, \quad \pi_2^n(B) = \tfrac{1}{2} + \tfrac{1}{2n},$$

then this converges to the strategy profile $\pi = (\pi_1, \pi_2)$. Moreover, a direct computation shows that the beliefs $\{\mu^{\pi_n}\}$ that are Bayes consistent with π_n are:

$$\mu_2^{\pi_n}(Y) = 1 - \tfrac{1}{2n}, \quad \mu_2^{\pi_n}(X) = \tfrac{1}{2n}$$

$$\mu_1^{\pi_n}(G) = \tfrac{1}{2} - \tfrac{1}{2n}, \quad \mu_1^{\pi_n}(H) = \tfrac{1}{2} + \tfrac{1}{2n},$$

$$\mu_1^{\pi_n}(E) = \tfrac{1}{2} - \tfrac{1}{2n}, \quad \mu_1^{\pi_n}(F) = \tfrac{1}{2} + \tfrac{1}{2n}.$$

Since these sequences also converge to the belief system μ, we have shown that μ is consistent with π.

We now claim that the pair (π, μ) is a sequential equilibrium of the game. We shall do this by checking that at each information set the behavior strategy π maximizes the expected payoff of the players given the belief system μ.

- **STEP I:** *We consider the information set* $I = \{G, H\}$.

Clearly, I is owned by player 1, and we have $\mu_1(G) = \mu_1(H) = \tfrac{1}{2}$. At this information set, the arbitrary behavior strategy P is of the form $P(L') = p$ and $P(R') = 1 - p$, where $0 \le p \le 1$. The expected payoff of player 1 for this behavior strategy is given by the formula

$$E(p, I) = \tfrac{1}{2}\big[3p + 2(1 - p)\big] + \tfrac{1}{2}\big[3p + 4(1 - p)\big]$$

$$= \tfrac{1}{2}\big[(3p + 2 - 2p) + (3p + 4 - 4p)\big] = 3,$$

which is independent of p. This shows that player 1 has nothing to gain by playing a behavior strategy other than

$$\pi_1(L') = \tfrac{1}{6} \quad \text{and} \quad \pi_1(R') = \tfrac{5}{6}.$$

- **STEP II:** *We consider the information set* $I_1 = \{E, F\}$.

At the information set I_1 we have $\mu_1(E) = \mu_1(F) = \frac{1}{2}$. So the expected payoff of player 1 for the arbitrary behavior strategy $P(L) = p$ and $P(R) = 1 - p$, where $0 \leq p \leq 1$, is given by

$$E(p, I_1) = \tfrac{1}{2}\big[4p + 0 \times (1 - p)\big] + \tfrac{1}{2}\big[p + 2(1 - p)\big] = 1 + \tfrac{3}{2}p \leq 2.5\,.$$

The behavior strategy that then maximizes player 1's payoff is to play L with a probability of 1 and R with a probability of 0, as this gives the highest expected payoff of 2.5.

- **STEP III:** *We consider the information set $I_2 = \{X, Y\}$.*

Clearly, the information set I_2 belongs to player 2. Since $\mu_2(Y) = 1$, the expected payoff of player 2 is determined by how the game is played starting from the node Y. The arbitrary behavior strategy P of player 2 at Y is $P(T) = p$ and $P(B) = 1 - p$, where $0 \leq p \leq 1$. Computing the expected payoff of player 2 at the information set I_2, we get

$$E(p, I_2) = \tfrac{1}{2}\big[p \times \tfrac{1}{6} \times 0 + p \times \tfrac{5}{6} \times 4 + (1 - p)\tfrac{1}{6} \times 5 + (1 - p)\tfrac{5}{6} \times 3\big] = \tfrac{5}{3}\,.$$

Again, this value is independent of p, and so player 2 will gain nothing by deviating from $\pi_2(T) = \pi_2(B) = \frac{1}{2}$.

- **STEP IV:** *We consider the information set consisting of the root alone.*

In this case, if player 1 plays p and a and $1 - p$ at b, then an easy computation shows that his expected payoff is

$$E(p, O) = \tfrac{5}{2} \times p + 3(1 - p) = 3 - \tfrac{p}{2}\,.$$

This is maximized when $p = 0$, which means that player 1 must play a with probability zero and b with probability 1. Thus it is optimal for player 1 to play b at the root.

Therefore, we have verified that none of the players can gain at any of their information sets by deviating from π. Thus the claim that (π, μ) is a sequential equilibrium is true, as the pair is sequentially rational.

In Theorem 5.8 we stated that a sequential equilibrium is always subgame perfect. This immediately raises the question as to whether a subgame perfect equilibrium is necessarily a sequential equilibrium. The next example demonstrates that this is not the case.

Example 5.11

Consider the sequential game with imperfect information shown in Figure 5.10. Notice that this game has only one proper subgame, the one starting at the node X. It should be easy to verify that the strategy profiles $(\{b\}, \{T, L\})$ and $(\{a\}, \{T, R\})$ are both subgame perfect equilibria.

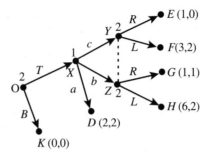

Figure 5.10

We claim the following.

1. The subgame perfect equilibrium $\big(\{b\}, \{T, L\}\big)$ is supported by the strategy profile $\pi = (\pi_1, \pi_2)$ given by

$$\pi_1(b) = 1 \quad \text{and} \quad \pi_1(a) = \pi_1(c) = 0,$$

and

$$\pi_2(T) = 1, \ \pi_2(B) = 0, \ \pi_2(R) = 0, \ \text{and} \ \pi_2(L) = 1.$$

The belief system $\mu = (\mu_1, \mu_2)$ at the information set $\{Y, Z\}$ given by

$$\mu_2(Y) = 0 \quad \text{and} \quad \mu_2(Z) = 1$$

is consistent with the strategy profile π, and the pair (π, μ) is a sequential equilibrium.

2. The subgame perfect equilibrium $\big(\{a\}, \{T, R\}\big)$ is not a sequential equilibrium.

We verify these claims separately. First, we show that the pair (π, μ) is a sequential equilibrium. Consider the sequence of completely mixed strategy profiles $\{\pi^n = (\pi_1^n, \pi_2^n)\}$ defined by

$$\pi_1^n(b) = 1 - \frac{1}{n} \quad \text{and} \quad \pi_1^n(a) = \pi_1^n(c) = \frac{1}{2n},$$

and

$$\pi_2^n(T) = 1 - \frac{1}{n}, \ \pi_2^n(B) = \frac{1}{n}, \ \pi_2^n(R) = \frac{1}{n}, \ \text{and} \ \pi_2^n(L) = 1 - \frac{1}{n}.$$

Clearly, $\pi^n \to \pi$.

A direct computation of the system of beliefs $\mu^{\pi_n} = (\mu_1^{\pi_n}, \mu_2^{\pi_n})$ that is Bayes consistent with π^n shows that at the information set $\{Y, Z\}$ we have

$$\mu_2^{\pi_n}(Y) = \frac{\pi_1^n(c)}{\pi_1^n(c) + \pi_1^n(b)} = \frac{\frac{1}{2n}}{1 - \frac{1}{2n}} \longrightarrow 0 = \mu_2(Y)$$

and

$$\mu_2^{\pi_n}(Z) = \frac{\pi_1^n(b)}{\pi_1^n(c) + \pi_1^n(b)} = \frac{1 - \frac{1}{n}}{1 - \frac{1}{2n}} \longrightarrow 1 = \mu_2(Z).$$

These show that the belief system μ is consistent with the strategy profile π. Next we check that the pair (π, μ) satisfies the expected payoff maximization condition.

If player 2 plays R with probability p and L with probability $1 - p$, then his expected payoff at the information set $\{Y, Z\}$ is

$$E(Y, Z) = p \times 1 + (1 - p) \times 2 = 2 - p.$$

This is clearly maximized when $p = 0$. This means that player 2 cannot gain by deviating from his strategy profile π_2 at the information set $\{Y, Z\}$.

Assume now that player 1 at node X plays c with probability p_1, b with probability p_1, and a with probability $1 - p_1 - p_2$. Then the expected payoff for player 1 starting from X is

$$E(X) = p_1 \times 3 + p_2 \times 6 + (1 - p_1 - p_2) \times 2 = 2 + p_1 + 4p_2.$$

Taking into account that $p_1 \geq 0$, $p_2 \geq 0$, and $p_1 + p_2 \leq 1$, we see that $E(X)$ is maximized when $p_1 = 0$ and $p_2 = 1$. This shows that player 1 cannot gain by changing his behavior strategy at node X.

Next assume that player 2 starting at O plays T with probability q and B with probability $1 - q$. Then his expected payoff starting at O is

$$E(O) = q \times 1 \times 1(2) = 2q.$$

This is clearly maximized when $q = 1$, and so player 2 cannot gain by changing his strategy at O. We have thus proven that $\big(\{b\}, \{T, L\}\big)$ is a sequential equilibrium.

We now show that the subgame perfect equilibrium $\big(\{a\}, \{T, R\}\big)$ cannot be a sequential equilibrium. To see this, let P be an arbitrary probability distribution on the information set $\{Y, Z\}$; we assume that $P(Y) = s$ and $P(Z) = 1 - s$. Also, assume that player 2 by playing R with probability p and L with probability $1 - p$ maximizes his expected payoff at the information set $\{Y, Z\}$. This expected payoff is given by

$$E^*(Y, Z) = s\big[p \times 0 + (1 - p) \times 2\big] + (1 - s)\big[p \times 1 + (1 - p) \times 2\big]$$
$$= 2 - (1 + s)p.$$

Clearly, $E^*(Y, Z)$ is maximized when $p = 0$ so that player 2 by deviating from his strategy $[\pi_1(R) = 1$ and $\pi_2(L) = 0]$ profile can improve his expected payoff. This shows that the subgame perfect equilibrium $\big(\{a\}, \{T, R\}\big)$ cannot be a sequential equilibrium, as player 2 at the information set $\{Y, Z\}$ can gain by playing a different strategy.

EXERCISES

1. Verify that the extensive form game with imperfect information shown in Figure 5.9 has no pure strategy Nash equilibria.

2. Consider the sequential game with imperfect information shown in Figure 5.10. Verify that the strategy profiles $(\{b\}, \{T, L\})$ and $(\{a\}, \{T, R\})$ are both subgame perfect equilibria. Show also that these are the only pure strategy Nash equilibria.

3. Consider the sequential game shown in Figure 5.7. Verify that the pair (π, μ), where

$$\pi(a) = \pi(t) = \pi(R) = 0, \quad \pi(b) = \pi(L) = 1,$$

and

$$\mu(B) = 1 \quad \text{and} \quad \mu(C) = 0,$$

is a sequential equilibrium.

4. Consider the game shown in Figure 5.11. Show that the pair (π, μ), where the behavior strategy profile π is given by

$$\pi(a) = \pi(T) = \pi(R) = \pi(R') = 0$$
$$\pi(b) = \pi(B) = \pi(L) = \pi(L') = 1$$

and the system of beliefs μ satisfies

$$\mu(X) = \mu(E) = \mu(G) = 0 \quad \text{and} \quad \mu(Y) = \mu(F) = \mu(H) = 1$$

is a sequential equilibrium.

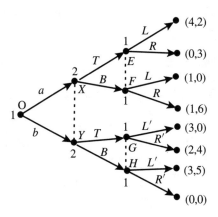

Figure 5.11

5. Consider the sequential game version of the game of matching pennies shown in Figure 5.12.

    a. Show that the strategy profiles (N, D') and (D, D') are the only pure strategy Nash equilibria of this game.

    b. Assume that player 1 plays N with probability α and player 2 plays N' with probality β; so every behavior strategy profile for this game is a pair (α, β). Also let μ be the system of beliefs for the information set $I = \{b, c\}$ induced by (α, β); that is, $\mu(c) = \alpha$ and $\mu(b) = 1 - \alpha$. Show that the pairs $\big((\alpha, 0), \mu\big)$ are the only sequential equilibria for this game.

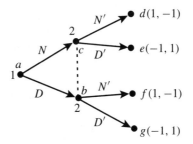

Figure 5.12

6. Consider the "truth telling" game shown in Figure 5.13. Show that the strategy profile $(G, T, \{b, d'\})$ is a Nash equilibrium and that it generates a sequential equilibrium.

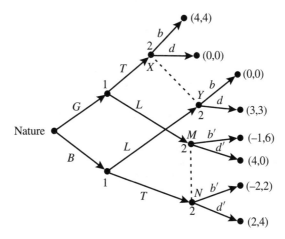

Figure 5.13

7. Go back to the game shown in Figure 5.13. Suppose that player 2 can find out at low cost whether player 1 is telling the truth. Does this change the nature of the equilibrium? Analyze in detail. [Hint: The game now is a sequential game with perfect information.]

8. Prove Theorem 5.8. That is, show that every sequential equilibrium is a subgame perfect equilibrium in the sense that, when restricted to any subgame, it is also a sequential equilibrium for the subgame.

5.6 APPLICATIONS: SIGNALING GAMES

It should have become clear from our discussion so far that the concept of sequential equilibrium is useful in solving sequential games when these games do not have subgames. An important class of sequential games, called *signaling games*, usually do not have subgames, and thus solving them involves some ideas of sequential rationality of the kind that sequential equilibrium uses. There are two players in a signaling game; we will call them player 1 and player 2. Nature moves first and chooses among a number of different options. This choice is then revealed to player 1, who then has to send a signal to player 2 about the information he has received. Player 2 then has to make a decision based on this information.

Signaling games are important because they can be used to depict many real-life situations. For instance, when you walk into a used-car lot, you are involved in a signaling game with the seller. Nature reveals the type of the car to the dealer, who then sends a signal to the buyer: the price asked for the car. The buyer, who is player 2, then decides whether or not to buy the car. The health insurance market is also an example of a signaling game. You as a buyer of insurance has information about your health that the insurance company does not have. The insurance company can receive a signal about the status of your health by taking a quick medical examination and then deciding on that basis whether to sell you insurance. Here we look at some examples of signaling games.

Example 5.12 (Financing a Project)

An entrepreneur E is seeking financing for a certain venture that he cannot finance with his own funds. The project is widely known to be viable, but only the entrepreneur knows precisely the value of the project. The entrepreneur knows that the project can either be worth H or L after an investment of I dollars. Since the entrepreneur does not have funds to finance the project, he needs to get a *venture capitalist* to fund it. In return for investing in the project, the entrepreneur can offer the capitalist an equity stake of e, where $0 \leq e \leq 1$.

We assume that this is a two-period operation. The investment takes place in period 1, and the return is realized in the second period. The rate of return i on the investment can be thought of as the current rate of interest or as the opportunity cost of capital.

The venture capitalist, whom we will call player C, can either accept the offer of equity e or reject it. At the time the offer is made, player C knows only that the project is worth H dollars with probability p and L dollars with probability $1 - p$. The number p is nature's choice and is treated by the players as a parameter. Therefore, the venture capitalist makes his decision of whether or not to accept the offer on the basis of the offer e and his knowledge of the chances of success of the project. Thus the game that the two players are engaged in is a signaling game in which the entrepreneur (the sender of the signal) sends the signal e, and the venture capitalist (the receiver of the signal) reacts on the basis of the signal.

The signaling game, which is a game of imperfect information with no subgames, is shown in Figure 5.14. If

$$H - I > L - I > (1 + i)I,$$

then the venture capitalist, player C, who knows that the project is worth H with probability p and L with probability $1 - p$, will accept an offer e only if

$$p(eH - I) + (1 - p)(eL - I) \geq (1 + i)I . \tag{5.1}$$

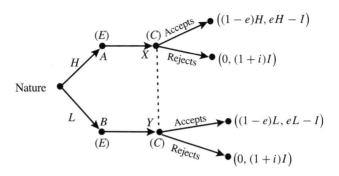

Figure 5.14

That is, once player C has to choose at his information set, he realizes that he is at node X with probability p and at node Y with probability $1 - p$. Given this belief, it is rational for player C to accept the offer only if e satisfies (5.1). Further, given the information that player C has, the beliefs are sequentially rational. Knowing this, player E, the entrepreneur, then offers player C an e that satisfies (5.1). This leads to a sequential equilibrium in which:

1. Player C has beliefs given by p and $1 - p$ at the nodes in his information set,
2. Player E offers an equity stake e which is a little more than the smallest equity state $e^* < 1$ that makes (5.1) an equality independently of whether he observes H or L (here $e^* = \frac{(2+i)I}{pH+(1-p)L}$), and
3. Player C accepts the offer e, since it is sequentially rational; see Exercise 1 at the end of the section.

Therefore, in case $e^* = \frac{(2+i)I}{pH+(1-p)L} < 1$, the project is financed, and the venture capitalist gets an equity stake e that is a little more than e^*.

In the solution that we have just obtained, the signal e fails to send any information about whether the project is going to be worth H or L. The equity e offered by the entrepreneur, therefore, has to be higher than what the venture capitalist would accept if he knew that the project was worth H. This is so because, if the venture capitalist knew that the project was worth H, then he would be willing to accept an equity share e_h satisfying

$$e_h H - I \geq (1 + i)I$$

and an equity share e_ℓ satisfying

$$e_\ell L - I \geq (1 + i)I$$

if he knew that the project was only worth L. Since the entrepreneur has an incentive to offer the lowest possible equity stake to the venture capitalist, the entrepreneur would always want to tell the capitalist that the project was worth H. The venture capitalist knows this and disbelieves any message sent by the entrepreneur about the worth of the project.

Example 5.13

In Example 5.12, we saw that the project would be financed provided that the parameters satisfy certain conditions. However, in case

$$H - I > (1 + i)I > L - I$$

and

$$p(eH - I) + (1 - p)(eL - I) < (1 + i)I \qquad (5.2)$$

then the solution in Example 5.12 does not work, as player C will be better off rejecting any offers. This is unfortunate, as the project is not financed, even though it ought to be financed if it is worth H. Thus, in this case, it can be checked (see Exercise 3 at the end of the section) that the sequential equilibrium in the signaling game is:

1. Player C believes that the project is worth H with probability p;
2. Player C rejects every offer of an equity stake e that satisfies (5.2);
3. Player E will offer e, satisfying
   a. $e(H - I) \geq I(1 + i)$ if the project is worth H dollars, and
   b. $e = 0$ if the project is worth L dollars.

The only way in which the project can be financed in this case is, if the entrepreneur offers to borrow I dollars from the capitalist, when he knows that the project is worth H, and has to return $\alpha(H - I)$ dollars, where $\alpha(H - I)$ satisfies:

$$\alpha(H - I) \geq (1 + i)I .$$

Since the capitalist in this case knows that the entrepreneur will make such an offer only if he knows that the project is worth H, the capitalist will take the offer.

We now turn our attention to another example of a signaling game.

Example 5.14 (Job Market Signaling)

The game that we present here is motivated by the work of Spence.[3] In this game, nature reveals the type of the individual to the individual, who then knows whether she is a high-ability type H or a low-ability type L. A firm F (player 1), which is deciding what wage to offer an individual, does not know the type of the individual and only observes the level of education e. The firm thus has to offer the wage $w(e)$ based on the level of education e. The individual (player 2) then picks a level of education e and enters the labor market. It is commonly known that one-half of the individuals are of type H and the other half are of type L.

In the analysis that follows we concern ourselves only with linear wage contracts. In particular, we suppose that the wage functions are of the form $w(e) = me + 0.1$,

---

[3]A. M. Spence, "Job market signaling," *Quarterly Journal of Economics* **87** (1973), 355–374.

where m is a non-negative real number. The value 0.1 can be thought of as the wage of an individual with zero level of education.

We assume that for any given level of education e, the individual who is of type H is more productive than the individual who is of type L. Specifically, we assume that the high-ability individual is worth $2e$ to the firm if she acquires the education level e, and is worth only e if she is of low ability. The profit of the firm is then given by $2e - w(e)$ if the individual is of high ability, and by $e - w(e)$ if the individual is of low ability.

The utility (or payoff) of the individual depends on both the wage she receives as well as the cost of acquiring education. The utility of the high-ability individual when she acquires the education level e is

$$u_H(e) = w(e) - \tfrac{1}{2}e^2$$

and the utility of the low-ability individual is

$$u_L(e) = w(e) - \tfrac{3}{4}e^2 .$$

Clearly, this means that the low-ability individual finds it more costly to acquire education. It is a sequential game with imperfect information that is played as follows.

- The firm, player 1, makes a wage offer $w(\cdot)$. The wage offer gives the wage as a function of the level of education e. As mentioned before, we assume that the wage function is of the form $w(e) = me + 0.1$, where m is a non-negative real number.
- Nature reveals the type of the individual to the individual.
- The individual, player 2, then sends the signal e about her type, which is her chosen level of education. The signal e may or may not reveal the type of the individual to the firm.
- The firm then offers $w(e)$ to the individual.
- In turn, the individual either accepts or rejects the offer, and both receive the payoffs shown in Figure 5.15.

The tree of the signaling game that the firm and the individual play is shown in Figure 5.15. Since there are infinitely many values for m ($m \geq 0$), there are actually infinitely many possibilities for the node N (nature). The possible nodes of N are the points of the half-line OP. Once the node N is reached, nature reveals the type of the individual to the individual; so that either node B or C is reached. Clearly, there are infinitely many possibilities for the nodes B and C; in Figure 5.15 they are the points of the half-lines $O'P'$ and $O''P''$, respectively. From node B or C, the individual sends the signal e by choosing the level of education, and reaches either node X or Y. Again, since e can be any non-negative number, there are infinitely many possible nodes for X and Y. These possible nodes are the points of the half-lines EQ and TK, respectively, shown in Figure 5.15. Obviously, the set $\{X, Y\}$ is an information set for player 1. At his information set $\{X, Y\}$, player 1 makes the offer $w(e)$, which brings the game either to node V or to node W. From there the final decision of player 2 will terminate the game.

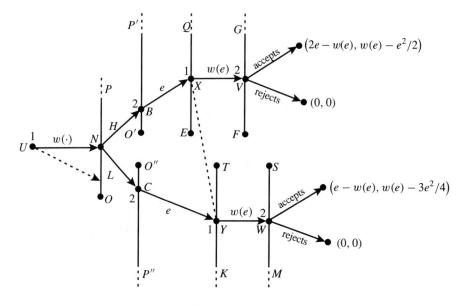

Figure 5.15

In this signaling game, player 2 (the individual) sends the signal, namely, her level of education e. Player 1 (the firm) is the receiver and responds to the signal e by offering the wage $w(e)$. In such a signaling game, the solution depends on the wage function $w(\cdot)$. We now proceed to solve this game.

We first describe precisely the payoff functions and the strategies of the players in this game. We shall use the abbreviations A for "accepts" and R for "rejects." Clearly, the strategy of player 1 is the function $w(\cdot)$, which in this case is completely determined by the number m; that is, a strategy for player 1 (the firm) is simply a real number $m \geq 0$. A strategy of player 2 (the individual) is now a pair $(\{e_L, e_H\}, s)$ such that:

a. s is a function on the nodes V and W of the half-lines FG and SM, respectively, which chooses A or R.

b. e_H is a function from the nodes B of the half-line $O'P'$ to the nodes X of the half-line EQ. Since the node B on the half-line $O'P'$ is completely determined by the node N (i.e., the number m), e_H is a real-valued function, that is, $e_H = e_H(m)$ or $e_H : [0, \infty) \to [0, \infty)$.

c. Similarly, e_L is a function from the nodes C of the half-line $O''P''$ to the nodes Y of the half-line TK. Again, $e_L = e_L(m)$ or $e_L : [0, \infty) \to [0, \infty)$.

In terms of this notation, the payoffs of the players are

$$u_1\left(m, (\{e_L, e_H\}, s)\right)$$

$$= \begin{cases} \frac{1}{2}[2e_H(m) - me_H(m) - 0.1] + \frac{1}{2}[e_L(m) - me_L(m) - 0.1], & \text{if } s(V) = s(W) = A \\ \frac{1}{2}[2e_H(m) - me_H(m) - 0.1], & \text{if } s(V) = A, \ s(W) = R \\ \frac{1}{2}[e_L(m) - me_L(m) - 0.1], & \text{if } s(V) = R, \ s(W) = A \\ 0, & \text{if } s(V) = R, \ s(W) = R, \end{cases}$$

$$u_2^L\big(m, (\{e_L, e_H\}, s)\big) = \begin{cases} me_L(m) - \frac{3}{4}e_L(m)^2 + 0.1, & \text{if } s(W) = A \\ 0, & \text{if } s(W) = R \end{cases}$$

$$u_2^H\big(m, (\{e_L, e_H\}, s)\big) = \begin{cases} me_H(m) - \frac{1}{2}e_H(m)^2 + 0.1, & \text{if } s(V) = A \\ 0, & \text{if } s(V) = R. \end{cases}$$

The two formulas above for the payoff of player 2 reflect the two types of individuals. The payoff of the firm is, of course, its expected payoff.

As mentioned before, the game starts with player 1 offering the wage contract (function) $w(\cdot)$ given by $w(e) = me + 0.1$. Player 2 responds to this offer by choosing a level of education e that maximizes her utility. If the individual (player 2) is of high ability, then she will choose a level of education e to maximize

$$u_H(e) = w(e) - \tfrac{1}{2}e^2 = me - \frac{e^2}{2} + 0.1.$$

It can be checked that this payoff function is maximized when $u_H'(e) = m - e = 0$. This gives the *optimal* strategy of player 2 when she is of type H, which is

$$e_H^*(m) = m.$$

The maximum value of $u_H(e)$ now is $u_H(m) = \frac{m^2}{2} + 0.1 > 0$, which implies that player 2's strategy s^* at the node V must be A; that is, $s^*(V) = A$.

In case the individual is of low ability, then she maximizes

$$u_L(e) = w(e) - \tfrac{3}{4}e^2 = me - \tfrac{3}{4}e^2 + 0.1.$$

Again, this payoff function is maximized when $u_L'(e) = m - \frac{3}{2}e = 0$. So, in this case, the *optimal* strategy of player 2 when she is of type H is

$$e_L^*(m) = \tfrac{2}{3}m.$$

The maximum value of $u_L(e)$ now is $u_L(\frac{2}{3}m) = \frac{m^2}{3} + 0.1 > 0$, which implies that player 2's strategy s^* at the node W must also be A; that is, $s^*(W) = A$.

Now the firm (player 1) anticipates player 2's choices of education levels. However, since player 1 is uncertain about the type of player 2, he must choose an m that maximizes his expected payoff. Since one-half of the individuals is of type H and the other half is of type L, player 1 believes that he is at node X (see Figure 5.15) with probability $\frac{1}{2}$ and at node Y with probability $\frac{1}{2}$. Thus the expected payoff of the firm at his information set $\{X, Y\}$ is

$$E(m) = \tfrac{1}{2}\big[2e_H^*(m) - me_H^*(m) - 0.1\big] + \tfrac{1}{2}\big[e_L^*(m) - me_L^*(m) - 0.1\big].$$

Since the firm knows that $e_H^*(m) = m$ and $e_L^*(m) = \frac{2}{3}m$, the expected payoff of the firm can be written as:

$$\begin{aligned} E(m) &= \tfrac{1}{2}(2m - m^2 - 0.1) + \tfrac{1}{2}\big(\tfrac{2}{3}m - \tfrac{2}{3}m^2 - 0.1\big) \\ &= \tfrac{1}{2}\big(\tfrac{8}{3}m - \tfrac{5}{3}m^2 - 0.2\big). \end{aligned}$$

Clearly, this function is maximized when $E'(m) = \frac{8}{3} - \frac{10}{3}m = 0$, or when $m^* = \frac{4}{5} = 0.8$.

So the "solution" of the game is the profile $\left(m^*, \left(\{e_L^*(m), e_H^*(m)\}, s^*\right)\right)$ given by

$$m^* = 0.8, \quad e_L^*(m) = \tfrac{2}{3}m, \quad e_H^*(m) = m,$$

$$s^*(V) = \begin{cases} A, & \text{if } w(e) - \frac{1}{2}e^2 \geq 0 \\ R, & \text{if } w(e) - \frac{1}{2}e^2 < 0 \end{cases} \quad \text{and} \quad s^*(W) = \begin{cases} A, & \text{if } w(e) - \frac{3}{4}e^2 \geq 0 \\ R, & \text{if } w(e) - \frac{3}{4}e^2 < 0. \end{cases}$$

This strategy profile translates to: Player 1 offers the wage function $w(e) = 0.8e + 0.1$, and player 2 accepts the offer and acquires the level of education $e_H = 0.8$ if she is of type H and the level $e_L = \frac{2}{3} \times 0.8 = \frac{1.6}{3} = 0.533$ if she is of type L. Moreover,

1. Player 1's expected payoff is $E(0.8) = 0.433$, and
2. Player 2's payoff is $u_H(0.8) = 0.42$ if she is of type H and $u_L\left(\frac{1.6}{3}\right) = 0.313$ if she is of type L.

Clearly, by construction $\left(m^*, \left(\{e_L^*(m), e_H^*(m)\}, s^*\right)\right)$ is a Nash equilibrium. We leave it as an exercise for the reader to verify that this strategy profile is in addition a sequential equilibrium for this game.

In the preceding example, the solution we have obtained separated the two types of individuals in the sense that

$$e_L = \tfrac{2}{3} \times 0.8 = 0.533 < e_H = 0.8.$$

So, by looking at the choice of educational levels, the firm is capable of distinguishing between the two types. For this reason, this kind of sequential equilibrium in signaling games is called a *separating equilibrium*.

In the next example, we shall obtain an equilibrium where the two types choose exactly the same level of education. In such a case, the equilibrium is called a *pooling equilibrium*.

Example 5.15 (Job Market Signaling Revisited)

We go back to the job market signaling game shown in Figure 5.15. The difference now is that the wage contract is no longer of the linear form $w(e) = me + 0.1$. Instead, the wage contract is a two-step wage offer of the form

$$w(e) = \begin{cases} 0 & \text{if } e < \hat{e} \\ \overline{w} & \text{if } e \geq \hat{e}. \end{cases}$$

That is, the wage offer has a "trigger" at the educational level $\hat{e} > 0$ as illustrated in Figure 5.16. The firm needs to determine the trigger $\hat{e}$ as well as the wage $\overline{w} > 0$.

In this game, we assume that the profit of the firm is $1.5e - w(e)$ if the individual is of high ability, and $e - w(e)$ if the individual is of low ability. It is also common knowledge that one-fourth of the individuals are of type H and the other three-fourths are of type L. The utility functions of the high- and low-ability types are now given by

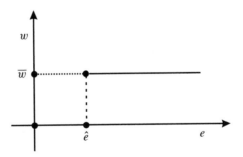

Figure 5.16   The wage function.

$$u_H(e) = w(e) - \tfrac{3}{4}e^2 \quad \text{and} \quad u_L(e) = w(e) - e^2.$$

As in the preceding example, the game starts with the wage offer (wage function) $w(\cdot)$. Player 2, the individual, after observing her type, responds by choosing an education level e. The firm then offers the individual the wage $w(e)$, and subsequently, the individual decides whether to accept or reject the offer. If the individual observes that she is a high-ability type, she chooses e to maximize her utility function

$$u_H(e) = w(e) - \tfrac{3}{4}e^2.$$

She chooses $e = \hat{e}$ if $\overline{w} - \tfrac{3}{4}\hat{e}^2 > 0$ and accepts the wage offer, and chooses $e = 0$ otherwise.

If the individual finds that she is of low ability, then she chooses e to maximize her utility function

$$u_L(e) = w(e) - e^2.$$

She chooses $e = \hat{e}$ if $\overline{w} - \hat{e}^2 > 0$ and accepts the wage offer, and chooses $e = 0$ otherwise and rejects the wage offer.

The firm, knowing all this, offers a wage function that maximizes his expected payoff. The expected payoff of the firm at the information set $\{X, Y\}$ is

$$E(\overline{w}) = \tfrac{1}{4}\big[1.5e - w(e)\big] + \tfrac{3}{4}\big[e - w(e)\big].$$

Since the wage function either gives a wage of zero or some fixed positive wage $\overline{w}$, in order to maximize profits, the firm either sets $\overline{w} \simeq \tfrac{3}{4}e^2$ (that is, sets the wage $\overline{w}$ just a little above $\tfrac{3}{4}e^2$), or $\overline{w} \simeq e^2$. We now distinguish two cases.

CASE I.
$\overline{w} \simeq \tfrac{3}{4}e^2.$

This implies $e = \tfrac{2}{3}\sqrt{3\overline{w}}$. Since $e^2 > \tfrac{3}{4}e^2 \simeq w(e)$, we have $u_L(e) = w(e) - e < 0$, and so the low-ability type will decline the offer. Consequently, in this case, the expected payoff of the firm is:

$$E(\overline{w}) = \tfrac{1}{4}\left(\tfrac{3}{2} \times \tfrac{2}{3}\sqrt{3\overline{w}} - \overline{w}\right) = \tfrac{1}{4}\left(\sqrt{3\overline{w}} - \overline{w}\right).$$

Differentiating, we get $E'(\overline{w}) = \tfrac{1}{4}\left(\tfrac{\sqrt{3}}{2\sqrt{\overline{w}}} - 1\right)$. Solving the equation $E'(\overline{w}) = 0$, we get the expected utility maximizer value $\overline{w} = \tfrac{3}{4} = 0.75$. This implies $e = 1$. The expected profit of the firm for such a wage offer is thus:

$$E(\overline{w}) = \tfrac{1}{4}\left(\tfrac{3}{2} \times 1 - \tfrac{3}{4}\right) = 0.1875. \tag{5.3}$$

CASE II.
$\overline{w} \simeq e^2$.

In this case, $e \simeq \sqrt{\overline{w}}$ and since $e^2 > \tfrac{3}{4}e^2$, the individual irrespective of type will accept the offer. So, in this case, the expected profit of the firm is:

$$E(\overline{w}) = \tfrac{1}{4}\left(\tfrac{3}{2}\sqrt{\overline{w}} - \overline{w}\right) + \tfrac{3}{4}\left(\sqrt{\overline{w}} - \overline{w}\right) = \tfrac{9}{8}\sqrt{\overline{w}} - \overline{w}.$$

Differentiating, we get $E'(\overline{w}) = \tfrac{9}{16\sqrt{\overline{w}}} - 1$. It is now easy to check that the firm maximizes expected profit when $E'(\overline{w}) = 0$. Solving this equation yields $\sqrt{\overline{w}} = \tfrac{9}{16}$, and so $\overline{w} = \tfrac{81}{256} = 0.3164$. This gives $e \geq \hat{e} = \tfrac{9}{16}$, and the expected profit

$$E(\overline{w}) = \tfrac{9}{8} \times \tfrac{9}{16} - \left(\tfrac{9}{16}\right)^2 = \tfrac{81}{256} = 0.3164.$$

Since this expected profit is higher than the one given in (5.3), the firm will offer the contract $\overline{w} = \tfrac{81}{256} = 0.3164$. This implies $\hat{e} = \tfrac{9}{16} = 0.5625$, and, moreover, the individual by choosing $e = 0.5625$ maximizes her utility irrespective of her type.

We have therefore arrived at the following equilibrium.

- Player 1, the firm, offers the wage function

$$w(e) \simeq \begin{cases} 0, & \text{if } e < 0.5625 \\ 0.3164, & \text{if } e \geq 0.5625. \end{cases}$$

- The individual irrespective of her type accepts the offer and chooses $e = 0.5625$.

- The firm, at the information set $\{X, Y\}$, offers the wage $\overline{w} \simeq 0.3164$.

- The individual irrespective of her type accepts the offer.

It can be verified that this gives us a sequential equilibrium with the belief system μ given by $\mu(X) = \tfrac{1}{4}$ and $\mu(Y) = \tfrac{3}{4}$.

In this example the two types end up choosing exactly the same level of education. Thus the equilibrium here is a *pooling equilibrium*, as the signal (which is the level of education) does not reveal the type of the individual. It is also worth noting that the firm finds it profitable to employ both types of workers at the same wage. This raises the following very intriguing question: *Is there anything to be gained by having high ability?*

EXERCISES

1. Consider the game of Example 5.12 shown in Figure 5.14. Assume that the share equity e satisfies the inequality

$$\left[p(eH - I) + (1 - p)(eL - I)\right] \geq (1 + i)I .$$

Then show that the strategy "*accepts*" at the information set $\{X, Y\}$ is sequentially rational. [Hint: If C plays "accepts" with probability q and "rejects" with probability $1 - q$, then $q = 1$ maximizes the expected payoff of player C.]

2. In the game of Example 5.12 shown in Figure 5.14, what is the smallest share equity e that the entrepreneur can offer to the venture capitalist so that the venture capitalist accepts the offer? [Hint: $e = \frac{(2+i)I}{pH+(1-p)L}$.]

3. Verify that if the parameters of Example 5.12 shown in Figure 5.14 satisfy the inequality

$$(2 + i)I > e\left[pH + (1 - p)L\right],$$

then the project is not financed.

4. Consider the signaling game of Example 5.14 whose game tree is shown in Figure 5.15. Show that the Nash equilibrium $\left(m^*, (\{e_L^*(m), e_H^*(m)\}, s^*)\right)$ obtained there is a sequential equilibrium with the system of beliefs μ at the information set $\{X, Y\}$ given by

$$\mu(X) = 1, \ \mu(Y) = 0, \ \text{if } e = m, \quad \text{and} \quad \mu(X) = 0, \ \mu(Y) = 1, \ \text{if } e = \tfrac{2}{3}m .$$

5. Consider the job market signaling game of Example 5.14 with the following parameters:

$$w(e) = \tfrac{1}{4}e^2 + me + 0.1$$
$$u_H(e) = w(e) - \tfrac{1}{2}e^2$$
$$u_L(e) = w(e) - \tfrac{3}{4}e^2 .$$

Asssume that the profit of the firm is given by $3e - w(e)$ if the individual is of high ability and $e - w(e)$ if she is of low ability. Find the separating equilibrium of the game. What is the expected profit of the firm? [Answers: $m = \tfrac{14}{17}$, $e_H = 2m$, $e_L = m$; the expected profit of the firm is 1.34.]

6. Again consider the signaling game of Example 5.14 with the same utility and profit functions but with a two-step wage function as in Example 5.15. Does this signaling game have a pooling equilibrium?

7. One can argue that when the wage offer is linear in a job market signaling game, there is a separating equilibrium because the high-ability worker is more productive. Suppose that for a given level of education both types of workers are equally productive, but the high-ability type can acquire education at lower cost. What would be the nature of the sequential equilibrium? [Hint: Change the payoffs in the game of Figure 5.15 when the high-ability worker accepts to $(e - w(e), w(e) - \tfrac{1}{2}e^2)$.]

8. What would be the wage offer if in a job market signaling game the firm uses a two-step wage offer in the game of the previous exercise? [Hint: Observe that $E(w) = e - w$.]

9. In the signaling games of the previous two exercises will the firm use a two-step wage offer or a linear wage offer?

10. Does an individual derive any benefits from being the high-ability type in a pooling equilibrium? Explain your answer.

S I X | AUCTIONS

Auctions have been used to sell and buy goods since prehistory and even today auctions are used quite frequently. Sotheby's of London, with branches in most of the wealthy metropolitan centers of the world, is in the business of auctioning rare art and antiques to wealthy buyers. Local municipalities use some form of auctioning to hire contractors for specific projects. Offshore oil leases are regularly auctioned to the major oil companies as well as independent wildcatters. One of the largest auctions, with billions of dollars changing hands, took place quite recently (July 1994). The United States government "auctioned licenses to use the electromagnetic spectrum for personal communications services: mobile telephones, two-way paging, portable fax machines, and wireless computer networks."[1] As we see, auctions are used in many different contexts.

Auctions, as we briefly discussed in Chapter 2, can be written as games. There we analyzed an auction in which bids were made simultaneously for a single good by bidders who knew the worth of the good. But this is only one kind of an auction. There are auctions in which only a single unit of an indivisible good is sold, and there are auctions in which a single seller sells n different goods. The airwaves auction was of the latter kind. Auctions can also be classified according to whether the winner pays the winning bid or the second-highest bid. In some auctions the bidders know what the value of the item is worth to the individual, whereas in other auctions there is a great deal of uncertainty about it. In auctions of offshore drilling rights, the bidders have only some estimate of the true value of the lease.

An auction can take many different forms. The bidders can make their bids *simultaneously* and put them in sealed envelopes, or they may *bid sequentially*, with the auctioneer calling out the successive bids. An auction may also be a *first-price auction*, in which the winner pays the highest bid, or it might very well be a *second-price auction*, where the winner pays only the second-highest bid.

In this chapter, we use the tools of game theory to analyze auctions by classifying them according to the amount of information bidders have about the value of the object being auctioned, and about each other's valuation of the object. We first look at *auctions with complete information*, in which the bidders know each other's valuation of the object.

---

[1]R. P. McAfee and J. McMillan, "Analyzing the Airwaves Auction," *Journal of Economic Perspectives* **10** (1996), 159–175.

We then analyze *individual private value auctions* in which a bidder knows only her own valuation. And, finally, we look at *common-value auctions* in which a bidder only receives a noisy signal about the value of the object.

6.1 AUCTIONS WITH COMPLETE INFORMATION

An *auction* is a gathering of n persons (called *bidders* or *players* numbered from 1 to n) for the sole purpose of buying an object (or good). The winner of the object is decided according to certain rules that have been declared in advance. We assume that the good for sale in an auction is worth v_i to the ith bidder. Without any loss of generality, we can suppose that

$$v_1 \geq v_2 \geq \cdots \geq v_n .$$

Auctions are classified according to their rules as well as according to the information the bidders have about the *value vector* $(v_1, v_2, \ldots, v_n)$. An auction in which every bidder knows the vector $v = (v_1, v_2, \ldots, v_n)$ is called an auction with *complete information*; otherwise it is an auction with *incomplete information*. In this section, we shall discuss the *first-price sealed-bid* and the *second-price sealed-bid* auctions.

We first look at a *first-price sealed-bid* auction. As the name suggests, the rules for this auction are the following. Each bidder i makes a bid b_i; that is, she chooses a number $b_i \in [0, \infty)$, and places it in a sealed envelope. After the envelopes are collected, the person in charge of the auction (the *auctioneer*) opens the envelopes and reveals the bids to everyone. The winner is declared to be the player with the highest bid who can then get the object by paying the auctioneer her bid. In case there are r players with the highest bid, we assume that the winner is declared by some random draw among the r highest bidders—so that each player among the r highest bidders (the *finalists*) has a probability $\frac{1}{r}$ of getting the object.

In a first-price sealed-bid auction, bidder i's utility (or payoff) function is given by

$$u_i(b_1, \ldots, b_n) = \begin{cases} 0, & \text{if } b_i < m \\ \frac{1}{r}(v_i - b_i), & \text{if } i \text{ is among the } r \text{ finalists}, \end{cases}$$

where $b = (b_1, \ldots, b_n)$ is the vector of bids and $m = \max\{b_1, \ldots, b_n\}$. Thus, if player i is the winner with the highest bid, then player i pays the highest bid and ends up with the difference between her valuation of the good and the amount she pays. If she does not have the highest bid, then her payoff is zero. It should be noted that if there are more than one finalists, then the payoffs of the bidders are expected payoffs. Notice that a bidder gets a positive payoff only if she wins and pays less than her valuation of the good. *Given this, what should she bid?* The claims in the next result provide the answer.

Theorem 6.1   In a first-price sealed-bid auction every player i bids

$$b_i \leq v_i .$$

Moreover, for a complete information first-price sealed-bid auction we have the following.

1. If $v_1 > v_2$ (i.e., if player 1 is the only player with the highest valuation), then player 1 wins by bidding an amount b_1 such that $v_2 < b_1 < v_1$. (In order to get a large payoff, player 1, of course, bids b_1 close to v_2.)
2. If there are two or more players with the highest valuation, then every finalist bids $b_i = v_1$.

Proof: If $b_i > v_i$ and player i wins, then $u_i = \frac{1}{r}(v_i - b_i) < 0$. If player i does not win, then $u_i = 0$. Note, in contrast, that player i can guarantee at least $u_i = 0$ if she bids $b_i \leq v_i$. Thus every bidder i should bid $b_i \leq v_i$.

From the observation above we know that for each $i \geq 2$ we have $b_i \leq v_2$. Thus player 1 wins by bidding $v_2 < b_1 < v_1$.

If the bid b_i of a finalist i satisfies $b_i < v_i = v_1$, then she will lose if another bidder j with the high-valuation bids b_j such that $b_i < b_j \leq v_1$. Therefore, the bid of every finalist must equal v_1, the highest valuation of the object.

In other words, the preceding theorem informs us that:

In a first-price sealed-bid auction with complete information, player 1 (the player with the highest valuation) is always a finalist and if $v_1 > v_2$, then she wins by making a bid greater than (but sufficiently close to) the second highest valuation.

It is clear that one can consider an auction as a strategic form game with n players. The strategy set S_i of player i is $[0, \infty)$; the set of all possible bids b_i. The payoff function of player i is the utility function just described. Now let us examine whether this game has a Nash equilibrium, and if so, what is the relationship of a Nash equilibrium to the solutions described in Theorem 6.1. As before, we distinguish two separate cases.

CASE I.
There is only one bidder with the highest valuation, that is, $v_1 > v_2$.

In this case, we claim that the game does not have a Nash equilibrium simply because bidder 1 can always keep improving her payoff by bidding b_1 closer and closer to v_2. However, notice that she should never bid $b_1 \leq v_2$.

In addition, observe that bidder 1 always receives a payoff less than $v_1 - v_2$, but she can win and receive a payoff that is arbitrarily close to $v_1 - v_2$. That is, for any $\epsilon > 0$, no matter how small, by bidding b_1 so that $v_2 < b_1 < v_2 + \epsilon$, she gets a payoff that is within ϵ of $v_1 - v_2$. Whenever players in a game can come arbitrarily close to their highest payoffs by choosing appropriate strategy combinations, we say that the game has *ϵ-Nash equilibria* or *approximate Nash equilibria*. Thus, in this case, the game does not have a Nash equilibrium, but it does have an approximate Nash equilibrium.

CASE II.

There are at least two bidders with the highest valuation.

In this case, it can be checked that the vector of bids $(v_1, v_2, \ldots, v_n)$ is a Nash equilibrium. It should also be clear that this is not the only Nash equilibrium of the game.

We now go on to see what happens in a *second-price sealed-bid auction*[2] with complete information. One needs to recall that, according to the rules, in a second-price auction the winner is declared to be again the one with the highest bid, but in this case she pays the second highest bid. We assume again that if there are r finalists (where $1 < r \leq n$) with the highest bid, then the winner is determined by some random draw and *pays the highest bid*.

Now let $b = (b_1, b_2, \ldots, b_n)$ be a vector of bids. For each player i, we let

$$m_{-i} = \max\{b_j \colon j \neq i\}.$$

With this notation in place, bidder i's utility (or payoff) function in a second-price sealed-bid auction is now given by

$$u_i(b_1, \ldots, b_n) = \begin{cases} 0, & \text{if } b_i < m_{-i} \\ \frac{1}{r}(v_i - m_{-i}), & \text{if } b_i = m_{-i} \text{ and we have } r \text{ finalists} \\ v_i - m_{-i}, & \text{if } b_i > m_{-i}. \end{cases}$$

In this case, we have the following facts.

Theorem 6.2   In a second-price sealed-bid auction every player i bids

$$b_i \leq v_i.$$

Moreover, for a second-price sealed-bid auction with complete information:

1. if $v_1 > v_2$ (i.e., if player 1 is the only player with the highest valuation), then player 1 wins by bidding any amount b_1 such that $v_2 < b_1 < v_1$, and
2. if there are more that one finalists, then the vector of bids $(v_1, v_2, \ldots, v_n)$ is a Nash equilibrium.

Proof: Assume that $b_i > v_i$. We distinguish four cases.

a. $m_{-i} > b_i$.

In this case some other bidder has the highest bid. So bidder i gets a payoff of zero, which she can also get by bidding v_i.

b. $m_{-i} = b_i$.

In this case the bidder is one among $r > 1$ bidders with the highest bid, and she recieves a payoff of $\frac{1}{r}(v_i - m_{-i}) < 0$. However, the bidder i can receive the higher payoff of zero by bidding v_i.

c. $v_i \leq m_{-i} < b_i$.

---

[2]These auctions are often called Vickrey auctions after Richard Vickrey, one of the winners of the 1996 Nobel Prize in economics.

In this case bidder i wins, pays the second highest bid m_{-i} and gets a payoff of $v_i - m_{-i} \leq 0$. However, if she had bid v_i, then she would have either lost (in which case she would have got a payoff of zero), or she would be among the $r > 1$ winners (in which case her expected payoff is zero). In either case, by bidding v_i she gets a payoff that is at least as high as the payoff she received by bidding b_i.

d. $m_{-i} < v_i$.

In this case player i wins and gets the payoff of $v_i - m_{-i}$. Note that the player can get the same payoff by bidding v_i.

1. Repeat the arguments of the proof of Theorem 6.1.
2. We shall prove that $(v_1, v_2, \ldots, v_n)$ is a Nash equilibrium when we have two finalists. The general case can be proved in a similar manner and is left for the reader. So assume $v_1 = v_2$. We first show that bidder 1 cannot improve her payoff by bidding $b_1 \neq v_1$.

From the first part, we know that $b_1 \leq v_1$. Now consider $b_1 < v_1$. Then we have $b_2 = v_2 = v_1 > b_1$, and so bidder 1 is a loser and gets a payoff of zero, the same payoff he gets by bidding v_1. This shows that bidder 1 cannot gain by deviating from v_1. An identical argument can be made for bidder 2.

Since again from the first part we know that $b_i \leq v_i < v_1$ for $3 \leq i \leq n$, we see that bidder i gets a payoff of zero, which cannot be improved by biddings other than the v_i.

In comparing the outcomes of the first-price and the second-price auction, we noticed that in case there is only one bidder with the highest valuation, then in both kinds of auctions the auctioneer is guaranteed to receive something close to the second highest value v_2. In case there is more than one bidder with the highest valuation, the first-price auction guarantees a payoff to the auctioneer that is equal to the highest valuation. As we saw, this also happens to be true in the second-price auction. Therefore, from the auctioneer's point of view the two types of auctions give him almost the same payoffs.

In the second-price auction, however, the Nash equilibrium in the bidding game at which bidder 1 bids close to v_2 is rather unstable, as bidder 2 may deviate without any cost to him to bidding lower than v_2. The auctioneer in this case may end up with a lower than anticipated second highest bid, thus causing a loss of profit. This may be a reason as to why second-price auctions are very rarely used in practice. There is a possibility that auctioneers may make less in a second-price auction than they do in a first-price auction.

In all that we have said so far, the bidding is done simultaneously. In many practical auctions, however, the bidding is done sequentially with the auctioneer starting the bidding by quoting a price. In the complete information case the sequential bidding may end quickly if player 1 bids v_2. Once this happens none of the other bidders would up the ante, as they get a negative payoff with certainty. The resulting outcome then is exactly the same as the one in the first-price sealed-bid auction.

1. Consider a first-price sealed-bid auction and view it as a strategic form game with n players, where the strategy set S_i of player i is $[0, \infty)$, the set of all possible bids b_i. If $v_1 = v_2$, then verify that the valuation vector $(v_1, v_2, \ldots, v_n)$ is a Nash equilibrium.

2. Show that if in a complete information first-price sealed-bid auction there are at least two bidders with the highest possible valuation of the object, then at the Nash equilibrium $(v_1, \ldots, v_n)$ the payoff of each player is zero.

3. Consider a second-price sealed-bid auction and view it as a strategic form game with n players, where the strategy set S_i of player i is $[0, \infty)$, the set of all possible bids b_i. Assume that $v_1 > v_2 > v_3 \geq v_4 \geq \cdots \geq v_n$. Show that any vector of bids $(v_2, b_2, b_3, \ldots, b_n)$, where $v_2 > b_2 \geq v_3$ and $v_i \geq b_i$ for $3 \leq i \leq n$, is a Nash equilibrium.

4. A local municipality is floating a tender for the construction of a park. There are five local contractors who want to bid for the contract. The bidder who makes the lowest bid gets the contract. Write down the strategic form game for this and explain how the contractors will bid if they know each other's cost for constructing the park.

5. A rare fossil has been discovered in West Africa. It has been decided that the fossil will be auctioned. It is known to the auctioneer that two museums attach the same value of $\$5$ million to this fossil, while the next possible buyer values it at $\$4$ million. Should the auctioneer use a first-price sealed-bid auction or a second-price auction? What does the auctioneer expect to get?

6. If in the preceding exercise it is known that one museum values the fossil at $\$5$ million another at $\$4.5$ million and the rest no more than $\$4$ million each, how would your answer change?

7. Suppose that the valuations of potential bidders in an auction are not known. Do you think that if bidders are asked to bid sequentially, then the bidders would bid up to their true valuation? Explain your answer.

8. Let us introduce some notation for an n-bidder auction. If $b = (b_1, b_2, \ldots, b_n)$ is a vector of bids, then we let $m = \max\{b_1, \ldots, b_n\}$. If $A = \{i: b_i = m\}$, then the second highest bid m_s is given by

$$m_s = \max\{b_i: i \notin A\},$$

provided that $A \neq \{1, 2, \ldots, n\}$. If $A = \{1, 2, \ldots, n\}$, then we let $m_s = m$, the common value of the b_i.

Consider a second-price sealed-bid type of auction with complete information that is played as follows. The highest bidder wins and pays the second highest bid m_s. That is, bidder i's utility (or payoff) function is given by

$$u_i(b_1, \ldots, b_n) = \begin{cases} 0, & \text{if } b_i < m \\ \frac{1}{r}(v_i - m_s), & \text{if } b_i = m \text{ and } A \text{ has } r < n \text{ finalists} \\ \frac{1}{n}(v_i - m), & \text{if } b_i = m \text{ for each } i. \end{cases}$$

Is $(v_1, v_2, \ldots, v_n)$ a Nash equilibrium for this auction game?

9. Consider a first-price sealed-bid auction and view it as a strategic form game with n players, where the strategy set S_i of player i is $[0, \infty)$; the set of all possible bids b_i. If $v_1 = v_2 > v_3 \geq v_4 \geq \cdots \geq v_n$, find all Nash equilibria of this auction game.

6.2 INDIVIDUAL PRIVATE VALUE AUCTIONS

An *individual private value auction* is an auction in which the bidders only know their own valuation of the item, though they may have some idea about the valuation of the other bidders. For instance, when you are at an auction of a rare piece of art, you know how much you are willing to pay for it, but you have only a vague idea about how much the others value it.

In this section, we study in detail an auction with two bidders who use "linear rules" as their bidding strategies. In this first-price sealed-bid individual private value auction, each bidder i has her own valuation v_i of the object, and the bidder with the highest bid wins. In case both bid the same amount, the winner is decided by a draw. So, as before, the payoff functions of the players are given by

$$u_1(b_1, b_2) = \begin{cases} v_1 - b_1, & \text{if } b_1 > b_2 \\ \frac{v_1 - b_1}{2}, & \text{if } b_1 = b_2 \\ 0, & \text{if } b_1 < b_2 \end{cases}$$

and

$$u_2(b_1, b_2) = \begin{cases} v_2 - b_2, & \text{if } b_2 > b_1 \\ \frac{v_2 - b_2}{2}, & \text{if } b_2 = b_1 \\ 0, & \text{if } b_2 < b_1. \end{cases}$$

Here, as mentioned above, we are assuming that if the bidders make the same bid, then the winner is decided by the toss of a coin so that the probability of winning is $\frac{1}{2}$. Thus the utility in this case is the expected payoff from winning the auction.

Unlike the bidders in the auctions of Section 6.1, here the bidders do not know the true valuation of the object by the other bidder. Though each player is uncertain (due to lack of information) about the true valuation of the other player, each player has a belief (or an estimate) of the true valuation of the others. Since player i does not know player j's true valuation v_j of the object, she must treat the value v_j as a random variable. This means that the belief of player i about the true value of v_j is expressed by means of a distribution function F_i. That is, player i considers v_j to be a random variable with a distribution function F_i. Thus player i believes that the event $v_j \leq v$ will happen with probability

$$P_i(v_j \leq v) = F_i(v).$$

(See Section 1.5 for the definition of a distribution.)

We note from the outset that since this is a game, each bidder can arrive at an optimal bid only after guessing the bidding behavior of the other players. Naturally, the bids b_1 and b_2 of the players must be functions of the two valuations v_1 and v_2. In other words, $b_1 = b_1(v_1)$ and $b_2 = b_2(v_2)$.

Given the lack of information on the part of the players, the best that any player can do is to choose a bid that maximizes her expected payoff. Notice that the expected payoffs of the players are given by

$$E_1(b_1, b_2) = P_1(b_1 > b_2)u_1(b_1, b_2) + P_1(b_1 = b_2)u_1(b_1, b_2)$$
$$+ P_1(b_1 < b_2)u_1(b_1, b_2)$$
$$= (v_1 - b_1)P_1(b_1 > b_2) + \tfrac{1}{2}(v_1 - b_1)P_1(b_1 = b_2)$$

and

$$E_2(b_1, b_2) = (v_2 - b_2)P_2(b_2 > b_1) + \tfrac{1}{2}(v_2 - b_2)P_2(b_2 = b_1).$$

Observe that the first term in the formula $E_1(b_1, b_2)$ describes the possibility that bidder 1 wins and receives the payoff $v_1 - b_1$, and the second term gives the payoff when there is a tie, in which case bidder 1's expected payoff is $\tfrac{1}{2}(v_1 - b_1)$.

So, in this auction, the strategy of a bidder, say, of bidder 1, is simply her bidding function $b_1(v_1)$, and her objective is to maximize her expected payoff given the bidding function $b_2 = b_2(v_2)$ of the second bidder. Thus the expected payoff functions can be written as

$$Eu_1(b_1|b_2) = (v_1 - b_1)P_1(b_1 > b_2) + \tfrac{1}{2}(v_1 - b_1)P_1(b_1 = b_2)$$

and

$$Eu_2(b_2|b_1) = (v_2 - b_2)P_2(b_2 > b_1) + \tfrac{1}{2}(v_2 - b_2)P_2(b_2 = b_1).$$

This now naturally leads to our old concept of a Nash equilibrium. A pair of bidding functions $\left(b_1^*(v_1), b_2^*(v_2)\right)$ is said to be a *Nash equilibrium* for the individual private value auction if for every bidding function $b_1(v_1)$ of player 1 we have

$$Eu_1\left(b_1|b_2^*\right) \le Eu_1\left(b_1^*|b_2^*\right),$$

and for each bidding function $b_2(v_2)$ of player 2 we have

$$Eu_2\left(b_2|b_1^*\right) \le Eu_2\left(b_2^*|b_1^*\right).$$

We now work out the details in a specific case. Assume that both players know that the valuation of the object lies between a lower value $\underline{v} \ge 0$ and an upper value $\bar{v} > \underline{v}$. Assume further that each bidder knows that the valuation of the other bidder is uniformly distributed on the interval $[\underline{v}, \bar{v}]$. That is, bidder i knows only that the true valuation v_j of bidder j is a random variable whose density function $f_i(v)$ is given by

$$f_i(v) = \begin{cases} \frac{1}{\bar{v}-\underline{v}}, & \text{if } \underline{v} < v < \bar{v} \\ 0, & \text{otherwise}. \end{cases}$$

In other words, player i believes that the likelihood of v_j having at most the value v is given by

$$P_i(v_j \le v) = \int_{-\infty}^{v} f_i(t)\, dt = \begin{cases} 0, & \text{if } v < \underline{v} \\ \frac{v-\underline{v}}{\bar{v}-\underline{v}}, & \text{if } \underline{v} \le v \le \bar{v} \\ 1, & \text{if } v > \bar{v}. \end{cases}$$

(See Example 1.15 for a discussion of the uniform distribution.) It should be clear that the following two "rationality" conditions must be satisfied:

$$\underline{v} \le b_2(\underline{v}) \le \overline{v} \quad \text{and} \quad \underline{v} \le b_1(\underline{v}) \le \overline{v}.$$

As both bidders have symmetric information about each other's valuation, each should use essentially the same reasoning to choose an optimal strategy. We therefore have the following result.

Bidding Rules in the Two-Bidder Case

Assume that in a two-bidder individual private value auction the valuations of the bidders are independent random variables uniformly distributed over an interval $[\underline{v}, \overline{v}]$. Then the linear bidding rules

$$b_1(v_1) = \tfrac{1}{2}\underline{v} + \tfrac{1}{2}v_1 \quad \text{and} \quad b_2(v_2) = \tfrac{1}{2}\underline{v} + \tfrac{1}{2}v_2$$

form a symmetric Nash equilibrium.

The graph of a linear rule is shown in Figure 6.1. We now proceed to verify that the pair of linear bidding rules

$$b_1^*(v_1) = \tfrac{1}{2}\underline{v} + \tfrac{1}{2}v_1 \quad \text{and} \quad b_2^*(v_2) = \tfrac{1}{2}\underline{v} + \tfrac{1}{2}v_2$$

is a symmetric[3] Nash equilibrium of the individual private value auction. Because of the symmetry of the situation, it suffices to work out the details for bidder 1. We start by computing the probability of winning for player 1. As far as bidder 1 is concerned, v_2 is a random variable that is uniformly distributed over the interval $[\underline{v}, \overline{v}]$. Therefore,

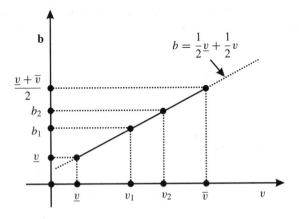

Figure 6.1   The linear bidding rule.

---

[3]In the language of game theory an equilibrium is known as a *symmetric Nash equilibrium* if each player uses the same strategy.

$$P_1(b_1 > b_2^*) = P_1\big(\{v_2 \colon b_1 > \tfrac{1}{2}\underline{v} + \tfrac{1}{2}v_2\}\big)$$
$$= P_1\big(\{v_2 \colon v_2 < 2b_1 - \underline{v}\}\big)$$
$$= P_1\big(\{v_2 \colon v_2 \le 2b_1 - \underline{v}\}\big)$$
$$= P_1\big(v_2 \le 2b_1 - \underline{v}\big)$$
$$= \begin{cases} 0, & \text{if } b_1 < \underline{v} \\ \frac{2(b_1-\underline{v})}{\bar{v}-\underline{v}}, & \text{if } \underline{v} \le b_1 \le \tfrac{1}{2}(\underline{v}+\bar{v}) \\ 1, & \text{if } b_1 > \tfrac{1}{2}(\underline{v}+\bar{v}) . \end{cases}$$

The graph of this function is shown in Figure 6.2(a).

Also, because v_2 has a uniform distribution (which is a continuous distribution), we have $P_1(b_1 = b_2) = P_1\big(\{v_2 \colon b_1 = \tfrac{1}{2}\underline{v}+\tfrac{1}{2}v_2\}\big) = P_1\big(\{v_2 \colon v_2 = 2b_1-\underline{v}\}\big) = 0$. This implies

$$Eu_1\big(b_1|b_2^*\big) = P_1(b_1 > b_2^*)(v_1 - b_1)$$
$$= \begin{cases} 0, & \text{if } b_1 < \underline{v} \\ \frac{2(b_1-\underline{v})(v_1-b_1)}{\bar{v}-\underline{v}}, & \text{if } \underline{v} \le b_1 \le \tfrac{1}{2}(\underline{v}+\bar{v}) \\ v_1 - b_1, & \text{if } b_1 > \tfrac{1}{2}(\underline{v}+\bar{v}) . \end{cases}$$

The graph of this function is shown in Figure 6.2(b).

Now it is easy to see that the maximum of the expected payoff function $Eu_1(b_1|b_2^*)$ takes place in the closed interval $\big[\underline{v}, \tfrac{1}{2}(\underline{v}+\bar{v})\big]$. Clearly, the maximizer satisfies the equation

$$Eu_1'(b_1|b_2^*) = \tfrac{2}{\bar{v}-\underline{v}}(v_1 - 2b_1 + \underline{v}) = 0$$

or $b_1 = \tfrac{1}{2}\underline{v} + \tfrac{1}{2}v_1$. This shows that the pair of linear bidding rules $\big(b_1^*(v_2), b_2^*(v_2)\big)$ is a Nash equilibrium for the individual private value auction.

We add a note of caution here. Though we have found explicit solutions for Nash equilibrium bidding rules, the reason we were able to do so is because we made the assumption that the distribution of the valuations were uniform. Thus, the linear bidding rules we obtained above may not be equilibrium bidding rules if the distribution is other than uniform.

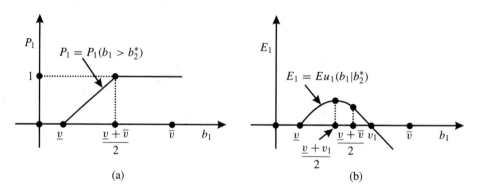

(a)   (b)

Figure 6.2

Let us now see how these linear bidding rules work out in a simple example.

Example 6.3

Suppose two bidders are bidding for a painting that each knows is worth between $100,000 and $500,000, and that each bidder's valuation of the painting is uniformly distributed over the interval $[100,000, 500,000]$. Thus in this case $\underline{v} = 100,000$ and $\overline{v} = 500,000$. The equilibrium bidding rules in this case are:

$$b_i(v_i) = \tfrac{1}{2}v_i + 50,000, \ \ i = 1, 2.$$

If bidder 1's true valuation is $200,000, then she bids $b_1 = \$150,000$, and if bidder 2's true valuation is $250,000, then bidder 2 bids $b_2 = \$175,000$. The auctioneer in this case collects $175,000, and bidder 2 gets the painting for $175,000.

The analysis that we have done so far has been restricted to the case of two bidders. Since auctions usually have more than two bidders, it is important to understand auctions with many players. We illustrate the arguments for the general case by looking at an individual private value auction in which there are three bidders. The case for n bidders can be argued in exactly the same way, and we leave the details as an exercise for the reader.

As before, each bidder i views the valuations of the other players as random variables that are commonly known to be uniformly distributed on the interval $[\underline{v}, \overline{v}]$. Of course, each individual bidder knows her own true valuation. Since this is a first-price sealed-bid auction, given a vector of bids (b_1, b_2, b_3), the payoff function of bidder i is given by

$$u_i(b_1, b_2, b_3) = \begin{cases} v_i - b_i, & \text{if } b_i > b_j \text{ for all } j \neq i \\ \frac{1}{r}(v_i - b_i), & \text{if } i \text{ is among the } r \text{ finalists} \\ 0, & \text{otherwise.} \end{cases}$$

The expected payoff of player i is given by

$$E_i(b_1, b_2, b_3) = P_i(b_i > b_j: \text{ for all } j \neq i) \, u_i(b_1, b_2, b_3).$$

Again, since the random variables v_j for $j \neq i$ are all uniformly distributed, the probability that any two bids are equal is zero, and thus the expected utility is unaffected by having ties. Because of the symmetry of the situation, it is reasonable to expect that bidders use the same optimal bidding rules. As in the two-bidder case, we have the following analogous result.

Bidding Rules in the Three-bidder Case

Assume that in a three-bidder individual private value auction the valuations of the bidders are independent random variables uniformly distributed over an interval $[\underline{v}, \overline{v}]$. Then the *linear bidding rules*

$$b_i(v_i) = \tfrac{1}{3}\underline{v} + \tfrac{2}{3}v_i, \ \ i = 1, 2, 3,$$

form a symmetric Nash equilibrium.

To verify that the linear bidding rules

$$b_i^*(v_i) = \tfrac{1}{3}\underline{v} + \tfrac{2}{3}v_i \,, \quad i = 1, 2, 3$$

form a Nash equilibrium, we proceed as in the two-bidder case. Again, because of the symmetry of the situation, it suffices to verify the Nash equilibrium behavior for bidder 1. We assume that each bidder bids independently, a reasonable assumption in the case of a sealed-bid auction. In probability theory, this is expressed by saying that the random variables are *independent*, which means that

$$P_1(b_1 > b_2 \text{ and } b_1 > b_3) = P_1(b_1 > b_2)P_1(b_1 > b_3) \,.$$

Consequently, we have

$$P_1(b_1 > b_2^* \text{ and } b_1 > b_3^*) = P_1(b_1 > b_2^*)P_1(b_1 > b_3^*)$$

$$= P_1\big(\{v_2 \colon b_1 > \tfrac{1}{3}\underline{v} + \tfrac{2}{3}v_2\}\big)P_1\big(\{v_3 \colon b_1 > \tfrac{1}{3}\underline{v} + \tfrac{2}{3}v_3\}\big)$$

$$= \begin{cases} 0, & \text{if } b_1 < \underline{v} \\ \frac{9(b_1 - \underline{v})^2}{4(\overline{v} - \underline{v})^2}, & \text{if } \underline{v} \le b_1 \le \tfrac{1}{3}\underline{v} + \tfrac{2}{3}\overline{v} \\ 1, & \text{if } b_1 > \tfrac{1}{3}\underline{v} + \tfrac{2}{3}\overline{v}. \end{cases}$$

Therefore, given that players 2 and 3 use the rules b_2^* and b_3^*, the expected payoff of player 1 is given by

$$Eu_1\big(b_1|b_2^*, b_3^*\big) = P_1(b_1 > b_2^* \text{ and } b_1 > b_3^*)(v_1 - b_1)$$

$$= P_1(b_1 > b_2^*)P_1(b_1 > b_3^*)(v_1 - b_1)$$

$$= \begin{cases} 0, & \text{if } b_1 < \underline{v} \\ \frac{9(b_1 - \underline{v})^2(v_1 - b_1)}{4(\overline{v} - \underline{v})^2}, & \text{if } \underline{v} \le b_1 \le \tfrac{1}{3}\underline{v} + \tfrac{2}{3}\overline{v} \\ v_1 - b_1, & \text{if } b_1 > \tfrac{1}{3}\underline{v} + \tfrac{2}{3}\overline{v} \,. \end{cases}$$

For $\underline{v} < v_1 < \tfrac{1}{3}\underline{v} + \tfrac{2}{3}\overline{v}$ its graph is shown Figure 6.3.

Clearly, this function attains its maximum inside the closed interval $\big[\underline{v}, \tfrac{1}{3}\underline{v} + \tfrac{2}{3}\overline{v}\big]$. Differentiating, we get:

$$Eu_1'\big(b_1|b_2^*, b_3^*\big) = \frac{9(b_1 - \underline{v})(-3b_1 + \underline{v} + 2v_1)}{4(\overline{v} - \underline{v})^2}$$

$$Eu_1''\big(b_1|b_2^*, b_3^*\big) = \frac{9(-3b_1 + 2\underline{v} + v_1)}{2(\overline{v} - \underline{v})^2} \,.$$

Solving $Eu_1'\big(b_1|b_2^*, b_3^*\big) = 0$ for b_1 yields $b_1^* = \tfrac{1}{3}\underline{v} + \tfrac{2}{3}v_1$, which means that the function $Eu_1\big(\cdot \,|b_2^*, b_3^*\big)$ has only one critical point in the interval $\big(\underline{v}, \tfrac{1}{3}\underline{v} + \tfrac{2}{3}\overline{v}\big)$. Since the second derivative satisfies

$$Eu_1''\big(b_1^*|b_2^*, b_3^*\big) = \frac{9}{2(\overline{v} - \underline{v})^2}(\underline{v} - v_1) < 0 \,,$$

we conclude that $Eu_1\big(\cdot \,|b_2^*, b_3^*\big)$ is maximized at b_1^*. This establishes that the triplet of linear bidding rules

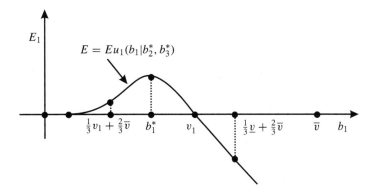

Figure 6.3 The graph of the expected payoff function Eu_1.

$$b_i^*(v_i) = \tfrac{1}{3}\underline{v} + \tfrac{2}{3}v_i\,,\quad i = 1, 2, 3\,,$$

is a Nash equilibrium.

Let us now go back to the second-price sealed-bid auction. Since the highest bidder who wins the auction pays only the second highest bid, the payoff functions in a second-price auction are given by

$$u_i(b_1, \dots, b_n) = \begin{cases} 0, & \text{if } b_i < m_{-i} \\ \tfrac{1}{r}(v_i - m_{-i}), & \text{if } b_i = m_{-i} \text{ and we have } r \text{ finalists} \\ v_i - m_{-i}, & \text{if } b_i > m_{-i}\,, \end{cases}$$

where $b = (b_1, b_2, \dots, b_n)$ is an arbitrary vector of bids and (as usual) $m_{-i} = \max\{b_j\colon j \neq i\}$.

In the case of the first-price auction, the bidding behavior in the individual private value case is quite different from the bidding in the complete information case. However, in contrast, the bidding in a second-price sealed-bid auction is identical for both cases. Indeed, as in the complete information case, the players will also always bid their true valuation in the case of individual private values. This remarkable result is stated and discussed below.

Theorem 6.4   Let $v = (v_1, v_2, \dots, v_n)$ be the vector of valuations. If the auction is a second-price sealed-bid auction, then bidder i's optimal bid is v_i.

Proof: We start by introducing some standard notation. Let $b = (b_1, b_2, \dots, b_n)$ be a vector of bids and let us isolate a player i. If b_{-i} is the $(n-1)$-dimensional vector of bids obtained from b by deleting the bid b_i of player i, then we shall denote the utility function $u_i(b_1, \dots, b_n)$ by $u_i(b_i, b_{-i})$. That is, for simplicity, we let

$$u_i(b_1, b_2, \dots, b_n) = u_i(b_i, b_{-i})\,.$$

We shall show that $b_i = v_i$ gives bidder i the highest payoff by establishing the following claims.

STEP I: $b_i \leq v_i$.

If $b_i > v_i$, then

$$
u_i(b_i, b_{-i}) = \begin{cases} v_i - m_{-i}, & \text{if } m_{-i} \leq v_i \\ v_i - m_{-i} < 0, & \text{if } v_i < m_{-i} < b_i \\ \frac{v_i - m_{-i}}{r} < 0, & \text{if } m_{-i} = b_i \text{ and we have } r \text{ finalists} \\ 0, & \text{if } m_{-i} > b_i, \end{cases}
$$

whereas if she bids v_i, then

$$
u_i(v_i, b_{-i}) = \begin{cases} v_i - m_{-i} & \text{if } m_{-i} < v_i \\ 0, & \text{if } m_{-i} \geq v_i. \end{cases}
$$

Thus, comparing the above payoffs, we see that $b_i > v_i$, implies $u_i(v_i, b_{-i}) \geq u_i(b_i, b_{-i})$.

STEP II: $b_i = v_i$.

From Step I, we know that $b_i \leq v_i$. Now assume by way of contradiction that $b_i < v_i$. Then,

$$
u_i(b_i, b_{-i}) = \begin{cases} v_i - m_{-i}, & \text{if } m_{-i} < b_i \\ \frac{v_i - m_{-i}}{r}, & \text{if } m_{-i} = b_i \text{ and we have } r \text{ finalists} \\ 0, & \text{if } m_{-i} > b_i. \end{cases}
$$

Again, comparing these payoffs, we see that $b_i < v_i$ implies $u_i(v_i, b_{-i}) \geq u_i(b_i, b_{-i})$. Therefore, we have established that the optimal bid for player i is v_i.

If we examine the preceding arguments closely, we will notice that the optimal bid of player i is v_i, irrespective of how the valuations of the other bidders are distributed. Thus a Nash equilibrium of a second-price sealed-bid auction with individual private values is the vector $v = (v_1, v_2, \ldots, v_n)$.

In comparing the first-price sealed-bid auction with the second-price sealed-bid auction, we find that the two types of auctions lead to quite distinct outcomes in the case of individual private values. This is in contrast with the complete information case. We saw in that case that the first-price sealed-bid auction generates as much revenue for the auctioneer as the second-price sealed-bid auction. In the case of individual private values, the second-price sealed-bid auctions can generate more revenue, as the following example demonstrates.

Example 6.5

Consider the auction of Example 6.3. In that example, if the painting was auctioned in a second-price sealed-bid auction, then player 1 would bid $200,000, and player 2 would bid $250,000. Thus, the painting would fetch $200,000, a considerably larger sum of money than the $175,000 that would be collected in a first-price auction.

Note, however, that if the valuation of bidder 2 is $350,000, then the highest bid in the first-price auction would be $225,000, and the auctioneer would collect $225,000. If a second-price auction is used, then it would again fetch $200,000. Consequently, it is difficult to determine which type of auction would generate the greater revenue in the case of individual private values.

1. Consider the auction described in Example 6.3. Now suppose that a third bidder enters the auction with a valuation $v_3 = \$125,000$. Will the bidding change? Does the auctioneer prefer the new biddings to the old ones?

2. Consider an individual private value auction with two bidders. Each player knows that the valuation of the other player is a uniformly distributed random variable on an interval $[\underline{v}, \overline{v}]$. Bidder 1 also knows that bidder 2's bidding function is given by

$$b_2(v_2) = (v_2 - \underline{v})^2 + \underline{v},$$

but bidder 2 does not know the bidding function of player 1. Find the best response bidding function $b_1(v_1)$ of player 1. [Answer: $b_1 = \frac{2}{3}\underline{v} + \frac{1}{3}v_1$.]

3. Suppose that two bidders are bidding for a piece of art that each knows is worth between $\$300,000$ and $\$800,000$, and that the other bidder's valuation of the piece of art is uniformly distributed over the interval $[300,000, 800,000]$. Player 2 knows that player 1's bidding function is given by

$$b_1(v_1) = \frac{1}{400,000}(v_1 - 300,000)^2 + 300,000$$

but player 1 does not know the bidding function of player 2. If the true valuations of the players are $v_1 = \$500,000$ and $v_2 = \$600,000$, find the bids of the players. [Answer: $b_1 = b_2 = \$400,000$.]

4. Consider an auction with two bidders in which player 1 knows that player 2's valuation is a random variable that is uniformly distributed on the interval $[\underline{v}, \overline{v}]$, and player 2 knows that player 1's valuation is also a random variable that is uniformly distributed on the interval $[v_*, v^*]$. Assume that $v_* < \underline{v} < v^* < \overline{v}$. Find the equilibrium linear bidding rules of the players in this auction. [Answers: $b_1(v_1) = \frac{1}{6}v_* + \frac{1}{3}\underline{v} + \frac{1}{2}v_1$ and $b_2(v_2) = \frac{1}{6}\underline{v} + \frac{1}{3}v_* + \frac{1}{2}v_2$.]

5. Verify that the graph of the expected payoff function of player 1

$$Eu_1(b_1|b_2^*, b_3^*) = \begin{cases} 0, & \text{if } b_1 < \underline{v} \\ \frac{9(b_1-\underline{v})^2(v_1-b_1)}{4(\overline{v}-\underline{v})^2}, & \text{if } \underline{v} \le b_1 \le \frac{1}{3}\underline{v} + \frac{2}{3}\overline{v} \\ v_1 - b_1, & \text{if } b_1 > \frac{1}{3}\underline{v} + \frac{2}{3}\overline{v}. \end{cases}$$

is as shown in Figure 6.3. Also determine the highest expected payoff of player 1. [Answer: The highest expected payoff of player 1 is $\frac{(v_1-\underline{v})^3}{3(\overline{v}-\underline{v})^2}$.]

6. Assume that in an individual private value auction with n bidders each bidder knows that the valuations of the others are independent random variables uniformly distributed on the interval $[\underline{v}, \overline{v}]$. Show that the vector of bids

$$\left(\frac{1}{n}\underline{v} + \frac{n-1}{n}v_1, \frac{1}{n}\underline{v} + \frac{n-1}{n}v_2, \ldots, \frac{1}{n}\underline{v} + \frac{n-1}{n}v_n\right)$$

is a symmetric Nash equilibrium for the auction. What is the expected payoff of each bidder at this Nash equilibrium? Also, what happens to this Nash equilibrium and the expected payoffs as $n \to \infty$?

6.3 ENGLISH AUCTIONS

One of the most popular type of auctions is the one in which the auctioneer uses a sequential bidding procedure. There are quite a few variants of sequential bid auctions. The most widely used is a variant of the *English auction* in which the auctioneer calls successively higher bids and a bidder then indicates whether she is willing to make that bid. The bidder who makes the last bid in this sequence of bids then wins the auction and pays that bid. In Japan a slightly different form of the English auction is used. The price is posted using an electronic display and the price is raised continuously. A bidder who wishes to be active at the current price depresses a button. When she releases the button she has withdrawn from the auction. The Dutch often use a sequential bidding procedure to auction tulips and tulip bulbs. The auction, however, starts with a high price and the price is continuously lowered until a bidder agrees to pay the bid. These auctions are called *Dutch auctions* and are obviously quite different from the English auctions. Here we analyze the standard version of the English auction. Such an auction is again a gathering of n persons for the sole purpose of buying an object under the following rules.

1. The auctioneer (the person in charge of the auction) starts the bidding by announcing a price b_0 for the object. This is *round* (or *stage*) zero of the auction. The quoted price b_0 is the *floor price* of the object at round zero. We assume that $b_0 > 0$.

2. Once the price b_0 is announced by the auctioneer, the players start bidding in a sequential fashion, that is, in succession one after the other. Successive bids must be higher than the prevailing floor price. Thus the first person who announces a price $b_1 > b_0$ brings the auction to round 1, and the price b_1 is now the floor price of round 1. The next player who bids a price $b_2 > b_1$ brings the auction to round 2 and to the floor price b_2, and so on. At each stage of the auction every player has the right to bid again, even if she had bid in earlier rounds.[4] Consequently, the floor price b_k at stage k is the result of the successive bids

$$0 < b_0 < b_1 < b_2 < \cdots < b_k.$$

3. If at some round k no one bids higher, then the player with the last bid b_k is declared to be the winner, and the auction ends. The player with the last bid then pays the amount b_k to the auctioneer and gets the object.

Since the process of bidding in an English auction is drastically different from a sealed-bid auction, it is, of course, quite natural to wonder whether the final bid would be different from the sealed-bid auction. Again we start discussing English auctions by assuming that each bidder i has a true valuation v_i of the item. As before, without loss of generality, we may assume that the valuations are ranked in the order

$$v_1 \geq v_2 \geq \cdots \geq v_n.$$

---

[4]It is understood here that rational bidders will not make two consecutive bids since by doing so they simply lower their expected payoffs of winning the auction. The making of two successive bids by the same player is tantamount to bidding against himself!

Since an English auction is still an individual private value auction, the bidders do not know the valuations of the others and know only their own valuations of the item. We shall see that one of the advantages of an English auction is that the bidders do not really need to know the distribution of possible valuations to bid optimally. We go on to examine the nature of an optimal strategy in an English bid auction.

Claim 1: *No bidder will bid more than her valuation.*

In order to justify this claim, we must interpret it in the framework of expected payoffs. Assume that a bidder i bids $b_k > v_i$ at the kth round of bidding. Then her belief about her chances of winning the auction is expressed by a number $0 \leq p \leq 1$, where

$$p = \text{the probability that } b_k \text{ is the highest bid}$$

and, of course, $1 - p$ is the probability that some other bidder will bid a higher price at the $(k+1)$th round. So player i, by bidding $b_k > v_i$ at the kth round expects a payoff of

$$p(v_i - b_k) + (1 - p) \times 0 = p(v_i - b_k) \leq 0,$$

which is negative if p is not zero. However, notice that she can have an expected payoff that is at least as high, by bidding no more than her valuation v_i.

Claim 2: *Bidder i will bid as long as the last bid is below v_i.*

To establish this claim, there are two cases to consider. First, if bidder i made the last bid b_k, then bidder i will not bid as long as there are no further bids, in which case bidder i wins and receives the payoff $v_i - b_k$. However, if $b_k > v_i$, then this payoff is negative and she would have been better off at the kth round, either by not bidding at all, or, in case $b_{k-1} < v_i$, by bidding b_k such that $b_{k-1} < b_k \leq v_i$.

If the floor price after k rounds of bidding is $b_k < v_i$, and bidder i did not make the last bid, then bidder i will bid an amount b_{k+1} on the $(k+1)$th round such that $b_k < b_{k+1} \leq v_i$ as the expected payoff from bidding at the $(k+1)$th round is:

$$p(v_i - b_{k+1}) + (1 - p) \times 0 = p(v_i - b_{k+1}) \geq 0.$$

This expected payoff is positive if bidder i thinks that there is a positive probability p that b_{k+1} is the highest bid. In this case, the expected payoff from not bidding is zero, irrespective of the beliefs of player i.

We can now use the preceding two claims to determine the winning bid in an English auction. Clearly, the bidding stops as soon as the floor price b_t at the tth round of bidding exceeds or is equal to v_2, the second highest valuation. Since the second highest bidder has no incentive to bid $b_t > v_2$, the bid must have been made by bidder 1, and hence, $b_t \leq v_1$. Therefore, in an English auction, the winning bid b^* must always satisfy $v_2 \leq b^* \leq v_1$.

We emphasize here that the winning bid is independent of the information or beliefs that players have about each other's valuations. The final bid is simply a consequence of the true valuations of the bidders.

One needs to compare the preceding conclusion with the outcome in a sealed-bid auction. Recall that in a sealed-bid auction the bid made by the bidders is not independent of their beliefs about the valuations of the others. One thus faces the following intriguing question: *Given a choice of the two forms of auctions, which one of the two would an auctioneer choose?*

The answer, as we shall see below, depends on the valuations of the players as well as on their beliefs about each other's true valuations.

Example 6.6

Let us go back to Example 6.3, in which there are two bidders with valuations $v_1 = \$250,000$ and $v_2 = \$200,000$. If the auction is an English auction, the bidding would stop as soon as the bid went over $200,000. Thus the auctioneer will net a little over $200,000 for the item. In the case of the sealed-bid auction, where the beliefs of the bidders about the valuations of the others are uniformly distributed between $100,000 and $500,000, the winning bid is only $175,000. Thus, in this case, the English auction generates significantly more revenue for the auctioneer than the sealed-bid auction.

In contrast, if we now change the parameters to

$$\underline{v} = \$200,000\,, \quad v_1 = \$300,000\,, \quad \text{and} \quad v_2 = \$200,000\,,$$

then the sealed-bid auction would get a winning bid of $250,000, and the English auction could get a winning bid of only $200,000. Thus in this case the sealed-bid auction generates substantially more revenue than the English auction.

From the example above it should be clear that a sealed-bid auction may outperform an English auction in some cases, whereas it may go the other way in some other cases. It is, therefore, no wonder that we see both kinds of auctions used frequently, as the type of auction that is better from the auctioneer's point of view depends on the expected group of bidders and their valuations of the item. In other words, the amount an auctioneer nets from an auction depends on the way the auction is designed.

Let us examine the following variant on a sequential bid auction.[5] The item being auctioned is a dollar and is being auctioned under the following rules.

1. The highest bidder gets the dollar.
2. The highest bidder as well as the second highest bidder must both pay their bids.

Notice that the difference between this auction and the usual sequential bid auction is that *both* the highest bidder as well as the second highest bidder must pay their bids, but *only* the highest bidder wins the object.

---

[5]The auction was first used by Professor Martin Shubik at Yale University.

This auction has one Nash equilibrium. Namely: *The bidder who makes the first bid makes a bid of a dollar and the rest then bid nothing.* We verify this by way of the following assertions.

- No player bids more than a dollar in a Nash equilibrium.

If you are the first bid and you bid $b > 1$, then your payoff is given by

$$u(b) = \begin{cases} 1 - b < 0, & \text{if you win} \\ -b < 0, & \text{if you are the second highest bid} \\ 0, & \text{otherwise.} \end{cases}$$

Clearly, you are better off by bidding zero for the dollar, as your payoff in that case is always zero. Thus the payoff of bidding more than one dollar is not higher than the payoff of bidding zero.

- A bid that is less than a dollar cannot be a winning bid in a Nash equilibrium.

To see this, let $b_1 < b_2 < \cdots < b_{k-1} < b_k$ be the successive bids in the auction which form a Nash equilibrium. If $k = 1$, then $b_k = 1$. Otherwise, any bidder j different from i can bid b such that $b_k < b < 1$ and win the auction and get a positive payoff.

When $k > 1$, then again $b_k = 1$. Otherwise, if $b_k < 1$, then the bidder j with the bid b_{k-1}, can have a winning bid b such that $b_{k-1} < b < 1$ and avoid the penalty b_{k-1}.

Thus the only candidates for an equilibrium are the outcomes in which the first bidder bids one dollar and no one else makes a bid.

In case the first bidder bids one dollar, any bidder who wants to win will have to bid more than a dollar. But from our first claim this strategy is dominated by bidding zero. Hence, it is an optimal strategy for every bidder other than the one who bid one dollar to abstain from bidding. Our second claim then guarantees that this is the only Nash equilibrium of the auction.

While this auction has a single Nash equilibrium, it is an auction that has a rather fascinating characteristic. If the first bid happens to be less than a dollar, then the bidding can unravel dramatically in such a way that the bid that finally wins the dollar is well above a dollar. Suppose for instance, the first bid is 50 cents. A second bidder then has a chance of winning by making a bid of, say, 75 cents. But once this second bid has been made, the bidder who made the first bid at 50 cents has to bid higher, as, otherwise, he loses 50 cents, since if the bidding stops, his bid is the second highest bid. This bidder then bids between 75 cents and a dollar. The bidder with the bid of 75 cents now is at the risk of becoming the one with the second highest bid and thus will want to make a higher bid. But will the bidding process stop once it reaches one dollar? The answer is no if there is a bidder who has already made a second bid. If the second highest bid is 90 cents, then the bidder with this bid will want to beat the highest bid (say \$1) by quoting \$1.05, since if he wins, then he loses only 5 cents, whereas if he does not bid, his loss is 90 cents. But then the bidder with the bid of \$1 will now bid higher, say \$1.10. This apparently perverse (but seemingly rational) bidding will continue until the bidding reaches very high and possibly absurd levels, whose only constraint is the size of each bidder's budget. This phenomenon has been observed in many auctions of this type around the world. For instance, for how much do you think you can auction a twenty dollar bill? Quite predictably, in some cases the bidding reached as high as $15,000!⁶

EXERCISES

1. We have seen that the final bid in an English auction is $b^* \geq v_2$, where v_2 is the valuation of the second highest bidder. How does this compare to the winning bid in a second-price sealed-bid auction?

2. Recall that in a Dutch auction the bidding starts with a high price that is continuously lowered until a bidder agrees to pay the bid. How would the winning bid in a Dutch auction compare to the winning bid in an English auction? Explain fully.

3. As an auctioneer you know that among the bidders there is one bidder with a very high valuation and you also know that none of the bidders knows this. What auction would you choose?

4. Consider an auction where the auctioneer knows that there are two bidders with very high valuations for the object and none of the bidders knows this. What form of an auction would the auctioneer choose?

5. A failed S & L is often auctioned to private bidders by the *Resolution Trust Commission* (RTC). Before bidding, a bidder can get all the necessary information to determine its value to him. The auctions have been first-price sealed-bid auctions. Do you think that this form of auction generates the maximum revenue for the RTC? If not, what type of auction should the RTC have used?

6.4 COMMON-VALUE AUCTIONS

A *common-value auction* is a first-price sealed-bid auction in which

- The underlying true value of the object is the same for all bidders (hence the name *common-value auction*), and
- The bidders receive information about the true value of the object by means of "signals."

In a common-value auction, the bidders have the least amount of information. In addition to not knowing the valuations of the others, they are also uncertain about their own valuations. In such auctions, each bidder receives a "noisy" signal about the true value of the object, and on the basis of this signal she forms an estimate of its value. Consequently, in a common-value auction, the valuation of bidder i is viewed as a random variable not only by the other bidders but also by bidder i herself.

Typical examples of common-value auctions are auctions of offshore oil leases. In these auctions, the bidders, who are typically the big oil-producing firms and some independent

⁶*The Indianapolis Star*, Business Monday, week of April 14, 1997.

wild catters, do not have a precise idea of the value of the leases. They form an estimate of the value of the lease on the basis of some signal they observe. The U.S. government, which auctions these tracts of ocean, provides a legal description of the location of the area being leased. The bidders are responsible for gathering whatever information they can about the tract. In this case, the information provided by geologists and seismologists is usually the noisy signal observed by the bidders.

From now on we shall use v to denote the random value of the object and ω_i to indicate the signal received by bidder i. The value v of the object is correlated with the arbitrary signal ω via a *joint density function* $f(v, \omega)$, which every bidder knows. The density function $f(v, \omega)$ represents the probability of observing v and ω simultaneously.[7] We illustrate the concept of the joint density function by considering the following simple example. Assume that v can take two possible values, say, v_1 and v_2, and a bidder can receive one of three possible signals, ω_1, ω_2, and ω_3. The following table gives the joint density function $f(v, \omega)$ at these points.[8]

A joint density function

v/ω	v_1	v_2
ω_1	0.1	0.2
ω_2	0.2	0.2
ω_3	0.2	0.1

Suppose now that a bidder observes the signal ω_2. *Then what can she conclude about the value v of the object?* She should observe that with this information she can update the probabilities of the possible values v_1 and v_2. These new probabilities—which are called the *conditional probabilities*—can be computed (as we did in Chapter 3) by the formula

$$P(v_1|\omega_2) = \frac{P(v = v_1 \ \& \ \omega = \omega_2)}{P(\omega = \omega_2)} = \frac{0.2}{0.4} = 0.5\,,$$

where $P(\omega = \omega_2)$ was computed from the formula

$$P(\omega = \omega_2) = P(v = v_1 \ \& \ \omega = \omega_2) + P(v = v_2 \ \& \ \omega = \omega_2)$$

$$= 0.2 + 0.2 = 0.4\,.$$

Similarly, we get

$$P(v_2|\omega_2) = 0.5\,.$$

The *conditional expected value*, which is given by

$$E(v|\omega_2) = v_1 P(v_1|\omega_2) + v_2 P(v_2|\omega_2) = 0.5v_1 + 0.5v_2\,,$$

---

[7]In probability terminology the density function $f(v, \omega)$ satisfies $f(v, \omega) \geq 0$ for all v and ω and $\int_{-\infty}^{\infty} \int_{-\infty}^{\infty} f(v, \omega)\, dv d\omega = 1$.

[8]The reader should notice at once that the "discrete" joint density function satisfies the property $\sum_{i=1}^{2} \sum_{j=1}^{3} f(v_i, \omega_j) = 1$.

provides the answer to the question posed above.

Note further that given the signal $\omega = \omega_2$, a bidder now has a conditional distribution over the values v_1 and v_2, which she uses to calculate the conditional expected value of the object. This new distribution on the values of v is called the *conditional distribution* of v given ω.

Now let us return to our discussion of the common-value auction. As we saw, each bidder bids after observing a signal that conveys to her some information about the value of the object. After observing a signal ω, the bidder will re-evaluate her expected value of the object conditioned on the signal. This revised expected value—called the *conditional expected value*—is written as $E(v|\omega)$. If v takes a finite number of values, say, $v_1, \ldots, v_k$, then

$$E(v|\omega_j) = \sum_{i=1}^{k} v_i P(v_i|\omega_j),$$

where

$$P(v_i|\omega_j) = \frac{P(v = v_i \ \& \ \omega = \omega_j)}{P(\omega = \omega_j)}$$

and

$$P(\omega = \omega_j) = \sum_{i=1}^{k} P(v = v_i \ \& \ \omega = \omega_j).$$

In case v is a continuous random variable, then the sums are replaced by integrals.[9]

Hence, when bidder 1 receives the signal ω_1 and the vector of bids is $(b_1, \ldots, b_n)$, her expected payoff is

$$E_1(b_1, \ldots, b_n) = \begin{cases} \frac{1}{r}[E(v|\omega_1) - b_1], & \text{if bidder 1 is among } r \text{ finalists} \\ 0, & \text{otherwise}. \end{cases}$$

In general, the expected payoff of bidder i is

$$E_i(b_1, \ldots, b_n) = \begin{cases} \frac{1}{r}[E(v|\omega_i) - b_i], & \text{if bidder } i \text{ is among } r \text{ finalists} \\ 0, & \text{otherwise}. \end{cases}$$

Since a bidder cannot observe the signals of the others, she conditions her bid on the signal ω_i alone. Thus, in general, the bid of a player is a function of the signal that she observes. That is, the bid of player 1 is a function $b_1(\omega_1)$, and the bid of player i is $b_i(\omega_i)$.

As in the case of individual private value auctions, we study the bidding behavior in common-value auctions by analyzing the case of two bidders. From now on, in order to make our model as simple as possible, we shall assume the following.

- *The bidders observe signals that are independent realizations of random variables that are uniformly distributed on the interval* [0, 1].
- *The object that is being auctioned is known to take only two possible values: a high value v_h and a low value v_ℓ.*

---

[9]Here we have $E(v|\omega) = \int_{-\infty}^{\infty} s P(s|\omega) \, ds$, where $P(s|\omega) = \frac{f(s,\omega)}{\int_{-\infty}^{\infty} f(t,\omega) \, dt}$.

- *The joint density function of the random value v of the object and the signal ω is given by*

$$f(v, \omega) = \begin{cases} \omega, & \text{if } v = v_h \\ 1 - \omega, & \text{if } v = v_\ell. \end{cases}$$

From this joint density function, we see that the likelihood that the value is high increases with the signal. Thus, when $\omega = \frac{1}{2}$, the conditional probability that the value is high is

$$P(v_h | \omega) = \frac{f\left(v_h, \frac{1}{2}\right)}{f\left(v_\ell, \frac{1}{2}\right) + f\left(v_h, \frac{1}{2}\right)} = \frac{1}{2}.$$

Similarly, when the signal is $\omega = \frac{3}{4}$, the conditional probability is $P(v_h | \omega = \frac{3}{4}) = \frac{3}{4}$. Therefore, we see that the signals observed by the bidders are useful in pinning down the probable true value of the object. As the signals ω are uniformly distributed over $[0, 1]$, before the bidders receive a signal, the prior probability that the value is high is given by

$$P(v = v_h) = \int_0^1 f(v_h, \omega)\, d\omega = \int_0^1 \omega\, d\omega = \frac{1}{2}.$$

After they receive the signal $\omega = k$, the conditional probability that $v = v_h$ is given by

$$P(v_h | k) = \frac{f(v_h, k)}{f(v_h, k) + f(v_\ell, k)} = \frac{k}{k + (1-k)} = k.$$

The *conditional expected value* when a bidder observes the signal $\omega = k$ is thus

$$E(v | \omega = k) = P(v_h | k) v_h + [1 - P(v_h | k)] v_\ell$$
$$= k v_h + (1 - k) v_\ell.$$

In the present case, as the signal is a number in $[0, 1]$, it would be reasonable to ask whether the bidders can find an "optimal" strategy that is "linear" in the observed signals. Before pursuing the "linear bidding rules" further, let us discuss the objective of each bidder. Assume in the general case that $b_1 = b_1(\omega_1)$ and $b_2 = b_2(\omega_2)$. Let us look at the objective of player 1 given that bidder 2 uses a bidding rule $b_2(\omega_2)$. She will win the auction if $b_1 > b_2$, she loses if $b_1 < b_2$, and she has a 50% chance of winning it when $b_1 = b_2$. Thus her probability of winning is

$$P_1(b_1 \geq b_2) = P_1\big(\{\omega_2 \colon b_1 \geq b_2(\omega_2)\}\big).$$

Therefore, when bidder 1 observes the signal ω_1 and bidder 2 uses the bidding rule $b_2(\omega_2)$, the expected payoff of bidder 1 from bidding b_1 is

$$Eu_1\big(b_1 | b_2(\omega_2)\big) = P_1(b_1 \geq b_2)\big[\, E(v | \omega_1) - b_1 \,\big] + P_1(b_1 < b_2) \times 0$$
$$= P_1\big(\{\omega_2 \colon b_1 \geq b_2(\omega_2)\}\big)\big[\, \omega_1 v_h + (1 - \omega_1) v_\ell - b_1 \,\big].$$

Similarly, when bidder 2 observes the signal ω_2 and bidder 1 uses the bidding rule $b_1(\omega_1)$, the expected payoff of bidder 2 from bidding b_2 is

$$Eu_2\big(b_2 | b_1(\omega_1)\big) = P_2\big(\{\omega_1 \colon b_2 \geq b_1(\omega_1)\}\big)\big[\omega_2 v_h + (1 - \omega_2) v_\ell - b_2 \,\big].$$

As before, we say that a pair of bidding rules $\left(b_1^*(\omega_1), b_2^*(\omega_2)\right)$ of a common-value auction is a *Nash equilibrium*, if

$$Eu_1\left(b_1|b_2^*(\omega_2)\right) \leq Eu_1\left(b_1^*|b_2^*(\omega_2)\right)$$

holds true for each bidding rule $b_1(\omega_1)$ of bidder 1, and

$$Eu_2\left(b_2|b_1^*(\omega_1)\right) \leq Eu_2\left(b_2^*|b_1^*(\omega_1)\right)$$

for each bidding rule $b_2(\omega_2)$ of player 2.

We now have the following important result regarding Nash equilibria in our common-value auction.

Bidding Rules in Two-Bidder Common-Value Auction

If the bidders observe signals ω_1 and ω_2 that are uniformly distributed over the interval $[0, 1]$, then the pair of linear bidding rules

$$b_1 = v_\ell + \tfrac{1}{2}(v_h - v_\ell)\omega_1 \quad \text{and} \quad b_2 = v_\ell + \tfrac{1}{2}(v_h - v_\ell)\omega_2$$

is a symmetric Nash equilibrium of the common-value auction.

To see this, let

$$b_1^*(\omega_1) = v_\ell + \tfrac{1}{2}(v_h - v_\ell)\omega_1 \quad \text{and} \quad b_2^*(\omega_2) = v_\ell + \tfrac{1}{2}(v_h - v_\ell)\omega_2 \,.$$

The graph of $b_1^*(\omega_1)$ is shown in Figure 6.4(a).

In order to show that the pair of bidding rules $\left(b_1^*(\omega_1), b_2^*(\omega_2)\right)$ is a Nash equilibrium, it suffices to show that

$$Eu_1\left(b_1|b_2^*(\omega_2) \leq Eu_1\left(b_1^*|b_2^*(\omega_2)\right)\right.$$

for any bidding rule $b_1(\omega_1)$. We start by observing that

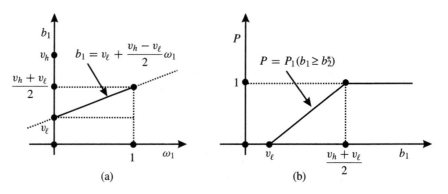

(a)   (b)

Figure 6.4

$$P_1\big(b_1 \geq b_2^*(\omega_2)\big) = P_1\big(\{\omega_2: b_1 \geq v_\ell + \tfrac{1}{2}(v_h - v_\ell)\omega_2\}\big)$$

$$= P_1\Big(\{\omega_2: \omega_2 \leq \tfrac{2(b_1 - v_\ell)}{v_h - v_\ell}\}\Big)$$

$$= P_1\Big(\omega_2 \leq \tfrac{2(b_1 - v_\ell)}{v_h - v_\ell}\Big)$$

$$= \begin{cases} 0, & \text{if } b_1 < v_\ell \\ \tfrac{2(b_1 - v_\ell)}{v_h - v_\ell}, & \text{if } v_\ell \leq b_1 \leq \tfrac{1}{2}(v_\ell + v_h) \\ 1, & \text{if } b_1 > \tfrac{1}{2}(v_\ell + v_h), \end{cases}$$

where the second line in the previous equation follows from the fact that ω_2 is a random variable that is uniformly distributed on $[0, 1]$. Figure 6.4(b) illustrates the graph of this probability function. Hence the expected payoff of bidder 1 is

$$E_1(b_1) = Eu_1\big(b_1|b_2^*(\omega_2)\big)$$

$$= P_1\big(b_1 \geq b_2^*(\omega_2)\big)(c - b_1)$$

$$= \begin{cases} 0, & \text{if } b_1 < v_\ell \\ \tfrac{2(b_1 - v_\ell)}{v_h - v_\ell}(c - b_1), & \text{if } v_\ell \leq b_1 \leq \tfrac{1}{2}(v_\ell + v_h) \\ c - b_1, & \text{if } b_1 > \tfrac{1}{2}(v_\ell + v_h), \end{cases}$$

where $c = \omega_1 v_h + (1 - \omega_1)v_\ell$. The graph of the function $E_1(\cdot)$ is shown in Figure 6.5.

It should be clear that the maximum of $E_1(\cdot)$ takes place inside the interval $\big[v_\ell, \tfrac{v_\ell + v_h}{2}\big]$. Thus the function $E_1(\cdot)$ attains its maximum when

$$E_1'(b_1) = \frac{2(c - b_1 - b_1 + v_\ell)}{v_h - v_\ell} = \frac{2[2v_\ell + (v_h - v_\ell)\omega_1 - 2b_1]}{v_h - v_\ell} = 0.$$

This implies $2v_\ell + (v_h - v_\ell)\omega_1 - 2b_1 = 0$, or $b_1 = v_\ell + \tfrac{1}{2}(v_h - v_\ell)\omega_1$. We have thus established that the rule $b_1^*(\omega_1)$ maximizes bidder 1's expected payoff. By the symmetry of the situation, a similar bidding rule is valid for bidder 2. In other words, the pair of bidding rules $(b_1^*(\omega_1), b_2^*(\omega_2))$ is indeed a Nash equilibrium of the common-value auction.

We now examine the outcome in a common-value auction when the bidders use such optimal bidding rules.

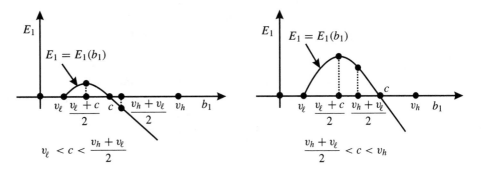

Figure 6.5

Example 6.7

A painting, which is claimed to be a genuine Renoir, is being auctioned. There is some doubt about its authenticity, and even experts are divided on the issue. If it is authentic, then the painting is worth one million; otherwise, the painting is simply a good copy and would sell for only $100,000. There are two individuals who are interested in the painting and have asked for permission to test whether the painting is genuine. They test the painting independently. The two potential buyers then will offer a bid on the basis of the signal they receive from the test. The signals are randomly distributed over [0, 1] in a uniform way, and the joint density function of the value of the painting and the signal is given by

$$f(v, \omega) = \begin{cases} \omega & \text{if } v = 1,000,000 \\ 1 - \omega & \text{if } v = 100,000 . \end{cases}$$

After the two bidders conducted their tests, bidder 1 received the signal $\omega_1 = \frac{1}{2}$ and bidder 2 received the signal $\omega_2 = \frac{3}{4}$. If the bidders use their Nash equilbrium bidding rules, then bidder 1 will bid

$$b_1 = v_\ell + \tfrac{1}{2}(v_h + v_\ell)\omega_1 = \$100,000 + \$225,000 = \$325,000 .$$

Bidder 2 will bid $b_2 = \$100,000 + \$337,500 = \$437,500$. Bidder 2 then wins the auction and pays $437,500.

Notice that the amount that the auctioneer gets depends on the signal that the winner receives.

We now go on to discuss the general case of n bidders, all of whom bid independently after receiving their own private signals about the value of the object. As in the two-bidder case, we assume that it is commonly known that the object takes two values, v_ℓ and v_h. Let $(b_1, \ldots, b_n)$ be the vector of bids. As before, we let

$$m_{-i} = \max\{b_j \colon j \neq i\} .$$

Also recall that the expected payoff of bidder i is

$$E_i(b_1, \ldots, b_n) = \begin{cases} \frac{1}{r}[E(v|\omega_i) - b_i], & \text{if bidder } i \text{ is among } r \text{ finalists} \\ 0, & \text{otherwise} . \end{cases}$$

As before, the symmetry of the situation suggests that it might be possible to find a symmetric Nash equilibrium. It turns out that one can establish the following basic equilibrium property of common-value auctions.

Bidding Rules in an n-Bidder Common-Value Auction

Assume that in an n-bidder common-value auction the bidders observe signals that are independent random variables that are uniformly distributed over the interval [0, 1]. Then the linear bidding rules

$$b_i = v_\ell + \tfrac{n-1}{n}(v_h - v_\ell)\omega_i , \quad i = 1, \ldots, n,$$

form a symmetric Nash equilibrium for the common-value auction.

1. Consider an n-bidder common-value auction in which the bidders observe signals that are independent random variables uniformly distributed over the interval $[0, 1]$. Assume that each bidder i uses the linear bidding rule $b_i = v_\ell + \frac{n-1}{n}(v_h - v_\ell)\omega_i$.

   a. Show that the probability of bidder i winning the auction is

   $$P_i(b_i > m_{-i}) = \begin{cases} 0, & \text{if } b_i < v_\ell \\ (\frac{n}{n-1})^{n-1}\frac{(b_i-v_\ell)^{n-1}}{(v_h-v_\ell)^{n-1}}, & \text{if } v_\ell \le b_i \le v_\ell + \frac{n-1}{n}(v_h - v_\ell) \\ 1, & \text{if } b_i > v_\ell + \frac{n-1}{n}(v_h - v_\ell), \end{cases}$$

   where $m_{-i} = \max\{b_j: j \ne i\}$.

   b. Show that the expected payoff of bidder i from bidding b_i is given by

   $$E_i(b_i|m_{-i}) = \begin{cases} 0 & \text{if } b_i < v_\ell \\ (\frac{n}{n-1})^{n-1}\frac{(b_i-v_\ell)^{n-1}(c_i-b_i)}{(v_h-v_\ell)^{n-1}}, & \text{if } v_\ell \le b_i \le v_\ell + \frac{n-1}{n}(v_h - v_\ell) \\ c_i - b_i, & \text{if } b_i > v_\ell + \frac{n-1}{n}(v_h - v_\ell), \end{cases}$$

   where $c_i = v_h\omega_i + (1 - \omega_i)v_\ell$.

   c. Sketch the graphs of the functions $P_i(b_i > m_{-i})$ and $E_i(b_i|m_{-i})$.

2. Assume that in an n-bidder common-value auction the bidders observe signals that are independent random variables uniformly distributed over the interval $[0, 1]$. Show that the symmetric linear bidding rules

   $$b_i = v_\ell + \frac{n-1}{n}(v_h - v_\ell)\omega_i, \quad i = 1, \ldots, n,$$

   form a Nash equilibrium for the common-value auction.

3. Consider a common-value auction with two bidders and an object that is known to take only two possible values, v_ℓ and v_h. Bidders observe signals that are independent realizations of random variables that are uniformly distributed on the interval $[0, 1]$, and bidder 2 uses a linear rule $b_2(\omega_2) = a_2 + m_2\omega_2$, where $v_\ell \le a_2$, $m_2 > 0$, and $a_2 + m_2 \le v_h$. What should be the bidding rule $b_1(\omega_1)$ of bidder 1 that is the best response to $b_2(\omega_2)$?

4. Consider a two-bidder common-value auction in which the joint density function is given by

   $$f(v, \omega) = \begin{cases} \frac{2}{\pi}e^{-v(1+\omega^2)}, & \text{if } v \ge 0 \text{ and } \omega \ge 0 \\ 0, & \text{otherwise}. \end{cases}$$

   a. Compute the conditional expected value $E(v|\omega)$.
   [Answer: $E(v|\omega) = (1 + \omega^2)^{-3}$.]

   b. Assume that player 2 uses the rule $b_2 = \omega_2$ and player 1 knows that ω_2 is a random variable that is uniformly distributed on the interval $[0, 1]$. Compute the expected payoff of player 1 and sketch its graph. [Answer:

   $$Eu_1(b_1|b_2) = \begin{cases} 0, & \text{if } b_1 < 0 \\ b_1[(1 + \omega_1^2)^{-3} - b_1], & \text{if } 0 \le b_1 \le 1 \\ (1 + \omega_1^2)^{-3} - b_1, & \text{if } b_1 > 1. \end{cases}$$

   c. What is the best response bidding rule of player 1 under the assumptions of part (b)?
   [Answer: $b_1(\omega_1) = \frac{1}{2}(1 + \omega_1^2)^{-3}$.]

BARGAINING

In the preceding chapter we used game-theoretic arguments to understand auctions of various kinds. We saw that auctions are special types of markets in which buyers bid for an object. However, there are many other forms of markets in which, instead of buyers simply bidding for the good, buyers and sellers actually make offers and counteroffers. To analyze and understand such markets, we need a different approach from the one used in the preceding chapter. In this chapter, we discuss theories of bargaining and trade. The housing market as well as the market for automobiles are good examples of markets in which the good is traded only after the buyer and the seller have reached an agreement on the price. In these cases, the agreement is reached only after a certain amount of bargaining.

When one enters the housing market, say as a buyer, the individual looks at houses that are for sale at some listed price. The buyer then makes a decision about which of these houses is the most desirable and within the individual's budget. Once the decision is made, the buyer makes an offer to the seller, usually at a price lower than the listed price. The seller then either accepts the offer or makes a counter-offer that is somewhere between the original list price and the offer of the buyer. The buyer can accept the counteroffer, or make another counteroffer, or possibly terminate the bargaining process. Another example of a market that uses such a bargaining process is the automobile market, which also starts the bargaining process with a list price quoted by the seller. Clearly, such markets are quite different from auctions and, as we shall see, can be sequential games. Theories of bargaining, however, are much more broadly used and applied, not just to understand the housing and the automobile markets, but also to solve problems such as division of a pie, sharing of common resources, and allocating costs.

We start by discussing the *axiomatic theories* of bargaining. These theories are developed on the presumption that the bargaining outcome must satisfy certain reasonable properties. Typically, these theories are used to divide an amount of money or resource among competing interests, or to allocate costs among individuals, where the allocating mechanism needs to satisfy certain notions of equity and efficiency.

In Section 7.1, we discuss *Nash's bargaining solution*. In Section 7.2, we study monotonicity in bargaining and the *Kalai–Smorodinsky solution*. In Sections 7.3 and 7.4, we investigate the *core* and the *Shapley value*, both of which can be viewed as concepts that use elements of bargaining among coalitions or groups. Finally, in Section 7.5, we discuss bargaining in which the strategic element is fundamental. Since such bargaining processes are sequential, we call them *sequential bargaining*.

7.1 THE NASH SOLUTION

Here we discuss and present a solution of the following classic problem:

- *How should a number of individuals divide a pie?*

Stated in this way, the problem seems to be fairly narrowly defined. However, understanding how to solve it provides valuable insights into how to solve more complex bargaining problems.

We start with a discussion of Nash's solution to a two-person bargaining problem. Such a bargaining problem arises in many contexts. When a buyer and a seller negotiate the price of a house, they are faced with a bargaining problem. Similarly, two trading countries bargaining over the terms of trade, a basketball player discussing his contract with the owners of a team, or two corporations arguing over the details of a joint venture are all examples of such two-person bargaining.

In all these bargaining situations, there is usually a set S of alternative outcomes, and the two sides have to agree on some element of this set. Once an agreement has been reached, the bargaining is over, and the two sides then receive their respective payoffs. In case they cannot agree, the result is usually the status quo, and we say there is *disagreement*. It is quite clear that the two sides will not engage in bargaining, unless there are outcomes in S that give both sides a higher payoff than the payoffs they receive from the status quo. Thus, if (d_1, d_2) are the payoffs from the disagreement point, then the interesting part of S consists of those outcomes that give both sides higher payoffs than the disagreement payoffs. We can thus define a bargaining problem as follows.

DEFINITION 7.1   A *two-person bargaining problem* (or *game*) consists of two persons (or players) 1 and 2, a set S of *feasible alternatives* (or *bargaining outcomes* or simply *outcomes*), and a utility function u_i on S for each player i, such that

1. $u_1(s) \geq d_1$ and $u_2(s) \geq d_2$ for every $s \in S$, and
2. At least for one $s \in S$ we have $u_1(s) > d_1$ and $u_2(s) > d_2$.

Notice that condition (2) guarantees that there is a feasible alternative that makes both players strictly better off relative to the disagreement point. This condition makes the bargaining problem nontrivial. Formally, we can write a bargaining problem as a triplet

$$\mathcal{B} = \big(S, (u_1, d_1), (u_2, d_2)\big),$$

where S, u_1, and u_2 satisfy properties (1) and (2) of Definition 7.1.

Now notice that to every alternative $s \in S$ there corresponds a pair of utilities $\big(u_1(s),$ $u_2(s)\big)$. Such a pair will be called a *utility allocation*. Thus, with every bargaining game, we can associate its set of utility allocations

$$\mathcal{U} = \big\{(u_1(s), u_2(s))\colon s \in S\big\}.$$

In case we need to designate to which game $\mathcal{U}$ belongs, we shall write $\mathcal{U}_S$ instead of $\mathcal{U}$. Clearly, $\mathcal{U}$ is a subset of the $u_1 u_2$-plane. The set $\mathcal{U}$ will play an important role in our discussion in this section.

As with any game, here, too, we are interested in finding a satisfactory "solution" to the bargaining game. We formally define a *solution* for a bargaining problem to be a *rule* (i.e., a function) that assigns to each bargaining game $\mathcal{B}$ a subset $s(\mathcal{B})$ of the set of its outcomes S. We can think of the set $s(\mathcal{B})$ as the collection of all mutually satisfactory agreements of the bargaining game $\mathcal{B}$ or, simply, as the *solutions* of the bargaining game. Obviously, any such rule ought to satisfy certain reasonable conditions. We discuss below some of these conditions.

We first look at the concept of Pareto efficiency.

- *Pareto optimality or efficiency*: An outcome $s^* \in S$ is said to be *Pareto optimal* (or *Pareto efficient*) if there is no other outcome $s \in S$ satisfying

  1. $u_1(s) \geq u_1(s^*)$ and $u_2(s) \geq u_2(s^*)$, and

  2. $u_i(s) > u_i(s^*)$ for at least one player i.

A bargaining outcome that is Pareto efficient guarantees that there is no further possibility of strictly improving the utility of one of the players, while leaving the other at least as well off as she was before. In other words, when the bargaining outcome is Pareto efficient, in order to give one player more, we have to give the other player less.

DEFINITION 7.2   A solution rule $s(\cdot)$ is said to be *Pareto optimal* if for every game $\mathcal{B}$ the set $s(\mathcal{B})$ consists of Pareto optimal outcomes.

Another property that a bargaining solution rule ought to have is the independence of irrelevant alternatives.

- *Independence of Irrelevant Alternatives*: A solution rule $s(\cdot)$ is said to be *independent of irrelevant alternatives* if for every bargaining game $\mathcal{B} = \big(S, (u_1, d_1),$ $(u_2, d_2)\big)$ and for every subset T of S satisfying $(d_1, d_2) \in \mathcal{U}_T$ and $s(\mathcal{B}) \subseteq T$, we have

$$s(\mathcal{B}_T) = s(\mathcal{B})$$

where $\mathcal{B}_T$ is the bargaining game

$$\mathcal{B}_T = \big(T, (u_1, d_1), (u_2, d_2)\big).$$

This condition captures the intuition that any acceptable bargaining solution rule should remain acceptable if we throw away alternatives that have already been considered to be less desirable by both players.

It can also be argued that the bargaining solution should be independent of changes in the scale of the utility functions. This then leads us to the following property.

- *Independence of Linear Transformations*: A bargaining solution $s(\cdot)$ is said to be *independent of linear transformations* if for any bargaining game

$$\mathcal{B} = \big(S, (u_1, d_1), (u_2, d_2)\big)$$

and any linear utility functions of the form $v_i = a_i + b_i u_i$, where the a_i and b_i are constants with $b_i > 0$ for each i, the bargaining game

$$\mathcal{B}^* = \big(S, (v_1, b_1 d_1 + a_1), (v_2, b_2 d_2 + a_2)\big)$$

satisfies $s(\mathcal{B}^*) = s(\mathcal{B})$.

This guarantees that the bargaining solution rule will not be affected by changing the scale or units in which we measure utility. In other words, the solution should not be sensitive to linear transformations of the utility functions.

We now proceed to describe a solution rule that satisfies all these conditions. We start by associating to each bargaining game $\mathcal{B} = \big(S, (u_1, d_1), (u_2, d_2)\big)$ the function $g_{\mathcal{B}} \colon S \to \mathbb{R}$ defined by

$$g_{\mathcal{B}}(s) = \big[u_1(s) - d_1\big]\big[u_2(s) - d_2\big]$$

and let $\sigma(\mathcal{B})$ be the set of all maximizers of the function $g_{\mathcal{B}}$; that is,

$$\sigma(\mathcal{B}) = \big\{s \in S \colon \ g_{\mathcal{B}}(s) = \max_{t \in S} g_{\mathcal{B}}(t)\big\}.$$

Note here that when $g_{\mathcal{B}}$ does not have any maximizer over the set S, then $\sigma(\mathcal{B}) = \emptyset$, the empty set.

We shall call $\sigma(\cdot)$ *the* Nash solution rule *and for any bargaining game* $\mathcal{B}$ *we shall refer to the members (if there are any) of* $\sigma(\mathcal{B})$ *as the* Nash solutions *of* $\mathcal{B}$.

A nice mathematical property of $\mathcal{U}$ that guarantees that $\sigma(\mathcal{B})$ is nonempty is that of compactness. The set of utility allocations $\mathcal{U}$ is said to be *compact* if it is bounded (i.e., it is contained inside a circle or a box) and closed (i.e., it contains its boundary points). Some

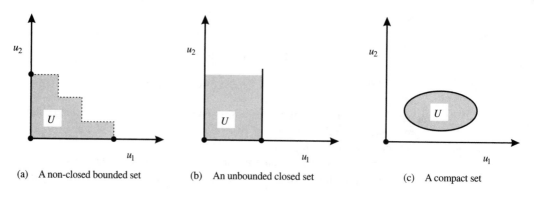

Figure 7.1

examples of the set $\mathcal{U}$ are shown in Figure 7.1. The compactness assumption guarantees that continuous functions on $\mathcal{U}$ always attain their maxima and minima. We formally state this important property here.

- If $f : X \to \mathbb{R}$ is a continuous function on a compact set X, then there exist x_1, x_2 in X such that

$$f(x_1) \le f(x) \le f(x_2)$$

holds for all $x \in X$.

So, if the set of utility allocations $\mathcal{U} = \big\{(u_1(s), u_2(s)) : s \in S\big\}$ of a bargaining game $\mathcal{B}$ is a compact set, then the continuous function $g : \mathcal{U} \to \mathbb{R}$, defined by

$$g(u_1, u_2) = (u_1 - d_1)(u_2 - d_2),$$

has at least one maximizer. That is, there exists some $(u_1^*, u_2^*) \in \mathcal{U}$ satisfying

$$g(u_1, u_2) \le g(u_1^*, u_2^*)$$

for all $(u_1, u_2) \in \mathcal{U}$. Now notice that any $s^* \in S$ such that $u_1(s^*) = u_1^*$ and $u_2(s^*) = u_2^*$ satisfies $s^* \in \sigma(\mathcal{B})$. This implies that $\sigma(\mathcal{B})$ is nonempty, which means that any bargaining game $\mathcal{B}$ with a compact set of utility allocations has at least one Nash solution.

We are now ready to state the first part of the central result of this section, which is due to J. Nash.[1] It describes the basic properties of the Nash solution rule.

Theorem 7.3 (Nash)   On the class of bargaining games with compact sets of utility allocations, the Nash rule $\sigma(\cdot)$ is Pareto optimal, independent of irrelevant alternatives, and independent of linear transformations.

[1]"The Bargaining Problem," *Econometrica* **18** (1950), 155–162.

Proof: Assume that $\mathcal{B}$ is a bargaining game having a compact set of utility allocations $\mathcal{U}$ and let

$$M = \max\{g_\mathcal{B}(s):\ s \in S\},$$

where $g_\mathcal{B}(s) = [u_1(s) - d_1][u_2(s) - d_2]$. Let $s^* \in \sigma(\mathcal{B})$, i.e, $g_\mathcal{B}(s^*) = M$. The geometry of the situation can be seen in Figure 7.2.

To see that s^* is Pareto optimal, suppose by way of contradiction that there exists some $s \in S$ such that $u_1(s) > u_1(s^*)$ and $u_2(s) \geq u_2(s^*)$. Since there is a feasible alternative $t \in S$ satisfying $u_1(t) > d_1$ and $u_2(t) > d_2$, it follows that $g_\mathcal{B}(s^*) \geq g_\mathcal{B}(t) > 0$. Therefore,

$$u_1(s) > u_1(s^*) > d_1 \quad \text{and} \quad u_2(s) \geq u_2(s^*) > d_2.$$

Consequently,

$$\begin{aligned} g_\mathcal{B}(s) &= [u_1(s) - d_1][u_2(s) - d_2] \\ &> [u_1(s^*) - d_1][u_2(s^*) - d_2] \\ &= g_\mathcal{B}(s^*), \end{aligned}$$

contradicting the fact that s^* is a maximizer of $g_\mathcal{B}$. Hence s^* is Pareto optimal. Therefore, every outcome in $\sigma(\mathcal{B})$ is Pareto optimal.

To verify that $\sigma(\cdot)$ is independent of irrelevant alternatives, we observe that if $\sigma(\mathcal{B})$ consists of all maximizers of $g_\mathcal{B}$ over S, then certainly this set will not change if we consider the set of all maximizers of $g_\mathcal{B}$ over a subset T of S satisfying $(d_1, d_2) \in \mathcal{U}_T$ and $\sigma(\mathcal{B}) \subseteq T$.

To establish the independence of linear transformations, for each player i let $v_i(s) = b_i u_i(s) + a_i$ be an arbitrary linear transformation of the utility function u_i with $b_i > 0$. Let $\mathcal{B}^* = (S, (v_1, b_1 d_1 + a_1), (v_2, b_2 d_2 + a_2))$ and

$$g_{\mathcal{B}^*}(s) = [v_1(s) - b_1 d_1 - a_1][v_2(s) - b_2 d_2 - a_2].$$

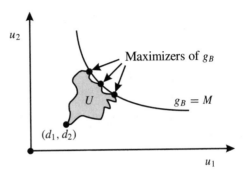

Figure 7.2

Then

$$g_{\mathcal{B}^*}(s) = \left[v_1(s) - b_1 d_1 - a_1\right]\left[v_2(s) - b_2 d_2 - a_2\right]$$
$$= \left[b_1 u_1(s) + a_1 - b_1 d_1 - a_1\right]\left[b_2 u_2(s) + a_2 - b_2 d_2 - a_2\right]$$
$$= b_1 b_2 \left[u_1(s) - d_1\right]\left[u_2(s) - d_2\right]$$
$$= b_1 b_2 g_{\mathcal{B}}(s).$$

Thus an outcome $s^* \in S$ maximizes $g_{\mathcal{B}}$ if and only if it maximizes $g_{\mathcal{B}^*}$. This implies $\sigma(\mathcal{B}^*) = \sigma(\mathcal{B})$.

To obtain further properties of the Nash solution rule, we need the notions of convexity and symmetry.

DEFINITION 7.4   The set of utility allocations $\mathcal{U}$ of a bargaining game is said to be:

a. *Convex*, if it contains every point on the line segment joining any two of its points, and
b. *Symmetric*, if $(u_1, u_2) \in \mathcal{U}$ implies $(u_2, u_1) \in \mathcal{U}$.

Geometrically, symmetry means that the set $\mathcal{U}$ is symmetric with respect to the bisector line $u_1 = u_2$. These properties are illustrated in the sets shown in Figure 7.3.

In order to introduce a fourth condition on the solution rules, we need the following definition.

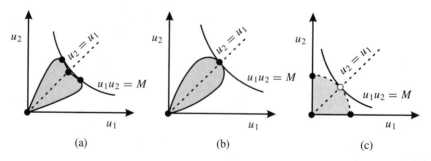

(a)   (b)   (c)

Figure 7.3   (a) A symmetric, compact and nonconvex set. (b) A symmetric, compact and convex set. (c) A symmetric, nonclosed, bounded and convex set.

DEFINITION 7.5   A bargaining game $\mathcal{B}$ is said to be:

1. *Convex*, if its set of utility allocations is convex and compact.
2. *Symmetric*, if $d_1 = d_2$ and its set of utility allocations is symmetric and compact.

We can now state the fourth condition.

- *Symmetry: A solution rule $s(\cdot)$ is said to be* symmetric *if for every symmetric bargaining game $\mathcal{B}$ we have $u_1(s) = u_2(s)$ for each $s \in s(\mathcal{B})$.*

That is, a bargaining solution rule is symmetric, provided that at each symmetric bargaining game it treats both players equally in the sense that, if the players receive the same disagreement payoff, then they should receive equal payoffs at any agreement point.

The second part of Nash's theorem is stated below.

Theorem 7.6 (Nash)   If $\mathcal{B}$ is a convex bargaining game, then there exists exactly one utility allocation (u_1^*, u_2^*) such that

$$\sigma(\mathcal{B}) = \left\{ s \in S: \ u_1(s) = u_1^* \ \text{and} \ u_2(s) = u_2^* \right\}.$$

If $\mathcal{B}$ is also symmetric, then $u_1^* = u_2^*$.

In particular, the Nash solution rule $\sigma(\cdot)$ on the class of convex and symmetric bargaining games, besides being Pareto optimal, independent of irrelevant alternatives, and independent of linear transformations, is also symmetric.

Proof: Let $\mathcal{B}$ be a convex bargaining game and consider the continuous function $g: \mathcal{U} \to \mathbb{R}$ defined by

$$g(u_1, u_2) = (u_1 - d_1)(u_2 - d_2).$$

Since $\mathcal{U}$ is compact and g is continuous there exists a maximizer of g, say, (u_1^*, u_2^*). Now assume that there exists another maximizer $(\bar{u}_1, \bar{u}_2)$ of g different from (u_1^*, u_2^*). The convexity of the set of utility allocations $\mathcal{U}$ implies $\left(\frac{1}{2}(u_1^* + \bar{u}_1), \frac{1}{2}(u_2^* + \bar{u}_2)\right)$ is also a utility allocation that satisfies $g\left(\frac{1}{2}(u_1^* + \bar{u}_1), \frac{1}{2}(u_2^* + \bar{u}_2)\right) > g(u_1^*, u_2^*)$, which is a contradiction. For details of the last argument see Exercise 11 at the end of this section.

For the last part, assume that the convex bargaining game $\mathcal{B}$ is also symmetric. Since the Nash solution rule is independent of linear transformations, we can normalize the utility function so that $d_1 = d_2 = 0$. Thus $g_{\mathcal{B}}(s) = u_1(s)u_2(s)$. This means that in order to maximize this function, it suffices to maximize the function $f(x, y) = xy$ over the compact, convex, and symmetric set $\mathcal{U}$. The mathematical notions of compactness and continuity guarantee that there is a maximizer $(x_0, y_0) \in \mathcal{U}$. We claim that (x_0, y_0) is uniquely determined and $x_0 = y_0$.

To see this, notice first that the symmetry of $\mathcal{U}$ implies that (y_0, x_0) is also a utility allocation. From the convexity of $\mathcal{U}$ it follows that

$$\tfrac{1}{2}(x_0, y_0) + \tfrac{1}{2}(y_0, x_0) = \left(\tfrac{1}{2}(x_0 + y_0), \tfrac{1}{2}(x_0 + y_0)\right)$$

belongs to $\mathcal{U}$. Therefore,

$$\tfrac{1}{2}(x_0 + y_0) \times \tfrac{1}{2}(x_0 + y_0) \leq x_0 y_0.$$

Working the algebra, we get $x_0^2 + 2x_0 y_0 + y_0^2 \leq 4x_0 y_0$. This implies

$$(x_0 - y_0)^2 = x_0^2 - 2x_0 y_0 + y_0^2 \leq 0$$

and consequently $(x_0 - y_0)^2 = 0$. Hence, $x_0 = y_0$.

We have just shown that there exists a unique utility allocation of the form (x_0, x_0) that maximizes the function $f(x, y) = xy$ over $\mathcal{B}$. Now it is easy to see that $\sigma(\mathcal{B}) = \{s \in S: u_1(s) = u_2(s) = x_0\}$.

The geometric interpretation of the conclusions of this theorem can be seen in Figure 7.4. Let us use a simple example to examine the nature of the Nash solution rule.

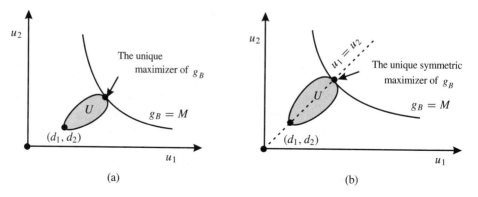

Figure 7.4 (a) A convex bargaining game. (b) A convex symmetric bargaining game.

Example 7.7

Suppose two individuals are bargaining over a sum of money, say, $100. If they cannot agree on how to divide the money, none of them gets any money. The bargaining set S in this case consists of all pairs (m_1, m_2) of non-negative real numbers such that $m_1 + m_2 \leq 100$, where m_i denotes the amount of money that player i receives. That is,

$$S = \left\{(m_1, m_2): m_1 \geq 0, \ m_2 \geq 0, \ \text{and} \ m_1 + m_2 \leq 100\right\}.$$

The utility that any individual gets is measured by the amount of money she receives. Therefore, the utility functions of the players are

$$u_1(m_1, m_2) = m_1 \quad \text{and} \quad u_2(m_1, m_2) = m_2.$$

Notice that if there is disagreement, the players get $d_1 = d_2 = 0$. It is clear from this that the bargaining game is convex and symmetric. Also, notice that for this bargaining game we have

$$g(m_1, m_2) = u_1(m_1, m_2)u_2(m_1, m_2) = m_1 m_2.$$

By Theorem 7.6, there exists a unique maximizer of g which is the only Nash solution of the bargaining game. This solution is Pareto optimal, independent of irrelevant alternatives, independent of linear transformations, and symmetric. This unique maximizer of g is $m_1^* = m_2^* = 50$. Thus the Nash solution of the bargaining game is to give $50 to each; see Figure 7.5.

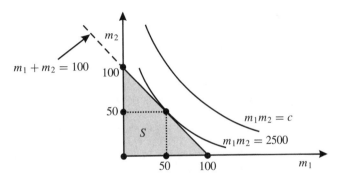

Figure 7.5

The power of Theorem 7.6 lies in its assertion that every symmetric convex bargaining game has a solution that satisfies all the desired conditions. This is best seen by going back to Example 7.7. In that example any division (m_1, m_2) of the $100 that satisfies $m_1 + m_2 = 100$ is Pareto optimal, independent of irrelevant alternatives, and invariant to linear transformations. However, the only pair that would also satisfy symmetry is $m_1 = m_2 = $50. This brings to focus very sharply the message of Nash's theorem, which asserts that the Nash solution rule provides a unique symmetric solution to every convex and symmetric bargaining game. Moreover, one can establish the remarkable fact that Nash's solution rule is the one and only solution rule with this property; see Exercise 12 at the end of this section.

Let us look at another example of a bargaining problem.

Example 7.8

An individual has listed her house at $120,000. Her reservation price for the house is $100,000. She knows that at any price less than $100,000 she is better off not selling the house. A potential buyer looks at the house and is willing to buy it at the price of \$120,000, which also happens to coincide with his reservation price. However the buyer would, of course, be better off getting the house at less than \$120,000.

We clearly have a bargaining problem. In this case there are two individuals who can make a potential net gain of \$20,000 and so the question is how should the two divide this among themselves. If the payoffs of the individuals are simply the money they receive, then (according to Nash's solution) the two individuals would agree to divide the amount \$20,000 equally and complete the transaction at a price of \$110,000.

Thus Nash's bargaining solution provides an intuitively satisfactory and sharp answer to a pricing problem in the housing market.

In the example that we just saw, there is a unique Nash solution to the bargaining problem that satisfies the conditions of Pareto efficiency, independence of irrelevant alternatives, independence from linear transformations, and symmetry. Indeed, in the above example, the Nash solution gives us exactly what we think the solution ought to be. In many cases, however, this approach to the bargaining problem fails to provide a satisfactory solution. The following example shows why this may happen. The example also highlights the importance of convexity in Theorem 7.6.

Example 7.9

Suppose a couple is trying to decide whether they should go to a football game or to a Broadway show. The set of outcomes is thus given by

$$S = \{\text{go to football, go to broadway, disagreement}\}.$$

In case they go to the Broadway show, the utility of individual A is $u_A = 4$, and the utility of individual B is $u_B = 1$. If they go to the football game, their utilities are reversed, and $u_A = 1$ and $u_B = 4$. In case they disagree, the payoffs are $u_A = u_B = 0$.

Clearly, when we use the approach of Theorem 7.3 to find the solution to the bargaining problem, we end up with two answers:

1. Either both go to the broadway show, or
2. Both go to the football game.

This is all we can say if we use Theorem 7.3. But in this case one can argue that the two individuals should really toss a coin to determine where they should go. But then, should the coin be a fair coin? That is, should they decide to go to one or the other place with a probability of one-half?

If the coin chooses the alternative of going to the Broadway show with a probability p, and the alternative of going to the football game with a probability of $1 - p$, then the expected payoffs of the two individual are given by

$$Eu_A = 4p + (1 - p) = 3p + 1 \quad \text{and} \quad Eu_B = p + 4(1 - p) = 4 - 3p.$$

Now if we choose p to maximize $(Eu_A - 0)(Eu_B - 0)$, then p maximizes the function

$$g(p) = (3p + 1)(4 - 3p) = -9p^2 + 9p + 4.$$

The maximum is obtained when p satisfies the first-order condition

$$g'(p) = -18p + 9 = 0,$$

which gives $p = \frac{1}{2}$. Thus we find that the individuals should indeed choose a fair coin. This seems to be a reasonable way of solving the bargaining problem, and we find that allowing individuals to extend the set of alternatives to include *joint randomization* or *correlation* leads to a more satisfactory solution to the bargaining problem.

The notion of correlation that we introduced in the preceding example is closely associated with the convexity of the set of utility allocations

$$\mathcal{U} = \big\{(u_1(s), u_2(s)): s \in S\big\}.$$

Recall that a *probability distribution* over a collection of outcomes $\{s_1, s_2, \ldots, s_k\}$ is any vector $(p_1, p_2, \ldots, p_k)$, where $p_i \geq 0$ for each i and $\sum_{i=1}^{k} p_i = 1$. We now formally define the notion of correlation.

DEFINITION 7.10   A *correlated utility allocation* over a set of outcomes $\{s_1, s_2, \ldots, s_k\}$ with probability distribution $(p_1, p_2, \ldots, p_k)$ is the two-dimensional vector given by

$$\left(\sum_{i=1}^{k} p_i u_1(s_i), \sum_{i=1}^{k} p_i u_2(s_i) \right).$$

The set of all correlated utility allocations will be denoted by $C(\mathcal{U})$.

Notice that the probability distribution $(p_1, p_2, \ldots, p_k)$ jointly randomizes over the alternatives $(s_1, s_2, \ldots, s_k)$. In mathematical terminology, the set of all correlated utility allocations $C(\mathcal{U})$ is known as the *convex hull* of $\mathcal{U}$, and is the smallest convex set that contains $\mathcal{U}$. That is, if individuals are allowed to correlate over alternatives, then the set $\mathcal{U}$ of feasible utility allocations becomes a convex set.

We can see this quite clearly in the case of Example 7.9. The set of utility allocations is

$$\mathcal{U} = \big\{(0, 0), (1, 4), (4, 1)\big\},$$

which is shown in Figure 7.6(a).

The set of all feasible payoffs when we allow for correlation consists of all pairs (u_1, u_2) that lie inside or on the edges of the triangle with vertices $(0, 0)$, $(1, 4)$, and $(4, 1)$. This set is the shaded triangle shown in Figure 7.6(b), which is clearly a convex set.

Every point in the triangle can be obtained by properly correlating over the set $\mathcal{U}$. For instance, the correlated utility allocation when $(1, 4)$ is chosen with probability $\frac{1}{3}$, $(4, 1)$ is chosen with probability $\frac{1}{3}$, and $(0, 0)$ is chosen with probability $\frac{1}{3}$, is a point in the interior

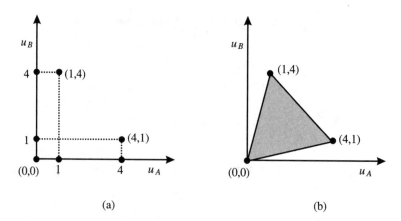

Figure 7.6

of the triangle. Thus the set of correlated utility allocations $C(\mathcal{U})$, shown in the shaded triangle of Figure 7.6(b), can be written algebraically as

$$C(\mathcal{U}) = \big\{ p(0,0) + q(4,1) + (1-p-q)(1,4): p \geq 0,\ q \geq 0,\ \text{and}\ p+q \leq 1 \big\}$$
$$= \big\{ (1-p+3q, 4-4p-3q): p \geq 0,\ q \geq 0,\ \text{and}\ p+q \leq 1 \big\}.$$

The notion of correlation extends to general sets of utility allocations. As in the case of Example 7.9, when we use correlation, the payoffs become expected payoffs to which we apply a solution rule (for instance, Nash's solution rule). The solution is then a probability distribution. For an application see Exercise 9 at the end of the section.

The Nash bargaining solution that we have discussed so far works well under the condition of symmetry. However, many bargaining games are essentially asymmetric either because of differing attitudes towards risk between the players or because of the difference in payoffs in case of a disagreement, or even because of some asymmetry in the set of utility allocations $\mathcal{U}$. In the case of differing attitudes towards risk or difference in the disagreement payoffs, the Nash solution rule still works quite well. Recall that the Nash solution set $\sigma(\mathcal{B})$ of a bargaining game $\mathcal{B}$ consists of all maximizers of the function $g_{\mathcal{B}}(s) = \big[u_1(s) - d_1\big]\big[u_2(s) - d_2\big]$:

$$\sigma(\mathcal{B}) = \Big\{ s \in S: g_{\mathcal{B}}(s) = \max_{t \in S} g_{\mathcal{B}}(t) \Big\}.$$

So a change in risk aversion will be reflected in the utility functions, and thus it will change the Nash solution accordingly. Similarly, a difference in the payoffs from a disagreement will change the d_i, and hence it will change the function $g_{\mathcal{B}}$, which in turn will affect the Nash solution. Indeed, it can be checked that when d_1 increases (due, for instance, to an outside option), then the Nash solution would increase the amount that player 1 gets. In the case of both types of asymmetries the Nash solution continues to provide a reasonable and intuitive answer to the asymmetries, because they either modify the utility function or the disagreement payoffs.

The Nash solution, however, will give unsatisfactory answers in case the set of utility allocations of the bargaining game is asymmetric. In the next section we look in detail at this weakness of the Nash solution rule and discuss an alternative solution to bargaining games that performs better when the bargaining game has an asymmetric set of utility allocations.

1. Show that every Pareto optimal bargaining outcome is independent of linear transformations.

2. Consider the function $g(m_1, m_2) = m_1 m_2$ of Example 7.7. Show that on the set of feasible alternatives

$$S = \{(m_1, m_2): m_1 \geq 0, \ m_2 \geq 0, \ \text{and} \ m_1 + m_2 \leq 100\}$$

the function g attains its maximum value only at the pair $(m_1^*, m_2^*) = (50, 50)$.

3. Consider the bargaining problem of Example 7.7. Show that each bargaining outcome in the set

$$T = \{(m_1, m_2): m_1 \geq 0, \ m_2 \geq 0, \ \text{and} \ m_1 + m_2 = 100\}$$

is Pareto optimal.

4. Consider the bargaining problem with a set of alternatives $S = (0, 1)$ (the open interval from 0 to 1) and utility functions $u_1(s) = 1 - s$ and $u_2(s) = -\ln(1 - s)$.
   a. Sketch the graphs of the utility functions.
   b. Show that every outcome is Pareto optimal.
   c. Prove that this bargaining problem has exactly one Pareto optimal and symmetric outcome. [Hint: If $t = -\ln t$, then $t \approx 0.567$.]

5. Consider the bargaining problem $\mathcal{B}$ of the preceding exercise.
   a. Sketch the set $\mathcal{U}$ of all utility allocations and show that $\mathcal{U}$ is closed but fails to be bounded, convex, and symmetric.
   b. Sketch the graph of the function $g(s) = -(1 - s) \ln(1 - s)$.
   c. Find the Nash solution set $\sigma(\mathcal{B})$.

6. Two persons are bargaining over a real estate property with the set of feasible alternatives given by

$$S = \{(s_1, s_2): s_1 \geq 0, \ s_2 \geq 0, \ \text{and} \ s_1 + s_2 \leq 1\}.$$

Their utility functions are

$$u_1(s_1, s_2) = s_1 + s_2 \quad \text{and} \quad u_2(s_1, s_2) = s_1 + \sqrt{s_2}.$$

What should be the bargaining outcome if both players are looking for a Pareto efficient solution? Also compute the payoffs of the players at this solution outcome.

7. If you examine the bargaining game of Example 7.7 carefully, you will notice that the players are risk neutral. Why? Suppose instead that player 1 is risk averse and has the utility function

$$u_1(m_1, m_2) = \sqrt{m_1}.$$

Find the Nash solution for this bargaining game. Discuss the implications for the Nash solution rule.

8. Suppose you are bargaining over the price of a Toyota Camry. The list price of the version that you want is $20,000. The invoice price is $18,000.

    a. Assuming that the utility functions are proportional to the money received, set up the bargaining game and find its Nash solution.
    b. Now suppose that a dealer located 60 miles away has agreed to sell the car at $18,500. Reformulate the bargaining game with this outside option and find its Nash solution.

9. Suppose an entrepreneur is engaged in negotiations with a venture capitalist on alternative strategies to follow. The alternatives are to: (1) invest in the business for the next five years before marketing the product, (2) develop a slightly different product within three years and market it, and (3) invest only for the next year and sell the business to a big rival firm. Consider the entrepreneur to be player 1 and the venture capitalist to be player 2. The normalized payoffs of the players from the three alternatives are (4, 1), (3, 3), and (2, 5), respectively. In case of a disagreement, there is no investment and the payoff is (0, 0).

    a. Describe the sets $\mathcal{U}$ and $C(\mathcal{U})$.
    b. Discuss the conditions of Nash's Theorem 7.6 in this case.
    c. What is the solution to the bargaining game if we apply Nash's solution rule to the set $\mathcal{U}$?
    d. What is the solution if we apply the Nash solution rule to the set $C(\mathcal{U})$?

10. For a given bargaining game $\mathcal{B} = \big(S, (u_1, d_1), (u_2, d_2)\big)$ we associate the function $h_{\mathcal{B}} \colon S \to \mathbb{R}$ defined by

$$h_{\mathcal{B}}(s) = [\, u_1(s) - d_1 \,] + [\, u_2(s) - d_2 \,],$$

and consider the set

$$\sigma_1(\mathcal{B}) = \{ s \in S \colon h_{\mathcal{B}}(s) = \max_{t \in S} h_{\mathcal{B}}(t) \}.$$

Show that $\sigma_1(\cdot)$ is a solution rule for the class of all bargaining games. What properties does $\sigma_1(\cdot)$ satisfy?

11. Complete the details of the first part of Theorem 7.6. That is, establish the following uniqueness property of the Nash solution rule. If $\mathcal{B}$ is a convex bargaining game, then there exists a unique utility allocation (u_1^*, u_2^*) such that

$$\sigma(\mathcal{B}) = \{ s \in S \colon u_1(s) = u_1^* \quad \text{and} \quad u_2(s) = u_2^* \}.$$

[Hint: Consider the function $g(u_1, u_2) = (u_1 - d_1)(u_2 - d_2)$ defined on $\mathcal{U}$, and suppose that (u_1^*, u_2^*) and $(\bar{u}_1, \bar{u}_2)$ are two maximizers of g. That is, $g(u_1^*, u_2^*) = g(\bar{u}_1, \bar{u}_2) = M$, where M is the maximum of g over $\mathcal{U}$. Now note that the point $\big(\frac{u_1^* + \bar{u}_1}{2}, \frac{u_2^* + \bar{u}_2}{2}\big)$ belongs to $\mathcal{U}$ and satisfies

$$g\left(\tfrac{u_1^* + \bar{u}_1}{2}, \tfrac{u_2^* + \bar{u}_2}{2}\right) = \tfrac{1}{2}\left[(u_1^* - d_1)(u_2^* - d_2) + (\bar{u}_1 - d_2)(\bar{u}_2 - d_2)\right]$$
$$+ \tfrac{1}{4}(u_2^* - \bar{u}_2)(\bar{u}_1 - u_1^*)$$
$$= M + \tfrac{1}{4}(u_2^* - \bar{u}_2)(\bar{u}_1 - u_1^*)$$
$$> M$$

which is a contradiction.]

12. Show that Nash's solution rule is uniquely determined in the sense that: If another solution rule $s(\cdot)$ is Pareto optimal and symmetric, and $\mathcal{B}$ is a symmetric and convex bargaining game, then

$$s(\mathcal{B}) \subseteq \sigma(\mathcal{B}),$$

which means that $s(\mathcal{B})$ and $\sigma(\mathcal{B})$ both give rise to the same unique utility allocation (u^*, u^*).

7.2 MONOTONICITY IN BARGAINING

In the previous section we discussed the Nash solution rule to bargaining games. We saw there that the Nash solution rule provided an intuitively appealing solution to symmetric bargaining games. We also mentioned that the Nash solution rule works quite well for bargaining games with asymmetries in risk aversion and disagreement points. However, it may fail to provide a satisfactory solution to bargaining games when the set of utility allocations is asymmetric. In some of these cases the Nash solution rule seems quite unreasonable. The most common situation in which the Nash solution rule fails to provide a satisfactory result is one in which the "pie" either contracts or expands in a way that makes the set of utility allocations asymmetric. A classic example is the amount received by creditors in a bankruptcy case.

In such cases, as long as the business is solvent, the creditors can expect to get their loans repaid in proportion to the size of the loan. However, when the business becomes insolvent, the Nash solution rule prescribes an equal division of the remaining assets among the creditors. This division rule, however, makes little sense when the sizes of the outstanding loans are different. It makes a lot of sense in these cases to argue that the assets ought to be divided in proportion to the size of the loans.

In this section, we study an alternative solution rule for bargaining games that does not satisfy the condition of symmetry but satisfies a monotonicity condition. We shall see that this solution rule for bargaining games is much more appealing as a solution rule to bargaining games with asymmetries. The next example illustrates what happens to the Nash solution rule in the case of a bankruptcy.

Example 7.11 (A Bankruptcy Game)

Bankruptcy cases arise usually when the assets of a firm become worth less than its liabilities. Thus, for instance, bankruptcy cases may arise when Savings & Loans make loans that are backed by collaterals that have depreciated in value, when the value of the real estate company owned by a developer falls below that of the total amount of the developer's debts, or when the assets of a firm become worth less than the total debts of the firm. In all these cases, if K denotes the value of the assets, and D_i the debt owed by the firm to creditor i, then bankruptcy occurs when

$$K < \sum_i D_i .$$

Because the value of the assets is now less than the amount that is owed to the creditors, the firm cannot fulfill its financial obligations and declares bankruptcy. The problem that now arises is about the fraction of K each creditor is given.

Assume that there are two creditors and the bankruptcy condition $K < D_1 + D_2$ is satisfied. The resulting bargaining game has the following characteristics. Its bargaining set is

$$S = \left\{ (c_1, c_2) \colon c_1 + c_2 \le K \right\} .$$

If the creditors are risk neutral, then we may represent their utilities as

$$u_1(c_1, c_2) = c_1 \quad \text{and} \quad u_2(c_1, c_2) = c_2 ,$$

that is, as functions of the amount of money they get. In this case, the disagreement point is $(-D_1, -D_2)$, in which the creditors receive none of the assets and are left with loans that are never repaid. Since the Nash solution is invariant to linear transformations, we can shift the disagreement point to $(0, 0)$. The problem is then reduced to a bargaining problem of sharing K dollars between two risk-neutral players with the constraint that creditor 1 cannot receive more than D_1 and creditor 2 cannot receive more than D_2. We can assume that $D_1 > D_2$ and distinguish two cases.

CASE I.
$D_2 > \frac{K}{2}$

In this case, the Nash solution rule gives each player $\frac{K}{2}$ dollars; see Figure 7.7(a).

CASE II.
$D_2 \le \frac{K}{2}$

Since $D_1 + D_2 > K$, it easily follows that we have the bargaining game shown in Figure 7.7(b). Observe that creditor 2 is paid off fully and creditor 1 gets $K - D_2$.

The resolution of the bankruptcy problem that is prescribed by Nash's solution is more than a little discomforting, as it treats both creditors absolutely equally, even though one may be owed a much larger sum. However, if $D_1 > D_2$, then it can be argued that creditor 1 should get a larger share of the assets K than creditor 2. Indeed, one may argue that the amount of the assets K of the firm should be divided among the two creditors in proportion to the claims of the creditors. That is, the division (c_1^*, c_2^*) of the assets K should satisfy

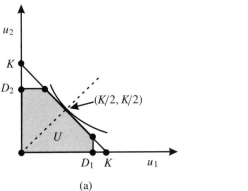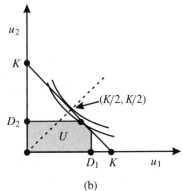

(a)   (b)

Figure 7.7

$$\frac{D_1}{D_2} = \frac{c_1^*}{c_2^*} \quad \text{and} \quad c_1^* + c_2^* = K \,.$$

Solving this system gives $c_1^* = \frac{D_1}{D_1+D_2} K$ and $c_2^* = \frac{D_2}{D_1+D_2} K$.

In other words, K is divided among the two creditors in proportion to the debt that the creditors are owed. For instance, if $K =$ \$1 million, $D_1 =$ \$1 million, and $D_2 =$ \$500,000, then the rule described above would give \$666,667 to creditor 1 and \$333,333 to creditor 2. In contrast to this, Nash's bargaining solution will give \$500,000 to each of the two creditors. Obviously, Nash's solution here does not seem to be quite acceptable.

If one examines Nash's solution to the bankruptcy problem carefully, it becomes clear that when the bargaining problem is fundamentally asymmetric, as is the case in the example above, then the Nash solution will often provide unreasonable answers. The condition that causes this difficulty with the Nash solution is symmetry. It is possible to replace the condition of symmetry with an alternate condition. One of the more interesting among these alternative conditions is that of *monotonicity*. This property requires a bargaining solution to give at least as much utility to a player when the set of bargaining alternatives expands as she is given in the original bargaining game. Formally, we can state this condition as follows.

- *Monotonicity*: A solution rule $s(\cdot)$ is said to be *monotone* if for any bargaining game $\mathcal{B} = \big(S, (u_1, d_1), (u_2, d_2)\big)$ and any subset T of S the solution set $s(\mathcal{B})$ dominates the solution set $s(\mathcal{B}_T)$ of the bargaining game $\mathcal{B}_T = \big(T, (u_1, d_1), (u_2, d_2)\big)$ in the following sense: For each $s \in T$ there exists some $s' \in S$ satisfying

$$u_1(s') \geq u_1(s) \quad \text{and} \quad u_2(s') \geq u_2(s) \,.$$

We first show that Nash's solution rule does not satisfy monotonicity. Examine the bargaining games shown in Figure 7.8. In Figure 7.8(a) the bargaining game is symmetric and the Nash solution rule leads to the payoff pair $(2, 2)$. In Figure 7.8(b), the bargaining game is *not* symmetric, and the Nash solution rule leads to the payoff pair $(1, 4)$. This shows that even though the set of utility allocations $\mathcal{U}_T$ of the game in Figure 7.8(a) is a strict subset of the set of utility allocations $\mathcal{U}$ of the game in Figure 7.8(b), player 1 gets less under the Nash solution rule in that game. Thus, in situations with asymmetries, as found in bargaining games of the type shown in Figure 7.8(b), we need to use a slightly different set of criteria. A solution rule that performs well under asymmetries was introduced by E. Kalai and M. Smorodinsky.[2] This solution rule is the subject of the discussion that follows.

In order to understand this rule, we need some preliminary discussion. For simplicity, we shall assume that the sets of utility allocations of our bargaining games lie in the positive orthant of the $u_1 u_2$-plane.

Given a bargaining game $\mathcal{B} = \big(S, (u_1, d_1), (u_2, d_2)\big)$, let

$$\mu_1 = \max_{s \in S} u_1(s) \quad \text{and} \quad \mu_2 = \max_{s \in S} u_2(s),$$

whenever the maxima exist. (If the set of utility allocations of $\mathcal{B}$ is compact, then it should be clear that μ_1 and μ_2 are well defined.) The *Kalai–Smorodinsky line* (or the KS-*line*) of the bargaining game $\mathcal{B}$ is the line in the $u_1 u_2$-plane passing through the origin and having slope $k = \frac{\mu_2}{\mu_1}$. That is, the equation of the KS line is given by

$$u_2 = k u_1.$$

If $(d_1, d_2) \neq (0, 0)$, then the KS line is, of course, the line of the $u_1 u_2$-plane passing through the points (d_1, d_2) and (μ_1, μ_2). In this case the KS line has slope $k = \frac{\mu_2 - d_2}{\mu_1 - d_1}$, and its equation is given by

$$u_2 - d_2 = k(u_1 - d_1).$$

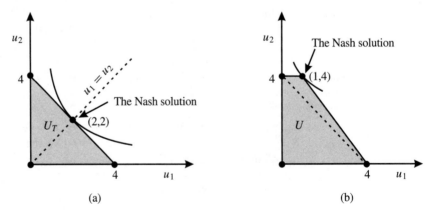

(a)   (b)

Figure 7.8

[2]"Other solutions to Nash's bargaining problem," *Econometrica* **43** (1975), 513–518.

The *Kalai–Smorodinsky utility allocation* (or the KS-*utility allocation*) of the bargaining game $\mathcal{B}$ is the "farthest northeast point $(\overline{u}_1, \overline{u}_2)$ on the KS line that lies in the set of utility allocations $\mathcal{U}$." Formally, if we consider the set $\mathcal{K} = \{ s \in S : (u_1(s), ku_2(s)) \in \mathcal{U} \}$, then

$$\overline{u}_1 = \max_{s \in \mathcal{K}} u_1(s) \quad \text{and} \quad \overline{u}_2 = k\overline{u}_1 .$$

Its geometric meaning is shown in Figure 7.9. If $\mathcal{K} = \emptyset$ (the empty set), then the bargaining game does not have a KS utility allocation. It should also be clear that a bargaining game can have at most one KS utility allocation. That is, a bargaining game $\mathcal{B}$ either has exactly one KS utility allocation or else it has none. If a bargaining game has a compact set of utility allocations $\mathcal{U}$, then [given that $(d_1, d_2) \in \mathcal{U}$] it easily follows that it has a KS utility allocation. In other words, a bargaining game with a compact set of utility allocations has exactly one KS utility allocation.

We now define the *Kalai–Smorodinsky solution rule* (or simply the KS *solution rule*) $\kappa(\cdot)$ by

$$\kappa(\mathcal{B}) = \{ s \in S : u_1(s) = \overline{u}_1 \quad \text{and} \quad u_2(s) = \overline{u}_2 \} .$$

If the bargaining game $\mathcal{B}$ does not have a KS utility allocation, then $\kappa(\mathcal{B}) = \emptyset$.

Below we list the basic properties of the Kalai–Smorodinsky solution rule.

- The Kalai–Smorodinsky solution rule is independent of linear transformations but fails to be independent of irrelevant alternatives.
- Every convex bargaining game $\mathcal{B}$ has a KS utility allocation, and the Kalai–Smorodinsky solution set $\kappa(\mathcal{B})$ is nonempty and consists of Pareto optimal bargaining outcomes.
- If $\mathcal{B}$ is a convex and symmetric bargaining game, then the Kalai–Smorodinsky and Nash solutions of $\mathcal{B}$ coincide:

$$\kappa(\mathcal{B}) = \sigma(\mathcal{B}) .$$

The bargaining game shown in Figure 7.10 demonstrates that the Kalai–Smorodinsky solution rule is not independent of irrelevant alternatives.

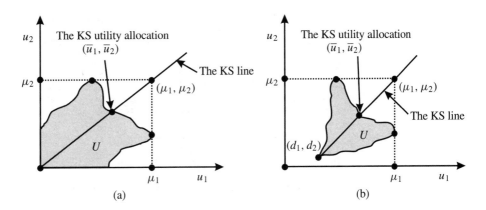

(a)   (b)

Figure 7.9

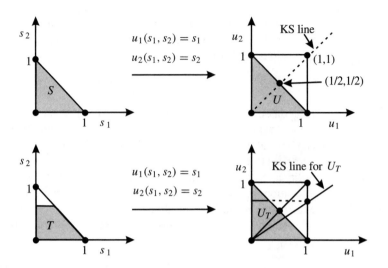

Figure 7.10   Failure of independence of irrelevant alternatives.

To see that the Kalai–Smorodinsky solution rule is independent of linear transformations, let $\mathcal{B} = \big(S, (u_1, d_1), (u_2, d_2)\big)$ be a bargaining game. The KS line of this bargaining game $\mathcal{B}$ has slope $k = \frac{\mu_2 - d_2}{\mu_1 - d_1}$, and so the KS solution is

$$\kappa(\mathcal{B}) = \big\{s \in S: u_1(s) = \bar{u}_1 \quad \text{and} \quad u_2(s) - d_2 = k(\bar{u}_1 - d_1)\big\}.$$

Now let $\mathcal{B}^*$ denote the bargaining game obtained by an arbitrary linear transformation $v_1 = b_1 u_1 + a_1$ and $v_2 = b_2 u_2 + a_2$ with $b_1 > 0$ and $b_2 > 0$. For this bargaining game $\mathcal{B}^*$ the disagreement point (d_1^*, d_2^*) is given by

$$d_1^* = b_1 d_1 + a_1 \quad \text{and} \quad d_2^* = b_2 d_2 + a_2,$$

and the slope of its KS line is

$$k^* = \frac{\mu_2^* - d_2^*}{\mu_1^* - d_1^*} = \frac{b_2 \mu_2 + a_2 - (b_2 d_2 + a_2)}{b_1 \mu_1 + a_1 - (b_1 d_1 + a_1)} = \frac{b_2(\mu_2 - d_2)}{b_1(\mu_1 - d_1)} = \frac{b_2}{b_1} k.$$

Now assume that an alternative $s \in S$ satisfies $v_1(s) = \bar{v}_1$ and $v_2(s) - d_2^* = k^*(\bar{v}_1 - d_1^*)$. Then we have

$$v_1(s) = b_1 u_1(s) + a_1 = \bar{v}_1 = b_1 \bar{u}_1 + a_1$$

if and only if $u_1(s) = \bar{u}_1$. Moreover, $v_2(s) - d_2^* = k^*(\bar{v}_1 - d_1^*)$ means

$$[b_2 u_2(s) + a_2] - (b_2 d_2 + a_2) = k^*[b_1 \bar{u}_1 + a_1 - (b_1 d_1 + a_1)],$$

or $b_2[u_2(s) - d_2] = \frac{b_2}{b_1} k(\bar{u}_1 - d_1)$, which is equivalent to $u_2(s) - d_2 = k(\bar{u}_1 - d_1)$. Thus

$$\begin{aligned} \kappa(\mathcal{B}^*) &= \big\{s \in S: v_1(s) = \bar{v}_1 \quad \text{and} \quad v_2(s) - d_2^* = k^*(\bar{v}_1 - d_1)\big\} \\ &= \big\{s \in S: u_1(s) = \bar{u}_1 \quad \text{and} \quad u_2(s) - d_2 = k(\bar{u}_1 - d_1)\big\} \\ &= \kappa(\mathcal{B}). \end{aligned}$$

This shows that the Kalai–Smorodinsky solution rule is independent of linear transformations.

Let us examine the nature of the KS solution rule by seeing how it works in a bargaining problem. The example that follows is the classic bargaining game between labor and management.

Example 7.12 (A Wage Bargaining Game)

The labor union and the management of a firm often bargain over the wage. We can write down a simple form of this bargaining game. Let W_m be the wage that the workers can get if the bargaining process breaks down. Let L be the size of the union membership. The firm can sell its output at a fixed price p. That is, the firm sells in a perfectly competitive product market. The output of the firm is a function $f(\cdot)$ of the amount of labor employed. Thus, if the firm employs L workers, the output of the firm is $f(L)$ and the revenue $R = pf(L)$. If the firm then pays a wage W, then the profit of the firm is given by

$$pf(L) - LW = R - LW.$$

As usual, the management pays a certain dividend D to the shareholders out of the profit of the firm.

The union and the management bargain over the wage W. In case of disagreement, the profit of the firm is zero, and the workers get the wage W_m. Otherwise, the union gets LW, and the firm gets $R - LW - D$. We designate player 1 to be the firm and player 2 to be the union. The bargaining game is thus given by $d_1 = 0, d_2 = LW_m$, and

$$u_1(W, D) = R - LW - D \quad \text{and} \quad u_2(W) = LW,$$

where $W_m \leq W \leq \frac{R}{L}$ and $0 \leq D \leq R - LW$ together with $(0, 0)$ define the set S of bargaining outcomes. The set S is shown in Figure 7.11(a). It can be checked that the set of utility allocations of this bargaining game is the darkened convex and compact set shown in Figure 7.11(b). Notice, however, that the same figure shows that, although the bargaining game is convex, it fails to be symmetric.

The slope of the KS line is given by

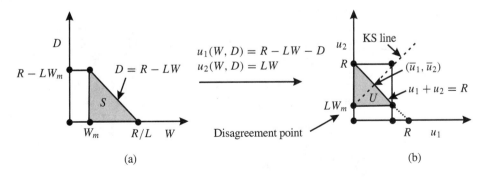

(a)   (b)

Figure 7.11

$$k = \frac{R - LW_m}{R - LW_m} = 1 .$$

Therefore, the KS line is given by

$$u_2 = u_1 + LW_m .$$

Letting $u_2 = R - u_1$, we get $R - u_1 = u_1 + LW_m$. Solving for u_1 yields

$$\bar{u}_1 = \frac{R - LW_m}{2} \quad \text{and} \quad \bar{u}_2 = \frac{R + LW_m}{2} .$$

Since $\bar{u}_2 = LW^*$, we see that the wage settlement W^* for the KS solution is given by

$$W^* = \frac{R + LW_m}{2L} . \tag{7.1}$$

Notice further that in the KS solution $D^* = R - LW^* = \frac{R - LW_m}{2}$.

Let us see what this means in a very specific example. Assume that $f(L) = 10\sqrt{L}$, $L = 25$, $p = 10$ and $W_m = 10$. In this case, $R = 100\sqrt{25} = 500$, and so substituting into the formula (7.1) yields $W^* = 15$. This value of W^* is well above the reservation wage of \$10, but well below the maximum wage of $\frac{R}{L} = \$20$.

We stated before that the KS solution rule satisfies a monotonicity property and argued that it provides a much more intuitively plausible solution to bargaining games when there are asymmetries. The next result shows precisely why the KS solution rule satisfies a monotonicity condition.

Theorem 7.13   Let $\mathcal{B} = \big(S, (u_1, d_1), (u_2, d_2)\big)$ be a bargaining game, and let T be a subset of S such that $\mathcal{U}_T$ contains the disagreement point (d_1, d_2). Further, let

$$\big(\bar{u}_1(S), \bar{u}_2(S)\big) \quad \text{and} \quad \big(\bar{u}_1(T), \bar{u}_2(T)\big)$$

denote the Kalai–Smorodinsky utility allocations of the two bargaining games $\mathcal{B}$ and $\mathcal{B}_T = \big(T, (u_1, d_1), (u_2, d_2)\big)$. If the slope of the KS line of $\mathcal{B}$ is equal to the slope of the KS line of $\mathcal{B}_T$, then

$$\bar{u}_1(S) \geq \bar{u}_1(T) \quad \text{and} \quad \bar{u}_2(S) \geq \bar{u}_2(T) .$$

Proof: Let k denote the slope of the common Kalai–Smorodinsky line of the two bargaining games. Furthermore let $\mathcal{K}_T = \big\{s \in T \colon \big(u_1(s), ku_2(s)\big) \in \mathcal{U}_T \big\}$ and $\mathcal{K} = \big\{s \in S \colon \big(u_1(s), ku_2(s)\big) \in \mathcal{U} \big\}$. Clearly, $\mathcal{K}_T \subseteq \mathcal{K}$, and so

$$\bar{u}_1(T) = \max_{s \in \mathcal{L}} u_1(s) \leq \max_{s \in \mathcal{K}} u_1(s) = \bar{u}_1(S) .$$

This implies $\bar{u}_2(T) = k\bar{u}_1(T) \leq k\bar{u}_1(S) = \bar{u}_2(S)$.

The Kalai–Smorodinsky solution rule, as well as the Nash solution rule provide us with solutions that satisfy certain normative properties. However, in some bargaining games, one set of conditions seems to make more sense than another, whereas in other bargaining problems quite a different set of conditions seems to be more appropriate. So far we have restricted our discussion to bargaining between two individuals. Frequently, the distribution of the surplus occurs between more than two individuals. This is especially true of markets. In situations where the surplus is generated by an exchange of goods or services between individuals, the distribution of the surplus also has features of bargaining, but the bargaining process is a little different from what we have seen thus far. In many bargaining problems individuals try to get the best offer they can get by using other options or alternatives. The next section looks at how n different individuals arrive at agreements that satisfy a "group rationality condition."

EXERCISES

1. The set of utility allocations $\mathcal{U}$ of a bargaining game is the closed triangle with vertices $(0, 0)$, $(1, 2)$, and $(2, 0)$, where $(0, 0)$ is also the point of disagreement. Draw a picture of $\mathcal{U}$ and find the Nash and Kalai–Smorodinsky utility allocations of the bargaining game.

2. Consider the bankruptcy game of Example 7.11. Show that if $K = \$1$ million, $D_1 = \$1$ million, and $D_2 = \$500,000$, then the KS solution rule gives \$666,667 to creditor 1 and \$333,333 to creditor 2.

3. Again consider the bankruptcy game of Example 7.11. If $K = \$800,000$, what are the amounts the KS solution rule give to each creditor? What happens if $K = \$1.2$ million? Is the KS solution rule monotonic in this case?

4. We found the KS solution rule for the wage bargaining game of Example 7.12. What is the Nash solution rule for this wage bargaining game? Are the Nash and KS solution rules giving different answers? Which of the two solution rules do you think would be more appropriate?

5. Show that every convex bargaining game always has a Kalai–Smorodinsky utility allocation.

6. If $\mathcal{B}$ is a convex and symmetric bargaining game, then show that the Kalai–Smorodinsky and Nash solutions of $\mathcal{B}$ coincide; that is, $\kappa(\mathcal{B}) = \sigma(\mathcal{B})$.

7. Show that if $\mathcal{B}$ is a convex bargaining game, then the Kalai–Smorodinsky solution $\kappa(\mathcal{B})$ is nonempty and consists of Pareto optimal bargaining outcomes.

8. Let $\mathcal{B} = \left(S, (u_1, d_1), (u_2, d_2)\right)$ be a convex bargaining game. Assume that the set of utility allocations is symmetric with respect to the KS line and that the KS line has slope one. Show that $\kappa(\mathcal{B}) = \sigma(\mathcal{B})$; that is, show that in this case the Kalai–Smorodinsky and the Nash solutions coincide.

9. Consider Theorem 7.13. Show that if the bargaining games $\mathcal{B}$ and $\mathcal{B}_T$ have different KS lines, then the KS utility allocations need not satisfy monotonicity.

7.3 THE CORE OF A BARGAINING GAME

In the preceding two sections we discussed bargaining games with two players. Quite frequently, however, bargaining problems involve more than two individuals. This is especially true in markets where individuals trade their endowments. Such trading processes usually involve more than two players. Multiperson bargaining games also arise in the context of decision making by teams. Quite often, members of a team have conflicting interests. In such cases, the team must make a proposal that all members of the team would find acceptable.

The purpose of this section is to attempt to address these issues. Thus we analyze multiperson bargaining games by introducing the concept of the *core*. The idea of the core was introduced by F. Edgeworth[3] and describes the minimal requirements that any reasonable agreement should possess.

We start by describing the basic model of a multiperson bargaining game. As in the case of the bargaining problem with two players, there is a set S of alternatives, a utility function for each individual, and a disagreement point that describes the status quo.

> **DEFINITION 7.14**   An *n-person bargaining game* (or *problem*) consists of a set $N = \{1, 2, \ldots, n\}$ of n persons (or players), a set S of *feasible alternatives* (or bargaining outcomes or simply outcomes), a utility function $u_i: S \to \mathbb{R}$ for each player i, and a disagreement point $(d_1, \ldots, d_n)$ such that:
>
> 1. $u_i(s) \geq d_i$ holds for all $s \in S$ and each $i = 1, \ldots, n$, and
> 2. There is at least one s in S for which $u_i(s) > d_i$ for every i.

At first glance, the bargaining problem just described seems to be a straightforward generalization of the two-person bargaining problem. There is, however, a fundamental difference. In an n-person bargaining game it is possible for some group of players to get together and form what is called a *coalition*. Such a coalition of players can agree on the alternatives that its members can implement, and, conceivably, it can guarantee higher payoffs to its members than they would otherwise receive as members of the *grand coalition*, the coalition N of all n players. Therefore, when the grand coalition proposes an alternative, the proposal must give every player as much satisfaction as she could expect to receive as a member of any other coalition. Consequently, in discussing any reasonable alternative in the bargaining problem, we need to describe the payoffs that players would receive as members of an arbitrary coalition.

We assume that for each coalition C there exists a specific non-empty set $S_C \subseteq S$ that represents the bargaining outcomes available to the coalition C. Thus, given an n-person bargaining game, there exists a function (called an *effectivity function*) that assigns to each

[3] F. Y. Edgeworth, *Mathematical Psychics*, Kegan Paul, London, 1881.

coalition C a subset S_C of S. The set S_C, which can be empty, is the set of alternatives that can be implemented by just the members in the coalition C. Since the grand coalition N can implement every alternative in S, it should be clear that $S_N = S$. The set of feasible bargaining outcomes S_C for a coalition C gives rise to the set $v(C)$ of all payoffs that the members of C can get from using only the alternatives in S_C. In general, the set $v(C)$ consists of all vectors $(v_1, \ldots, v_n) \in \mathbb{R}^n$ for which there exists some $s \in S_C$ satisfying $v_i = u_i(s)$ for all $i \in C$.

From the above discussion, it should be apparent that every n-person bargaining game has an effectivity function assigned to it, which explicitly describes the alternatives available to every coalition. This then leads to the notion of the characteristic function, which is defined as follows.

> **DEFINITION 7.15**   The *characteristic* (or the *coalition*) *function* of an n-person bargaining game with effectivity function $C \mapsto S_C$ is the function
>
> $$v: \mathcal{N} \to \mathcal{P}(\mathbb{R}^n)$$
>
> where $\mathcal{N}$ is the set of all subsets of N excluding the empty set (i.e., the set of all coalitions), and $\mathcal{P}(\mathbb{R}^n)$ is the set of all subsets of $\mathbb{R}^n$.

In contrast to the effectivity function that describes the alternatives S_C that are feasible for a coalition C, the characteristic function describes the payoffs or the utilities that the members of a coalition C can get from the alternatives in S_C. Thus for each coalition C the set $v(C)$ is a subset of $\mathbb{R}^n$, and the interpretation is that $v(C)$ describes the set of all utility allocations that the coalition C can get for its members. Since an element of $v(C)$ is an n-dimensional vector $(u_1, \ldots, u_n)$, only the coordinates of the vector that correspond to the players in the coalition C have any meaning, as the other coordinates can either be set at zero or allowed to vary as one wishes. It should be noted that $v(C)$ is not necessarily a subset of $v(N)$.

It is customary to relegate the effectivity function $C \mapsto S_C$ to the background and consider only the characteristic function of the bargaining game. As a matter of fact, once the characteristic function $v: \mathcal{N} \to \mathcal{P}(\mathbb{R}^n)$ has been specified, the utility functions play a minimal role. For this reason, an n-person bargaining game is quite often defined by many people as simply a group of n players $\{1, 2, \ldots, n\}$ together with its characteristic function $v: \mathcal{N} \to \mathcal{P}(\mathbb{R}^n)$.

Now let us see with an example how an n-person bargaining game can be written in its characteristic function form.

Example 7.16 (Joint Venture)

Consider the case of three power companies located in adjacent geographical areas. Each has a well-defined jurisdiction to which it is the sole distributor of power. However, the location and vintage of the plants are such that if the power companies agree to trade power supplies within their jurisdictions, they would be able to supply power more cheaply. One way of describing what happens, under the various scenarios, is by writing down the bargaining game in its characteristic function form.

In this case the values of the characteristic function for coalitions of size 1 are given by

$$v(\{1\}) = \big\{(0, x_2, x_3): x_2, x_3 \in \mathbb{R} \big\},$$
$$v(\{2\}) = \big\{(x_1, 0, x_3): x_1, x_3 \in \mathbb{R} \big\},$$
$$v(\{3\}) = \big\{(x_1, x_2, 0): x_1, x_2 \in \mathbb{R} \big\}.$$

For instance, the set $v(\{1\})$ indicates that the profit of the first company, without being in a partnership, has been normalized down to zero, while the profits of the other two companies are designated by x_2, x_3 (which as unknowns can take any values). Here a profit of zero simply means that the company earns only a normal profit, indicating that it only makes an average rate of return on its capital.

For coalitions of size 2, we have

$$v(\{1, 2\}) = \big\{(0.5, 0.5, x_3): x_3 \in \mathbb{R} \big\},$$
$$v(\{2, 3\}) = \big\{(x_1, 0.5, 0.5): x_1 \in \mathbb{R} \big\},$$
$$v(\{1, 3\}) = \big\{(0.6, x_2, 0.4): x_2 \in \mathbb{R} \big\},$$

and finally, for the grand coalition we get

$$v(\{1, 2, 3\}) = \big\{(0.8, 1, 0.5)\big\}.$$

As mentioned before, the convention is to ignore the payoffs of the members not in the coalition. Thus a coordinate associated with a player i not in the coalition is designated by an unknown variable x_i, which can be thought of as taking any arbitrary value.

In the discussion that follows, we also use the convention adopted in the literature, and simply write the characteristic function without mentioning the payoffs of those not in the coalition. For instance, we will write $v(\{1\}) = \{0\}$ instead of the set of vectors $\big\{(0, x_2, x_3): x_2, x_3 \in \mathbb{R} \big\}$, and for the coalition $\{1, 2\}$ we write $v(\{1, 2\}) = \{(0.5, 0.5)\}$.

Here is another example of a bargaining game written in its characteristic function form.

Example 7.17 (A Trading Game)

Consider an economy with three goods, labeled by the variables x, y, and z. There are three individuals in the economy each of whom is endowed with some amounts of these goods. The individuals all have the same utility function given by

$$u(x, y, z) = \sqrt{xyz}, \quad x \geq 0, \ y \geq 0, \ z \geq 0.$$

The first individual, player 1, has the endowment $e_1 = (1, 0, 1)$, the second individual (player 2) has the endowment $e_2 = (0, 1, 1)$, and player 3 has the endowment $e_3 = \left(\frac{1}{2}, \frac{1}{2}, \frac{1}{2}\right)$.

In this trading game, the coalitions can essentially allow all trades that can be formed by the aggregate endowment of the coalition. Thus a coalition of size 1 can only allow the consumer to consume up to her endowment, while in a coalition of size 2 an individual can trade with the other player in the coalition. This means that for coalitions of size 2 the effectivity function is given by

$$S_{\{1,2\}} = \left\{ \left((x_1, y_1, z_1), (x_2, y_2, z_2)\right): x_1 + x_2 \leq 1, \ y_1 + y_2 \leq 1, \ z_1 + z_2 \leq 2 \right\},$$

$$S_{\{1,3\}} = \left\{ \left((x_1, y_1, z_1), (x_3, y_3, z_3)\right): x_1 + x_3 \leq 1.5, \ y_1 + y_3 \leq 0.5, \ z_1 + z_3 \leq 1.5 \right\},$$

$$S_{\{2,3\}} = \left\{ \left((x_2, y_2, z_2), (x_3, y_3, z_3)\right): x_2 + x_3 \leq 0.5, \ y_2 + y_3 \leq 1.5, \ z_2 + z_3 \leq 1.5 \right\}.$$

The set $S_{\{1,2\}}$ is shown in Figure 7.12. The point $A\,(x_1, y_1, z_1)$ in the the solid box shown in Figure 7.12 is an arbitrary bundle given by the coalition $\{1, 2\}$ to individual 1. Notice that every point in the solid corresponds to an alternative in $S_{\{1,2\}}$.

We now describe the characteristic functions of the coalitions. If C is a coalition, then $v(C)$ consists of all vectors $(v_1, v_2, v_3) \in \mathbb{R}^3$ such that there exist non-negative vectors $\{(x_i, y_i, z_i): i \in C\}$ satisfying

$$\sum_{i \in C}(x_i, y_i, z_i) \leq \sum_{i \in C} e_i \quad \text{and} \quad v_i \leq \sqrt{x_i y_i z_i} \ \text{ for each } i \in C.$$

Notice that the values v_i for $i \notin C$ are free. For instance, we have

$$v(\{1\}) = \left\{(v_1, v_2, v_3): v_1 \leq 0, \ v_2, v_3 \in \mathbb{R} \right\},$$

$$v(\{2\}) = \left\{(v_1, v_2, v_3): v_2 \leq 0, \ v_1, v_3 \in \mathbb{R} \right\},$$

$$v(\{3\}) = \left\{(v_1, v_2, v_3): v_3 \leq \tfrac{1}{8} = 0.3536, \ v_1, v_2 \in \mathbb{R} \right\},$$

$$v(\{1, 2\}) = \left\{(v_1, v_2, v_3): \exists \, (x_1, y_1, z_1) \geq 0, \ (x_2, y_2, z_2) \geq 0 \ \text{satisfying}\right.$$

$$x_1 + x_2 \leq 1, \ y_1 + y_2 \leq 1, \ z_1 + z_2 \leq 2 \ \text{and}$$

$$\left. v_1 \leq \sqrt{x_1 y_1 z_1}, \ v_2 \leq \sqrt{x_2 y_2 z_2} \right\}$$

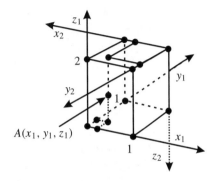

Figure 7.12

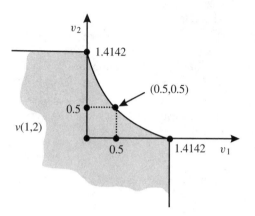

Figure 7.13

$$v(\{1, 2, 3\}) = \big\{(v_1, v_2, v_3): \exists\, (x_1, y_1, z_1) \geq 0,\; (x_2, y_2, z_2) \geq 0,$$
$$(x_3, y_3, z_3) \geq 0 \text{ with } x_1 + x_2 + x_3 \leq 1.5,\; y_1 + y_2 + y_3 \leq 1.5,$$
$$z_1 + z_2 + z_3 \leq 2.5 \text{ and } v_1 \leq \sqrt{x_1 y_1 z_1},\; v_2 \leq \sqrt{x_2 y_2 z_2},$$
$$v_3 \leq \sqrt{x_3 y_3 z_3}\big\}.$$

The set $v(\{1, 2\})$ is shown in Figure 7.13.

If the entire endowment of the grand coalition is given to one individual, then the individual's utility is 2.37, whereas the others get zero utility. However, if the endowment is divided equally among the three, then the consumption bundle of each is $(0.5, 0.5, 0.8333)$. The corresponding utilities are $(0.46, 0.46, 0.46)$. Thus the utility allocations $(2.37, 0, 0)$, $(0, 2.37, 0)$, $(0, 0, 2.37)$, and $(0.46, 0.46, 0.46)$ all belong to the set $v(\{1, 2, 3\})$.

One of the central features of n-person bargaining situations is that coalitions can often offer their members better payoffs than the grand coalition. In such cases, a coalition that can guarantee higher payoff to its members will, of course, want to exit from the grand coalition. In these situations, we say that the coalition *blocks* the proposal of the grand coalition. Formally, an outcome $s \in S$ is said to be **blocked** by a coalition C if there exists some $(v_1, \ldots, v_n) \in v(C)$ satisfying

$$v_i > u_i(s) \quad \text{for all}\;\; i \in C.$$

The fact that some proposals by the grand coalition can be blocked, guarantees that the only proposals by the grand coalition that have a realistic chance of acceptance are the alternatives to which no coalition can object. This idea is the central feature of the notion of a core outcome, which we define below.

DEFINITION 7.18   Any outcome of an *n*-person bargaining game that cannot be blocked by any coalition is called a *core outcome*. The set of all core outcomes is called the *core*.

A utility allocation of the form $(u_1(s^*), u_2(s^*), \ldots, u_n(s^*))$, where s^* is a core outcome, is called a *core utility allocation*. The set of all core utility allocations of a bargaining game with characteristic function v is denoted by Core(v). Clearly, Core(v) is a subset of $v(N)$. Observe that a utility allocation $(u_1, \ldots, u_n) \in v(N)$ belongs to Core(v) if and only if there is no coalition C and some $(v_1, \ldots, v_n) \in v(C)$ satisfying $v_i > u_i$ for all $i \in C$.

It should now be evident that any "solution" to any *n*-person bargaining game should belong to the core. As otherwise, some coalition will object to the proposed solution. It is also worth noting at this point that every core outcome satisfies the following *efficiency condition*: If s^* is a core oucome, then there is no other outcome s satisfying $u_i(s) > u_i(s^*)$ for each player i. (If there is an outcome s satisfying $u_i(s) > u_i(s^*)$ for each player i, then the grand coalition N blocks s^*.)

An important issue that needs to be addressed for an *n*-person bargaining game is whether it has a nonempty core. Obviously, this is of immediate interest, since a game with an empty core has no chance of offering an acceptable alternative to which every coalition agrees. A condition for an *n*-person game (together with some other standard assumptions) that guarantees that the core is nonempty is called *balancedness*, and it will be discussed below.

Recall that the symbol χ_C denotes the *indicator function* of C, that is, the function $\chi_C: N \to \mathbb{R}$ defined by $\chi_C(k) = 1$ if $k \in C$ and $\chi_C(k) = 0$ if $k \notin C$.

DEFINITION 7.19   A family C of coalitions is said to be *balanced* whenever we can find non-negative weights $\{w_C: C \in C\}$ (called a *family of balancing weights*) such that

$$\sum_{C \in C} w_C \chi_C = \chi_N .$$

Equivalently, a family C of coalitions is balanced whenever there exist non-negative scalars $\{w_C: C \in C\}$ (the balancing weights) such that if we let $C_i = \{C \in C: i \in C\}$ (i.e., C_i consists of all coalitions of C to which player i belongs), then

$$\sum_{C \in C_i} w_C = 1$$

holds for each $i = 1, 2, \ldots, n$. Unfortunately, it is not easy to check whether or not a given family of coalitions is balanced. For instance, if $N = \{1, 2, 3\}$, then the families

$$C_1 = \{\{1\}, \{2\}, \{3\}\} \quad \text{and} \quad C_2 = \{\{1, 2\}, \{2, 3\}, \{1, 3\}\}$$

are both balanced—for C_1 take balancing weights $\{1, 1, 1\}$ and for C_2 take $\{\frac{1}{2}, \frac{1}{2}, \frac{1}{2}\}$—while the family $C_3 = \{\{1\}, \{1, 2\}, \{1, 3\}\}$ is not balanced.

DEFINITION 7.20 (Bondareva)   An n-person bargaining game is said to be *balanced*[4] whenever every balanced family C of coalitions satisfies

$$\bigcap_{C \in C} v(C) \subseteq v(N).$$

Another property of sets needed for our discussion is that of *comprehensiveness*. A subset A of a Euclidean space $\mathbb{R}^n$ is said to be **comprehensive** whenever $(u_1, \ldots, u_n) \in A$ implies $(v_1, \ldots, v_n) \in A$ for all vectors $(v_1, \ldots, v_n) \in \mathbb{R}^n$ that satisfy $v_i \leq u_i$ for all i. A two-dimensional comprehensive set is shown in Figure 7.14.

We now state one of the fundamental results in the literature, due to H. E. Scarf, concerning the existence of core allocations.

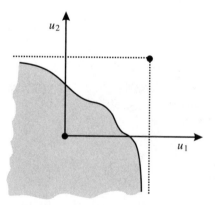

Figure 7.14   A comprehensive, closed, and bounded from above set.

[4] The important notion of balancedness was introduced to game theory by the Russian economist Olga Bondareva in: "Kernel theory in *n*-person games," *Vestnik Leningrad Univ. Math.* **17** (1962), 141–142.

Theorem 7.21 (Scarf)   Assume that the characteristic function v of an n-person bargaining game satisfies the following properties.

1. Each $v(C)$ is closed.
2. Each $v(C)$ is comprehensive.
3. If $u \in v(C)$ and $w \in \mathbb{R}^n$ satisfy $u_i = w_i$ for all $i \in C$, then $w \in v(C)$.
4. Each $v(C)$ is bounded from above in $\mathbb{R}^C$; that is, for each coalition C there exists some $M_C > 0$ such that $u_i \leq M_C$ for all $u \in v(C)$ and all $i \in C$.

If the bargaining game is balanced, then it has a core outcome.

This important theorem was proved in 1967 by H. E. Scarf [19]. Since then many attempts have been made to present a simple proof of this result. The simplest proof so far seems to be the one presented by L. Shapley and R. Vohra [22]; see also [1, p. 45].

The balancedness condition that is central in guaranteeing that the core is nonempty at first sight looks fairly technical. One way to understand this condition is to note that the weights that each player is given for belonging to different coalitions in a balanced collection sums to 1. Thus, if the balanced collection consists of two coalitions, then the weight that a player gets in each of the two coalitions must sum to one. In essence, the weights in a balanced collection indicate a player's presence and "importance" in the coalitions. In other words, the balancedness condition indicates that a player gets at least as much utility for being a member of the grand coalition as she gets from belonging to a balanced family of coalitions. Even though the condition of balancedness seems a little awkward, it has proven to be the most useful of the conditions that guarantee the nonemptiness of the core.

In many bargaining games, the payoff of an individual is simply the amount of money that he or she receives. In such cases, one may add up the payoffs of all individuals in a coalition and represent the sum or the total payoff by a number rather than a set of vectors. In these situations, we simply denote this real number by $v(C)$ and interpret it as the characteristic function of the bargaining game. The number $v(C)$ is also known as the *worth* of the coalition C. Since $v(C)$ is now a number representing the total sum of the payoffs of the members of C, $v(C)$ can be divided among the members of the coalition C in any way they choose, so that if u_i is the amount that individual i receives, then

$$\sum_{i \in C} u_i = v(C).$$

The reason that $v(C)$ can be interpreted as the characteristic function of the coalition is that $v(C)$ can also be identified with the following closed and comprehensive subset of $\mathbb{R}^n$:

$$\left\{ (u_1, \ldots, u_n) \in \mathbb{R}^n : \sum_{i \in C} u_i \leq v(C) \right\}.$$

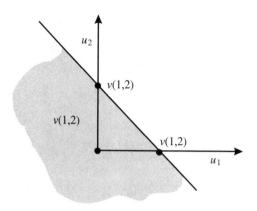

Figure 7.15

We shall use $v(C)$ to designate both the sum of the total payoff of the members of the coalition C as well as the set described above; the meaning of $v(C)$ will be clear from the context. In Figure 7.15 the number $v(C)$ and the set $v(C)$ are illustrated for the coalition $C = \{1, 2\}$.

Since the payoff of a member of a coalition can be increased or decreased by giving the individual less or more money, that is, by making *side payments*, such bargaining games are often called *side-payment games*; they are also known as *transferable utility games*. Bargaining games that do not allow side payments are known in the literature as *non-side-payment games*. The trading game that we discussed earlier in Example 7.17 is an example of a non-side-payment game, whereas the bargaining game of Example 7.24 (which will be discussed below) is an example of a side-payment game.

The core of side-payment games is characterized as follows.

Theorem 7.22   In a side-payment n-person bargaining game v, a vector $(u_1, \dots, u_n)$ $\in v(N)$ belongs to the core if and only if

$$\sum_{i \in C} u_i \geq v(C)$$

holds for each coalition C.

For a side-payment game we have the following result regarding the nonemptiness of the core.

Theorem 7.23 (Bondareva)   An n-person side-payment bargaining game has a nonempty core if and only if for each balanced collection C of coalitions there exist balancing weights $\{w_C: C \in C\}$ such that

$$\sum_{C \in \mathcal{C}} w_C v(C) \le v(N).$$

For a proof and a discussion concerning this theorem see [7, Section 5.2]. In the next example we look at a bargaining game that is a side-payment game and examine its core. In this bargaining game we shall use direct arguments to establish that the core is nonempty.

Example 7.24 (Markets for Indivisible Goods)

In many markets the buyers and sellers enter into transactions in which they exchange a commodity that is indivisible. Examples of such markets are the housing markets, the used car markets, or even the markets for medical interns. In these markets there is a set $\{1, \ldots, I\}$ of buyers and a set $\{1, \ldots, J\}$ of sellers. Each seller has a unit of the indivisible good. Seller j values its unit at b_j. Buyer i values seller $j's$ unit of the good at a_{ij}. Thus in this market if seller j meets buyer i, then the total profit of the buyer and the seller from entering a market transaction is $\max\{a_{ij} - b_j, 0\}$. We can, in fact, think of the buyer and the seller forming a coalition. The characteristic function of this coalition is

$$v(i, j) = \max\{a_{ij} - b_j, 0\} = \begin{cases} a_{ij} - b_j & \text{if } a_{ij} > b_j \\ 0 & \text{if } a_{ij} \le b_j. \end{cases}$$

While it is easy to define the characteristic function of a coalition of a buyer and a seller, we can also define the characteristic function for every coalition. For instance, if a coalition C is a subset of either the set of buyers or sellers, then there is no profitable transaction, and so, in this case

$$v(C) = 0.$$

For a coalition C that contains both buyers and sellers, assume without loss of generality that the number of buyers is less than or equal to the number of sellers in C. In this case, let

$$k: \{1, \ldots, I\} \cap C \to \{1, \ldots, J\} \cap C$$

be an *assignment map* that assigns buyers to sellers within the coalition C in one-to-one fashion. For each such assignment k, we define the total profit of the coalition as the sum of the profits generated by each pair. Thus for an assignment k the total profit is

$$\pi(k) = \sum_{i \in \{1, \ldots, I\} \cap C} v(i, k(i)).$$

Now if $\mathcal{K}$ denotes all assignment maps that match buyers to sellers within C, then the characteristic function of the coalition C is defined by

$$v(C) = \max_{k \in \mathcal{K}} \pi(k).$$

Let $y_i \geq 0$ be the payoff of the buyer i, and let $z_j \geq 0$ be the payoff of the seller j. We then solve the following optimization problem:

$$\text{minimize} : \sum_{i=1}^{I} y_i + \sum_{j=1}^{J} z_j$$

such that

$$y_i + z_j \geq v(i, j) \text{ for all } i \text{ and } j .$$

Let $y^* = (y_1^*, \ldots, y_I^*)$ and $z^* = (z_1^*, \ldots, z_J^*)$ be a solution of this problem. We claim that

$$\sum_{i=1}^{I} y_i^* + \sum_{j=1}^{J} z_j^* = v(N) ,$$

where now N is the set of all sellers and buyers together. Standard linear programming techniques (which are too technical to be reproduced here) guarantee that $\sum_{i=1}^{I} y_i^* + \sum_{j=1}^{J} z_j^* = v(N)$; for details, see [18, pp. 153–155].

Next we claim that (y^*, z^*) is a profit allocation to the buyers and the sellers that is in the core of the game. To see this, let C be a coalition. Pick an assignment $k : \{1, \ldots, I\} \to \{1, \ldots, J\}$ that assigns buyers to sellers within the coalition C such that $\pi(k) = \sum_{i \in \{1, \ldots, I\} \cap C} v(i, k(i)) = v(C)$. Then, according to the preceding minimization problem, we have

$$\sum_{i \in \{1, \ldots, I\} \cap C} y_i^* + \sum_{j \in \{1, \ldots, J\} \cap C} z_j^* \geq \sum_{i \in \{1, \ldots, I\} \cap C} v(i, k(i)) = v(C) .$$

This shows that the profit allocation (y^*, z^*) cannot be blocked by any coalition. Therefore, it is a payoff allocation in the core.

EXERCISES

1. Consider the three-person bargaining game whose characteristic function v is given by

$$v(\{1\}) = v(\{1, 2\}) = \{(x, y, z) \in \mathbb{R}^3 : x \leq 1\}$$
$$v(\{2\}) = v(\{2, 3\}) = \{(x, y, z) \in \mathbb{R}^3 : y \leq 1\}$$
$$v(\{3\}) = v(\{1, 3\}) = \{(x, y, z) \in \mathbb{R}^3 : z \leq 1\}$$
$$v(\{1, 2, 3\}) = \{(x, y, z) \in \mathbb{R}^3 : x^2 + y^2 + z^2 \leq 3\} .$$

Find Core(v). [Answer: Core(v) = $\{(1, 1, 1)\}$]

2. Consider the two-person bargaining game having the characteristic function defined by

$$v(\{1\}) = \{(x, y) \in \mathbb{R}^2 : x \leq 1\}$$

$$v(\{2\}) = \{(x, y) \in \mathbb{R}^2 \colon\ y \le \tfrac{1}{2}\}$$

$$v(\{1, 2\}) = \{(x, y) \in \mathbb{R}^2 \colon\ x < 4 \text{ and } y \le \tfrac{x-3}{x-4}\}.$$

    a. Show that the bargaining game is balanced and satisfies the hypotheses of Scarf's Theorem 7.21 (and hence its core is non-empty).

    b. Determine Core(v). [Answer: Core$(v) = \{(x, \tfrac{x-3}{x-4})\colon\ 1 \le x \le 2\}$.]

3. Consider a bargaining game with three players; that is, $N = \{1, 2, 3\}$. Show that the family of coalitions $C = \{\{1\}, \{1, 2\}, \{1, 3\}\}$ is not balanced.

4. Show that if C is a balanced collection of coalitions, then every player must belong to at least one coalition of C.

5. Prove Theorem 7.22.

6. If an n-person side-payment bargaining game v has a nonempty core, then show that

$$v(C) + v(N \setminus C) \le v(N)$$

holds for each coalition C.

7. Assume that in a side-payment bargaining game we have $v(C) \le v(N)$ for each coalition C. If C is a balanced collection of coalitions with a family of balancing weights $\{w_C \colon C \in C\}$, is

$$\sum_{C \in C} w_C v(C) \le v(N)$$

true?

8. Describe the core outcomes of Example 7.16.

9. Consider the game described in Example 7.17 with three goods and n players. Show that the game is balanced.

10. Consider a market with two buyers and three sellers where each seller has one unit of an indivisible good to sell. Assume that:

$$a_{11} = 4, \ a_{12} = 2, \ a_{13} = 7$$
$$a_{21} = 3, \ a_{22} = 5, \ a_{23} = 7$$
$$b_1 = 3, \ b_2 = 4, \ b_3 = 5.$$

Find a profit-maximizing assignment for this market. Is this assignment unique?

11. If in an n-person bargaining game the set $v(N)$ is a closed subset of $\mathbb{R}^n$, then show that the core is a closed subset of $\mathbb{R}^n$. If the core of a bargaining game is closed, is $v(N)$ necessarily a closed set?

7.4 ALLOCATION RULES: THE SHAPLEY VALUE

In the previous section we discussed the core of a bargaining game. While the core clearly has the desirable property of being stable against blocking by coalitions, in many cases of interest, the outcomes in the core are not unique and are confusingly large. In some instances, as in the majority voting game (see Exercise 5 at the end of the section), the core might be empty. If one examines a bankruptcy game or a bargaining game in which a sum of money is divided between n individuals, then one finds that (since intermediate coalitions cannot divide the money by themselves) the core coincides with the set of all Pareto optimal outcomes. In such cases one would like to find another rule that would assign a unique payoff vector to the players in the game. Of course, the payoff vector that one should designate as the solution should be intuitively plausible and reasonable.

The *Shapley value* of a side-payment game, introduced by L. S. Shapley[5] in 1953, provides an appealing method of deciding the share of each individual in an n-person game. The Shapley value has been used as an allocation rule in a wide variety of contexts. It has been used to analyze problems in areas as diverse as the management of water resources, allocation of taxes, public utility pricing, internal pricing of long distance telephone calls in a large organization, airport landing fees, etc.

In this section, we investigate the nature of the solution provided by the Shapley value for an n-person side-payment bargaining game. So let $v: \mathcal{N} \rightarrow \mathbb{R}$ be a side-payment game in characteristic function form. We shall say that a player i is a *dummy player* if $v(C \cup \{i\}) = v(C)$ holds for each coalition. That is, a player is a dummy if he contributes nothing to any coalition by being a member of that coalition.

A *permutation* π of the players is simply a one-to-one function $\pi: N \rightarrow N$. That is, a permutation is a rearrangement of the players in a game. As usual, if C is a coalition of players, we define the two coalitions $\pi(C)$ and $\pi^{-1}(C)$ by

$$\pi(C) = \{\pi(i): i \in C\} \quad \text{and} \quad \pi^{-1}(C) = \{i \in N: \pi(i) \in C\}.$$

Now for each permutation π we define a new game $\pi v: \mathcal{N} \rightarrow \mathbb{R}$ by

$$\pi v(C) = v(\pi^{-1}(C)) \quad \text{or} \quad \pi v(\pi(C)) = v(C).$$

In other words, the game πv is the same as the game v, with the roles of the players interchanged by the permutation π. It should be emphasized, however, that the amount $\pi v(C)$ that a coalition C gets in the game πv is the same as the amount that the coalition $\pi^{-1}(C) = \{i \in N: \pi(i) \in C\}$ gets in the game v. We can now introduce the concept of a Shapley value.

---

[5] "A value for n-person games," in: H. W. Kuhn and A. W. Tucker, Eds., *Contributions to the Theory of Games II* (Annals of Mathematical Studies, Princeton University Press, Princeton, New Jersey, 1953), Volume 28, pp. 307–312.

DEFINITION 7.25   A *Shapley value* (or simply a **value**) is a rule ϕ that assigns to each n-person side-payment game v an n-dimensional vector $\phi(v) = \big(\phi_1(v), \phi_2(v), \ldots, \phi_n(v)\big)$ satisfying the following properties.

1. *Efficiency*: $\sum_{i=1}^{n} \phi_i(v) = v(N)$.
2. *Symmetry*: For any permutation π of v and each player i we have $\phi_{\pi(i)}(\pi v) = \phi_i(v)$. This means that the value $\phi_i(v)$ does not depend on the labeling of the player i but rather on its position in the game relative to the characteristic function v.
3. *Linearity*: If u and v are any two n-person side-payment games and α and β are scalars, then

   $$\phi(\alpha u + \beta v) = \alpha \phi(u) + \beta \phi(v)$$

   where $\alpha u + \beta v$ denotes the n-person side-payment game defined by $(\alpha u + \beta v)(C) = \alpha u(C) + \beta v(C)$.
4. *Irrelevance of Dummy Players*: If i is a dummy player, then $\phi_i(v) = 0$.

Recall that for any integer n the factorial $n!$ is defined by

$$n! = 1 \times 2 \times 3 \times (n\text{-}1) \times n$$

with $0! = 1$. The number $n!$ coincides with the number of all possible permutations of a set with n elements. As usual, $|C|$ designates the number of players in the coalition C. We also adhere to the convention that for any n-person bargaining game v we let $v(\emptyset) = 0$.

In 1953, L. S. Shapley also established the following remarkable result.

Theorem 7.26 (Shapley)   The class of all side-payment games has a unique Shapley value. Moreover, for any n-person side-payment game v, the components of the Shapley value $\phi(v) = \big(\phi_1(v), \phi_2(v), \ldots, \phi_n(v)\big)$ are given by the formulas

$$\phi_i(v) = \sum_{C \subseteq N \setminus \{i\}} \frac{|C|!(|N|-|C|-1)!}{|N|!} \big[v(C \cup \{i\}) - v(C)\big]$$

for each $i = 1, 2, \ldots, n$.

The amount $v(C \cup \{i\}) - v(C)$ appearing in the above formula is called the *marginal worth of player i* when she joins the coalition C.

If we examine the formula for the Shapley value, we will notice that the amount given to a player i is actually the *expected marginal worth* of player i. The number of coalitions that a player i can join is, of course, the same as the number of coalitions that can be formed by the set of players $N \setminus \{i\}$. For each coalition C that does not contain player i there are

$|C|!(|N| - |C| - 1)!$ ways of ordering the players in the game such that the players in C are just ahead of i in the ordering, and the players in $N \setminus (C \cup \{i\})$ are just behind player i. Since there are $|N|!$ ways of ordering the $|N|$ players, the probability that the members of the coalition C are just ahead of i in an ordering is

$$\frac{|C|!(|N| - |C| - 1)!}{|N|!} .$$

Thus $\frac{|C|!(|N| - |C| - 1)!}{|N|!}$ can be interpreted as the probability of the coalition C forming ahead of player i and then i joining C. It can be shown that $\sum_{C \subseteq N \setminus \{i\}} \frac{|C|!(|N| - |C| - 1)!}{|N|!} = 1$; see Exercise 3 at the end of this section. Therefore, the expected marginal worth of player i in the game is

$$\phi_i(v) = \sum_{C \subseteq N \setminus \{i\}} \frac{|C|!(|N| - |C| - 1)!}{|N|!} \left[v(C \cup \{i\}) - v(C) \right]$$

which is precisely the amount indicated by the Shapley value.

Hence the Shapley value of a game gives each player the *average* of the marginal worth that a player adds by joining a coalition that is just ahead of her in some ordering of the players. An alternative interpretation of the Shapley value is that it indicates the "expected power" of an individual in a game. Thus the Shapley value has at least two different interpretations. The description of the Shapley value that is the most appropriate depends on the context in which it is used. In bargaining games the Shapley value is best thought of as an allocation rule that gives every player his average or expected marginal worth.

It is of some interest at this point to examine what the Shapley value allocates to each player in the simplest possible bargaining game, a game in which two individuals have to divide a sum of money among themselves. The characteristic function of this game can be written as

$$v(\{1\}) = v(\{2\}) = 0 \quad \text{and} \quad v(\{1, 2\}) = M .$$

Note that player 1 can only join the coalition $\{2\}$, and his marginal worth in this case is $v(\{1, 2\}) - v(\{1\}) = M$. Since there is only one way in which the coalition $\{2\}$ can be placed ahead of 1, we see that

$$\phi_1(v) = \frac{0!1!}{2!} \left[v(\{1\}) - v(\emptyset) \right] + \frac{1!0!}{2!} \left[v(\{1, 2\}) - v(\{2\}) \right]$$
$$= \frac{0!1!}{2!} \times 0 + \frac{1!0!}{2!} M = \frac{M}{2} .$$

A similar argument shows that $\phi_2(v) = \frac{M}{2}$. In this case the Shapley value provides a perfectly reasonable solution to the game. In the example that follows we use the Shapley value to allocate the cost of running an airport.

Example 7.27 (Setting Landing Fees)

The cost of building and running an airport consists of two types of expenses: a fixed capital cost of building the airport and a variable cost that depends on the types of planes that use the airport. The operating or the variable cost of each landing can be attributed directly to the landing. The capital cost of building the airport, however, needs to be divided in some way among all users of the facility. Usually, the capital cost of building the airport depends most directly on the "type" of airplane that needs the largest runway. In this example, we will abstract from the question of the frequency of landings and the need for multiple runways and focus on the issue of building a single runway for T different types of airplanes.

Let K_t denote the cost of a runway that is adequate for a plane of type t, where $t = 1, \ldots, T$. We will assume that

$$0 < K_1 < K_2 < \cdots < K_T,$$

that is, the larger the type, the larger the cost of using the runway. We now describe the side-payment game that we will use to *allocate the cost* of the runway among the different users. Let n be the estimated total number of landings over the life of the runway.

A coalition C in this bargaining game is a subset of $N = \{1, 2, \ldots, n\}$. Let N_t denote the (estimated) set of landings by an airplane of type t. Clearly, $N = \bigcup_{t=1}^{T} N_t$ and $N_t \cap N_s = \emptyset$ for $t \neq s$. For each coalition C, let

$$t(C) = \max\{t \in \{1, 2, \ldots, T\}: C \cap N_t \neq \emptyset\},$$

that is, $t(C)$ is the largest type of airplane having landings in the coalition C. The characteristic function v of the game is now defined by

$$v(C) = -K_{t(C)}.$$

That is, the value of a coalition is the capital cost needed for building the runway for the most expensive type of plane in the coalition. We should note that $v(N) = -K_T$, so that the entire cost of building the airport is covered by the fees collected from the entire set of landings. We will use $K_0 = 0$ to denote the value of $v(\emptyset)$. That is, $v(\emptyset) = -K_0$.

In this bargaining game, if $i \in N_1$, then

$$v(C \cup \{i\}) - v(C) = \begin{cases} K_0 - K_1, & \text{if } C = \emptyset \\ 0, & \text{otherwise}. \end{cases}$$

Similarly, if $i \in N_2$, then

$$v(C \cup \{i\}) - v(C) = \begin{cases} K_0 - K_2, & \text{if } C = \emptyset \\ K_1 - K_2, & \text{if } C \subseteq N_1 \\ 0, & \text{otherwise}. \end{cases}$$

In general, if $i \in N_t$, then

$$v(C \cup \{i\}) - v(C) = \begin{cases} K_{t(C)} - K_t, & \text{if } t(C) < t \\ 0, & \text{if } t(C) \geq t. \end{cases}$$

Therefore, if $i \in N_t$, then the Shapley value $\phi_i(v)$ satisfies

$$\phi_i(v) = \sum_{C \subseteq N_1 \cup N_2 \cup \cdots \cup N_{t-1}} \frac{|C|!(|N|-|C|-1)!}{|N|!} \left[v(C \cup \{i\}) - v(C) \right].$$

This expression for the Shapley value of the game is, however, not very useful, as it is computationally complex. We shall use a different approach to compute the Shapley value. Let us define the set

$$A_\ell = \bigcup_{t=\ell}^{T} N_t \,.$$

We now define T n-player side-payment games with characteristic functions $v_1, \ldots, v_T$ given by

$$v_\ell(C) = \begin{cases} 0, & \text{if } C \cap A_\ell = \emptyset \\ K_{\ell-1} - K_\ell, & \text{if } C \cap A_\ell \neq \emptyset. \end{cases}$$

We claim that

$$v(C) = \sum_{\ell=1}^{T} v_\ell(C)$$

for every coalition C. To see this, note that if $\ell \leq t(C)$, then $C \cap A_\ell \neq \emptyset$, while if $\ell > t(C)$, then $C \cap A_\ell = \emptyset$. Thus

$$\sum_{\ell=1}^{T} v_\ell(C) = \sum_{\ell=1}^{t(C)} (K_{\ell-1} - K_\ell) = K_0 - C K_{t(C)} = v(C) \,.$$

Therefore, by the additivity property of the Shapley value, we have

$$\phi(v) = \sum_{\ell=1}^{T} \phi(v_\ell) \,. \tag{7.2}$$

Next, we shall compute $\phi_i(v_\ell)$ for each i. Note first that from the definition of v_ℓ it follows that

$$v_\ell(C \cup \{i\}) - v_\ell(C) = \begin{cases} K_{\ell-1} - K_\ell, & \text{if } C \cap A_\ell = \emptyset \text{ and } i \in A_\ell \\ 0, & \text{otherwise} \,. \end{cases}$$

Therefore, for each $i \in A_\ell$, the Shapley value is given by

$$\phi_i(v_\ell) = \sum_{C \subseteq N \setminus A_\ell} \frac{|C|!(|N|-|C|-1)!}{|N|!} \left(K_{\ell-1} - K_\ell \right) \,.$$

In particular, we have $\phi_i(v_\ell) = \phi_j(v_\ell)$ for all $i, j \in A_\ell$. For $i \notin A_\ell$, we have $\phi_i(v_\ell) = 0$. This then gives

$$\left(\sum_{t=\ell}^{T} |N_t| \right) \phi_i(v_\ell) = \sum_{i \in A_\ell} \phi_i(v_\ell) = v_\ell(N) = K_{\ell-1} - K_\ell \,.$$

Consequently,

$$\phi_i(v_\ell) = \frac{K_{\ell-1} - K_\ell}{\sum_{t=\ell}^{T} |N_t|} \,.$$

Hence the Shapley value for the game v_ℓ satisfies

$$
\phi_i(v_\ell) = \begin{cases} 0, & \text{if } i \notin A_\ell \\ \dfrac{K_{\ell-1} - K_\ell}{\sum_{t=\ell}^{T} |N_t|}, & \text{if } i \in A_\ell \end{cases}
$$

for each i and ℓ. Now recalling from (7.2) that $\phi_i(v) = \sum_{\ell=1}^{T} \phi_i(v_\ell)$ and that $i \in N_k$ implies $i \in A_\ell$ for $\ell \le k$, we obtain

$$
\phi_i(v) = \sum_{\ell=1}^{k} \frac{K_{\ell-1} - K_\ell}{\sum_{t=\ell}^{T} |N_t|}, \quad i \in N_k, \quad k = 1, 2, \ldots, T. \tag{7.3}
$$

This is the expression for the Shapley value of the game.

Let us see what kind of landing fees the Shapley value gives us in a numerical example. Suppose a runway that can accommodate five different types of airplanes can be built at a cost of \$10 million. The capital cost of the runway must be recovered in ten years. It has been estimated that there will be a total of 10,000 landings over the next ten years.

The costs of building the runway for the five different types of airplanes are:

$$
K_1 = \$1,000,000, \quad K_2 = \$2,000,000, \quad K_3 = \$3,500,000
$$

$$
K_4 = \$7,500,000, \quad K_5 = \$10,000,000.
$$

Of the five different types of airplanes, it is expected that type 1 will land 5,000 times so that $N_1 = 5,000$. Similarly, $N_2 = 2,000$, $N_3 = 1,000$, $N_4 = 1,000$, and $N_5 = 1,000$. If we now compute the Shapley value of this game using the expression (7.3) derived before, we get

$$
\phi_i(v) = \frac{K_0 - K_1}{N_1 + N_2 + N_3 + N_4 + N_5} = \frac{-1,000,000}{10,000} = -100
$$

for all $i \in N_1$. For $i \in N_2$ we have

$$
\phi_i(v) = \sum_{\ell=1}^{2} \frac{K_{\ell-1} - K_\ell}{\sum_{t=\ell}^{5} |N_t|} = \frac{K_0 - K_1}{N_1 + N_2 + N_3 + N_4 + N_5} + \frac{K_1 - K_2}{N_2 + N_3 + N_4 + N_5} = -300.
$$

For $i \in N_3$, we have $\phi_i(v) = -800$; for $i \in N_4$, $\phi_i(v) = -2,800$ and finally, for $i \in N_5$, we have $\phi_i(v) = -5,300$. Thus the schedule of landing fees is given by:

$$
\$100 \text{ for type } 1, \quad \$300 \text{ for type } 2, \quad \$800 \text{ for type } 3
$$

$$
\$2,800 \text{ for type } 4, \quad \$5,300 \text{ for type } 5.
$$

What we notice here is that the landing fees reflect the increment in cost, due to the different types and the frequency of the landings. Thus type 5 has the largest landing fee, since to accommodate this type of airplane, the increment in the cost of building the runway is \$2,500,000, while the expected number of landings for this type is only 1,000. The fee structure that we, therefore, obtained by using the Shapley value seems to be both intuitive and reasonable.

We now present another application of the Shapley value in a slightly different context. We consider the problem of determining the tax that each household in a community should pay towards a public project, say, for building a bridge. The tax assessed on each household should satisfy certain minimal conditions. The tax should ideally reflect the benefit that each household would derive from the project, and the revenue from the tax should be enough to finance the project. The next example shows how the Shapley value can be used to determine these taxes.

Example 7.28 (Allocating the Tax Burden)

We consider the problem of taxing for the purpose of making available a public good, for example, a bridge. There are n potential users of the bridge designated as players $1, \ldots, n$. Here we have two possibilities: either the bridge is built (B) or else it is not built (NB). If the bridge is built, individual i derives utility $u_i(B) > 0$, otherwise the utility is zero. The utility $u_i(B)$ will be interpreted as the maximum amount that individual i would be willing to pay for the bridge. Each individual i has a net worth of W_i, and we assume that the cost K of building the bridge is such that $\sum_{i=1}^{n} W_i > K$. That is, if the community wants to build the bridge, then there are sufficient resources in the community to do so. We will further assume that the community as a whole would derive a net benefit from building the bridge. That is, $\sum_{i=1}^{n} u_i(B) > K$.

The building of the bridge is going to be financed by taxing each household in an appropriate manner. Notice that the surplus (net benefit) that the community derives from building the bridge is

$$\sum_{i=1}^{n} u_i(B) - K .$$

The surplus that each individual derives is given by

$$u_i(B) - t_i$$

where t_i is the tax paid by individual i. The total revenue from the taxes should cover the cost of building the bridge; that is, $\sum_{i=1}^{n} t_i = K$. Therefore, we have the following important fact.

- The total surplus of the community is the sum of the surpluses derived by the individuals in the community.

Because of this fact, in order to determine a fair tax system, it seems appropriate to use the Shapley value to determine the share of the surplus that goes to each individual.

We now describe the characteristic function of the side-payment game that represents the problem of taxation outlined above. For any coalition C we let

$$v(C) = \begin{cases} \max\{ \sum_{i \in C} u_i(B) - K, 0\}, & \text{if } \sum_{i \in C} W_i > K \\ 0, & \text{otherwise} . \end{cases}$$

Thus the value of a coalition is the total surplus of the individuals in the coalition if the coalition has enough wealth to build the bridge. In this case, the marginal worth of an individual i is given by

$$v(C \cup \{i\}) - v(C) = \begin{cases} u_i(B), & \text{if } v(C) > 0 \\ \sum_{j \in C \cup \{i\}} u_j(B) - K, & \text{if } v(C) = 0 \text{ and } v(C \cup \{i\}) > 0 \\ 0, & \text{if } v(C) = v(C \cup \{i\}) = 0. \end{cases}$$

This formula has the following interpretation. The marginal worth of player i is simply the amount the player is willing to pay [namely $u_i(B)$] if coalition C can build the bridge by itself [that is, when $v(C) > 0$]. When coalition C cannot build the bridge by itself, and by adding player i it can do so, then the marginal worth of player i is the entire surplus of the coalition $C \cup \{i\}$. If none of the above occurs, then the narginal worth of player i is zero.

The Shapley value of this game is now given by

$$\phi_i(v) = \sum_{\{C \subseteq N \setminus \{i\}: \, v(C) > 0\}} \frac{|C|!(|N| - |C| - 1)!}{|N|!} u_i(B)$$

$$+ \sum_{\{S \subseteq N \setminus \{i\}: \, v(C \cup \{i\}) > 0, \, v(C) = 0\}} \frac{|C|!(|N| - |C| - 1)!}{|N|!} \left(\sum_{j \in C \cup \{i\}} u_j(B) - K \right).$$

The taxes $(t_1^*, \ldots, t_n^*)$ that allocate the surplus in a fair manner among the individuals must satisfy

$$\phi_i(v) = u_i(B) - t_i^*$$

for $i = 1, \ldots, n$. In other words, according to the Shapley value allocation rule, each individual i must pay the amount of tax $t_i^* = \phi_i(v) - u_i(B)$.

Let us see what the tax rule we have obtained above gives us by taking a look at a numerical example. Suppose there are four households who plan to construct a swimming pool they can share. The cost of constructing the swimming pool is $10,000. The wealths of the households are:

$$W_1 = \$50,000, \quad W_2 = \$75,000, \quad W_3 = \$100,000, \quad W_4 = \$200,000.$$

The housholds are willing to pay the following amounts:

$$u_1 = \$5,000, \quad u_2 = \$4,000, \quad u_3 = \$6,000, \quad u_4 = \$8,000.$$

Thus none of the households is willing to spend enough to build a pool that costs $10,000. The only way the pool will be built is if the households pool their resources, and contribute a certain amount towards the construction of the pool. But in order to do this, the households must decide how to allocate the cost among themselves. Clearly, they are willing to build the pool, as the joint surplus is $13,000. We can use the Shapley value as in the preceding example to find the fair share of the cost for each household.

The characteristic function of the game that represents the situation just described is as follows:

$$v(\{1\}) = v(\{2\}) = v(\{3\}) = v(\{4\}) = 0$$

$$v(\{1, 2\}) = v(\{3, 2\}) = 0, \quad v(\{1, 3\}) = 1,000, \quad v(\{3, 4\}) = 4,000$$

$$v(\{2, 4\}) = 2,000, \quad v(\{1, 4\}) = 3,000$$

$$v(\{1, 2, 3\}) = 5,000, \quad v(\{1, 3, 4\}) = 9,000, \quad v(\{2, 3, 4\}) = 8,000$$

$$v(\{1, 2, 4\}) = 7,000, \quad v(\{1, 2, 3, 4\}) = 13,000.$$

Thus

$$
\begin{aligned}
\phi_1(v) &= \tfrac{1!2!}{4!}\Big\{\big[v(\{1, 3\}) - v(\{3\})\big] + \big[v(\{1, 4\}) - v(\{4\})\big]\Big\} \\
&\quad + \tfrac{2!1!}{4!}\{[v(\{1, 2, 3\}) - v(\{2, 3\})]\} \\
&\quad + \tfrac{2!1!}{4!}\{[v(\{1, 3, 4\}) - v(\{3, 4\})] + [v(\{1, 2, 4\}) - v(\{2, 4\})]\} \\
&\quad + \tfrac{3!0!}{4!}\big[v(\{1, 2, 3, 4\}) - v(\{2, 3, 4\})\big] \\
&= \tfrac{2}{24} \times 4,000 + \tfrac{2}{24} \times (5,000 + 5,000 + 5000) + \tfrac{6}{24} \times 5,000 \\
&= \tfrac{34,000}{12} = 2,833.33.
\end{aligned}
$$

Consequently, applying the conclusion of Example 7.28, we get

$$t_1^* = u_1 - \phi_1(v) = 5,000 - 2,833.33 = 2,166.67.$$

Similarly, we have

$$
\begin{aligned}
\phi_2(v) &= \tfrac{1}{12} \times 2000 + \tfrac{1}{12} \times [4000 + 4000 + 4000] + \tfrac{1}{4} \times 4000 \\
&= \tfrac{26,000}{12} = 2,166.67
\end{aligned}
$$

so that

$$t_2^* = 4,000 - 2,166.67 = 1,833.33.$$

For player 3, we have

$$
\begin{aligned}
\phi_3(v) &= \tfrac{1}{12} \times 5000 + \tfrac{1}{12} \times (5000 + 6000 + 6000) + \tfrac{1}{4} \times 6000 \\
&= \tfrac{40,000}{12} = 3333.33.
\end{aligned}
$$

Hence

$$t_3^* = 6,000 - 3,333.33 = 2,666.67.$$

Finally,

$$
\begin{aligned}
\phi_4(v) &= \tfrac{1}{12} \times (3,000 + 2,000 + 4,000) + \tfrac{1}{12} \times (7,000 + 8,000 + 8,000) \\
&\quad + \tfrac{1}{4} \times 8,000 \\
&= \tfrac{56,000}{12} = 4,666.67
\end{aligned}
$$

so that

$$t_4^* = 8{,}000 - 4{,}666.67 = 3{,}333.33 \, .$$

Therefore, the share of the cost (or the tax) for each household is

$$t_1^* = 2{,}166.67, \quad t_2^* = 1{,}833.33, \quad t_3^* = 2{,}666.67, \quad \text{and} \quad t_4^* = 3{,}333.33 \, .$$

Since, as expected, $t_1^* + t_2^* + t_3^* + t_4^* = 10{,}000$, we have found a normative way of allocating the cost of building the swimming pool among the four households. Notice that the distribution of cost across the households is determined by the amount each household is willing to pay for the swimming pool. The wealth of the households plays no role, except in determining the feasibility of households to generate enough resources to build the pool.

We have seen that the Shapley value is a useful allocation rule that can be used in a wide variety of situations. A particularly meaningful way of thinking about this allocation rule is to view it as a rule that distributes the surplus generated in bargaining games according to the expected marginal worth of the participants. If an individual is expected to add little to a partnership or a group, then the amount allocated by the Shapley value is going to be small, whereas if the amount an individual adds to different groups is large, then the Shapley value gives a larger share of the surplus to this individual. Thus the Shapley value can be viewed as a rule that divides the surplus fairly between the participants, where the concept of fairness is not that of equity, but rather one in which the amount an individual receives is determined by his contribution.

The Shapley value can, therefore, be viewed as providing a normative solution to a bargaining game. In many instances, such normative rules may not work, and the solution to a bargaining game is then determined by the strategic choices made by the players. In many bargaining games the method of dividing the surplus takes the form of making offers and counteroffers, and usually in such situations there is a sequence of moves made by the players. In the section that follows, we discuss bargaining games in which the solution is determined by such strategic interactions among the participants.

EXERCISES

1. In Example 7.27 of setting the landing fee for each $i \in N_t$, we used the formula

$$v(C \cup \{i\}) - v(C) = \begin{cases} K_{t(C)} - K_t, & \text{if } t(C) < t \\ 0, & \text{if } t(C) \geq t \, . \end{cases}$$

   Verify this formula.

2. Verify that the Shapley value satisfies the properties of efficiency, symmetry, linearity, and irrelevance of dummy players as described in Definition 7.25.

3. Show that for each i we have $\sum_{C \subseteq N \setminus \{i\}} \frac{|C|!(|N|-|C|-1)!}{|N|!} = 1$.

4. The n-person side-payment game in characteristic function form as is described below is called the *majority voting game*. We assume that in this side-payment game the number of players $|N| = n$ is an odd number. The characteristic function is

$$v(C) = \begin{cases} 1, & \text{if } \frac{|C|}{n} \geq \frac{1}{2} \\ 0, & \text{otherwise} \, . \end{cases}$$

That is, a coalition has a value of 1 if it is the majority and a value of 0 if it is a minority. Find the Shapley value of this game.

5. Show that the majority voting game with $2n + 1$ players described in the previous exercise has an empty core.

6. Suppose we need to construct an airport in which ten different types of airplanes can land. The airport can be constructed at a cost of $1 billion. The capital cost of constructing the airport needs to be recovered over 20 years. Over this period we expect to have 100,000 landings by the different types of airplanes. Let N_i denote the number of landings by planes of type i. Then the expected number of landings by the different types of airplanes is given as follows:

$$N_1 = 20,000, \quad N_2 = 10,000, \quad N_3 = 10,000, \quad N_4 = 15,000$$
$$N_5 = 5,000, \quad N_6 = 6,000, \quad N_7 = 7,000, \quad N_8 = 7,000$$
$$N_9 = 15,000, \quad N_{10} = 5,000.$$

The cost of building the runway for first five types is:

$$K_1 = K_2 = K_3 = K_4 = K_5 = \$500,000,000.$$

The costs for building an airport that can accommodate the other types are:

$$K_6 = K_7 = \$750,000,000, \quad K_8 = K_9 = \$900,000,000,$$

$$K_{10} = \$1,000,000,000.$$

Compute the optimal landing fees for the different types of planes.

7. Suppose an irrigation canal can be built at a cost of $100 million that can serve five different categories of farmlands. The five different types of farmlands are at different distances from the source of the canal, and, as such, the costs of extending the canal to serve the different categories of farmlands are different. The costs, which are incremental, are given by

$$K_1 = \$10,000,000, \quad K_2 = \$30,000,000, \quad K_3 = \$50,000,000,$$
$$K_4 = \$70,000,000, \quad K_5 = \$100,000,000.$$

There are 1,000 farmlands of each type.

    a. Describe a method for setting fees for use of the irrigation canal. Explain why you chose this method.

    b. Find the fee that each type of farm pays according to the method you described.

8. Suppose a bridge needs to be built for a community of 10,000. The bridge will cost $1,000,000.

    a. If each individual in the community is willing to pay the same amount for the bridge, what should be the share of each individual in the cost of building the bridge? Explain your answer.

b. If half the individuals in the community value the bridge at twice that of the value of the bridge to the other half of the community, how would your allocation of the cost change? Are you using the same allocation rule in both parts?

9. An n-person side-payment game v is said to be *convex* if for every pair of coalitions C and T we have

$$v(C \cup T) + v(C \cap T) \geq v(C) + v(T).$$

Let v be a convex side-payment game.

a. Show that if $C \subseteq T$, then for any $i \notin T$ we have

$$v(T \cup \{i\}) - v(T) \geq v(C \cup \{i\}) - v(C).$$

b. For any coalition C, define the side-payment game v_C with players the members of the coalition C via the formula $v_C(T) = v(T)$ for all coalitions T of C (i.e., $T \subseteq C$). Show that if $S \subseteq T$, then for any player $i \in S$ we have

$$\phi_i(v_C) \leq \phi_i(v_T).$$

c. Using the results in (a) and (b) show that the Shapley value of a convex side-payment game v is a core allocation—and conclude from this that every convex sidepayement game has a non-empty core.

10. Consider a firm that has 100,000 shareholders. Of this, three shareholders own significant fractions of the shares. Shareholder 1 holds 25 percent of the shares, shareholder 2 owns 30 percent of the shares and the third major shareholder owns 35 percent of the shares. The remainder of the shares are held by the smaller shareholders, with no one holding more than 1 percent of the total. Any decision in the firm is settled by the approval of stockholders who own a majority of the shares.

a. Describe the majority voting game v for this problem. That is, describe the characteristic function of the game that assigns a value of 1 to the winning coalitions and zero to the others.

b. Find the Shapley value of this game.

c. Give an interpretation of the Shapley value.

11. Suppose three firms 1, 2, 3 are looking into a joint venture that is expected to increase the value of the firms. The estimated market value of the various joint venture possibilities among the firms is given by

$$v(1) = v(2) = v(3) = \$1,000,000,000$$

$$v(1, 2) = v(2, 3) = v(1, 3) = \$3,000,000$$

$$v(1, 2, 3) = \$5,000,000,000$$

where $v(i)$ denotes the market value of firm i when it has not entered into any joint ventures, $v(i, j)$ denotes the market value of the joint venture when firm i enters into an agreement with firm j, and $v(1, 2, 3)$ denotes the market value of the joint venture of the three firms.

    a. Describe a method of finding the expected increase in the value of the firms when they enter into the joint venture.

    b. Using this method, find the expected increase in the value of each firm when they enter into the joint venture.

    c. Do you think it is in the interest of the firms to enter into the joint venture?

7.5 TWO-PERSON SEQUENTIAL BARGAINING

We have studied the bargaining game in some detail in the preceding sections. Our focus was principally on the question of how to divide the surplus so that the allocation rules satisfy certain normative properties. The Nash bargaining solution, the KS solution, and the Shapley value were all solutions to the bargaining game that belong to this genre. Even the core has features that gives it the flavor of being a normative solution concept.

In this section we proceed to discuss bargaining games from a positivist's perspective. That is, instead of worrying about what properties a solution ought to satisfy, we concern ourselves with trying to predict what will actually happen when the bargaining process is sequential. In particular, we will be concerned with understanding what will happen in a bargaining game when the bargaining process actually takes the form of a series of offers and counteroffers. In these cases, the bargaining process becomes a sequential game, and strategic play becomes important.

A typical two-person sequential bargaining game takes place when a potential buyer and the seller of a house make bids and counterbids. The game starts with a list price announced by the seller when she puts the house up for a bid. A potential buyer will usually make a bid that is somewhat lower than the list price, but above what the buyer believes the seller is likely to accept. The seller, of course, has the option to reject, and she will do so if she believes that there is a buyer who would be willing to bid higher. This bargaining process can be described by a two-person sequential game in which the first move is made by the seller, followed by a move of the buyer, after which the seller moves again, and so on.

In Chapters 4 and 5 we studied how to solve sequential games with perfect and imperfect information. Here we will make use of that knowledge to understand sequential bargaining. The basic model that we shall analyze in this section is the bargaining game described in Definition 7.1. We will simplify that model by assuming symmetry and normalizing the size of the total surplus to one. The utilities of the two players are given by the fraction of the surplus received by the player. In case there is disagreement, the utilities of both players are taken to be zero. Therefore, the set S of bargaining alternatives of this game is

$$S = \left\{ (s_1, s_2) \colon s_1 \geq 0, \ s_2 \geq 0, \ \text{and} \ s_1 + s_2 \leq 1 \right\}.$$

The utility functions of the players are

$$u_1(s_1, s_2) = s_1 \quad \text{and} \quad u_2(s_1, s_2) = s_2.$$

Therefore, the set of utility allocations of the bargaining game is

$$\mathcal{U} = \left\{ (s_1, s_2) \colon (s_1, s_2) \in S \right\}.$$

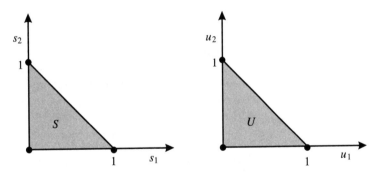

Figure 7.16

The bargaining set S and its set of utility allocations U in this case coincide, and they are shown in Figure 7.16.

However, as the bargaining game is now played strategically, the utilities achieved by the players depend on the equilibrium of the game played between the players. Since the bargaining procedure is one of making alternating offers, the bargaining game is a sequential game, and the most likely agreement is one that is given by an "equilibrium" of the game.

The game of alternating offers is played over time periods $t = 1, 2, \ldots$. We shall indicate the share of the pie received by player i in period t by $s_{t,i}$ and the utility of player i by $u_i(s_{t,1}, s_{t,2}) = s_{t,i}$. The game starts with player 1 making an offer in period $t = 1$ of taking $s_{1,1}$ so that player 2 gets $s_{1,2} = 1 - s_{1,1}$. Player 2 can either accept or reject the offer. If the offer is accepted, the game ends. If the offer is rejected, the game proceeds to period $t = 2$. Player 2 now must make an offer $s_{2,1}$ to player 1 so that player 2 gets $s_{2,2} = 1 - s_{2,1}$. Player 1 can now either accept or reject. If player 1 accepts, then the game ends; otherwise, the play proceeds to period $t = 3$, where player 1 must make a counteroffer. The game (whose graph is shown in Figure 7.17) continues in this fashion and conceivably could continue for an indefinitely long period. The reader should keep in mind that here offers and counteroffers are always quoted as the share of the pie that goes to player 1.

Since the sequential game is played over time, if a player prefers to have his share of the pie earlier rather than later, then there is a cost to waiting. This preference for consumption

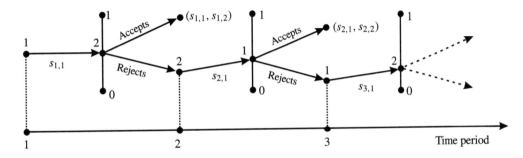

Figure 7.17

in the present over the future is indicated by a positive rate of time preference. The *rate of time preference* is the amount of a unit of consumption that an individual is willing to give up in order to be able to consume today, rather than in the next period. Thus, if the rate of time preference is r, then the individual is indifferent between consuming c units today or $(1 + r)c$ units tomorrow. Equivalently, c units tomorrow are the same as $\frac{1}{1+r}c$ units today. As usual, we let $\delta = \frac{1}{1+r}$ and call it the *discount rate*; clearly $0 < \delta < 1$. Thus, if the bargaining process settles after t periods with an agreement given by $(s_{t,1}, 1 - s_{t,1})$, then the utilities of the two players with discount rates δ_1 and δ_2, respectively, are given by

$$u_1(s_{t,1}, 1 - s_{t,1}) = \delta_1^{t-1} s_{t,1} \quad \text{and} \quad u_2(s_{t,1}, 1 - s_{t,1}) = \delta_2^{t-1}(1 - s_{t,1}).$$

With these "discounted" utilities, we can explicitly compute the *cost of delay in bargaining*, which is simply the cost of waiting until the next period. For player 1 the cost of delay in period t for the share s in next period $t+1$ is given by

$$\delta_1^t s - \delta_1^{t-1} s = \delta_1^{t-1}(1 - \delta_1)s,$$

which is the difference in the payoff that is solely due to having waited for a period starting in period t. Note that the cost of delay in this case is not a constant, as it depends on the share of pie that goes to the player.

Since the game is a sequential game with perfect information, it is natural to look for a subgame perfect equilibrium. We start by examining a three-period finite-horizon version of the bargaining game. This game is shown in Figure 7.18.

We solve the game by using backward induction. We note that in the final stage of period 3, player 2 will accept if $0 \le s_{3,1} < 1$ and will be indifferent if $s_{3,1} = 1$. Thus player 1, at the beginning of time period 3, knowing that player 2 will not reject, offers $s_{3,1} < 1$ but very close to 1 (i.e., $s_{3,1} \approx 1$), in which case player 2 gets zero (or almost zero). Player 1 in this case gets δ_1^2.

Therefore, at the beginning of period 2, player 2 must make an offer $s_{2,1}$ to player 1 such that

$$\delta_1 s_{2,1} \ge \delta_1^2 \quad \text{or} \quad s_{2,1} \ge \delta_1$$

as, otherwise, player 1 rejects and the play proceeds to period 3, where player 2 ends up getting zero. Since under the constraint $s_{2,1} \ge \delta_1$, the value $s_{2,1}^* = \delta_1$ maximizes the payoff $\delta_2 s_{2,2} = \delta_2(1 - s_{2,1})$ of player 2 in period 2, player 2 must make the offer of $s_{2,1}^* = \delta_1$ to

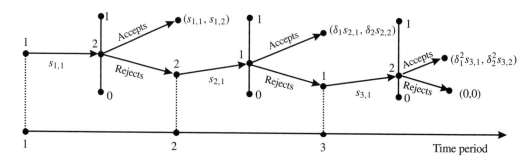

Figure 7.18

player 1 at the beginning of period 2. In particular, if player 2 makes the offer $s_{2,1}^* = \delta_1$ at the beginning of period 2, then player 1 accepts and gets the payoff δ_1^2, and player 2 receives the payoff $\delta_2(1 - \delta_1)$.

Now at the beginning of period 1, player 1 anticipates that player 2 will make the offer $s_{2,1}^* = \delta_1$ if the play proceeds to period 2. This means that player 2 will reject unless the offer $s_{1,1}$ is such that $1 - s_{1,1} \geq \delta_2(1 - \delta_1)$ or $s_{1,1} \leq 1 - \delta_2(1 - \delta_1)$. This implies that player 1 will maximize his payoff by offering

$$s_{1,1}^* = 1 - \delta_2(1 - \delta_1).$$

When player 1 makes this offer, he compares the payoff of $1 - \delta_2(1 - \delta_1)$ to the payoff he gets if he waits until period 2, when he expects to be offered $s_{2,1}^* = \delta_1$. Since $1 - \delta_2(1 - \delta_1) \geq \delta_1^2$ is trivially true, player 1 (who plays optimally) must offer $s_{1,1}^* = 1 - \delta_2(1 - \delta_1)$.

We have thus obtained the following subgame perfect equilibrium strategy combination of the game.

Theorem 7.29   Assume that in a three-period bargaining game player 1's strategy is

- Period 1: Offer $s_{1,1} = 1 - \delta_2(1 - \delta_1)$;
- Period 2: Accept if $s_{2,1} \geq \delta_1$ and reject otherwise;
- Period 3: Offer $s_{3,1} = 1$ (or $s_{3,1} < 1$ and $s_{3,1}$ very close to 1).

Player 2's strategy is

- Period 1: Accept if $s_{1,1} \leq 1 - \delta_2(1 - \delta_1)$ and reject otherwise;
- Period 2: Offer $s_{2,1} = \delta_1$;
- Period 3: Accept.

Then the resulting strategy combination is a subgame perfect equilibrium that yields the bargaining agreement

$$s_{1,1}^* = 1 - \delta_2(1 - \delta_1) \quad \text{and} \quad s_{1,2}^* = \delta_2(1 - \delta_1). \tag{7.4}$$

In general, the bargaining agreement given in (7.4) will not be the same as the $(\frac{1}{2}, \frac{1}{2})$ solution that would be obtained by using the normative solution concepts of the previous sections.

While we have been able to get a clear answer to the three-period bargaining game that we have just analyzed, the three-period bargaining game raises significant questions about whether a three-period game really captures the essence of sequential bargaining. Indeed, it is very likely that players actually can make offers and counteroffers for any number of periods. A situation in which a player can always make a counteroffer cannot be written as a "finite-horizon game." This then leads us to investigate what happens in an "infinite-horizon" version of the bargaining game. While it is true that no bargaining process goes on forever, the reasoning that leads to an agreement is often best described using an infinite-horizon game.

To analyze an infinite-horizon game it is useful to study the equilibrium of a finite-horizon game in which the payoffs in the terminal period of the game are "continuation payoffs." A *continuation payoff* is a payoff that a player expects to get if the game is allowed to continue rather than terminate. Thus, instead of a payoff of $(0, 0)$, the payoff that the players receive when player 2 rejects player 1's offer in period 3 is $\left(\delta_1^2 x, \delta_2^2(1-x)\right)$, where x is the share of the pie player 1 receives if play continues.

In other words, $(x, 1-x)$ is the expected agreement in case the bargaining continues. Thus player 1 at the beginning of period 3 knows that player 2 will accept an offer $s_{3,1}$ only if

$$\delta_2^2(1 - s_{3,1}) \geq \delta_2^2(1 - x) \quad \text{or} \quad s_{3,1} \leq x .$$

Therefore, player 1 makes the offer $s_{3,1}^* = x$. In this case, player 1 gets $\delta_1^2 x$. Hence, at the beginning of period 2, player 2 has to make an offer $s_{2,1}$ such that

$$\delta_1 s_{2,1} \geq \delta_1^2 x \quad \text{or} \quad s_{2,1} \geq \delta_1 x$$

as, otherwise, player 1 rejects, and the play proceeds to period 3. Therefore, at the beginning of period 2, player 2 makes the offer $s_{2,1}^* = \delta_1 x$, which maximizes his payoff $\delta_2^2(1 - s_{2,1})$. In that case, player 2's payoff is $\delta_2(1 - \delta_1 x)$, which exceeds $\delta_2^2(1 - x)$.

If player 1 anticipates this at the beginning of period 1, then player 1 will make an offer $s_{1,1}$ such that

$$1 - s_{1,1} \geq \delta_2(1 - \delta_1 x) \quad \text{or} \quad s_{1,1} \leq 1 - \delta_2(1 - \delta_1 x) .$$

Thus $s_{1,1}^* = 1 - \delta_2(1 - \delta_1 x)$, and player 2's payoff is $\delta_2(1 - \delta_1 x)$. Player 1's payoff here is larger than $\delta_1 x$, as $1 - \delta_1 x > \delta_2(1 - \delta_1 x)$.

Note that the preceding equilibrium agreement depends on the continuation payoff x. This brings us to the following important question: *What is the proper value for x?* Clearly, x should take a value that is consistent with playing an equilibrium in the game. But if that is so, then x should also be the offer at the beginning of period 1, since the bargaining process that takes place at the beginning of period 3 is an exact replica of the bargaining process that takes place starting from period 1. Consequently, the equilibrium x^* should satisfy the equation $x^* = 1 - \delta_2\left(1 - \delta_1 x^*\right)$, or

$$x^* = \frac{1 - \delta_2}{1 - \delta_1 \delta_2} .$$

Thus we have established the following important result.

Theorem 7.30   Assume that in a bargaining game the two players have discount rates δ_1 and δ_2, respectively. If players can make any number of offers (so that the bargaining game can be viewed as an infinite-horizon game), then the equilibrium solution to the bargaining game is given by

$$\left(x^*, 1 - x^*\right) = \left(\frac{1 - \delta_2}{1 - \delta_1 \delta_2}, \frac{\delta_2(1 - \delta_1)}{1 - \delta_1 \delta_2}\right). \tag{7.5}$$

If we examine the agreement (7.5) obtained in the preceding theorem carefully, we will notice that the equilibrium bargaining agreement depends on the discount rates δ_1 and δ_2. If $\delta_1 = \delta_2 = \delta$, then player 1 (the player who makes the first offer) gets $\frac{1}{1+\delta}$, and player 2 gets $\frac{\delta}{1+\delta}$. If $\delta < 1$, then $\frac{\delta}{1+\delta} < \frac{1}{1+\delta}$. Thus, even if the players have exactly the same time preference, player 1 gets a larger share of the pie than player 2 in the strategic bargaining game. It should be noted at this point that the smaller the discount factor (that is, the more impatient the players are), the smaller is the share of the pie that player 2 receives.

The next example illustrates Theorem 7.30.

Example 7.31 (An Automobile Purchase)

An individual has decided that he wants to buy a Ford Explorer. This sport utility vehicle is usually listed at \$30,865.00 and has an invoice price of \$27,786.00. The buyer knows that the seller may accept a price somewhere between the list price and the invoice price, but will most likely refuse to sell when the offer made is below the invoice price. The buyer is fairly patient, with a discount factor of $\delta_1 = 0.95$ over a seven-day period. The seller would like to sell the car at a reasonable price, but has a discount factor of $\delta_2 = 0.9$ over the same seven-day period. The bargaining process starts with the buyer, who is player 1, making the first move by offering a price for the car. The seller, who is player 2, has the option of accepting the offer or rejecting it and making a counteroffer.

The bargaining process described above can be viewed as a sequential bargaining game in which the buyer makes the first offer by quoting a price that is somewhere between the list price and the invoice price. The seller then responds by either accepting the offer or by making a counteroffer. It is not unreasonable to assume that it takes around a week for each of the respondents to make up their mind about serious offers and counteroffers. Here we ignore casual talk that can take place over a very short span of time but is not decisive. Since conceivably an unlimited number of offers and counteroffers can be made, this sequential bargaining game is an infinite-horizon bargaining game of the type that we have just analyzed. So, according to Theorem 7.30, the solution to this bargaining process is given by

$$\left(x^*, 1 - x^*\right) = \left(\frac{1-0.9}{1-0.95\times0.9}, \frac{0.9(1-0.95)}{1-0.95\times0.9}\right) = \left(0.6897, 0.3103\right),$$

where x^* is the share of the pie that goes to the buyer and $1 - x^*$ is the share of the pie that goes to the seller. The size of the pie in this case is \$30,865.00 $-$ 27,786.00 $=$ \$3,079. Since $x^* = 0.6897$, the buyer will get

$$0.6897 \times \$3,079 = \$2,123.59$$

of the total pie and the seller gets the rest. The price that the buyer thus offers the seller is

$$p^* = \$30,865 - \$2,123.59 = \$28,741.41\,.$$

This is a price that the seller would most likely accept in which case the bargaining ends quickly, with the car being sold for approximately \$28,700.

Clearly, in the case of strategic bargaining, the rate of time preference plays a crucial role in determining the nature of the agreement. This observation about the time preference raises an important question: *What happens when the rates of time preferences are not known by the players?*

Next we shall examine a bargaining game in which the discount factor of player 2 can take one of two values: δ_h with probability p_h and δ_ℓ with probability $1 - p_h$. We assume that

$$0 < \delta_\ell < \delta_1 < \delta_h < 1.$$

This bargaining game will be referred to (for simplicity) as the *sequential bargaining game with imperfect information*. We first look at the sequential game with imperfect information that terminates after three periods with the payoff of $(0, 0)$ if there is no agreement. The graph of this bargaining game is shown in Figure 7.19.

We now proceed to find an equilibrium of the game. As before, in period 3, player 2, whether he is of type h or ℓ, will accept an offer $s_{3,1}^* < 1$ but very close to 1 (i.e., $s_{3,1}^* \approx 1$), as a rejection leads to a payoff of zero. Thus, in period 3, player 1 proposes $s_{3,1}^* = 1$ (in fact, makes an offer $s_{3,1}^*$, which is less but very close to 1) and both types accept. In this case, player 1's payoff is δ_1^2 and player 2 gets zero.

Given this offer in period 3, in period 2, player 2 (h or ℓ) will propose (as in the perfect information case) $s_{2,1}^* = \delta_1$ and player 2 will accept and get:

$$\delta_h(1 - \delta_1) \quad \text{if player 2 is type of } h, \text{ and}$$

$$\delta_\ell(1 - \delta_1) \quad \text{if player 2 is of type } \ell.$$

In period 1, if player 1 knew that player 2 is of type h, then player 1 would offer $s_{1,1} = 1 - \delta_h(1 - \delta_1)$, otherwise he would offer $s_{1,1} = 1 - \delta_\ell(1 - \delta_1)$. We now analyze two cases.

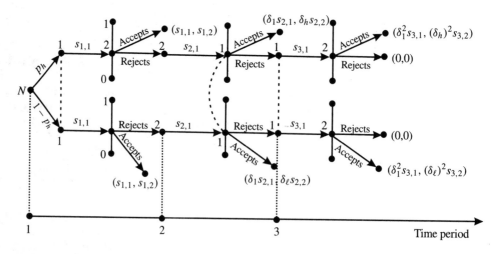

Figure 7.19

CASE I.

$s_{1,1} = 1 - \delta_\ell(1 - \delta_1)$.

In this case we claim that:

- If player 2 is of type ℓ, then player 2 accepts this offer.

Indeed, if player 2 rejects the offer and makes the counteroffer $s_{2,1}^* = \delta_1$ in period 2, then player 1 accepts. The payoff of player 2 in this case is $\delta_\ell(1 - \delta_1)$, which is exactly what he gets from the offer $s_{1,1}$ in period 1. Thus, if player 2 is of type ℓ, then he gains nothing from rejecting the offer made to him in period 1.

Next we also claim that:

- If player 2 is of type h, then player 2 will reject the offer.

Indeed, if player 2 rejects the offer, then, as before, the offer in period 2 is δ_1. Player 2 then gets a payoff of $\delta_h(1 - \delta_1) > \delta_\ell(1 - \delta_1)$, which implies that player 2 gains by rejecting the offer if he is of type h.

CASE II.

$s_{1,1} = 1 - \delta_h(1 - \delta_1)$.

In this case, since

$$\delta_h s_{1,2} = \delta_h(1 - s_{1,1}) = \delta_h^2(1 - \delta_1) > 0 \quad \text{and} \quad \delta_\ell s_{1,2} = \delta_\ell \delta_h(1 - \delta_1) > 0,$$

player 2 will accept the offer regardless of his type.

Player 1 now has to decide what to offer in period 1. His decision is based upon the following arguments. First of all, from Case II he knows that if he offers $s_{1,1} = 1 - \delta_h(1 - \delta_1)$, then player 2 will take it regardless of his type. He also knows (from Case I) that if player 2 is of type ℓ, then he will accept the offer $s_{1,1} = 1 - \delta_\ell(1 - \delta_1)$, but he will reject this offer if he is of type h. If this offer is rejected, then the offer from player 2 in period 2 is δ_1. Thus player 1's payoff in the case of rejection by player 2 in period 2 is δ_1^2. This means that player 1 must offer $s_{1,1} = 1 - \delta_\ell(1 - \delta_1)$, only if his expected payoff from making this offer

$$p_h \delta_1^2 + (1 - p_h)\big[1 - \delta_\ell(1 - \delta_1)\big]$$

exceeds the payoff from making the offer $s_{1,1} = 1 - \delta_h(1 - \delta_1)$. In other words, the following strategy summarizes player 1's choice in period 1:

- Player 1 offers $s_{1,1} = 1 - \delta_\ell(1 - \delta_1)$ if

$$p_h \delta_1^2 + (1 - p_h)[1 - \delta_\ell(1 - \delta_1)] > 1 - \delta_h(1 - \delta_1),$$

otherwise he offers $s_{1,1} = 1 - \delta_h(1 - \delta_1)$.

The preceding discussion shows that we have established the following result.

Theorem 7.32   In a sequential three-period bargaining game with imperfect information there is an equilibrium that is described as follows.

a. In period 1, player 1 offers $s_{1,1}^* = 1 - \delta_\ell(1 - \delta_1)$ if

$$p_h\delta_1^2 + (1 - p_h)[1 - \delta_\ell(1 - \delta_1)] > 1 - \delta_h(1 - \delta_1)$$

holds, otherwise offers $1 - \delta_h(1 - \delta_1)$. Player 2 rejects $s_{1,1}^*$ if he is of type h and accepts otherwise.

b. In period 2, player 2 offers $s_{2,1}^* = \delta_1$ regardless of his type. Player 1 accepts.

c. In period 3, player 1 believes that player 2 is of type h if his offer in period 1 was

$$s_{1,1}^* = 1 - \delta_\ell(1 - \delta_1)$$

and player 2 rejected the offer; otherwise his beliefs are unchanged from period 1.

If a bargaining game in which the type of one of the players is known only to the player is a game that allows for infinitely many rounds of offers and counteroffers, then the bargaining game is known as an *infinite-horizon sequential game with imperfect information*.

In the rest of the section, we analyze this version of our sequential bargaining game using arguments that are similar to the ones we used to solve the infinite-horizon game in the perfect information case. As before, the infinite-horizon game can be understood by using a finite-horizon game in which the payoffs in the terminal period are continuation payoffs.

In the game of Figure 7.20, the continuation payoffs are $(x_h, 1 - x_h)$ if player 2 is of type h and $(x_\ell, 1 - x_\ell)$ if player 2 is of type ℓ. If player 1 has not learned anything about the type

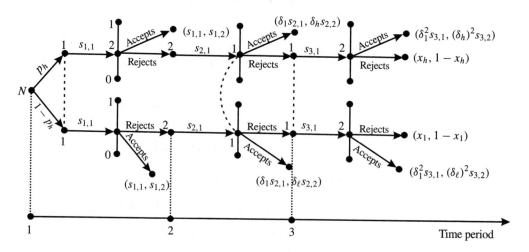

Figure 7.20

of player 2 by period 3, player 1 has no way of knowing whether the continuation payoff is x_h or x_ℓ. However, if player 1 has reached a firm conclusion about the type of player 2 that happens to be true, then player 1 has a firm belief about the continuation payoffs.

If player 1 knew that player 2 is of type h, then (according to Theorem 7.30) the continuation payoff would be

$$x_h = \frac{1 - \delta_1}{1 - \delta_1 \delta_h}.$$

Similarly, if player 2 is of type ℓ, then the continuation payoff is

$$x_\ell = \frac{1 - \delta_1}{1 - \delta_1 \delta_\ell}.$$

Surprisingly, the following result shows that in some situations player 1 will never offer $\frac{1-\delta_1}{1-\delta_1\delta_\ell}$.

Theorem 7.33   There is an equilibrium of an infinite-horizon bargaining game with imperfect information in which player 1 offers:

$$s_{1,1}^* = \begin{cases} 1 - \delta_\ell(1 - \delta_1 x_h), & \text{if } p_h \delta_1 x_h + (1 - p_h)[1 - \delta_\ell(1 - \delta_1 x_h)] \\ & \qquad > (1 - \delta_1)/(1 - \delta_1 \delta_h) \\ \frac{1-\delta_1}{1-\delta_1\delta_h}, & \text{if } p_h \delta_1 x_h + (1 - p_h)[1 - \delta_\ell(1 - \delta_1 x_h)] \\ & \qquad \leq (1 - \delta_1)/(1 - \delta_1 \delta_h). \end{cases}$$

Proof: When player 1 offers $s_{1,1} = 1 - \delta_\ell(1 - \delta_1 x_h)$, then player 2, if he is of type h, will reject the offer, as in period 2 he can offer $\delta_1 x_h$, which player 1 will accept if he believes that player 2 is of type h, and receive the payoff $1 - \delta_1 x_h$. This payoff is greater than $\delta_\ell(1 - \delta_1 x_h)$, which is the payoff he gets if he accepts $s_{1,1}$. On the other hand, if player 2 is of type ℓ, then the payoff to player 2 from either accepting or rejecting is exactly the same, in which case player 2 gains nothing by rejecting if he is of type ℓ. Therefore, player 2 will reject only if he is of type h. Given this information, player 1 believes that player 2 is of type h if there is a rejection and, in that case, makes the offer $x_h = \frac{1-\delta_1}{1-\delta_1\delta_h}$ in period 3. Thus the expected payoff of player 1 from making the offer $s_{1,1} = 1 - \delta_\ell(1 - \delta_1 x_h)$ is

$$p_h \delta_1 x_h + (1 - p_h)\Big[1 - \delta_\ell(1 - \delta_1 x_h)\Big].$$

If player 1 makes the offer $x_h = \frac{1-\delta_1}{1-\delta_1\delta_h}$, then player 2 will accept the offer regardless of type. Thus player 1 will make the offer

$$s_{1,1} = 1 - \delta_\ell(1 - \delta_1 x_h)$$

only if $p_h \delta_1 x_h + (1 - p_h)[1 - \delta_\ell(1 - \delta_1 x_h)] > \frac{1-\delta_1}{1-\delta_1\delta_h}$ holds, as then his expected payoff from making the offer is greater than the payoff from settling the bargaining issue by making the offer assuming that player 2 is of type h.

The obvious question that crops up now is whether there is an equilibrium in which player 1 can sensibly make the offer $x_\ell = \frac{1-\delta_1}{1-\delta_1\delta_\ell}$, that is, make an offer believing that player 2 is of type ℓ. Clearly, this will happen when the probability that player 2 is of type h is low and it is not sensible for player 1 to believe that player 2 is of type h when player 2 rejects an offer of x_ℓ. We leave the formal details of the analysis for the reader, but observe that the probability with which player 2 is of type h or ℓ clearly has a role in deciding what kind of offers would be made in an equilibrium. Indeed, it is of interest to note that, in some cases, the type of player 2 may never be revealed when an offer is made. In other cases, the type of offer may be such that it leads to a delay in reaching an agreement, as clearly happens in the case when player 1 makes an offer targeted at type ℓ, which is then rejected by a player of type h, and the bargaining is settled in period 2.

This aspect of an equilibrium offer, that there may actually be some delay in reaching an agreement, is quite often observed in practical bargaining. This aspect of equilibrium in sequential bargaining with imperfect information leaves us with some intriguing questions, since clearly there should never be any delay in reaching an agreement in case there is perfect information.

We finish the section (and the book) with an example that presents the details of a contract negotiation on a manuscript—such as this one.

Example 7.34 (Contract on a Manuscript)

An author is negotiating the terms of a contract with his publisher. The publisher starts the bargaining process by making an offer to the author. In such cases, the contract is usually written as a percentage of the gross earnings that goes to the author. Such an offer can lie between 0 and 40 percent, where an offer of 40 percent of the gross earnings means that the publisher is left with no profit. The share of the pie received by the publisher in this case is zero and the entire share of the profit goes to the author. On the other hand, if the contract specifies 20 percent of the gross earnings, then the share of the pie is one-half each for the publisher and the author.

Once the publisher makes an offer, the author can either accept the offer or reject it and come back with a counteroffer. Such a process of making offers and counteroffers can in principle go on for any number of periods, with a typical response time of a week between offers. Thus the bargaining process (on the contract on a manuscript) is a sequential bargaining game with the possibility of many offers and counteroffers. The sequential bargaining game starts with the publisher, whom we will think of as player 1, making an offer $s_{1,1}$, which we recall is the share (fraction) of the pie that goes to player 1. The discount factor of the publisher is known to be $\delta_1 = 0.8$ over a seven-day period (which is the time between offers). The publisher, however, is unsure about the discount factor of the author, but he knows that authors are either relatively patient with a discount factor of 0.85 or else hate bargaining and have a low discount factor of 0.75. The probability that the author is the one or the other type is one-half. Thus the sequential bargaining game is a game with imperfect information, where $\delta_h = 0.85$ and $\delta_\ell = 0.75$.

A solution to the sequential bargaining process is, therefore, found by examining an equilibrium of the bargaining game. Such an equilibrium is described in Theorem 7.33. In this example we have

$$x_\ell = \frac{1 - 0.8}{1 - 0.8 \times 0.75} = 0.5 \quad \text{and} \quad x_h = \frac{1 - 0.8}{1 - 0.8 \times 0.85} = 0.625.$$

Further,

$$p_h \delta_1 x_h + (1 - p_h)[1 - \delta_\ell(1 - \delta_h x_h)]$$
$$= \tfrac{1}{2} \times 0.8 \times 0.625 + \tfrac{1}{2}[1 - 0.75(1 - 0.85 \times 0.625)]$$
$$= 0.5742$$

Since this is less than $x_h = 0.625$, the publisher's offer (according to Theorem 7.33) is

$$s_{1,1} = x_h = 0.625$$

in the first period, which is the share of the gross profits that he retains. The author, in this case, accepts the offer, and the bargaining ends in the first period. The share of the gross revenue that is offered to the author is $0.4(1 - 0.625) = 15$ percent.

EXERCISES

1. Suppose a buyer is thinking of making an offer on a house that is listed at $150,000. The buyer can make an offer that the seller can accept, or that the seller can reject and make a counteroffer. The buyer then has the chance of accepting the counteroffer or rejecting it and making one final counteroffer. The bargaining then ends at this stage with an acceptance or a rejection by the seller.

    a. Sketch the sequential bargaining game when the discount factor is $\delta_1 = \delta_2 = 0.99$ between offers and counteroffers and the reservation price of the seller is known to be $135,000. (The reservation price is the price below which the seller will refuse to sell.) [Hint: The size of pie is $15,000.]

    b. Solve the three-period bargaining game that was sketched in part (a).

2. Suppose the bargaining process of the previous exercise can go on indefinitely. In this case what is the solution to the bargaining problem?

3. In the Automobile Purchase of Example 7.31, the bargaining takes place between a buyer and a seller with offers and counteroffers. Now suppose that the buyer has the option of going to another dealer who has agreed to sell the Ford Explorer to the individual for $28,000.

    a. Sketch the bargaining game between the buyer and the seller when the buyer has this "outside option" and the negotiating process is one in which the buyer makes an offer, waits for the counteroffer, and either takes it or rejects it and takes the outside option.

    b. Find a subgame perfect equilibrium of the game described in (a). Is the sale still executed at a price of $28,700? Explain fully.

4. Consider the game of Example 7.34. What happens in that game if the probability that the author is patient is 15%, that is, δ_h has a probability of 15%? How is the negotiation settled?

5. Suppose in the manuscript game of Example 7.34 that the author has an outside offer of 16 percent of the gross revenue. The publisher knows this and makes an offer in period 1, which the author is free to reject and make a counteroffer in period 2. In period 2, the negotiations terminate with the publisher either accepting the offer or rejecting it, in which case the author takes the other offer.

   a. Sketch the sequential game that is now played between the author and the publisher.

   b. Find a sequential equilibrium of this game. What are the terms of the agreement?

6. Show that in the bargaining game with perfect information, the share of the pie that goes to a player increases as the player's discount factor goes to 1, when the discount factor of the other player is fixed. What does this imply about what players would do if the discount factor is not fully known?

7. What happens to the bargaining solution in the perfect information game when the time period between offers and counteroffers gets close to zero? [Hint: Analyze this by first determining what happens to the discount factors and then take limits.]

8. Establish the following properties.

   a. If $\frac{\delta_1(1-\delta_\ell)}{1-\delta_1\delta_\ell} + \frac{\delta_1\delta_h(1-\delta_1)}{1-\delta_1\delta_h} > \delta_h$, then $\delta_h(1 - \delta_1 x_h) \leq 1 - x_\ell$.

   b. If $\frac{\delta_1(1-\delta_\ell)}{1-\delta_1\delta_\ell} + \frac{\delta_1\delta_h(1-\delta_1)}{1-\delta_1\delta_h} > \delta_h$ holds true, then there is a sequential equilibrium in which player 1 offers $s_{1,1} = x_\ell$ if

   $$p_h \delta_1 x_h + (1 - p_h)[1 - \delta_\ell(1 - \delta_1 x_h)] \leq \frac{1 - \delta_1}{1 - \delta_1\delta_\ell} = x_\ell$$

   otherwise player 1 offers $s_{1,1} = 1 - \delta_\ell(1 - \delta_1 x_h)$.

BIBLIOGRAPHY

1. C. D. Aliprantis, D. J. Brown, and O. Burkinshaw, *Existence and Optimality of Competitive Equilibria*, Springer–Verlag, Heidelberg & New York, 1990.

2. A. C. Chiang, *Fundamental methods of Mathematical Economics*, 3rd Edition, McGraw-Hill, New York & London, 1984.

3. J. W. Friedman, *Game Theory with Applications to Economics*, 2nd Edition, Oxford University Press, New York & Oxford, 1990.

4. D. Fudenberg and J. Tirole, *Game Theory*, MIT Press, Cambridge, MA, 1991.

5. R. Gardner, *Games for Business and Economics*, John Wiley & Sons, New York & Toronto, 1995.

6. R. Gibbons, *Game Theory for Applied Economists*, Princeton University Press, Princeton, NJ, 1992.

7. T. Ichiishi, *Game Theory for Economic Analysis*, Academic Press, New York & London, 1983.

8. R. Issac, *The Pleasures of Probability*, Springer–Verlag, Undergraduate Texts in Mathematics, Heidelberg & New York, 1995.

9. D. M. Kreps, *A Course in Microeconomic Theory*, Princeton University Press, Princeton, NJ, 1990.

10. H. W. Kuhn, Editor, *Classics in Game Theory*, Princeton University Press, Princeton, NJ, 1997.

11. R. D. Luce and H. Raiffa, *Games and Decisions*, John Wiley & Sons, New York & Toronto, 1957.

12. A. Mas-Colell, M. D. Whinston, and J. R. Green, *Microeconomic Theory*, Oxford University Press, New York & Oxford, 1995.

13. J. McMillan, *Games, Strategies and Managers*, Oxford University Press, New York & Oxford, 1992.

14. P. Morris, *Introduction to Game Theory*, Spinger–Verlag, New York & Heidelberg, 1994.

15. R. B. Myerson, *Game Theory: Analysis of Conflict*, Harvard University Press, Cambridge, MA, 1991.

16. J. F. Nash, Non-cooperative games, *Annals of Mathematics* **54** (1951), 286–295.

17. P. C. Ordeshook, *Game Theory and Political Theory*, Cambridge University Press, New York & London, 1986.

18. G. Owen, *Game Theory*, 2nd Edition, Academic Press, New York & London, 1982.

19. H. E. Scarf, The core of an N-person game, *Econometrica* **35** (1967), 50–69.

20. T. C. Schelling, *The Strategy of Conflict*, Harvard University Press, Cambridge, MA, 1960.

21. T. C. Schelling, *Micromotives and Microbehavior*, Norton Publishing Company, New York & London, 1978.

22. L. Shapley and R. Vohra, On Kakutani's fixed point theorem, the K-K-M-S theorem and the core of a balanced game, *Economic Theory* **1** (1991), 108–116.

23. K. Sydsaeter and P. J. Hammond, *Mathematics for Economic Analysis*, Prentice Hall, New York, 1995.

24. H. R. Varian, *Microeconomic Analysis*, 2nd Edition, Norton Publishing Company, New York & London, 1984.

25. J. von Neumann and O. Morgenstern, *Theory of Games and Economic Behavior*, Princeton University Press, Princeton, NJ, 1944.

INDEX

$\mathbb{N}$, 2
ϵ-Nash equilibrium, 65, 165
$\mathbb{R}$, 2
Core (v), 219

advantage of first mover, 110, 115
Allais' paradox, 37
allocation
    utility, 192
ancestor of node, 77
approximate Nash equilibrium, 165
assignment map, 223
auction, 164
    common-value, 182
    Dutch, 178
    English, 178
    first-price sealed-bid, 164
    first price, 163
    individual private, 169
    second price, 163
    with complete information, 164
    with incomplete information, 164
auction finalist, 164
auction model, 62
auctioneer, 164
automobile purchase, 243
axiom
    continuity, 28
    independence, 28

backward graph, 76
backward induction method, 81, 106
balanced bargaining game, 220
balanced family, 219
bankruptcy game, 205
bargaining, 191
bargaining game, 191, 214
    balanced, 220
    convex, 197
    symmetric, 197
    trading, 216
    two person, 191
    with imperfect information, 244
    n-person, 214
bargaining outcome, 191, 214

    core, 219
bargaining problem, 191, 214
    two person, 191
battle of the sexes, 46
Bayes' consistent strategy profile, 138
Bayes's formula, 91
Bayes, Thomas, 91
behavior strategy, 134
behavior strategy profile, 134
    completely mixed, 134
belief of player, 134
belief system, 134
    generated by strategy profile, 136
beliefs, 134
    consistent, 139
best response function, 64
bidder, 164
bidding rule
    linear, 171, 173
bimatrix form of a game, 69
blocking by a coalition, 218
branch, 77
budget line, 9
budget set, 9

chain rule, 8
characteristic function of bargaining game, 215
child of node, 77
choice
    noncredible, 119
choice function, 98
    respecting an information set, 98
choice of player, 98
choice set, 4
coalition, 214
coalition function of bargaining game, 215
column player, 69
common-value auction, 182
common property resources model, 58
compact set
    193
completely mixed behavior strategy profile, 134
compound lottery, 27
comprehensive set, 220
computation of mixed strategies equilibria, 71

concave function, 31
conditional distribution, 184
conditional expected value, 184
conditional probability, 91
consistent beliefs, 139
constraint
    incentive, 124
    individual rationality, 124
constraint function, 13
constraint set, 4
continuation payoff, 242
continuity axiom, 28
contract on a manuscript, 248
convex bargaining game, 197
convex function, 30
convex hull, 201
convex set, 196
convex sidepayment game, 237
core of bargaining game, 219
core outcome, 219
core utility allocation, 219
cost
    marginal, 59
    opportunity, 111
cost of delay in bargaining, 240
Cournot, Antoine-Augustin, 54
Cournot duopoly model, 54
critical point, 8

decision graph, 79
decision node, 96
density
    ideological, 66
density function, 21
    joint, 183
dependent variable, 2
derivative
    partial, 13
derivative of function, 8
descendant of node, 77
diagram of graph, 75
differentiable function, 8
directed graph, 75
disagreement, 191
discount rate, 240
distribution
    conditional, 184
    normal, 23
    probability, 201
    uniform, 22
distribution function, 18
distribution of random variable, 18
domain, 2
domain of function, 2
dominating strategy, 44
dummy player, 226
duopoly model
    Cournot, 54
    Stackelberg, 109
Dutch auction, 178

edge of graph, 75
effectivity function, 214
empty set, 18
English auction, 178
equilibrium, 69, 104
    interior, 71
    mixed strategies, 71
    Nash, 47, 104, 170, 186
    pooling, 158
    separating, 158
    sequential, 144
    subgame perfect, 118
    supported by non-credible behavior, 119
equilibrium path, 105
equilibrium pooling, 160
equivalent nodes, 97
event, 18
expectation, 20
expected payoff, 141
    of information set, 141
expected utility, 141
    of decision, 27
Expected utility theory, 26
expected value, 20
    conditional, 184
extensive form game, 98

family of balancing weights, 219
feasible alternative, 191, 214
feasible set, 4
finalist in an auction, 164
financing a project, 152
first-order test, 8
first-price sealed-bid auction, 164
first mover advantage, 110
first mover advantage, 115
first price auction, 163
floor price, 178
formula
    Bayes', 91
function, 2
    best response, 64
    choice, 98
    concave, 31
    contraint, 13
    convex, 30
    density, 21
    differentiable, 8
    distribution, 18
    effectivity, 214
    ideological density, 66
    indicator, 219
    objective, 4
    payoff, 49
    reaction, 64
    strictly concave, 31
    strictly convex, 31
    utility, 5
    utility over wealth, 27

gain by a player, 144

game, 44
   bankruptcy, 205
   bargaining, 191
   battle of sexes, 46
   in bimatrix form, 69
   in extensive form, 98
   in mixed strategies, 70
   in normal form, 49
   in normal form, 49
   in strategic form, 41
   in strategic form, 49
   lemons, 131
   majority voting, 235
   matching coins, 72
   matrix, 44
   of perfect information, 100
   partnership, 110
   prisoner's dilemma, 42
   sequential, 98
   sidepayment, 222
   signaling, 151
   takeover, 99
   transferable utility, 222
   wage, 211
   with imperfect information, 100, 116
   with perfect information, 100, 104
   zero-sum, 48
game tree, 96
global warming, 66
grand coalition, 214
graph
   backward, 76
   decision, 79
   directed, 75

Harsanyi, John C., 117

ideological density function, 66
imperfect information game, 100, 116
incentive constraint, 124
independence axiom, 28
independent of irrelevant alternatives rule, 192
independent of linear transformations solution, 193
independent variable, 2
indicator function, 219
individual
   risk averse, 30
   risk neutral, 30
   risk seeking, 30
individual private value auction, 169
individual rationality constraint, 124
infinite-horizon sequential game
   with imperfect information, 246
information set, 97
information set with recall, 102
input, 2
insurance, 31
interior equilibrium, 71

joint density function, 183

Kalai–Smorodinsky line, 208
Kalai–Smorodinsky solution rule, 209
Kalai–Smorodinsky utility allocation, 209
KS-line, 208
KS-solution rule, 209
KS-utility allocation, 209
Kuhn, Harold W., 106

Lagrange's method, 13
Lagrangean method, 14
Lagrangian, 14
landing fees, 228
lemons game, 131
length of path, 76
linear bidding rule, 171, 173
lottery
   compound, 27

majority voting game, 235
map
   assignemnet, 223
marginal cost, 59
marginal worth of player, 227
market equilibrium conditions, 55
market for lemons, 128, 129
matching coins game, 72
matrix game, 44
maximizer, 4
median voter model, 56
method
   backward induction, 81, 106
   Lagrangean, 14
mixed strategies game, 70
mixed strategy, 69
mixed strategy profile, 141
model
   auction, 62
   common property resources, 58
   Cournot duopoly, 54
   median voter, 56
   second price auction, 62
   voter, 66
monotone solution rule, 207
moral hazard, 112

Nash, John, 47, 117, 194, 197
Nash equilibrium, 47, 50, 104, 170, 186
   approximate, 165
   symmetric, 171
   ϵ, 65, 165
Nash equilibrium test, 51
Nash solution of bargaining game, 193
Nash solution rule, 193
node, 75
   belonging to a player, 96
   decision, 96
   of graph, 75
   owned by a player, 96
   terminal, 76
noncredible choice, 119
normal distribution, 23

standard, 23
nuclear deterrence, 108

objective function, 4
opportunity cost, 111
opportunity set, 4
optimal decision path, 80
optimal portfolio, 33, 34, 35
optimization problem, 4
optimizer, 4
optimum
    social, 61
outcome, 191, 214
    Pareto efficient, 192
    Pareto optimal, 192
output, 2

parent of node, 77
Pareto efficient outcome, 192
Pareto optimal outcome, 192
Pareto optimal solution rule, 192
partial derivative, 13
partnership game, 110
path, 75
    equilibrium, 105
    optimal decision, 80
    supported by a strategy profile, 105
path supported by a strategy profile, 105
payoff, 50
    continuation, 242
    expected, 141
payoff function, 49
perfect information game, 100, 104
player, 49
    column, 69
    dummy, 226
    row, 69
point
    critical, 8
    saddle, 49
    stationary, 8
pooling equilibrium, 158, 160
portfolio, 33, 34, 35
posterior probability, 92
power rule, 8
predeccessor, 75
preference reversal, 37
price
    reservation, 129
prior probability, 92
prisoner's dillema, 42
probability, 17
    conditional, 91
    of reaching a node, 135
    posterior, 92
    prior, 92
probability distribution, 201
probability profile, 69
probability space, 18
problem
    optimization, 4

product rule, 8
profile, 141
    mixed strategy, 141
    probability, 69
    pure strategy, 141
    strategy, 104
    strategy, 50
pure strategy, 69

quotient rule, 8

random variable, 18
rate of time preference, 240
reaction function, 64
real function, 2
real numbers, 2
reservation price, 129
risk averse individual, 30
risk neutral individual, 30
risk seeking individual, 30
root, 76
round zero of auction, 178
row player, 69
rule
    chain, 8
    independent of irrelevant alternatives, 192
    power, 8
    product, 8
    quotient, 8

saddle point, 49
sample space, 18
second-order test, 9
second price auction, 163
second price auction model, 62
Selten, Reinhard, 117
separating equilibrium, 158
sequential equilibrium, 144
sequential game, 98
    infinite-horizon, 246
sequential rationality, 144
set, 2
    budget, 9
    choice, 4
    compact, 193
    comprehensive, 220
    constraint, 4
    convex, 196
    empty, 18
    feasible, 4
    information, 97
    information with recall, 102
    opportunity, 4
    strategy, 49
    strategy profile, 50
set of natural numbers, 2
set of outcomes, 50
set of utility allocations
    symmetric, 196
Shapley value, 227
sidepayment game, 222

convex, 237
signaling game, 151
single person decision process, 80
social optimum, 61
solution
   independent of linear transformations, 193
   Pareto optimal, 192
   symmetric, 197
   Nash, 193
solution of game, 104
solution rule, 192
   Kalai–Smorodinsky, 209
   KS, 209
   monotone, 207
   Nash, 193
solution to a bargaining game, 192
space
   probability, 18
   sample, 18
Stackelberg duopoly model, 109
stage zero of auction, 178
standard deviation, 20
standard normal distribution, 23
strategic form game, 41, 49
strategy, 49, 99
   behavior, 134
   combination, 50
   dominating, 44
   mixed, 69
   profile, 50
   profile, 99
   pure, 69
   strictly dominant, 43
   strictly dominating, 44
strategy profile, 99, 104
   Baye's consistent, 138
   behavior, 134
strategy profile set, 50
strategy set, 49
strictly concave function, 31
strictly convex function, 31
strictly dominant strategy, 43
strictly dominating strategy, 44
subgame, 116
   trivial, 116
subgame perfect equilibrium, 118

subtree, 78
successor, 75
symmetric bargaining game, 197
symmetric Nash equilibrium, 171
symmetric solution, 197
system of beliefs, 134

takeover game, 99
tax burden, 232
terminal node, 76
test
   first-order, 8
   Nash equilibrium, 51
   second-order, 9
trading game, 216
transferable utility game, 222
tree, 76
   game, 96
trivial subgame, 116
two-person bargaining game, 191
two-person bargaining problem, 191

uniform distribution, 22
utility
   expected, 141
utility allocation, 192
   core, 219
   Kalai–Smorodinsky, 209
utility function, 5
   von Neumann–Morgenstern, 27
utility function over wealth, 27

value of a game, 227
variable
   dependent, 2
   independent, 2
variance, 20
venture capitalist, 152
vertex of graph, 75
von Neumann–Morgenstern utility function, 27
voter model, 66

wage game, 211
worth of coalition, 221

zero-sum game, 48